COTTON'S RENAISSANCE

Cotton's Renaissance is the story of one of the more remarkable feats in the annals of enterprise. At its center, the book shows how U.S. cotton growers lost half their market share in the 1960s and 1970s *and then won it back* through highly innovative marketing and organization. To place this unprecedented achievement in perspective, the authors analyze and interpret the responses of cotton growers over two hundred years to the timeless problems of nature, technology, markets, and politics. The upshot is a dramatic history of how growers learned – after more than a century and a half of trying to manage supply – how to drive and shape demand for their commodity. This key change in perspective and behavior was accomplished by the creation of a unique public–private company that helped thousands of growers to cultivate demand and to survive in an increasingly competitive global marketplace.

The impact of Cotton Incorporated on the markets for cotton was nothing less than an entrepreneurial coup in strategy and organization. In its "total marketing" effort to rebuild cotton's market share, it fostered substantial scientific, technological, and managerial improvements in the quality and performance of cotton. In doing so, it enhanced the efficiency not only of the farmers who grow cotton but also of the intermediaries who transform it into consumer goods. This account of the cotton industry's revival, which took place at every level of production and distribution, holds many important lessons for anyone interested in history, economics, marketing, or public policy.

Timothy Curtis Jacobson is a partner in The Winthrop Group, Inc., a consulting firm based in Cambridge, Massachusetts. He is the author of *Making Medical Doctors, An American Journey by Rail,* and *Waste Management: An American Corporate Story.*

George David Smith is Clinical Professor of Economics and International Business at New York University's Stern School of Business. He is also president of The Winthrop Group, Inc. His previous book-length publications include *Anatomy of a Business Strategy, From Monopoly to Competition,* and (with George P. Baker) *The New Financial Capitalists.*

COTTON'S RENAISSANCE

A STUDY IN MARKET INNOVATION

TIMOTHY CURTIS JACOBSON

The Winthrop Group, Inc.

GEORGE DAVID SMITH

Stern School of Business, New York University

CAMBRIDGE
UNIVERSITY PRESS

PUBLISHED BY THE PRESS SYNDICATE OF THE UNIVERSITY OF CAMBRIDGE
The Pitt Building, Trumpington Street, Cambridge, United Kingdom

CAMBRIDGE UNIVERSITY PRESS
The Edinburgh Building, Cambridge CB2 2RU, UK
40 West 20th Street, New York, NY 10011-4211, USA
10 Stamford Road, Oakleigh, VIC 3166, Australia
Ruiz de Alarcón 13, 28014 Madrid, Spain
Dock House, The Waterfront, Cape Town 8001, South Africa

http://www.cambridge.org

First published 2001

Printed in the United States of America

Typeface Sabon 10.25/13.5 pt.   *System* AMS-T$_{\text{E}}$X   [FH]

A catalog record for this book is available from the British Library.

Library of Congress Cataloging in Publication Data
Jacobson, Timothy C., 1948–
Cotton's renaissance : a study in market innovation / Timothy C. Jacobson,
George David Smith.
p.   cm.
Includes index.
ISBN 0-521-80827-8
1. Cotton trade – United States – History.   2. Cotton – Economic aspects – United
States – History.   3. Cotton farmers – United States – History.   4. Cotton
Incorporated – History.   I. Smith, George David.   II. Title.

HD9075 .J33   2001
338.1′7351′0973 – dc21   2001025824

ISBN 0 521 80827 8 hardback

For Christopher and Anne Jacobson
and
David Paton Gray-Smith

CONTENTS

CONTENTS

PREFACE

In the nineteenth century, cotton was the miracle fiber of the Industrial Revolution. Cotton textile manufacturing was the high-technology and high-growth business of the day, and American cotton was "King." The short staple, upland cotton of the Old South, once it was made profitable by the mechanical cotton gin, fed the insatiable mills of Old and New England, and much of Europe, too. It was the young nation's major export, earning much of the foreign exchange required to fuel the emerging U.S. economy. By mid-century, American cotton accounted for two thirds of the world's supply. Like all farm products, American cotton was subject to the vagaries of the weather, pests, and political risks, but generally it sold into fast-growing and weakly contested markets.

Now, at the dawn of the twenty-first century, cotton growing is a nearly $5 billion industry in the United States and remains one of America's major agricultural exports. The great bulk of U.S. cotton today still comes – as it has for more than 200 years – from family farms, and the people who grow it have a strong attachment to cotton both as a way of life and as a means to a livelihood. Theirs is no rosy agrarianism, however. The tough job of growing and harvesting crops drove out the last romantics, if ever there were any, long ago.

Despite enormous advances in technology and technique, the job has become much tougher in at least one critical respect: cotton growing has become a fiercely competitive enterprise worldwide. Produced in many countries, cotton trades more freely than ever as growers everywhere compete for markets in which there are often more than enough sellers and in which there are cost-competitive synthetic substitutes that consumers can always turn to. Competing in such markets demands a level of scientific and strategic sophistication that would surprise most people not familiar with the economics of modern agriculture. Cotton growing has become both capital- and knowledge-intensive. It requires ongoing investment in science, technology, management, and marketing as well as a broad-based knowledge of global affairs – from the weather in Australia to political conditions in Pakistan, from what's fashionable in Paris to what's happening in the world's genetic and biochemical laboratories.

Few people outside the business realize how difficult cotton is to grow in the modern world or that, for cotton growers, a nagging question – "Why grow cotton, anyway?" – must be asked each year. Most have answered it by dropping out. In 1970 there were some 300,000 cotton farms in the United States serving a declining market; by 2000 there were roughly 30,000 – the fittest survivors? – struggling to compete in a larger one. That it is a larger market is good news. That it remains a struggle to make a living in it is a harsh reality of the modern global economy. What keeps those sturdy cotton farmers going is the subject of our story.

Farmers supply the market, but their fate is much more the story of demand. Traditionally, agricultural producers thought chiefly about supply. Cotton growers, like all farmers, felt they had little control over their markets, much less over nature. Whenever they experienced serious problems, they tended to seek out political solutions. Yet something has changed. Since the 1960s, through industrywide research and promotion programs, cotton farmers have been learning how to shape demand. Like their fathers and grandfathers, they cannot control the weather. Nor can they make the seeds come up. They cannot do much about the price their product fetches in the market. Yet for 30,000 or so of them, cotton still works *because they have found a way to influence demand.*

As the following chapters show, a large part of the reason why U.S. farmers still export the world's largest share of cotton lies in a change in strategic thinking that led to an organizational invention, Cotton Incorporated. The strategic story is a history of how modern cotton growers came gradually to understand, almost counterintuitively, that their task was not simply to manage what they grew but rather to manage the demand for their product. The organizational story is how those growers who understood the problem first helped to create an institution unique in the annals of agriculture and marketing. The entrepreneurial "heroes" are many. At a critical moment in the 1960s, when cotton's markets were fast eroding under the assault of new synthetic fibers, a few alert growers knew that something had to change in the way they thought about and served their markets. Against considerable skepticism and some outright opposition from their peers and government officials, they created a new organization to help them do it. In doing so, they forged an alliance with rank "outsiders," visionary marketing strategists like J. Dukes Wooters and J. Nicholas Hahn, early presidents of Cotton Incorporated who fashioned what amounts to a revolution in commodity marketing.

The very name, "Cotton Incorporated" (never contracted to "Cotton Inc." or "CI"), was meant to evoke the spirit of unequivocal commercial seriousness, even though some of the functional substance was obviously absent. Describing itself as "the fiber company of America's cotton producers," Cotton Incorporated was an unusual sort of "company." It was headquartered far from the growing fields, in New York City. Its funding and staff were lean. (By 2000, a $60 million budget supported the work of some 160 employees in New York and Cary, North Carolina.) It neither produced cotton nor sold it. Rather, it performed the intermediate functions – research and development plus promotion – that more purely commercial, large-scale enterprises routinely performed in addition to producing and selling.

That it largely succeeded in this purpose can be illustrated with the following data points. In 1973, cotton's share of the U.S. textile fiber market had sunk to an all-time low of 33 percent (down from 63 percent in 1960). New "miracle" fibers, synthetically produced, were taking the market by storm. Yet by the end of the twentieth century, cotton's share had been restored to 60 percent! Has any other industry, or company, ever accomplished a market rebound of that magnitude? Exports of American cotton had grown, too. Few cotton farmers would argue that this change in fortune was fortuitous or accidental. The concerted "total marketing" efforts of Cotton Incorporated to stimulate consumer demand for cotton products – together with ongoing technical assistance to textile mills and research and development on agricultural science and technology – all contributed to this resurgent trend. Without the performance of these intermediate functions to match that of the same functions by the synthetic-fibers competition, not enough cotton fiber would be consumed to sustain America's cotton growers.

This study of how Cotton Incorporated did its work, and what impact it had on the cotton-growing industry, is framed as an economic history. The company's institutional roots go back as far as the New Deal; it evolved out of a series of efforts to create a nationally organized response to the chronic problems of cotton growers. Beyond that, there is the history of cotton growing itself and, for our purposes, how that history evolved from one of supply-side economics to one of demand cultivation. Hence our story goes all the way back to the time of Eli Whitney's cotton gin, the simple technological device that made cotton economical to grow and propelled it into the forefront of American economic life.

The study is organized as follows. An introductory chapter describes the modern world of the cotton grower (cotton farmers like to be called "growers") and the uncertain prospects that confront him (cotton growers are almost invariably male) as the twenty-first century unfolds. Part One consists of three chapters that telescope the changing structure and economic problems of cotton farming from the end of the eighteenth century through the Great Depression and its immediate aftermath, when cotton growers began to band together to seek political solutions to their economic problems. This development was much in keeping with the broader trend in American agriculture, which – although the most efficient and progressive in the world – became highly dependent on government support in the mid-twentieth century. Part Two encompasses a discussion of how cotton growers gradually changed their view of the market, including the events that led up to the creation of Cotton Incorporated and the development of its revolutionary strategy and structure.

Part Three deals with the functional activities of Cotton Incorporated and their impact on demand, first domestically and then worldwide. Chapter 6 focuses on promotion and advertising designed to "pull" more cotton into the market by altering consumer preferences, and it offers an analysis of how an agricultural commodity was transformed into a desirable branded good. Chapter 7 discusses how the building of consumer demand was accompanied by the technical assistance given by Cotton Incorporated to the growers' first line of customers, the textile mills. If brand promotion were to have any credibility and if the mills were to tailor products to satisfy shifting consumer needs, Cotton Incorporated would have to invest in research and development, including field operations technology and the science of cotton breeding. Those activities are the subject of Chapter 8. Chapter 9 examines Cotton Incorporated's attempts to expand markets for American cotton outside the United States. Ever since its emergence as a great staple crop in the early nineteenth century, cotton had been caught in a web of global interests; so it would be in the late twentieth century. The company's "total marketing" strategy would never serve growers effectively if it failed to demonstrate the linkage between local, down-on-the-farm issues and the farthest reaches of cotton's economy.

Finally, an Afterword attempts to tease out the implications of the history for the uncertain environment in which cotton growers continue to labor. Our ultimate purpose is not only to provide an account of American cotton growers' responses to changing market conditions over time but also to find the relevant lessons in the story. That is, after all, why history matters.

ACKNOWLEDGMENTS

This book is the outgrowth of a consulting study undertaken by The Winthrop Group, Inc. for Cotton Incorporated in order to document the evolution of the company and the response of U.S. cotton growers to competition. Primary credit for commencing serious historical study of the subject belongs to four growers in particular: Eddie Smith of Floydada, Texas, Morgan Nelson of Roswell, New Mexico, L. C. Unfred of New Home, Texas, and the late E. Hervey Evans, Jr., of Laurinburg, North Carolina. Current president and CEO of Cotton Incorporated, J. Berrye Worsham III, and vice-president Hugh Malone provided access to company files and research facilities and opened doors to growers and industry experts across the Cotton Belt. Company marketing and research staff in Cary, North Carolina, and in New York City shared generously of their time and knowledge. Kristin Wenzel and Anne Talamas gave essential administrative support. Ms. Talamas's sharp eye saved us from many an error. Gary Raines helped to compile data for charts and graphs. His patient diligence was indispensable to the project.

The manuscript was reviewed by technical experts at Cotton Incorporated for factual accuracy. In accordance with protocols generally accepted by professional business historians, we benefited from the counsel of a history committee consisting of producer representatives and chaired by David Blakemore of Campbell, Missouri. At our insistence, the committee was empowered to address factual errors and to suggest how we might find sources to address gaps in our story; conceptualization of the history and interpretation of the facts were entirely and exclusively our freedom and responsibility.

We also wish to acknowledge the insightful criticism of Professor Harold Livesay of Texas A&M University, who read the manuscript in various stages of its development. Professor Thomas K. McCraw of the Harvard Business School and Professor Richard Sylla of the Stern School of Business made useful suggestions on portions of the text.

Illustration credits: pp. 2, 164, 187, 188, 268, 269, 270, 298, 301, Cotton Incorporated; pp. 6, 10, 11, 17, 23, 25, 32, 34, 67, 72, Timothy C. Jacobson; pp. 48, 51, 73, 78, 79, 103, 104, 112, 121, 126, 131, 210 (top), 242, 248, 249, 250, 254, 260, 283, 306, National Cotton Council; p. 210 (bottom), Simon Griffiths; pp. 63, 64, Staplcotn; p. 69, USDA.

INTRODUCTION

Why Grow Cotton, Anyway?
Culture and Economy

It was a cheerful occasion, a celebration even. Cotton grower Moss Perrow and his fellow board directors were getting their first look at Cotton Incorporated's new headquarters and laboratory in Cary, North Carolina. The new building was, without doubt, the world's premier facility for cotton research. It had been "brought in," board chairman Hugh Summerville reported happily, "on time and on budget." Preston Sasser, head of research and development, was in charge of the building project, and he purred over the $20 million edifice – the Bell Labs, so to speak, of cotton. As the morning moved on, shouts of greeting and backslapping among sons of the soil punctuated upbeat presentations about what the various laboratories were working on. The weather was chilly, and the first of several ribbon cuttings was scheduled outdoors under the white-columned front portico, reminiscent (belying the high-tech gear inside) of an old southern veranda. It felt good – a big day for cotton. Perrow was impressed, but his mind was on work. "Well," he was overheard to say as he prepared to go home to South Carolina, "all we've got to do now is make a crop."

No easy business, making a crop. Selling it was even harder. Two months later, in April 2000, Keith Collins (chief economist for the U.S. Department of Agriculture) came to the same place to explain just how hard it would be. Addressing the thirteenth annual Engineered Fiber Selection (EFS) Conference of Cotton Incorporated, he delivered a sobering message. The textile industry representatives and cotton growers in attendance already knew that U.S. farm prices across the board had been falling steadily since posting record highs in 1996. High yields worldwide had met with severe recessions, first in East Asia starting in 1998 and then in Latin America in 1999. Demand was shrinking in relation to supply. The only thing that had prevented a full-fledged "farm crisis" in the United States were federal

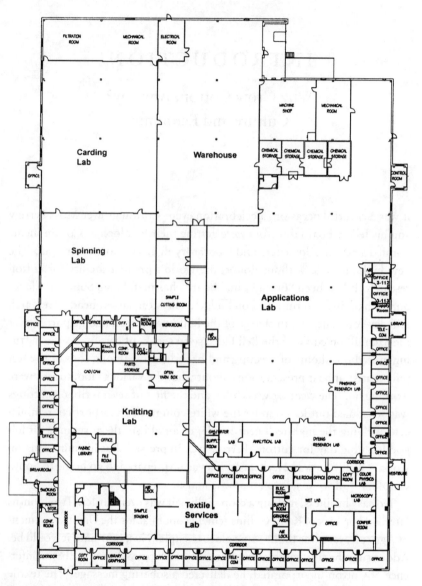

Footprint of Cotton Incorporated's research facility in Cary, North Carolina, opened 2000. The building brought all aspects of cotton fiber research under one roof, a concept first perfected by the manufacturers of synthetic textile fibers, who remain cotton's fierce competitors.

emergency support programs, some $27 billion in aid, aimed at preserving a survivable minimum of farm incomes. Farmers had protected themselves, to some degree, by avoiding debt and finding ways to generate off-farm income. Land values were also rising in a strong economy, but unless one sold off, it was only paper. One might have thought there was nothing unusual about any of this, from a historical perspective. This, too, would pass.

But longer-term threats were looming that might have dire consequences for cotton producers. The largest exporter of cotton in the world, the United States had produced its smallest crop in four years. (On the financial side, cotton growers' gross receipts came in at $4.1 billion, the lowest in ten years, although $2.6 billion of federal payments kept farm incomes up.) To make matters worse, U.S. textile mills took up only 10.1 million of the 17 million bales produced.

It was not that there was anything drastically wrong with consumer demand for cotton. The U.S. consumer preference for cotton had risen dramatically over the past generation and remained at least steady.[1] And world cotton consumption was rebounding to a high of over 90 million bales in 2000, a spike in demand driven by recovering world economies and the lowest cotton prices in fifteen years. But "cut-throat competition" from abroad was driving the U.S. textile business to distraction. Still, farmers could always export, and did so increasingly.[2] Yet the world market was not waiting expectantly on shipments of American fiber. Countries in Central and South Asia were already well established as major producers, and now China was on track to become a strong net exporter of cotton. Collins described China's transformation (beginning in the spring of 1998) from net importer to net exporter of cotton as "probably the single most important factor" explaining the continuing decline in prices.[3]

Surveying the 2000 crop season, Collins – typical two-armed economist that he was – painted a curious and contradictory scenario. On the

[1] Keith Collins to Cotton Incorporated EFS meeting, April 2000. In 1980, per-capita retail use of cotton was 15 pounds; in 1990, 24 pounds; in 2000, a record 34.5 pounds. This generated a total U.S. retail consumption of 20.5 million bale-equivalents. Domestic mill use of cotton was falling, and domestic cotton textile production was being supplanted by rising cotton textile imports. Imports in 2000 totaled 15 million bale-equivalents, double the level of ten years earlier; this versus U.S. textile exports of 4.5 million bale-equivalents.

[2] Ibid. U.S. raw cotton exports rebounded after a thirteen-year low of 4.3 million bales in 1998 to 6.5 million bales.

[3] Ibid. Adding exports and domestic mill use produced a total demand for U.S. cotton of 16.6 million bales. But that was still less than the size of the 1999 crop and resulted in a substantial carryover, which also helped explain continuing low prices.

one hand, a market was taking shape in which foreign stocks would fall and world prices would increase modestly. On the other hand, U.S. stocks would rise and prices would likely fall. He expected American cotton growers to plant 15.6 million acres of cotton of all kinds, their second-highest acreage in forty years, yet with the lowest prices in twenty-five years. With normal weather, that would amount to some 19 million bales; although with more production one hoped for more demand, the demand picture remained "somewhat mixed." Domestically, a robust economy was expected to keep retail cotton textile consumption high. But when one factored in the effect of textile imports on domestic mill demand and then calculated likely raw cotton exports, U.S. growers would still not find enough markets for all their cotton. Cotton growers in the audience could therefore look forward to another decline in their net incomes, unless government programs picked up the slack. To make matters worse, higher interest rates and notably higher oil prices were predicted, which would raise the cost of producing cotton by about 2 cents per pound.

Almost out of breath, or so it seemed to his audience, Collins summed up "extraordinary developments" in the markets facing the cotton industry today: 25-year-low prices, high acreage, strong exports, high farm program spending and support, and the prospect of the world's largest and most populous country (China) coming under the discipline of the World Trade Organization. "Enormous challenges" lay ahead, he said; "I can only wish you the best of luck."

In the awkward moment between the chief economist's "thank you" and a smattering of polite applause, one could hear a pin drop. Those still addicted to the comforting old vice hurried outside for a smoke. Moss Perrow had already fled to South Carolina to make his crop. But why, one might well ask, would he even bother to grow cotton, anyway?

VALLEY

Few people outside the business know that there are several ways, and many places, to grow cotton in the United States. Ted Sheely farms 6,600 acres in the central San Joaquin Valley of California near the town of Lemoore, between Fresno and Bakersfield. It is a medium-sized operation, irrigated, diversified, and employing 25 people year-round, which spikes up to 200 during vegetable harvest. Virtually all hands are Hispanic. Sheely runs it with minimal management structure; besides himself, there are one general foreman and two sub-foremen. He oversees his operations from a farm office converted from the same double-wide mobile home where he first brought his bride to live in 1974. During his 49 years, he has done every physical job there is to do on the farm, save for cropdusting (though he is a qualified pilot). On occasion, he still drives a tractor.[4]

Sheely drives the pick-up five miles from the office to his cotton field, signals the driver to come down from the big John Deere to take a break, and mounts the cab himself. He is dressed casually for the office, not the field, but in this particular cab he could wear his Sunday best without trepidation. He shuts the sealed door on the pressurized, air-conditioned interior and prepares to set off, back down the field. Enjoying a cigarette, the hired man lounges contentedly against the pick-up, one eye alert to see just how good the boss really is. It is a "listing" operation, which prepares the ground for next year's crop. The tractor driver who can guide a big rig across the half-mile-long field in the straightest line is typically in high demand and difficult to keep. The best drivers have a steady touch and rely on the power of sight. Sheely has lost such men to contract outfits that can pay higher wages for specialized skills. It is a weak point in the system, a problem that long begged for a technical solution.

This is the vast central valley of California, the flattest of agricultural landscapes, where it does not rain in the summer and where the commonest sight is of big tractors working immense fields, often shrouded in dust clouds of their own making. Responding to a comment that the air-conditioning must make a huge difference in driver comfort in this dusty, dirty operation, Sheely responds: "Of course, but this is what it's really for." He points to a purple and orange plastic box in the corner of the cab, labeled "Beeline Navigator," taps "Automatic" on the touch screen in front of him, engages the transmission, and commences his journey down the row. He does not touch the steering wheel.

As the rig rumbles down the field at precisely 6.5 miles per hour, Sheely peers out the back window (not the front) and explains that, under the relentless cost pressures of today's farming, it is essential to use human talent wisely and let technology do the rest. Beeline is a global positioning satellite (GPS) guidance control system, developed in Australia, that mechanizes machinery guidance in ground tillage and application operations. It eliminates conventional implement markers and permits the tractor to know its

---

[4] Following: Ted Sheely interview, September 29, 2000.

John Deere caterpillar-tread tractor equipped with global positioning guidance system, San Joaquin Valley, California. The driver looks backward to monitor the listing (land preparation) operation; the satellite/computer watch ahead, through dust clouds and darkness.

position to an accuracy of ±2 centimeters, "so even a hack tractor driver like myself," Sheely jokes, "can make it look pretty good."

How it looks relates to what it costs. Operating directly off satellites, the system is impervious to darkness, dust, and fog. Critical operations can be performed at night. This can potentially halve the time of those operations or double the acres covered in the same time. It also enables one to reduce capital investment in machinery. Sheely's John Deere cost $200,000 and the Beeline computer attachment $50,000, making for a quarter-million-dollar piece of equipment. "But the thing was, after you analyze it, and it didn't take much analysis," says Sheely, "that this tractor without the GPS technology worked only about 40 percent of the time because of fog and darkness. So I bought a 'second' tractor for $50,000. Good deal." The John Deere is back at the pick-up, and the hired hand again takes over. The man had felt threatened at first by the new gadgetry, Sheely admits. But he still has his job, although the skills once focused merely on steering can now be transferred to monitoring the actual tasks being performed. Sheely figures the hand has become more valuable, not less.

Ted Sheely believes in technology and is an optimist. He is also careful and diversifies. In addition to top-quality Acala upland cotton, he raises long staple American Pima cotton and a variety of vegetables. Thirty percent of his acreage is in tomatoes, and then there is garlic, garbanzo beans, and pistachio trees. Growing just vegetables, he admits, probably would be more rewarding than staying in cotton, but he cannot afford the risk – an untimely freeze could put him out of business. In business on his own, he evaluates risk carefully to make sure he is still in business next year. In the San Joaquin, the risk and reward of farming relate inevitably to water.

Because it rains little, water is Sheely's most critical resource. It shapes choices about what to plant and ultimately will decide the future of agriculture in the Valley. It was arrival of water from the north via the California aqueduct in the late 1960s that changed the face of this land and greatly increased its value. The price of water, too, has gone only up. When he started farming in the mid-1970s, he could count on the aqueduct meeting 100 percent of his needs, except in time of natural drought. His contract with the government today provides just 50 percent reliability, although he still grows 100 percent of the crops and must rely on pumping ground water to make up the difference, which is not a good long-term option. "These days, we suffer more of the regulatory droughts, created by environmentalism, than the natural droughts." This makes garbanzos attractive because they are a winter crop that needs no water during the summer, when it is essential to conserve a limited supply of groundwater for tomatoes and cotton. Laying out crop maps for the year ahead, Sheely weighs his plans against anticipated water and financial resources. "I need to make sure of having enough water and schedule our activities so we don't end up overloading our lines of credit."

Sheely grew up near Phoenix, Arizona, on a cotton farm still in the family after three generations. His father, Joe, was active in national cotton affairs before his death in a plane crash in 1979. An aerial photograph of the original Arizona holding hangs on the wall of Ted's office in Lemoore, and he uses it to illustrate his anxiety about the future – wherever cotton, water, and growth collide. "We have this little highway, you see," he says wryly. "It's called Interstate 10, and it goes along one side of our property. And they're building a new loop. Look." He points to row after row of new residential developments: "The city has encroached right to where we are. And so you can see: it will go out of cotton farming in my generation."

California has a population of some 30 million, over 90 percent of it classed as "urban." It is the second largest producer of cotton (after Texas) in the United States and the largest producer of many fruits and vegetables. Yet most Californians, as Sheely puts it, think "their clothes come from K-Mart and Wal-Mart, Macy's or Saks, and their groceries from Safeway." Farmers have a big educational job ahead of them. Sheely spends a lot of time with teachers, promoting the state's "Agriculture in the Classroom" program. His farm is pretty much an open book. "I have nothing to hide. I'll speak to the pesticides issues or whatever they want to know." He tries to explain how they, the consumer and the voter, dictate what he, the producer, does. Right now they are telling him they want, above all, high quality and low price, and this – "precision ag" (GPS-guided tractors), judicious use of insecticides, and aqueduct water, for example – is how they get it. Most visitors arrive laden with a lot of clichés about the wonders of "family farms" and the malevolence of "agribusiness" but without a clue about what a real cotton farm is like. They leave, Sheely hopes, somewhat better informed.

Sheely tries to educate politicians, too. He began, as is typical of cotton growers, at the local Farm Bureau, and eventually got involved with the National Cotton Council. He started going to Washington and learned to work the halls of Congress. "You need to be able to go up and knock on their door. I've always found that anybody that relies just on lobbyists is not nearly as successful as people who actually will go and look them in the eye and say, 'I am your constituent, and this is important.'" Typically, he encounters politicians who are "firemen," guided by no larger policy. But as the number of farmers – and thus the number of farm votes – declines, the ability to shape policy grows more problematic.

There needs to be some national strategy for agriculture that individual growers can work within, Sheely believes. He feels beset by regulation, high costs mandated from outside: farming in environmentally correct ways, as American growers must do, is expensive. Yet he must compete unprotected in world markets against countries less fastidious than the United States about environmental safety and where production costs are much lower. (Eighty percent of California's cotton crop is exported.) Just how much more efficient is he expected to become? How much more cost can be squeezed out at the margins? How many more Beeline silver bullets will he be able to lay his hands on? How many more will he be able to afford? He will do what the market tells him, season to season, but he would like to know what the larger game is. Does the United States have an interest in "protecting" its basic industries, including production of food and fiber? If so, then what is the regime that will permit its producers to stay profitable? Technology will help, but technology in a policy vacuum can't do it all.

Here in the San Joaquin Valley of California, on U.S. cotton's last and richest frontier, a year-to-year cocktail of relentlessly escalating costs, low prices, and competition from both foreign growth and synthetic fibers threatens to leave even cotton's largest, most efficient, and most technologically sophisticated growers with a nasty hangover. It is not a pleasant feeling, and it makes one think of alternatives. What else can be done with the assets at one's command – land, water, entrepreneurial know-how – than raise cotton?

"I still optimistically look to the future of farming," reflects Sheely. "I hope to see some relief in my lifetime, but I realize it will be challenging. I enjoy doing what I do and that's one of the things I try to encourage in my kids." He hopes one of them will choose (and be able) to follow him and keep the operation going. If not, then, "like in the case of my grandfather's farm in Arizona, we'll sell it and let them build houses on it." He hesitates. Growth is inevitable, and what he sees in Phoenix, with the city built right up to their property line, is at least reasonably well planned. But in the long run? "I kind of think once you get down the road, you can't take the houses off and start farming again."

PLAINS

A thousand miles to the east, on the High Plains of West Texas near Lubbock in what is known as "the world's biggest cotton patch," urban encroachment wouldn't seem to be a problem. Forty-nine-year-old grower Eddie Smith cruises the 3,000+ acre cotton operation that he farms with his father and son, in a big pick-up, under an immense and cloudless Texas sky.[5] It is July, and he is inspecting the pumps that bring up water from the Ogallala aquifer to irrigate the crop. The roar from the unmuffled 350-cubic-inch recycled automobile engines that power the pumps is deafening, but they have to be checked out visually twice a day. No water, no cotton.[6]

---

[5] Following: Eddie Smith interviews, December 10, 1999; July 20, 2000.

[6] Neither will last forever. The Ogallala aquifer, a Lake Huron–sized underground river extending from South Dakota to the Texas High Plains, was first tapped extensively for agriculture in the 1930s, when improved well-drilling techniques and gasoline-powered pumps enabled farmers economically to bring up the water from far greater depths than permitted by windmills. In a naturally parched place, the aquifer became equivalent to "rain on demand." Extraction

The High Plains surrounding Lubbock, Texas, have been called the "world's biggest cotton patch." Land and climate conspire to make the land good for little else besides cotton, unless it is the solitude afforded by Eddie Smith's canyon.

Pass one along the highway at 70 mph, even with the windows shut, and the Doppler-effect sensation is of a P-51 Mustang – or some other heavy-duty pre–jet fighter plane – swooping in for the kill. Smith adds a couple quarts of oil to one of the thirsty machines and moves on. There is cotton everywhere, except where there is sky. Over a rise, the cotton stops and gives way to prairie grass. The transmission lurches down into low gear and the four-wheel drive takes hold. Suddenly the prairie stops too, and the truck plunges down a rock path into Eddie Smith's canyon.

Not far from Smith's farm in Floyd County, between Lubbock and Amarillo, lies the Palo Duro Canyon, which is something of a scenic attraction in this largely flat part of the world. Sliced through by a stream called the White River, Smith's canyon is but an echo of its larger neighbor to the north, but the beauty intensifies as scale diminishes. In several ways, it is a private

rates, however, greatly exceeded the ability of the aquifer to recharge, and hydrologists foresaw an end to the water boom in twenty or thirty years. See J. R. McNeill, *Something New under the Sun: An Environmental History of The Twentieth-Century World* (New York: Norton, 2000), 151–4; John Opie, *Ogallala: Water for a Dry Land* (Lincoln: University of Nebraska Press, 1993).

Most Texas High Plains cotton is irrigated with water from the Ogallala aquifer, pumped from depths of 350–400 feet. The water is "free" (while it lasts); the pumps and irrigation infrastructure that bring it to the cotton are not.

place. He speaks of it as possessively as he does of his cotton, up over the rim of the prairie. He came upon it in a stroke of good fortune, and Smith, a quiet man, claims he will never let it go. "There's a lot of solitude here."

It is not that he won't have the opportunity. "You know, it's hard to believe, but this canyon land is worth more than that good cotton land up there." He could easily divide it up and sell off bits for developers to build on. The truck hits bottom and finds the cow path along the canyon floor. Smith's 25-year-old son, who has greater interest in ranching cattle than raising cotton, keeps some of the family's herd down here. There are three water holes.

One is natural, fed from a stream right out of the rock, a pond hedged with scraggly willows and cottonwood, home to thousands of frogs – for the coyotes and snakes, a tasty part of the food chain. The second is a tank kept full with water pumped up from the aquifer by a windmill, one of thousands that dot the western plains. Most now are only relics, wobbly metal towers tapering to the top twenty or thirty feet above the ground, the paddles of the wheel half-missing, the sail – which once guided the wheel to catch the wind – dangling precipitously. But not Smith's windmill. Even in a modest breeze (it is relatively sheltered, at the bottom of the canyon) it whirls away, the transmission shaft that connects the wheel up top with the pump down below, squeakily moving up and down – *whee-hah, whee-hah, whee-hah* – the water gurgling gently from the spout, into the flume, down to the tank. The third water hole employs more modern technology to fill its tank. It is solar powered, its heart a panel of dark glass cells that automatically track the march of the sun across the sky and so maximize the capture of nature's energy for economic use, just as the sail guides the wheel into the wind. The cells power the current that drives the electric pump that brings up the water. Smith says it works fine, though no better than the wind, which is pretty reliable out here, too. Both were there before he got the canyon, and he'll keep them till they quit: "Probably not before I do," he adds.

On the High Plains, as in the San Joaquin Valley, water is everything: whether down in the canyon to the gentle whir of the windmill or up with the cotton to the roar of the Chevy 350s. Smith made his first cotton crop in 1973, the year he graduated from college and went into partnership with his father. His father's father had farmed cotton before him since the 1930s, and his grandfather on his mother's side had farmed and been a prominent figure in the West Texas ginning industry. "I started at the 'ground level,' so to speak," he remembers, "walking the fields, hoeing. I sure was glad to get out of that." In high school, he graduated to a tractor, still dirty work, thinking all the while, "I'm never going to keep doing this. I despise this job." Tractor cabs in those days were just a shell to protect against the wind and cold, but "they definitely weren't soundproof. You always had earaches or headaches when you got out of them at the end of the day." But when he went to college, at Texas Tech in nearby Lubbock, it was to major in agricultural economics. College changed things; he began to look at the farm afresh and, besides, "there was just nothing more comfortable than to go home to the farm and work in that world."

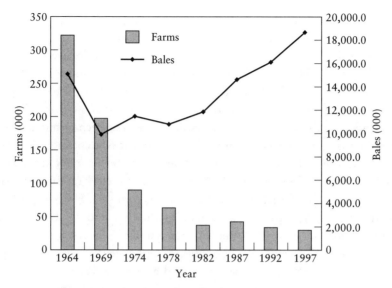

Figure 1. U.S. cotton production and number of cotton farms, 1964–1997. *Source:* U.S. Department of Agriculture, National Agricultural Statistics Service.

Starting with 300 acres, Smith today works over 3,000, and he got a taste early of how agriculture works when it works right. With the income from his first crop, he bought his first tractor and built his own first house. "Nineteen seventy-three was an excellent production year." The tractor had a cab, air conditioning, radio, the works. He looks back on that charmed beginning – "it was 70-cent cotton, and it cost a lot less to produce then" – and remembers thinking that if it was this easy, then what was wrong with his dad? Why hadn't he done any better than he had? "I'd love to have 70-cent cotton today," says Smith wistfully.

Today the farm is diversified, within natural limits. Part of the land he bought was a cattle operation: "So we became cowboys." Smith's son Eric, who also went to Texas Tech, likes ranching and is more at home on a horse than on his father's tractor. Along with the grandfather, the three of them work the entire operation in partnership. They have two full-time employees and add three or four more during the harvest, which on the High Plains usually comes around Thanksgiving and is the last harvest anywhere in the Cotton Belt. Labor, however, is a problem.

Even with mechanization, cotton still requires a lot of human tending, and Smith finds it harder and harder to get and keep good quality farm help. From conversation with growers elsewhere in the Belt, he concludes it is a typical problem on most farms. "We just can't keep good people: it's not so much that we can't afford to pay them, it's that they're just not available." It is a problem with regional variations. On the Texas High Plains, where cotton and indeed settlement has a relatively short history, population is sparse and the labor pool has always been shallow. Virtually all of it today is Hispanic. Over the years that Smith has been farming, however, he has seen a marked change. There simply used to be more people: "In 1973, it wasn't unusual to have a different farmer on every section of land, maybe two, three different farmers." Today, the landscape is empty of people, and the no-longer-bustling small prairie towns like Floydada, where Smith still lives, are stark reminders of this decline in numbers. (Other parts of the Cotton Belt have a different heritage, but like Texas today they suffer the same dearth of labor.) There are other employment alternatives, other places to go. Farming, for the hired hand at least, holds few remaining charms. "Maybe I'm just getting older, but it seems to be getting worse," Smith grumbles. "I know it used to be easier to hire people, and good people too, who wanted to work."

Like other businessmen, individual farmers work hard to manage labor and other factors of production as best they can, season to season, year to year. Successful cotton farming, however, takes not only labor but also leadership and a longer vision than this fall's harvest and next spring's planting.

In the 1970s, Smith concentrated mostly on building up his own farming operation. In the 1980s, he reached out to look after business more broadly. First, he served on his local gin board, then on the board of the Plains Cotton Cooperative Association and the American Cotton Growers, which had built one of the world's largest denim mills in the hamlet of Littlefield, Texas, 30 miles northwest of Lubbock. The real "springboard," though, was his selection, in 1990, to participate in the Cotton Leadership Program sponsored by DuPont and the Cotton Foundation of the National Cotton Council. The program, which began in the early 1980s, put a select group of young leaders through an intense, six-week course on all segments of the cotton industry. They traveled the country learning about technology, marketing, infrastructure, politics, and who the players were everywhere. DuPont's division of agricultural chemicals underwrote the enterprise, which was in its direct interest: cotton producers consumed a lot of DuPont chemicals. But Smith is convinced that DuPont had a more enlightened long-term motive, as well. "DuPont sees that cotton and the synthetics will always be intertwined in one facet or another." DuPont textile fibers was indeed cotton's competitor, "but they felt like there was a lot to gain from the technology on the cotton textile side of the business. It was a unique experience."

It reinforced something Smith had learned over the years: "If you want to do things, you have to step out. So I stepped out and started learning more about who was doing what, and why." So much goes on that is beyond the individual grower's reach. He cannot afford to go it alone, for the unorganized grower is the grower without a voice. The truth comes home to Smith when he considers the dwindling number of cotton producers, in West Texas and everywhere else in the United States, who still have the capability to produce more and better cotton than ever. They are clearly more efficient and better at what they do than any of those who aren't around anymore, yet the reward for their efficiency is diminished influence along the corridors of power: "We have less political clout."

So Smith will continue to "step out" for cotton. The alternatives, from where he stands, aren't too many or too attractive. In the cotton world, as it is, West Texas always gets the end of things: with the last crop to go to market, it is always the price follower, never the leader. Behind the Texas-style boast of "the world's biggest cotton patch" lurks the hard determinism of its particular combination of soil, moisture, length of growing season, and prevalence of hail, wind, and even snow. For it is not just that cotton grows best here, it is that not much else would be any good at all.

Unless it is cattle – or, down in the canyon, "second homes" for wealthy Austinites in search of scenery and maybe solitude. Eddie Smith likes cotton. But if he had the choice of buying more land for more cotton, or buying a second canyon – well, that might be a tough choice to make.

On the courthouse square in Smith's hometown of Floydada, the visitor will find an above-average historical museum filled with typical pioneer bric-a-brac, displays on local war heroes, and even a full-size sod house. But the real tour de force requires stepping further back – 400 years or so, in fact. Vasquez de Coronado, it seems, passed this way sometime between 1540 and 1542 searching for "Quivera," the mythical kingdom of gold. He found no gold, gave up and went back to Mexico City.

But he left behind artifacts that have kept buffs and university archaeologists digging up his old campsites for years. In the display case at the very front of the Floydada museum lies what is (up to now, anyway) the prize: the remnant of a chain-mail gauntlet, presumably worn by one of Coronado's intrepid, greedy band or perhaps even by the great explorer himself.

It was unearthed in a canyon not far from Smith's. (Campers then, like today, looked for water and shelter from the wind.) It is a handsome piece and certainly looks authentic. It is of value, however, because it is claimed to be part of the kit that the Spaniards brought with them, across 3,000 miles of ocean to the New World and then 2,000 miles more to the far northern reaches of their empire to a place not yet known as "Texas" – *not* because it is part of anything they found here. It is iron, not gold.[7]

Cotton has been called "white gold." The metaphor, generally, exaggerates, but not always. In the Deep South, it doesn't take many conversations with growers to stir ancestral memories of the halcyon 1850s, when King Cotton created an authentic American aristocracy not of birth but of money. In the Far West today, the sheer immensity of cotton's domain – 17,000 acres here, 20,000 acres there, 50,000 acres over yonder – suggests there is still wealth in this plant. Even to a young Eddie Smith back in 1973, it must have seemed as if, with cotton, he had indeed struck it rich.

Today, it is a different matter. Smith talks of solitude in the canyon, but his thoughts are never far from the cotton, blowing in the wind up over the rim of the prairie. The "gold" is as elusive for him as for old Coronado.

DELTA

Around Greenville, in Washington County, Mississippi, there is no need for pumps unless it is to keep the water *out*. Rainfall in the Yazoo–Mississippi Delta averages over 55 inches per year (compared with 18 inches on the Texas High Plains and 12 inches in the San Joaquin Valley), and for centuries flooding renewed the land each year with nutrients washed down on the streams that drained a continent: the Missouri, the Ohio, the Mississippi. For fecundity of soil, little in nature compares with the Delta: North America's own Fertile Crescent-cum-Nile Delta. Plus, it rains.

Washington County lies some 800 miles almost due east of Floyd County, Texas, and it too was once frontier. The Percy family has been farming this neighborhood since the 1830s. William Armstrong Percy III ("Billy"), along with his son and nephew, farm Trail Lake Plantation today, a medium-sized operation planted largely in cotton.[8] The Percys are an "old" southern

---

[7] See "South Plains Heritage Trail: A Self-Guided Tour of Historic Sites" (South Plains Heritage Trails Consortium, Lubbock, no date); and Nelson England, "Coronado in Texas," *Texas Highways* (December 1997), 38–42.

[8] Following: Billy Percy interview, August 6, 1999.

In the Yazoo–Mississippi Delta, nature supplies the water and also the insects. Weevil trap, part of the boll weevil eradication program, Washington County, Mississippi.

family, a "house," with ancestry traced back to the "Northumberland Percys" and the English Civil War.[9] To Billy Percy, the Delta is filled with family ghosts, many from the American Civil War (*the* "War") and its aftermath. There was William Alexander Percy, who "was a colonel and had a battalion from Mississippi. That's his battle flag on the wall, right behind you. He was called the 'Gray Eagle.' He came back from the war and was broke, like everybody was." And then there was the Gray Eagle's son, farmer and lawyer Leroy Percy, who became a U.S. senator; he sold the old family farm in Leland and bought the one that is now Trail Lake, near Arcola.

The notion that the Delta is not very old, or that Delta growers are themselves not that far removed from the frontier, would probably come as a surprise to Ted Sheely or Eddie Smith. But they belong to a new Southwest. The Delta belongs to what is known in American history as the "Old Southwest," a vast expanse of Alabama, Mississippi, Arkansas, and Louisiana. In the 1820s and 1830s, it became a magnet for planters and yeomen

[9] Bertram Wyatt-Brown, *The House of Percy: Honor, Melancholy and Imagination in a Southern Family* (New York: Oxford University Press, 1994), genealogies 359–62.

from Virginia and the Carolinas, whose lands were worn out by 200 years of tobacco culture and filled with too many slaves.

Much of the region was ideal for cotton and none of it more so than the Delta; of all the cotton-growing regions in the world, none has a richer lore. In literature, it has become the "most southern place on earth."[10] Here, William Faulkner conjured a universe matchless in American fiction – "Yoknapatawpha County" – peopling it, as in *Absalom, Absalom!,* with the protean likes of Thomas Sutpen and the sons and slaves who hacked from the Mississippi wilderness a land fit for cotton. David Cohn, Greenville native and cosmopolitan friend of the Percys, wrote about the Delta in the 1930s as the place where cotton was not just a crop "but a form of mysticism ... a religion and a way of life ... omnipresent here as a god is omnipresent ... omnipotent as a god is omnipotent, giving life and taking life away."[11] The Percy name appears prominently among the region's chroniclers, most memorably in William Alexander ("Will") Percy's lyrical elegy on Delta life in the early twentieth century, *Lanterns on the Levee: Memoirs of a Planter's Son.*

In 1929, Will, the "planter's son," adopted the orphaned sons of Leroy Pratt Percy (a Birmingham lawyer) and raised them until his own death in 1942. They did different things. "Walker ended up being an author; my father ended up being a farmer." And so in turn would his son Billy, for whom the farm seemed a natural fit. He liked to hunt and fish and worked all his summers there. "I just loved the farm." There was never any question in his mind. Nobody told him that was what he had to do.

"My father essentially retired from farming as soon as I got out of the Army in the early 1960s," remembers Billy. Although Billy, who had graduated the University of Virginia, always knew he would come home to farm, there was some question about how he would get worked into the business. Work for one of the managers? Try a small piece of ground for himself? His father simply told him to "go on out to the farm and take over. They were all waiting for me to come tell them what to do."

It is 170 years since the first Percys came here to unlock the land's agricultural potential, and Billy Percy's Delta is a different place from the Delta of any of his ancestors. Protecting the fields from the Mississippi's yearly floods has always been a problem for farmers, but before the Depression,

[10] Alone of cotton's provinces, the Delta even has its own metropolis: Memphis.
[11] David L. Cohn, *Where I Was Born and Raised* (Cambridge, Mass., 1948), 41, cited in James C. Cobb, ed., *The Mississippi Delta and the World: The Memoirs of David L. Cohn* (Baton Rouge: Louisiana State University Press, 1995), 61.

this burden had fallen largely on the shoulders of local levee boards, elected bodies conferred by the state constitution with taxing powers to build and maintain the levees. The task, however, exceeded local resources and the technology of the times, and the Great Flood of 1927, which turned the whole Delta into an inland sea for four months, turned flood control in the entire Mississippi Valley into a federal responsibility.[12]

The catastrophe found the Percys near the center of the action. Greenville and Washington County were probably the hardest hit, after levees had been breached just a few miles upriver. Uncle Will was head of the local Red Cross and headed up the relief efforts. His father, "the Senator," supervised from the background. Will's friend from World War I in France, then–U.S. Secretary of Commerce Herbert Hoover, set up shop in Memphis to spearhead federal assistance. The river never misbehaved quite like that again, and the federal government, through the Army Corps of Engineers, subsequently assumed authority for flood control. Bigger and better levees protected the land, while new channels diverted the river's flow to hasten it to the sea. Consensus about controlling the river shifted with the times, however. In the past twenty years, the environmental movement attacked the orthodoxy of flood control at its heart, arguing that maybe a flood was not so bad after all and that the river should once again be allowed to run its course. This view is not shared by many cotton producers.

There is still something of the frontier about the place, where rugged individualism coexists with the understanding that some jobs are too big for anyone to tackle alone. "Involvement" is a Delta tradition that is probably rooted in the experience of the old levee boards, which afforded planters at least the illusion of control over natural forces. The more lasting and far-reaching institutional expression of this impulse was the Delta Council, established as a sort of regional chamber of commerce.[13]

The Council represents all eighteen counties of the Delta. It started out with a twin agenda of agriculture and flood control; over the years, its focus has broadened to embrace industrial development, highways, education, and research. Billy Percy became involved within a few years of returning from college and the Army to manage Trail Lake, back in 1963. "It's a big deal around here." It is a lean organization, he notes. "By far the most

---

[12] See John M. Barry, *Rising Tide: The Great Mississippi Flood of 1927 and How It Changed America* (New York: Simon & Schuster, 1997).

[13] See Chapter 3, "Acts of God and Government."

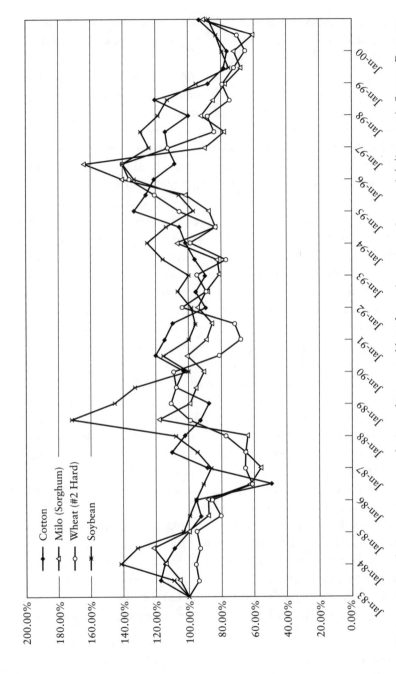

Figure 2. Index of relative movement of prices of cotton and key alternative crops, 1983–2001 (1/2/83 = 100). *Source:* Data provided by Cotton Incorporated and the New York Board of Trade.

extravagant thing they have ever done is to build that building over there, where we had the catfish lunch the other day, next to the Stoneville Experiment Station."

In the Delta, as everywhere else, the strength of cotton's organizations comes down to business judgments of individual growers, every year, on the ground. While to outside observers the Delta may look like a flat, fertile, well-watered Garden of Eden, to the growers who work its soil it is more properly seen as a set of business assets. Percy's own operation is highly concentrated on a single crop, with 90 percent planted in cotton. It is, he says, an asset-based decision. A few years ago, he acquired more and better land. He could perfectly well raise something besides cotton on it, and certainly would if something promised superior returns. Just now, not much does. "I was not necessarily making a cotton decision; it was the land type. I opted for high-priced land, which is better land even if you are going to grow soybeans or corn or whatever else." When everything is depressed, he finds cotton is still the best cash crop. He admits to some sentiment (he has, after all, been raising cotton for two thirds of his lifetime), but not much: "It is strictly a penciled-in number," he hurries to add.

Even so, he detects a difference between his and the coming generation. His son and nephew work Trail Lake now; one is an MBA, the other a lawyer. "They don't farm like I used to farm, by God." Much more oriented to the bottom line than are "some of us older guys, you have a bunch of young guys farming today with their computers out, with their budgets and watching every penny." There are alternatives. "We can easily switch to soybeans or corn; we grow them anyway." And then there is rice, a quarter-million acres' worth already in Mississippi; and catfish farming, which has put another 100,000 acres of good cotton land back under water in hundreds of intensively-managed ponds and has given the northwest corner of the state, when viewed from the air, something of the look of Minnesota. But Percy remains bullish on cotton. "We're not only going to have the best land, but the best farmers and best technology, too." But there is a caveat. "As long as our input costs don't get out of control, we will be just as efficient as anybody else."

Tens of thousands, of course, have left the Delta farms. Machines and insecticides took their place as the cotton farms became larger and more efficient. In a land once dense with labor – including slaves and their tenant descendants – a traveler can go for miles and see virtually no one. For a place as rich as the Delta, it is eerily empty. Farmers white and black gave up, following the same well-worn path up the Illinois Central to factory jobs in the North or out West.

To drive south from Memphis toward Greenville during high summer is to go to sea in cotton, under a blue dome almost worthy of a Texas sky. But for the occasional crop-dusting airplane, it is even quieter than the High Plains. (There is less wind and there are no pumps.) It is also to be reminded that, compared to the Delta, all U.S. cotton land is "marginal." The Delta could not be more opposite from Smith's High Plains, where the cotton ecology is far more fragile, or Sheely's San Joaquin, which is naturally starved for water. If cotton were to go the way of the buggy whip, the Delta would be its last American stronghold. But this is hardly the case, yet.

With respect to cost and price factors over which neither Valley nor Plains nor Delta grower has much control, cotton growers find themselves facing identical dilemmas and asking the same questions of public policy makers. "Whether, in fact, we remain a viable economic enterprise," as Percy puts the question, cannot be answered by any individual grower alone. Two generations ago, Percy's melancholy "Uncle Will" had his own way of putting it, in *Lanterns on the Levee*: "We have fields to plow and the earth smells good. Maybe in time someone will pay us more for our cotton than we spend making it."

PIEDMONT

In the United States, cotton began in the Southeast – old states that, before they were states, were colonies facing the Atlantic world. Johnny Gramling farms cotton today in Orangeburg County in the South Carolina Piedmont, 75 miles upcountry from Charleston and the coast. It is a flat to gently rolling landscape of sandy fields, hedged by woods of scrub oak and pine. Where the woods are today, chances are there once were fields; what are today's fields may well be tomorrow's woods. It is hot and damp here, and plants grow fast. Acres not tended (thousands, in the past, were simply abandoned, as cotton declined and population moved away) go quickly back to nature. A pine plantation grown for pulp matures here in twenty years or less.

Gramling's farm is down a long dirt road, off the state highway. But for the crunch of tires, stillness reigns here, too. It pays to follow directions closely, for there are few people around to ask the way. A sight, not a sound, announces that this is indeed the right place: a great white wooden house, added to here and there, porches wrapped around two sides, situated in the

Before the boll weevil came, in the early twentieth century, cotton prospered in the Southeast under a modified plantation system. Signs of that prosperity can be seen in the "plantation architecture" that remains popular to this day. Gramling homestead, Orangeburg, South Carolina, built ca. 1900.

center of scattered tumbledown outbuildings, after the old plantation style. Surely, this is the place to find Johnny Gramling. A closer look reveals it is empty.

A figure appears in the yard, waving toward a low-slung concrete-block farm–office affair, off to one side. This is the man. The sign reads "Gramling Hunting, Fishing & Camping, J. L. Gramling & Sons, 362 Jumbo Road." Conversation begins with the house. "Do you live there?" "No, I live across the way, [in] a little [red-brick rancher]." "Does anybody live there?" "Not much, well, just off and on." It is just like cotton in South Carolina.

"The old house that I stopped you at when you were fixing to drive in, that house was built in 1900," Gramling says of the "old home place." It is testimony to cotton's good times, before arrival in these parts of the boll weevil. The ruins around it reach back a bit farther. An old log structure, overgrown with vines, was once the kitchen. "It was built in 1765," ten years before the outbreak of the American Revolution in which South Carolina supplied so many battlefields. "How far back, then, does this farm go in your family?" "They settled here in 1735." He has the date firmly at hand. That was back when South Carolina was still a prosperous province of British North America and content to be so. It was also a good hundred years before Billy Percy's ancestors showed up in the Delta. "Old home place" is a phrase commonly used by farmers referring to the clan's first homestead. In South Carolina, however, "old" is older than just about any place else.

Back in the eighteenth century, it is unlikely that Gramling's ancestors grew much cotton here. Cotton then meant largely long staple "Sea Island" varieties grown in small quantities on the colony's coastal islands. Shorter staple "upland" (so called because it would grow on higher ground, upriver from the coast) was not unknown, but it was mostly limited to domestic use. All cotton in those days – before invention of the cotton gin, which made practical the separation of fiber and seed – was expensive. Hence the Gramlings probably grew the great southern staples of corn and hogs, with some wheat, vegetables, and cattle thrown in. Two centuries later, Johnny Gramling remembers from his 1930s boyhood the sights and smells of what was still, for many families like his, subsistence farming. "People manufactured a lot of their food locally. I can remember many a time shelling the corn off the cob and taking it over to the mill to get the grits. That's the way you got stuff then. We didn't have plastic or any of that stuff. You had a pint jar, and you used it til it finally broke!" There was even sugarcane in the neighborhood, and the Gramlings had a syrup mill. "When I was a kid, people would bring the cane over here to have it ground, and we'd get a certain amount of syrup for the grinding." (In the same manner, cotton farmers commonly paid for ginning their crop with part of the crop itself: the seed.)

Gramling also remembers the cotton, which came here commercially early in the nineteenth century as British demand for fiber exploded and entrepreneurial American planters scrambled – with their unique combination of resources in land, labor, and climate – to meet it. The land boomed and then eventually wore out. Free men and slaves trekked off together to Mississippi. The Old South shuddered as the Yankees came, first as invaders and then as investors. The New South brought textile mills that, along with fertilizer, revived the cotton. Then, almost Biblically, came the years of the locust – or, more precisely, the boll weevil. Gramling was born in 1931, during the very bottom of the plague.

"There had been cotton here a long time ago. Then it went to nothin'. When I was coming along as a kid, there just wasn't hardly any cotton planted around here." The old gin, down the road, fell to ruin. Gramling went away to the University of South Carolina in Columbia and starred in

When the boll weevil (pronounced "bow-evil") came, the cotton went and with it much of the labor force that once crowded the rural South. Today's cotton landscape is largely empty of people, and advanced agricultural practice produces as much cotton as once was raised on several times the acreage by thousands more farmers. Abandoned tenant house, Halifax County, North Carolina, 1999.

football. For a time, he made a career of it and played professionally in the Canadian League. He thought about going on to coaching but didn't like the odds. "Every Saturday, there's a winner and a loser and your chances over the long haul are just the same: 50–50." He probably had the wrong temperament, anyway. "I don't know, I just can't stand sitting there and having somebody criticize me and not be able to say anything back to them. That's what you've got to do as a coach or an athlete. You've got to keep your mouth shut." One morning in Canada, at breakfast in a coffee shop with a long counter, "this guy on the other side said, 'I don't know what the hell they keep that Gramling for. They ought to send him back to South Carolina!'" It wasn't too long before he went.

Not that the odds in farming were a lot better, but there were compensations. As a boy, he had loved the land and to hunt and fish. "I just wanted to come back and be here with my parents, rather than go off somewhere for good." When he returned, in the late 1950s, things down on the farm were beginning to look up. The family, still with numerous tenants, farmed around 1,000 acres, though only 200 or so were in cotton. Pesticides were getting better, and the battle against the weevil looked like it might turn at last. Cotton acreage went up to 700 or 800. But chemicals were expensive and cotton prices volatile. For a couple of years, again, he didn't plant any cotton at all. Soybeans, corn, and wheat went in instead, "whatever looked like was going to be the best return, which none of it was a real good deal."

Two things made him stick. One was boll weevil eradication, the grower-organized and -financed program to get rid of the pest for good, which came to this eastern edge of the Cotton Belt early, in the mid-1980s.[14] The cost of eradication, though steep at the start, quickly fell in subsequent years as farm after farm, county after county, was swept free and stayed free of weevils. Compared to the cost of trying to poison the bug into submission with insecticides alone, the program was a bargain. "It set this section of the country on fire," Gramling described eradication's impact in bringing cotton back from the dead. The Southeast returned to the status of major producer.

The second was the coming of the cotton research and promotion program, also governed and paid for by growers themselves. Gramling had been active in the Farm Bureau, and believed that cotton growers needed their own organization to promote cotton and improve its marketability. When Cotton Incorporated was organized in 1970, it helped keep him in the business.

Cotton promotion today, he is convinced, is stronger than ever, but price and profitability is a problem. "If we don't get something going on these prices, there's not going to be any people farming for long." Memories are still fresh in this part of the country of when the land went to something other than cotton. It could happen again. Ten or fifteen years ago, the government had a program encouraging reforestation in pulpwood, and it made a man think twice. "They were paying you to put it in. A guy would have been a whole lot better off if he planted everything in pine trees."

Other options are tempting. Urban and suburban encroachment presses harder on agriculture every year, and while Orangeburg or Columbia may not exactly be Phoenix, the trend strikes South Carolinian farmers with the same notions of opportunity. Not far from the Gramling place, the state capital sprawls relentlessly northeast along U.S. 1 toward Camden, another pre–Revolutionary War town, not that long ago hedged by cotton fields picked by hand. "You know, you've got property around someplace like Columbia or places like that: more advantageous to turn it into real estate."

---

[14] See Chapter 8, "The Necessary Illusion of Control."

Like a lot of cotton growers, Gramling has other business interests that help even out the agricultural cycle. He charges money, for instance, to fish in his teeming ponds.[15] But rational calculations have their limits. Emotional ties keep him on his land. So long as he can survive, he'll take his stand right where he is, which is where generations of his "people" have stood before him. However, he would just as soon not go broke in the meantime. He is grateful to have sons still working the place but frets about their futures here. Besides a depressed market, labor is scarce and virtually all of it is migrant (Hispanic). The weather can be fierce. The High Plains may contend with hail and snow and wind, but only the Southeast has hurricanes. Gramling remembers one monster (probably hurricane Hazel in 1955) that fairly flattened a good crop just ready to harvest. "If we hadn't still been picking by hand, we'd lost it all. The hands went through there and picked it up off the ground and off the stalks." (Nature can be counted on reliably to repeat herself; much of the North Carolina crop was lost to flooding caused by hurricane Fran, which devastated the Piedmont in 1999.)

"You know, we keep getting new pieces of machinery, updating this and that. Consequently, we can actually increase the yield some, or make it more economical to grow stuff, yet still" – it is somehow not adding up for him – "you're not making any more money."

"Sounds like you're chasing your tail."

"Yeah, and with taxes going up all the time."

FATHERS AND SONS

Cotton farms may be individual proprietorships, partnerships, or closely held corporations. Many display levels of technological and management sophistication equal to much larger organizations. Very few are "small"

---

[15] "Members will pay an annual fishing fee, payable in advance, and a fee for each day's fishing. The daily fee will be posted on the Fishing Boards at Gramling Fishing headquarters .... Members coming to fish will fill out a brown envelope and deposit a daily fishing fee, before fishing, and fill out and place a tag on the board at the Fishing Headquarters. This tag must designate which pond the member is fishing in. Upon leaving, if member fished in a pond with a number lower than 40, member will report fish caught in *each* pond by placing this information on his daily fishing tag and depositing tag .... Members are allowed one guest per visit and member will pay the daily fishing rate for that guest. Children under twelve years of age may fish free when accompanied by an adult member. Limit one child per member and one child per guest. Only one limit of fish can be caught by member and child or by guest and child. There is to be no running around that will disturb other members .... Members will use good sportsmanship at all times ...."

anymore (no more "forty acres" and certainly no more mules). But most do conform to an old simple vision of what a farm is, or ought to be: they are rooted deep in and enlivened by family identity, family loyalty, and family memory. There is also a hard economic reason for this: given extraordinarily high costs of entry, the "family way" is just about the only way for a young person to get started in agriculture today – short of winning the lottery and then turning around and betting the winnings on the other lottery of farming. The names of these cotton firms (Starrh & Starrh Cotton Growers, Hansen Ranches, Summerville Enterprises, Pennington Farms) record business and family relationships packed with unusual emotional power.

A poster familiar to anyone who has spent any time in coffee shops, gin offices, and farm kitchens across the Cotton Belt depicts two young boys in overalls, hands in pockets, eyes cast downward, taciturn beyond their years. "Been farmin' long?" runs the caption. It is a joke that masks the hope shared by many cotton farmers that there will be someone to carry on after them, preferably one of their own and most preferably (in that still patriarchal world) a son. This hope has a dimension found in few other lines of work: that by passing on the business of the farm and the firm, a man will be passing on and securing for yet another generation a way of life as well as means to a living. A lot of this is tied up with the notion that agriculture affords a man the satisfaction of independence rare in a corporatized world; this may seem ironic given agriculture's chronic economic distress, but it is not to be gainsaid.

A lot of it also involves attachment to physical place and the notion of stewardship – "love" is not too strong a word – for the land itself. Farmers are not rosy romantics, but few would do anything else. Though they complain endlessly about low prices, bad weather, and fickle politicians who don't understand their needs, most believe they are among the lucky ones of the earth, blessed with interesting and meaningful work. Partners with nature ("only the Good Lord can make the seeds come up"), farmers plant, nurture, harvest, and – year after year, through good prices or bad – experience first hand the satisfaction of creation. This is no small reward and is akin, some would say, to art.[16]

Johnny Gramling's sons already pretty much run the business. Billy Percy's son helps manage Trail Lake with a law degree. Eddie Smith's son tends the pumps and the cattle alongside his father. Ted Sheely visits every

[16] Jay Hardwick, Newellton, Louisiana, conversation with author, December 14, 2000.

morning with his second son, who always gets up early and, though only 10, likes to talk about the farm: "There's a chance he might." Two other men's sons have made up their minds and are getting ready.

Frank Summerville is a junior at Mississippi State University in Starkville, where his father studied before him.[17] He spends most of his time in the Department of Agricultural and Biological Engineering, where his curriculum for the Bachelor of Science degree is a fair map of the sort of ground that tomorrow's cotton producer must be prepared to negotiate. The Agricultural Engineering, Technology and Business (AETB) program "provides an educational opportunity for students interested in applying technical, business and management skills to problems in agricultural production, processing, commodity related business and finance, and natural resources utilization."[18] The program sees itself as a supplier to the agricultural industry of young people trained in a combination of "agricultural engineering technologies" and business and management skills. Within the course of study, there are several possible emphases: agricultural systems; natural resource and environmental management; and gin management and technology/processing.

Frank, who has been tinkering with things since he was a boy, has worked out his own specialization, which emphasizes manufacturing. He would like to invent an implement and then manufacture and market it. He thinks tractors and other equipment should be simpler and fixable "without a laptop." Affordable equipment is a critical issue particularly on smaller operations like the Summervilles' in Aliceville, Alabama. (They have bought only second-hand equipment for years, which helps keep debt low.) "Our biggest field is 55 acres, little patches here and there, and all that GPS and precision stuff doesn't work for us like it does out in the Delta."

The AETB program opens doors to a variety of career options. Frank looks forward to "food/fiber production" (or "farming," as the catalogue copy notes, parenthetically). "There's never been anything else I wanted to do." As a freshman, he studied engineering technology in agriculture, plant biology, chemistry, algebra, and English composition. As a sophomore: agricultural economics, physics, zoology, public speaking, and graphic communications. As a junior: principles of financial and managerial accounting,

[17] Following: Frank Summerville interview, November 20, 2000.
[18] Mississippi State University College of Agricultural and Life Sciences Catalogue 1999–2000, 80.

computers, land surveying, and internal combustion technology. Finally, as a senior he studied financial systems, building construction, human resources management, and soil and water management – with a humanities elective thrown in. Frank wants to put his education to use on the farm, and he is confident about his preparation. "I think I'll be able to handle it, except for the market and the weather."

Frank's father, Hugh, has been farming for over thirty years in addition to looking after broader business. He served as chairman of Cotton Incorporated in the late 1990s. "I've been in this industry since I was born," he explains. "My father was a producer, as was his father. In fact, I'm the sixth generation of our family that has produced cotton in Alabama." He hopes strongly that Frank's plans will work out and that the son will indeed follow after the father. "Cotton has been good to me," he is fond of saying.

But he can promise nothing, and he tells Frank sternly that he must have other interests than cotton if he is to prosper. Hugh raises pecans and sometimes butterbeans, and for many years he operated a gin and was involved in the agricultural chemical business. He also tells Frank to get involved and stay involved. "If we want our children and our grandchildren to have a strong cotton industry, we need to continue to invest in cooperative promotion and research efforts." Frank should graduate in a little over a year, and, if all goes according to plan, father and son should be in the business together soon after that. "It's a great way of life ... if you can find a way to make a living at it."[19]

Spence Pennington is a sophomore at Texas Agricultural and Mechanical University in College Station, an "Aggie."[20] His hometown is in Raymondville, Texas, in the subtropical lower Rio Grande Valley and as far south as cotton grows anywhere in the United States. He is majoring in agricultural economics, and his course of study looks not unlike Frank Summerville's. His plans, however, include a detour first. Like his father Joe before him (also an Aggie "ag" economics major), he is in A&M's ROTC Corps of Cadets and is attending school on an Air Force scholarship. He wants first to fly, then to farm.

The two ambitions afford an interesting contrast, which he could yet come to evaluate differently: the economic cocoon and occasional excitement of military life (outside Sweden, the last true bastion of the welfare

[19] Hugh Summerville interview, November 21, 2000.
[20] Following: Spence Pennington interview, November 17, 2000.

state?) versus the economic roller-coaster and different variety of excitement attached to living perennially close to the edge, as in production agriculture. Security or independence?

For now, Spence's mind is set, despite some stern fatherly warnings. "Seems like my dad is sometimes my greatest opponent," he says of the talks they have had over the years. But as the son went off to college determined to study "ag economics," the father did not stand in his way.

Like many farm boys, Spence grew up around machinery – both the real thing and, before he was ready for that, toys. Ben Franklin Stores up and down the Farm Belt have sold them for decades: sturdy die-cast replicas of tractors, plows, manure spreaders, and combines. His first was a red "International" tractor. ("My grandpa used to run 'all-red' and made the conversion to 'green' [John Deere] after a while."). Spence still has that red toy tractor. He also has stories, before he was there to remember, of his pregnant mother driving a tractor at two in the morning, hauling cotton trailers. They were harvesting in July and August. Spence was a September baby and so figures he was helping to make his first cotton crop "about eight months on the way." There are pictures of himself as a little boy, up in a cotton trailer, in the soon-to-vanish ritual of "stompin' cotton."

Farm life encourages early development of practical skills and an understanding of their economic purpose. "Chores" on a farm have a meaning that "taking out the trash" in a suburban home does not. For farm boys, driving a tractor is a hallowed rite of passage into the grown-up world. Spence got his first taste of the real thing in stages. "I'd driven with the hands forever; I'd sit in their laps and drive; they'd actually fall asleep every once in a while, so I'd just be out there driving; I guess I learned from some of the best." Then one day when he was 11 or 12, his father picked him up after school and took him out to the middle of a 550-acre field, put his son atop the biggest piece of equipment he owned (an 8650 John Deere four-wheel drive tractor), and let him go. Spence drove it all afternoon. There was a radio in the cab, so the father could keep an ear out, and the big field itself was a precaution: "He didn't want me to hit anything." There was no turning back.

A farm is also a remarkably transparent place. Children see a lot, and not all of it is pretty. As Spence matured during some of cotton's toughest times in the 1990s, he drew some conclusions about how the world of agriculture works. "It's kind of ironic, how I love equipment and tractors and all that kind of stuff, but I know the problem of agriculture is not production or equipment, it's the money side. We produce more than we ever

Most U.S. cotton comes from family farms, highly capital-intensive and managerially sophisticated business units. For young people who would be cotton growers, the cost of entry can be prohibitively high, unless there is a "family way." (Cotton pickers cost $250,000.) Spence Pennington (right), who is studying agricultural economics in college, hopes someday to farm with his father, Joe. Raymondville, Texas, 2000.

thought we could produce, more efficiently than we ever could before, but we just can't sell it." Like many young people, Spence has a high-minded side: for a farmer, it is consoling to remember that he is working to feed and clothe the world, take care of the land and so forth. But that is not enough. "I don't need to devote my life to making more, I need to devote my life to trying to get something for it." (Thus he will major in ag economics, not engineering, and only minor in agronomy.)

He remembers his father coming in from the field in the evening, too many times with a frown and a headache, to face the numbers. "A lot of our numbers then were in parentheses [negative]. That doesn't make you feel very good." Yet he did not draw the obvious conclusion and set his sights on becoming a lawyer, a doctor, or businessman. "I saw the worst [of agriculture], and *still* loved it."

Spence's father, Joe, entered the farming business because his own father had been in it before him and offered the opportunity (though he inherited no land and "paid for every acre I own 'at market'," Joe was able to use his father's equipment years before he could afford to buy his own).[21] In turn, Joe will give his son every opportunity that he can. He does not know if this will be enough. He remembers thinking that – when Spence came to him and said, "Dad, I want to come back and farm; I love the farm" – well, it was time for a serious talk.

But for right now, some distance between Spence and his father's farm is probably prudent. "I've watched my dad fight it all these years," Spence says, "so it's probably best for me to go away for a while." His Air Force trajectory presents three options. He could come back after the minimum four-year commitment that goes with his ROTC contract. Or, if he commits to becoming a pilot, it would be another twelve years (after college) before he could get back to the farm. Or, he could just stay in the military for twenty years and take his pension. "Then I could blow all my retirement money farming." Only then he probably wouldn't remember how to do anything. "I'd be so out of the loop that I wouldn't be able to be competitive at all."

The father will not say, like the son, that he loves to farm. "I have enjoyed it, but I enjoy it a hell of a lot more when I'm making money. The 1990s were very character-building years for me." Joe is only 51 and plans to be around a while longer yet. So Spence can go off and do his flying. That may be best, anyway. If he were ready today, Joe would have a hard time getting him started. When he comes back, maybe things will be better. "I hope when he does, times are good again, but I don't know."

Farmers are fatalistic optimists who run on a long charge of hope. You can hear it in the father's voice. "I've been telling my family that it will change one of these days – that it's just one of those cycles. But I think the change we're going to see is going to be a radical one." He hopes it will leave room for Spence.

COOPERATING TO INFLUENCE DEMAND

Competitiveness in cotton agriculture requires cooperation. Farmers, historically, are a fiercely independent-minded lot, which (some would say) has been their downfall when it comes to contending with the concentrated economic power of the institutions sometimes arrayed against them. The

---

[21] Joe Pennington interview, July 28, 2000.

New Mexico growers raise some of the highest-quality Acala upland cotton grown in the United States, all of it irrigated. Dairies increasingly compete for the same land and water. Three generations – Morgan Nelson (center), son-in-law Harold N. Houghtaling, Jr., and grandson Steven Houghtaling – tend their crop near Roswell, 2000.

conflict between wheat farmers and the railroads in the nineteenth century comes to mind. So does the relation between cotton farmers and mill owners in the twentieth century. It is the same principle of "involvement" that historically brought farmers together in local cooperative ventures, like Mississippi's Delta Council or the (Texas) Plains Cotton Cooperative, to advance and defend their mutual interests.

Cotton growers take pride in the organizational lineage that stretches from the Delta Council to other institutions that would give cotton a voice far beyond their local regions.[22] The National Cotton Council (1938), the Cotton Producers Institute (1960), the Cotton Board (1966), and Cotton Incorporated (1970) were successive attempts to serve grower interests on a

---

[22] The Staple Cotton Cooperative Association ("Staplcotn"), founded in Greenville in 1921, is the oldest continuously operating cotton marketing cooperative. See Noel Workman, *Staplcotn: The First 75 Years* (Greenville, 1996). See also Jack Lichtenstein, *Field to Fabric: The Story of American Cotton Growers* (Lubbock: Texas Tech University Press, 1990), a nicely detailed study of the Plains Cotton Cooperative and its role in promoting regional interests in cotton markets and quality.

national level. Each of these organizations served cotton in different ways. The National Cotton Council was a trade association and political lobby representing all segments of the cotton industry. The Cotton Producers Institute was a stopgap defense against the assault on cotton's markets by synthetic fibers. The Cotton Board was a quasi-public agency established by federal statute to oversee collection and distribution of grower funds to finance a cotton research and promotion program. All were efforts that focused mainly on cotton *supply* issues. Only after growers realized that they could actively influence the *demand* side of their business did the job of carrying out that program finally fall to Cotton Incorporated.

Eddie Smith talks hopefully about building on thirty years of experience in the management of demand. He is due to become chairman of Cotton Incorporated in 2002. It is a job that will require much uncompensated time and effort, just as it does for the company's hundred or so active board members. He paid his first dollar-a-bale "assessment" to support Cotton Incorporated in 1973, the year he brought in his first crop, the one that earned him enough to buy a tractor and a house. He has had good and not-so-good years since then but has not wavered in his conviction that his yearly assessment to the Cotton Board – which contracts with Cotton Incorporated to conduct research, technical development, and promotion for cotton – is the best money he ever spent. Back in the days when they were allowed, Smith never took a refund on his assessment, even in bad years, and he never had much patience with the "freeloaders" who did. How else, he says, could a bunch of cotton growers have a prayer of standing up to the likes of DuPont, the leading manufacturer and marketer of synthetic fibers?

Like Ted Sheely in California, Billy Percy in Mississippi, and Johnny Gramling in South Carolina, Eddie Smith's problems – high costs, low prices, stagnant yields, marginal profitability – are business problems, but with a strong political component. Government farm programs have long factored into the business of agriculture and are hard to separate from the brute logic of the market. Like all businessmen, Smith both loves and hates government assistance. It is good to have when one needs it, but it takes decisions out of the hands of individuals. Smith also abhors what he sees as the chronic instability in public policy and would simply like some clearer signals about what game he is expected to play. Now that the industry's research and promotion program is well financed (thanks to legislation making the assessments that fund Cotton Incorporated mandatory to growers

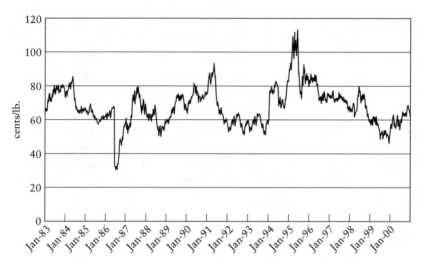

Figure 3. U.S. cotton prices since 1983. *Sources:* Data provided by Cotton Incorporated and the New York Board of Trade.

and importers of cotton textiles), a policy vacuum still threatens. "The Congress of the United States is going to have to define what they want out of U.S. agriculture," Smith says. Right now, he is frustrated at being told to compete in world markets, not so much against foreign growers as against the foreign governments that subsidize them. "Other countries do subsidize their agriculture," he declares emphatically – and far more than any farm aid provided by the U.S. government. "And we're competing with those countries."

Even so, from his West Texas perspective, relying on traditional forms of farm aid looks like a loser's game. In a free-trading world, the old supply management–oriented farm policies dating back to the New Deal simply will not work. If the United States cuts acreage in the hope of reducing supply and increasing price, then other producing countries will see the opportunity to fill the gap and take more market share: "And they'll take it!" Hence the pressure to increase demand and sustain competitive advantage in fiber quality only goes up, and with it Smith's support for the cotton growers' research and promotion program. With the costs of production soaring, he believes that margins can be maintained only on the top side, through increased demand.

Like most growers, conservative politically as they are, Smith feels a bit embarrassed at the thought of accepting subsidies. He would rather

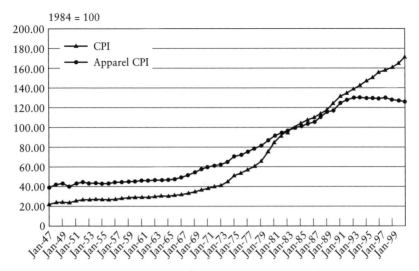

Figure 4. Consumer Price Index and Apparel Consumer Price Index (SA), 1947–2000 (1984 = 100). *Source:* U.S. Department of Agriculture, National Agricultural Statistics Service.

just compete, fair and square. Percy, Pennington, Sheely, Gramling, and Summerville would all agree. It is a credible claim, particularly when one considers the unforeseen circumstances that soon engulfed the good intentions of the 1996 "Freedom to Farm" Act. The policy of weaning farmers away from income supports and encouraging them to follow their instincts to plant what profited most discriminated against cotton, where infrastructure and equipment requirements made switching more difficult than, say, changing from wheat to corn. It also assumed that there would in fact be profit differentials between crops and that, if a producer found it difficult to profit with one crop, then something else would offer stronger markets and better returns. The problem was that, as the refrain went across the Cotton Belt, "everything tanked together." Because cotton was more vulnerable to begin with, its growers had warned that everything depended on at least some commodity prices staying high; if they didn't, serious trouble would follow. "As long as any one of the major commodities is in short supply and its price is high, it brings all the other prices up," Percy explained it for them all. "If soybeans are high, in order to get any cotton planted, the price of cotton has got to go up to compete for those acres. Otherwise, we are all going to plant soybeans. But what has happened to us now is that they are *all* at forty-year lows."

It is a situation which has put the federal government in the ironic position of doling out the record emergency assistance cited by USDA chief economist Collins, even as it professes a policy of increasing market incentives, and which puts growers in the unhappy position of accepting such assistance or going broke. There is little margin for error. Even if he has three or four great years in a row, with the capital that a cotton farmer has to employ, concludes Billy Percy without a smile, "I don't care how well you've done, one or two bad years and you are gone."

Like all industries, cotton growing is a product of its history. And Cotton Incorporated, which has been remarkably successful in increasing demand for cotton over the past thirty years, is the product of nearly two centuries of experience, much of it in vain, of trying to manage cotton supply. One cannot know what lies ahead for U.S. cotton growers, but a better understanding of its past might help better prepare for the future. It is far from irrelevant to begin with an appreciation for how cotton came to dominate the American agricultural economy in the nineteenth century and to see why it has remained important to the U.S. economy in the postindustrial age.

PART ONE
MANAGING SUPPLY

"THE SNOW OF SOUTHERN SUMMERS"

King Cotton and Its Markets in the Age of Industrial Revolution

Combine natural resources, financial capital, human talent, and energy – so that the end product is worth more than the sum of the inputs – and an economic "good" is what you get. The story of American upland cotton is a remarkable story of goods creation and subsequent economic growth. It began with the powerful conjunction of a particular demand and a particular supply, which were to fuel the economic and social transformation of the first two industrialized nations: the United Kingdom (and later, New England), which represented demand; and the southern United States, which represented supply.

The story of mass-produced cotton is peopled with a broad cast of characters having similar yet far from identical interests. For those among them who actually raised the cotton from seed, sun, and soil – and who have included (at different times and places) farmers, planters, growers, slaves, and sharecroppers – the story of upland cotton constitutes a hard lesson in how technological advancement in agriculture did not automatically yield progress. For progress to occur, markets had to be made, and the market for cotton was, until "modern times," severely limited by the high cost of the raw material. It came into its own as a mass-market commodity only at the end of the eighteenth century, when an entire modern industry began to emerge around the cotton plant, *the* industry that formed the very core of the Industrial Revolution. Around cotton coalesced new "high technologies" in steam power and automated machinery as well as coordinated marketing and managerial systems that linked the continuous stages of transformation from harvest to woven textile, from the field to the final customer.

Cultivated in pockets of the world since ancient times – aboriginal peoples of what is now New Mexico, for example, grew it for clothing 10,000

years ago – cotton was for most people a difficult fiber to use.[1] Before
the coming of inexpensive cotton cloth in the nineteenth century, most of
the inhabited world dressed uncomfortably and uncleanly in clothes made
from wool or dressed expensively in linens and silks. In northern countries, where sheep were abundant and cottage spinning and weaving well
developed, woolen textiles thrived for centuries, largely without competition. But wool was filled with oil; it was hard to wash and rough on the
skin. It itched, stored disease-bearing bacteria, and did little for the cause
of good hygiene among ordinary people. Southern countries, on the other
hand, with growing seasons long and warm enough to permit cultivation of
cotton, gradually gained experience of the plant's advantages when woven
into a textile. If what the North needed was good washable underwear
made from cotton, in the South cotton might suffice as cool outer garments
alone. North or South, the problem lay not with knowledge of the product
but rather with the price.

Hence cotton, as grown in the eighteenth century, was no substitute
for traditional clothing; compared to it, everything else was cheap. The
value-added multiple for top-end fine cotton muslin has been calculated at
around 900! Even for rougher qualities, the relative labor intensiveness of
cotton manufacture crippled its competitiveness among fibers. One or two
man-days of labor sufficed to produce a pound of woolen thread, two to
five for linen, six for silk. Labor-hungry cotton, however, consumed two
weeks.[2] Even so, cotton felt good to the touch, and when converted into
printed cloth it became highly fashionable in eighteenth-century England –
penetrating the market just enough to excite anxiety in the native woolen
industry, which campaigned unsuccessfully to block its importation and
growth. Even so, the appeal of printed cotton fabrics from the Far East
prompted local entrepreneurs to copy. By mid-century, Lancashire firms
were profitably manufacturing "fustian," a fabric with a cotton woof and a
linen warp, that spurred demand. The Near East and the West Indies supplied the raw cotton.

Cotton's growth in popularity was steady though at first unspectacular,
rising in England from some 3 million pounds in 1751 to over 5 million

[1] On cotton's origins, see C. L. Brubaker et al., "The Origin and Domestication of Cotton," in
C. Wayne Smith and J. Tom Cothren, eds., *Cotton: Origin, History, Technology and Production* (New York: Wiley, 1999), 3–32.
[2] Henry Hobhouse, *Seeds of Change: Five Plants That Transformed the World* (New York:
Harper & Row, 1986), 144ff.

pounds thirty years later. Then, something happened. By 1786, English imports of raw cotton nearly quadrupled to 19 million pounds. Five years after that, the number was 29 million pounds.[3] The explosion of demand for raw fiber was due to a well-known progression of inventions, as mechanization of the two chief processes of textile manufacture – spinning and weaving – addressed the problems of the high cost of finished cotton cloth.

The progression began with Kay's manually powered flying shuttle (1733), which increased the speed of weaving and thus also increased pressure on hand spinners to keep up. The water frame, patented by Arkwright in 1769, made possible the replacement of hand power with water power in spinning and combined the drawing out and the spinning of cotton fibers into a single operation. In 1770, Hargreaves patented the spinning jenny, in which one wheel drove as many as 100 spindles and produced a fine, strong yarn. Crompton's mule (1790) refined the spinning process further. Finally, Cartwright's power loom (patented in 1785 but not perfected until the early nineteenth century) enabled weaving to catch up with spinning and so restore balance between the key elements of the manufacturing process.

The story was not complete, however, without the addition of yet another new source of power. Water wheels drove the first mechanized mills, limiting those that could operate at scale to locations blessed with fast-running rivers. In the nineteenth century, steam engines would be perfected to extend cotton manufacture well beyond previous limits. With steam-powered machinery, spinning moved decisively out of the cottage and into the mill, where it sped the integration of spinning and weaving in factories. Advantages of scale and increased manufacturing capacity in turn enlarged demand for raw material and created yet another imbalance.[4]

Thus the growth of cotton was aided by technology, but neither its widespread diffusion nor its cost-saving potential were guaranteed. Adventurous entrepreneurs had to act: first to capitalize on technology in England's proto-industrial midlands, and then to spread the technology abroad. Only then would competition spur efficient gains and bring prices down. Seeking to monopolize the trade in cotton textiles, England enacted laws forbidding the export of any of the new textile technologies as well as emigration

[3] Stuart Bruchey, *Cotton and the Growth of the American Economy, 1790–1860* (New York: Harcourt, Brace & World, 1967), 43ff., table 2E.

[4] Ibid., 44–5. Also see Paul Joseph Mantoux, *The Industrial Revolution in the Eighteenth Century* (London: Jonathan Cape, 1961).

of craftsmen who possessed key mechanical knowledge. But when mill apprentice Samuel Slater memorized the details of Arkwright's water frame and other devices and made off for America in 1789, England's mills were doomed to competition. Slater landed in Rhode Island, where he built a modest spinning mill. Small groups of weavers continued to produce the finished cloth until Francis Cabot Lowell introduced a successful power loom in 1813; he opened an integrated textile factory in Massachusetts, the forerunner of America's own cotton textile industry.[5]

This progression of technology would in time crown cotton as "King" for more than a hundred years. It was cotton that primed the industrialization of the Atlantic world, leading to historically unprecedented economic growth. Cotton was an early, dramatic example of industry "leadership" in the growth process. Just as automobiles and electronics have functioned as leaders of economic growth in the twentieth century – with long linkages reaching backward and forward through the economy, spurring increases in income and employment – so cotton served in the nineteenth century, particularly before the Civil War. Nothing else approached it. A U.S. crop of 3,000 bales in 1790 grew to 330,000 in 1820, to 1.3 million in 1840, and to 3.8 million in 1860.[6] Between 1815 and 1860, cotton accounted for more than half the value of American exports; its earnings financed 60 percent of the nation's imports, including not just manufactured consumables but capital goods like railroad iron. Among leading branches of manufacture in the United States in 1860, cotton goods ranked second (behind only flour and meal) at $107 million and ranked first in value added by manufacture, $54 million. However, perhaps the most important consequence of the huge demand for cotton, as it related to economic growth, was creation of a market broad enough to promote specialized economic activity in different sectors and different geographic regions. As southern agriculture concentrated its resources in cotton, it grew more efficient and used its earnings to trade, in America's growing internal market, for the East's manufactured goods and financial and transportation services and for the West's foodstuffs. Specialization encouraged trade and boosted productivity of the whole economy.[7]

---

[5] Irving R. Starbird et al., *The U.S. Cotton Industry* (Washington, DC: U.S. Department of Agriculture Economic Research Service, 1987), 4.

[6] USDA, 1936; see Smith and Cothren, *Cotton*, table 3.1.1, p. 436.

[7] See Douglass C. North, *Growth and Welfare in the American Past* (Englewood Cliffs: Prentice-Hall, 1966), 75ff.; *The Economic Growth of the United States* (Englewood Cliffs: Prentice-Hall, 1961).

THE RIGHT PLANT

Cotton owed its American preeminence to the mechanization of English textile mills and the sudden disequilibrium that mechanization created between demand and supply. Egypt and the Caribbean islands were supplanted as sources of the cotton fiber that fed England's mills because of American Eli Whitney's mechanical solution to the problem of separating cotton fiber from cotton seed. This seemingly simple task was so time-consuming that it made raw cotton very expensive to process. Shortening it would revolutionize the industry and the world. Whitney's "cotton engine" was one of history's supreme examples of the right technological innovation answering the right market challenge at the right time – and, it should be added, at just the right price. The "gin" (short for "engine") or "saw gin" (because it sawed the fibers in order to extract the seed) was the instrument that enabled cotton growers to answer English demand by exploiting a different sort of cotton plant.

Two domesticated varieties of cotton then grew in the United States. "Sea Island" cotton was a "long staple" variety that had been introduced in the 1780s with seed brought from the Bahamas. Its silky, lengthy, sturdy fibers found quick favor and good prices in the English market, and production responded sharply, reaching 9 million pounds in 1805.[8] It had the additional advantage of seed that separated from the fiber easily – merely by squeezing the cotton between a pair of rollers. It was fussy, though, about where it grew. Climatic sensitivity confined long staple to a relatively short strip of land, 30 to 40 miles wide, along the South Carolina and Georgia coastline. Thus, while it sustained a premium price throughout the antebellum period of cotton's great ascendancy, its production never expanded beyond 16 million pounds, a mere fraction of what would become America's annual national cotton production as the nineteenth century advanced.

Gossypium hirsutum, or short staple "upland" cotton, was a hardier plant, better adapted to the South's vast interior. Its development as a viable commercial crop took a long time. A strain that probably originated in what is now Guatemala and southern Mexico, upland cotton derived its name from the territory above the Fall Line, which separated Tidewater

---

[8] Bruchey, *Cotton and the Growth of the American Economy,* 45; Starbird et al., *The U.S. Cotton Industry,* 3.

from Piedmont in the new nation's South Atlantic region. Spanish explorers had reported such cotton growing in Brazil and Peru in the sixteenth century; Columbus had come upon aboriginals clad in woven cotton fabrics before that. Upland cotton had been grown continuously in Virginia and the Carolinas since the 1620s, but the crop was an economically marginal proposition. It came with the grave handicap of a short sticky fiber, which made it hard to remove the green seeds within. One worker might remove seed from only one to two pounds of lint per day, and the consequent high labor cost of extracting the raw fiber made other crops (such as tobacco, rice, and indigo) more profitable.[9]

Whitney's gin changed all that. In a few short years, the leap in productivity from ginning upland cotton enabled southern states to supply the voracious demand of England's (and, to a lesser degree, New England's) entire cotton textile industry – and to profit handsomely in the process. The first cotton gin was an elegantly simple device inspired, it is said, by Whitney's observation of a plantation cat clawing the carcass of a dead chicken and coming up with clean feathers. His original machine consisted of a solid wooden cylinder studded with teethlike headless nails, which drew the *seed cotton* (the term for cotton picked but not yet ginned) through a wire mesh. A second revolving cylinder then brushed the seedless lint from the teeth of the first cylinder and dropped it into baskets for hand transport to an adjacent "press," which compacted the lint into a bale. The bale was the unit of measure in which the seedless cotton thence entered the market, bound for the mill. (The seed, in the early days, was regarded as waste.) With such a "cotton engine" at his disposal, a planter could produce not merely one but *fifty* pounds per day. As Whitney himself wrote of his discovery: "This machine may be turned by water or with a horse, with the greatest ease, and one man and a horse will do more than fifty men with the old machines. It makes the labor fifty times less, without throwing that class of People out of business."[10]

Once it became economically feasible, upland cotton culture in the American South moved forward in rhythm to an immutable yearly cycle, from preparation of the soil through to the harvest. The land was broken and rows were run in late winter, seed was planted in April, sprouts were thinned

[9] Joshua A. Lee, "Cotton as a World Crop," in *Cotton, Agronomy Monograph No. 24* (Madison, 1984); ibid., 4.

[10] Bruchey, *Cotton and the Growth of the American Economy*; Constance M. Green, *Eli Whitney and the Birth of American Technology* (New York, 1956).

and weeds were chopped well into July. The crop was then "laid by," and the plantation world had to abide until September or October for nature to bring forth her fruit. Bolls burst into puffs of white lint – Charleston poet Henry Timrod's "snow of southern summers" – and fieldhands with long sacks dragged behind them worked up and down the rows, stooped low, picking cotton. They emptied the sacks into baskets in the field, and mule-drawn wagons carried the baskets to the gin. Up to the point of ginning, the routine of cotton tillage relied on primitive implements and muscle power alone: the one-mule plow, the simple hoe, the human hand.[11]

TO GIN AND TO MARKET

The cotton gin in effect "corrected" a critical economic and technological imbalance between supply and demand, between the boundless fecundity of the southern land for growing *Gossypium hirsutum* and the boundless appetite of the mechanizing textile industry for consuming it. What amounted to a quantum shift in the supply of cotton would not have occurred so quickly had Whitney's great invention not been so simple and so easy to copy. If the machine's simplicity was well-suited to the rudimentary mechanical skill levels of an agrarian labor force, it was also an open invitation to imitators. Whitney took out a patent in 1794, and the gin's simplicity should have made it hard to match in performance by alternative means. Yet the prospects for enforcement were weak. The pirates, usually farmers who simply devised their own gins, prevailed, which kept

---

[11] Identified with the group of Charleston writers led by William Gilmore Simms in the 1850s, Timrod was generally regarded as "poet laureate of the Confederacy" and of the Cotton Kingdom at its zenith. The phrase "Snow of southern summers" appeared in the poem "Ethnogenesis" (1861), in which Timrod expressed the high hopes of the South at the beginning of the Civil War. "The Cotton Boll" (1861) affirmed the unity between cotton and the Confederacy and conjured an image of the southern landscape that transcended the political excitements of the moment and the florid style of the age:

> To the remotest point of sight,
> Although I gaze upon no waste of snow,
> The endless field is white;
> And the whole landscape glows,
> For many a shining league away,
> With such accumulated light
> As Polar lands would flash beneath a tropic day!

See Thomas Daniel Young et al., eds., *The Literature of the South* (Glenview: Scott, Foresman, 1968), 290ff.

The lone farmer plodding in the fields behind one or two mules was a common sight in cotton agriculture in many parts of the South well into the 1940s. Together, they supplied both the motive power and much of the know-how that drove the Cotton Kingdom.

the cost of the technology low.[12] Cotton gins proliferated and moved with the cotton, from the Old South of the Carolinas and Georgia into newer territories of Alabama, Mississippi, Tennessee, Louisiana, Arkansas, and Texas.

The image of the planter's white-columned "big house" came to dominate the architectural mythology of the antebellum plantation South, but it was the decidedly unromantic "gin house" that defined the economic reality. Most plantations of any size had one of their own, typically a two-story barn-like structure built according to a carpenter's pattern book. The working components – the gin stand, the running gear, and the press – could be purchased from a variety of regional manufacturers and agents.

[12] Patent law was then in the rudimentary stages of development in the United States. It is estimated that the machine that made cotton king in the American South and fueled the Industrial Revolution in Britain earned its inventor no more than $100,000.

To the modern eye, an antebellum-era gin house looks an odd mismatch of big shell to small innards. Power requirements made it so. The ground floor, dirt and typically open to the air on two or three sides, was given over to a treadmill, and it was the speed and endurance of the mules that drove it that determined the capacity of the gin. Great geared wheels and pulleys transformed plodding animal power into the concentrated mechanical energy needed to drive the saws and cylinders of the gin on the floor above. Hoisted manually by the basketful to the ginning floor above, seed cotton was fed into a device typically no bigger than two or three large sewing machines. The most popular gins by the eve of the Civil War contained sixty closely-packed lint-cutting saws and could extract enough seed to produce (depending on the efficiency of the mule power below) three to six 400-pound bales per day. The other energy requirement, of course, was human. In addition to the half dozen mules that drove the gin engine (and the others that were harnessed to the long poles that turned the giant wooden screw of the press), eight to fifteen laborers toiled hour after hour to hoist up the seed cotton and haul out the lint.[13]

This was a seasonal ritual, repeated every autumn at thousands of gins across the American South. Between the gins and the mills, cotton followed a path filled with middlemen. The central figure was the *factor,* who marketed the crop and supplied the planter with credit for making it. In colonial

[13] Charles S. Aiken, *The Cotton Plantation South Since the Civil War* (Baltimore: Johns Hopkins University Press, 1998), 12–13. Also Daniel A. Tomkins, *Cotton and Cotton Oil* (Charlotte, 1901, privately published); Ulrich B. Phillips, *Life and Labor in the Old South* (Boston: Little, Brown, 1929); Frederick Law Olmsted, *A Journey in the Seaboard Slave States* (New York: Dix & Edwards, 1856). A number of antebellum gins have been preserved, a few in working condition. One of the best mule-powered examples is the Henderson & Chisolm gin, probably built around 1850 in Georgia and restored today in Laurinburg (Scotland County), North Carolina.

Among architectural icons of the South's cotton landscape, next to the plantation house itself there is probably no more powerful image than the cotton gin. One of the best fictional representations can be found in novelist Ferrol Sam's account of a Georgia boyhood in the 1930s, *Run with Horsemen* (New York: Penguin, 1984, p. 363): "Mounted on timbers, the two-storied gin was completely covered with corrugated sheets of galvanized metal. It was filled with horribly complicated machinery that spun and rattled behind glass-covered lids in a dizzying whirl, separating seeds from the cotton. The noise level was soul-shattering, and conversation had to be conducted by yelling at maximum volume over a distance of no more than four inches. If the line of wagons dwindled, the operator blew a steam whistle to announce to all farmers within five miles that the gin was eager for business. Muted by distance, the whistle was a not unpleasant part of the rural scene, but added to the cacophony of the vibrating machinery, it was a totally unexpected screech that hurt the ears and made a small boy grab for his grandfather."

times, Tidewater tobacco planters had often dealt directly with factors in London. But in the postcolonial cotton culture, as planters pushed westward and spread out, factors also spread out from England and the North, deep into the Cotton Kingdom. Important interior towns like Columbia, Augusta, Montgomery, Nashville, and Memphis were filled with factors. On the edges of the cotton frontier, where volumes still were low, the village storekeeper might serve the same middleman function.

Cotton began its journey when a wagonload of bales left the gin for the factor's warehouse in a market town. A planter who lived near a river could avail himself of flatboats. The factor might sell the cotton directly, even without unloading it, or he might hold it for a more favorable market. Typically, planters gave factors wide leeway about when to sell and at what price, and factors typically shared information freely with planters.[14] Their commission (figured usually at 2.5 percent of the sale proceeds) depended on gleaning good information from coastal factors and from northern and English merchants and judging the market wisely. Factors operated in a crowded market and competed on the basis of their ability to dispose of the planter's crop at the optimum price and their readiness to supply the planter with credit to finance the crop from planting to harvest. The factor was a middleman in two directions. The cotton plantation system and the factorage system depended mutually, and heavily, on credit, which made it possible for planters to specialize in growing cotton and for factors to find the best markets for it.[15]

Factors were experts, with responsibility for making sales on behalf of planters. Selling directly in the factor's own inland market town might save transportion and insurance costs for shipment to a seaport, but buyers were more abundant on the coast and prices often higher. More buyers and more active demand made Charleston, Savannah, Mobile, and New Orleans the biggest cotton markets in the antebellum era. The local factor's business connections and partnerships in those cities enhanced his own competitive position and opened broader markets to his planter clients. Those markets could also extend beyond the South, and larger southern factorage houses enjoyed relationships with northern and European firms.

---

[14] Information on prices and sales in various markets appeared in newspapers in market centers, in the commercial journals (*Hunt's Merchants' Magazine*; *DeBow's Review*), and in circulars and specialized publications (*Price Currents*) published in major port cities.

[15] Harold D. Woodman, *King Cotton and His Retainers* (Lexington: University of Kentucky Press, 1968), 30–42; Bruchey, *Cotton and the Growth of the American Economy*, 224–5.

Cotton bales are bulky; in a region with poor roads but laced with streams and rivers, much cotton found its way to market on water. Steamboats loaded to the gunwales with cotton were a familiar sight throughout the South after the harvest came in.

For example, Baring Brothers and Company in England and also Brown Brothers and Company in New York and Baltimore took cotton on consignment from southern factors for later sale in England and maintained their own representatives in the southern ports as well.[16]

If a southern factor chose to move the cotton out for sale, it might travel directly from Savannah or New Orleans to Liverpool, the port that dominated English cotton commerce. Chances were good, however, that it would travel first to New York (and, if it were shipped directly, chances were good it would sail aboard a ship owned and insured by a New York firm). New York was a long-standing mercantile entrepôt, the primary destination and distribution center for manufactured goods imported from Britain, which increasingly included manufactured cotton textiles. New York's mercantile firms entered the supply side of the cotton trade quickly, after the War of 1812, securing bales from southern factors for transshipment to British mercantile houses eager to buy and ready to pay with exported manufactures.

[16] Woodman, *King Cotton and His Retainers,* 16–19.

Though plainly not the most direct arrangement, export of southern cotton to England via New York made perfect economic sense. A range of natural and institutional advantages accounted for New York's prominence in cotton. It had the finest harbor in the United States, with good sea access to the southeastern cotton ports as well as New England, and it developed packet lines sailing regular schedules to the South and to destinations across the Atlantic. At a critical point in its development, the state legislature required auctioneers, when cotton was largely sold that way, to sell to the highest bidder (other markets operated on a minimum bid system), which brought more buyers in. To the west, the Hudson–Mohawk corridor and (after 1825) the Erie Canal afforded access to the vast transmontane hinterland. New York could also claim long experience and specialized skills in international trade, and it was home to financial institutions with the capital necessary to finance future cotton crops at attractive rates. New York occupied one of the corners of what has been called the transatlantic "cotton triangle," reaching from the American South to New York to England. The image is somewhat misleading, however, since a considerable part of the trade moved along just two sides of the triangle: southern cotton first sailed north and then east; English manufactured goods first sailed west and then south. Such two-sidedness was testimony to New York's central role in the financing and marketing of southern cotton.[17]

The factor, where the route to an intricate world market began, was the seller's agent. Brokers, whose names also appear in the record of many sales transactions, acted as intermediaries between seller and buyer, frequently negotiating with the factor over the grade and classification of the cotton in question, which was of great importance in determining its value. Buyers themselves came in many descriptions. Some were speculators operating, as one Charleston factor described their activity, in the spirit of "cotton to be restored and resold later."[18] Others were the buyer-speculators who

---

[17] Glenn Porter and Harold Livesay, *Merchants and Manufacturers* (Baltimore: Johns Hopkins University Press, 1971), 18–19; Bruchey, *Cotton and the Growth of the American Economy*, 226–7.

[18] Edward Sullivan, a British visitor to New Orleans in the early 1850s, was more colorful: "During the whole winter the city is thronged with cotton speculators .... People make bets about the probable rise and fall in the price of cotton in the same way as a man does his bets on the 'Derby.' It appears that the real amount of the yield of cotton is never exactly known, and all the great speculators have touts, who are despatched [sic] into the different cotton districts to send information to their employers. As their accounts differ, so does the spirit of gambling increase, each man considering his information better than his neighbor's, and backing it

operated between southern and northern (or European) markets – buying, shipping, and then hoping to resell at a profit after transportation costs were deducted. A third sort were agent-buyers working on commission and buying on direct orders from northern or European merchants or cotton spinners. Such buyers also frequently traded on their own, sharing the risk and anticipating some of the reward.[19]

The demand that drove the system and paid the planters and all the middlemen was relentless, flattening competition from other textiles and enabling English and American manufacturers to push their product out the factory door with no need for marketing. In 1810, American-grown cotton made up almost half of the 79 million pounds of raw fiber consumed in England. In 1830, 70 percent of England's 248-million-pound importation came from the American South. On the eve of the Civil War, in 1860, southern planters supplied 92 percent of the over 1,000 million pounds shipped to the old mother country.[20] Nor should one forget the influence of the smaller but growing American textile industry. Located chiefly in New England, American textile mills supplied more than three fourths of all cotton cloth consumed in the United States by the mid-nineteenth century and consumed a third of the raw cotton fiber grown in the South.

Of course neither the growers, nor the textile mills, nor the intermediaries who sold cotton to the mills or textiles to retailers did any "marketing" in the modern sense of the term. There was no systematic information on the markets for cotton and no techniques for assessing the impact of weather conditions, demographics, political events, patterns of world trade, or, for that matter, consumer spending. Mills produced textiles on the basis of experience and hope, and they simply cut production and purchasing when gluts appeared, sending prices for raw cotton tumbling. Distant financial shocks might upset international trade in commodities, which would also reverberate back to the farms, catching growers unaware. But such vicissitudes, like the weather, were short-run shocks that paled in comparison to the long-term opportunity.[21] Cotton was a growth industry, and – as

accordingly." *Rambles and Scrambles in North and South America* (London, 1852), 217–18, cited in Woodman, *King Cotton and His Retainers*, 27.

[19] Ibid., 28–9.

[20] Hobson, *Seeds of Change*, 181.

[21] This is not to diminish the impact of cotton gluts or external shocks on the welfare of growers and market intermediaries, and even financial institutions. In 1839, amidst an economic depression, the Bank of the United States of Pennsylvania (the privatized vestige of the Federal

Table I. *Upland cotton production, exports,
and prices, 1790–1860*

Year	Crop (bales)	Exports (bales)	Price (cents; New York)
1790	8,889	889	26
1800	210,526	91,716	44
1810	269,360	208,950	16
1820	647,482	449,257	14
1830	1,038,847	773,000	10
1840	1,634,954	1,313,500	10
1850	2,454,442	1,988,710	12
1860	3,849,469	3,127,565	13

Sources: Stuart Bruchey, *Cotton and the Growth of the
American Economy, 1790–1860* (New York: Harcourt,
Brace & World, 1967); Ralph Gray and John M. Peterson,
Economic Development of the United States, rev. ed.
(Homewood, Ill.: Irwin, 1974).

with all growth industries – prices trended down gradually as output increased exponentially. Marketing, except insofar as it involved effective selling (moving the product to buyers), was not a critical issue.

Never before, and certainly not since, has the demand for any one crop fired economic growth to the degree that cotton did in the United States during the five decades before the Civil War. Without cotton, that economic growth would have been far less dramatic. Some other things would have been different, too.

THE DARK SIDE: ECONOMY OF THE SLAVE PLANTATION

Cotton's consequences were not all good. Inexpensive, washable clothing – which much of humanity had not enjoyed before the coming of the spinning

government's defunct central bank) issued short-term interest-bearing notes pegged to the price of cotton as a means to help settle the country's adverse trade balances. Other banks followed suit. To sustain the price of cotton, the bank's president, Nicholas Biddle, tried to shore up the price of cotton through a pooling scheme; this worked for a time but finally failed when cotton prices turned sharply downward in Liverpool. The bank went under in this one of history's many futile attempts to shore up long-term cotton prices by artificial means. See Bray Hammond, *Banks and Politics in America from the American Revolution to the Civil War* (Princeton University Press, 1957), 535ff.

jenny, the flying shuttle, and the cotton gin – was a good by any measure. So was the rapid economic growth stimulated by the fast-growing cotton industry, along with rising incomes and sheer cultural confidence experienced by the new industrialists in Victorian Britain and antebellum America. One of the "inputs," however, that enabled cotton so dramatically to bring home the goods was itself an absolute evil. The intertwined history of cotton and slavery in the United States almost destroyed the country in the 1860s and invites discomfiture to this day. They are examples, however, of a category of historical relation less causal than contingent: one came before, and subsequently touched, the other. The antecedence of slavery had a significant impact on the subsequence of cotton. In the antebellum period, slavery and cotton have contingent histories.

Slavery had existed in the British North American colonies since 1619 but, as practiced toward the end of the eighteenth century, tobacco-, rice-, and indigo-based slavery was a system past its prime, or so it seemed. The price of slaves fell 50 percent between 1775 and 1800, and there was reason enough to believe that human bondage in America was, after nearly 200 years, doomed to extinction.[22] James Madison, for instance, thought his slave-worked 2,000-acre plantation in middle Virginia was less profitable than Richard Rush's 10-acre farm in Pennsylvania worked by free labor. "The worst possible for profit," the fourth president described slave property in principle.[23] Most famously, George Washington manumitted all his slaves in his will. Thomas Jefferson probably would have done so but for the bankruptcy of his estate.

Expectations for the demise of slavery were foiled by the rise in cotton production from just a few thousand bales in 1790 to nearly 4 million in 1860. By then, the Cotton South that accomplished this prodigy of production was not, by and large, the old tobacco South replanted to cotton. It was accomplished by a newer region to the southwest – opened politically by American destruction of Spanish and Indian power in the lower Mississippi River valley, and opened economically by the profit potential of cotton raised for export. With the coming of cotton, a trickle of settlers became a "rush" of planters. "Alabama Fever" swept through the old South of Virginia, the Carolinas and coastal Georgia – lands tired out from tobacco

---

[22] Francis Butler Simkins and Charles P. Roland, *A History of the South*, 4th ed. (New York: Knopf, 1972), 128ff.
[23] Ibid.

culture and filled with too many slaves – luring thousands westward to fresher spaces. Virginia and South Carolina continued to represent the cultural voice of the South, but it was the new, "deep" South states of Alabama, Mississippi, Louisiana, and Arkansas that supplied the region's economic muscle, as cotton quickly established its comparative advantage over most alternative crops. By the 1830s, sugar and rice were confined to coastal marshlands. Wheat did poorly in the lower South, corn had no export market, and the market for tobacco was entering a half-century of unrelenting low prices. More than anything else, it was upland cotton that responded to the Old Southwest's warm but temperate climate and to its cheap and fertile land. The expansion of cotton culture favored plantation-scale operations, not ordinary family farms, and the labor input of plantations was well met by chattel slavery. Upland cotton made slavery profitable enough to prevent its demise, and its administration, on large plantations at least, could be highly efficient.

It is true that cotton was also raised on many small farms without slaves, and for the same reason that it was raised by slaveholding planters: it was highly profitable. The "yeoman tradition" was strong, and is strongly remembered, throughout the South. Cotton was, however, a new crop moving onto new land, and the potential profit from it justified high – even speculative – capitalization. Scale was important. A few acres could never produce enough cotton to support the processing facility (the gin and press) that readied the crop for competitive entry into the world market. Most cotton plantations covered more than 300 acres. Typically, there was a large labor force to match (100 laborers per 300–400 acres was common), and entire families worked the fields. Because plantation labor specialized in preparing for, planting, cultivating, and harvesting just one commercial crop, it became highly (albeit narrowly) skilled and hence efficient at its task. Finally, large scale and specialization put a premium on good management, all year round.[24] In the words of U. B. Phillips, one of the institution's earliest historians, slavery on the southern plantation was "controlled, provisioned, and

[24] The literature is voluminous. Basic texts include Kenneth M. Stampp, *The Peculiar Institution: Slavery in the Antebellum South* (New York: Random House, 1956); Stanley M. Elkins, *Slavery: A Problem in American Institutional and Intellectual Life* (University of Chicago Press, 1959); David B. Davis, *The Problem of Slavery in Western Culture* (Ithaca: Cornell University Press, 1966); Eugene D. Genovese, *The Political Economy of Slavery* (New York: Random House, 1965); *Roll Jordan Roll: The World the Slaveholders Made* (New York: Vintage, 1969); and Robert W. Fogel and Stanley Engerman, *Time on the Cross: The Economics of American Negro Slavery* (New York: Norton, 1995 ed.).

mobile."[25] Management was key, and the slave plantations, far from being the archaic medieval constructs of film and folklore, were modern and effective instruments of wealth creation.[26] Slaves worked on some 90 percent of cotton plantations; hired labor was hard pressed to compete with them. Slaves could be driven – not to the point of exhaustion or rebellion, but certainly far harder than free men would tolerate. And they worked, evidently, with enough effectiveness to repay their masters steadily at competitive rates of return. Aggregate annual returns on slave investments between 1800 and the Civil War have been estimated at around 10 percent. More impressive was the great increase in labor productivity. Slaves easily produced more than they consumed. On average, one slave laborer cost $30 to $40 to maintain annually, but he could produce three to four bales of cotton, which realized $100 or more for his owner. It added up. The crop value per slave was less than $18 in 1810 but climbed to more than $101 on the eve of the Civil War, even as the price for cotton declined from 0.147 cents to 0.111 cents per pound. Planter income, which had been $100 million in 1850, increased to $250 million ten years later. Prices and the value of the invested capital that the slaves represented rose steadily right up until the Civil War, to approximately $2 billion.[27]

This great gain in productivity, which redounded mainly to consumers of cotton, was accomplished in part because of the temperateness and fertility of the South itself, but also because of managerial efficiencies. Organized managerial hierarchies coordinated the work of specialized personnel in ways no less sophisticated than those of well-regulated industrial factories. Typically, field hands on larger plantations were divided into "gangs" dedicated to particular tasks, such as plowing or hoeing; each gang was overseen by a driver or foreman (also slaves), who in turn reported to a white overseer. Manning the plantations' maintenance and support functions were such craftsmen as mechanics, blacksmiths, wheelwrights, and carpenters. There were cooks, stablehands, tenders for cattle and hogs, seamstresses,

[25] Ulrich B. Phillips, *American Negro Slavery* (New York: Appleton, 1918), 401.

[26] "The notion that southern slavery was an old-fashioned institution, a hangover from the past, was false," observed British historian Paul Johnson. "It was a product of the Industrial Revolution, high technology, and the commercial spirit catering for mass markets of hundreds of millions worldwide. It was very much a part of the modern world. That is why it proved so difficult to eradicate." *A History of the American People* (New York: Basic, 1997), 312.

[27] Simkins and Roland, *A History of the South*, 129–30; Woodman, *Slavery and the Southern Economy*, 91–2.

and even midwives and nurses to assist with the all-important process of replenishing the labor supply.

It was this economic reality that overcame moral qualms to the point where, by the mid-nineteenth century, leading intellectual and political thinkers of the cotton-growing regions were fully able to rationalize slavery as a positive good. Never mind that all other Western powers had abolished slavery in their domains, or that the political and moral contradictions between the practice of human bondage and the profession of a democratic creed had become harder and harder to explain in terms of Christian or democratic principles. As Northern abolitionists – many of them scions of the cotton mills – grew more militant in their demands for the eradication of slavery, no argument was too convoluted or bizarre for the defenders of "the peculiar institution." What's done is done, argued some, like Thomas Dew, a professor at the College of William and Mary. Abolition could never be achieved with due compensation to slaveholders for the enormous loss of invested capital imbedded in their slaves. Besides, entrenched social and economic arrangements, no matter how "wrong, in the abstract," could not be unraveled without undermining the "deep and solid foundations of society." Among the more prominent apologists was George Fitzhugh, a Virginia lawyer who saw in the plantation a kind of virtuous socialist regime that bred intergenerational stability and beneficent interdependency between master and slave. He and other Southern apologists deplored the free-market practices of the British and Northern mills, where "wage slavery" debased labor and competition drove mills into bankruptcy.[28]

The intellectual defense of slavery was accompanied by a growing belief that – as slavery came to dominate national politics – cotton was an indispensable economic weapon in the growing ideological war between slaveholders and Northern abolitionists. Legislative compromises ensured that the Southern "slave" states, despite their relatively small populations, would be able to sustain representation equal to the "free" states in the Senate. Right up until South Carolina led the exodus of the cotton South from the Union in 1861 and Abraham Lincoln moved militarily to prevent it, it was hard to imagine what the North really could do about slavery in the South where it already existed (as opposed to the western territories, where

---

[28] See Stampp, *The Peculiar Institution,* chapter 10, "He Who Has Endured": "The pathos in the life of every master lay in the fact that slavery had no philosophical defense worthy of the name – that it had nothing to commend it to posterity, except that it paid" (p. 422).

it did not). "Would any sane nation make war on cotton?" South Carolina Senator James Henry Hammond famously put the question in 1857. "Without firing a gun, without drawing a sword, should they make war on us, we could bring the whole world to our feet. No, you dare not make war on cotton. No power on earth dares make war on cotton. Cotton is King." Thus were the lines drawn in the epic conflict of cultures and economic interests that would ultimately be resolved only by the bloodiest war in American history.

As it turned out, U.S. cotton production grew rapidly after the Civil War as both U.S. and world populations burgeoned to support a seemingly limitless demand for manufactured cotton textiles. The antebellum South had produced, at its apogee in 1860, just over 3.8 million bales. In 1929, the South produced just over 14.8 million bales, which still represented some 65 percent of all the world's production and a respectable share compared even with its best antebellum performance.[29] Put another way, by the 1890s, the United States still produced three times the crop of the rest of the world combined. In the 1910s, three fifths of the world's cotton was still American. Only in the early 1930s did the American crop for the first time slip below the total for the rest of the world, 13 million bales to 13.8 million in 1934.

Thus the misanthropic premise that cotton's economic foundations rested on slavery would prove false. Cotton would survive after slavery's traumatic end, as its history since the Civil War illustrates. The broader Southern economy was another matter; it stubbornly resisted attempts to industrialize. Despite a rousing and for the most part locally financed "cotton mill crusade" in the 1880s and 1890s, the South remained an industrial dwarf, capital-poor and dependent as ever on agricultural commodities – most of all, cotton – for its share of business in increasingly competitive world marketplaces.[30] As cotton agriculture grew, however, it became less anchored in the Old South. It moved geographically, progressed technologically, and eventually bore little resemblance to the plantation culture for which so many southern lads fell in battle. It did not happen quickly, however.

[29] Harold D. Woodman, *King Cotton and His Retainers, 1800–1925* (New York, 1968).

[30] On the cotton mill crusade, see Broadus Mitchell, *The Rise of Cotton Mills in the South* (Baltimore: Johns Hopkins University Press, 1921).

2

NATURE AND KNOW-HOW

Organization and Technology in the Postbellum Era

Raising cotton called for considerable special knowledge and know-how among its thousands of postbellum tillers. Much of their knowledge was far from scientific, but it was authentic enough, subtle and exceedingly pragmatic; it was based on experience, folk wisdom, and the almanac. In the moving testament *All God's Dangers: The Life of Nate Shaw,* oral historian Theodore Rosengarten transcribed one Alabama Black Belt farmer's life in cotton in a vernacular that would have been familiar all across the South and was still a living memory when recorded just twenty-five years ago.[1]

"Catch a seasonable time when the ground's in good shape to plow, as early as you can – don't plow it wet." Ned Cobb (the real "Nate Shaw") planted in April. "You take a middle-bustin' plow – the land broke, in good shape – that's a plow that carries two wings, throwin' dirt each way, makes you a nice bed." Then put down guano fertilizer and then spread seed in good straight rows with the help of a one-armed planter. "That rake planter has a spoon 'bout as wide as my fingers that runs into the ground just ahead of them seeds and them seeds feedin' out right behind that spoon." Then if the weather cooperated, "you can plant the first days of the week and by the middle of the next week, you got a pretty stand of cotton all over your field." Weeding and thinning ("chopping") came next and also depended on the weather: "If you chop it too early, decidin' wrong about what the weather's goin' to do, you go out there and thin out your crop, that bad weather come and get the balance of it." By late May, if all went well, the branches of the young plant "will just roll off with squares. And as them squares grow

---

[1] Theodore Rosengarten, *All God's Dangers: The Life of Nate Shaw* (New York, 1974); passages cited in Pete Daniel, *Breaking the Land: The Transformation of Cotton, Tobacco and Rice Cultures Since 1880* (Urbana: University of Illinois Press, 1986), 186ff.

they'll bloom." And when "the bloom falls the boll is right behind, and that little boll ain't a bit bigger than the tip of your little finger."

By the end of August, the lint would have emerged and turned, as William Faulkner gave words to V. K. Ratliff in *The Hamlet,* into "a surf of bursting bolls." Then, Ned Cobb and the rest of his family brought in the harvest. "The Bible says, once a man and twice a child – well, it's that way pickin' cotton. I picked at the end of my cotton-pickin' days how much I picked at the start," which was 100 pounds per day. In between, in his prime, he picked 300 pounds. It took 1,200 pounds to make a bale, and he stored his seed cotton in a cotton house until he figured he had enough. Then, "I'd drive my wagon up to the door of that house and load it all out, take it to the gin." Cotton was never "mixed" at the gin, and the bale Cobb carried away was composed of just the crop he had taken in minus the seed, which also had value. "Sometimes I'd sell the seeds to the ginner and the seed out of one bale of cotton would pay for ginnin' two bales."

What Cobb got for his bales when he took them to market depended on their grade. Cobb, a black man, was cynical, if not about cotton then about the cotton market: "Much of it is humbug, just like everything else, this gradin' business." But he was free to shop around and did, often with the help of a white friend: "Colored man's cotton weren't worth as much as a white man's cotton less'n it come to the buyer in a white man's hands." Whether a farmer's condition at the end of cotton's year was any different from the beginning depended on much beyond his control. Relying on credit for his "furnish" and with little control over the price he received for his product, the tenant typically found himself dogged by debt. "If you don't make enough to have some left you ain't done nothin', except givin' the other fellow your labor." Ned Cobb was lucky, shrewder than many, and had a wife who was good with numbers; he finally became a farm owner, though still a poor man. But how well he remembered the years when, as a sharecropper, he "made nuthin'."

Extended distress could breed hopelessness, or it could spur reform. Although the memories of Ned Cobb could have described cotton's world in either the 1870s or the 1920s, reform or "modernization" of the cotton culture was stirring. It came partly from within the traditional cotton South (through World War I, still synonymous with the cotton states of the old Confederacy) and partly from without. Modernization was a long, slow process, and something of a mixed blessing. It brought tumbling down the stubbornly traditional, labor-intensive, plantation-based agriculture of the years between the Civil War and the Great Depression, but at the human price of displacing from the land hundreds of thousands of "tenant" farmers, much like Cobb, who were ill prepared for the shock.[2]

PEASANT FARMING ON THE NEW PLANTATION

Shorn of its slave labor, the "cotton belt" South that stretched from North Carolina to Texas remained very much a plantation economy. The revolution in the labor system from slave to free actually obscured the fact that a traditional system of land tenure would change very slowly. The concentration of labor relative to capital remained much the same for decades. These facts held for all four of the main staple crops of the American South – tobacco, rice, sugar, cotton – cotton being by far the greatest.[3] The plantation form of commercial agriculture (and the culture that went with it) did not truly come to an end until washed away by the confluence of depression, government acreage controls, and mechanization after the 1920s.

Never again would cotton sustain the oligarchy of business and political power that the planters had represented before the Civil War. Instead, cotton and many of the people who grew it after the war, from lordliest planter to lowliest sharecropper, experienced increasing distress. As the crop grew, from 4.3 million bales in the early 1870s to 6.6 million in the early 1880s to 9 million in the early 1890s, the price fell from 15 cents to 9 cents and then to under 6 cents per pound. Cotton growers were certainly not alone among American agriculturalists in feeling the anxiety of falling prices in the late nineteenth century, although their difficulties had a unique dimension that related directly to the history of cotton's technology and markets.[4] Fueled

---

[2] See Daniel, *Breaking the Land,* 155ff.

[3] The following discussion is based on Lewis C. Gray, *History of Agriculture in the Southern States to 1860* (Washington, DC, 1933), vol. 1; and Aiken, *The Cotton Plantation South Since the Civil War* (Baltimore: Johns Hopkins University Press, 1998), chapter 1. "Plantation" is a word whose meaning has shifted over the years: from its earliest meaning simply as a new settlement (as in the plantation of Scots and English in Ireland, or the first plantation of English in North America, in Virginia), to a synonym for "farm," to the meaning it attained in the nineteenth century (and still retains) of a large commercial agricultural unit.

[4] On the social and psychological consequences of agricultural distress at the end of the nineteenth century, the classic account is Richard Hofstadter, *The Age of Reform* (New York: Knopf, 1956). See also Gavin Wright, *Old South, New South: Revolutions in the Southern Economy Since the Civil War* (Baton Rouge: Louisiana State University Press, 1996); and Gilbert C. Fite, *Cotton Fields No More: Southern Agriculture, 1865–1980* (Lexington: University Press of Kentucky, 1984).

BOLIVAR COUNTY, MISS.   1906

MOVING EARTH to build embankment for Miss. River Levee.

BOLIVAR COUNTY   1906

COTTON BEGINS JOURNEY from the gin to a compress.

BOLIVAR COUNTY   1910-15

HOE HAND BRIGADE ready to chop cotton on the Pole Knowlton farm before planters were improved and chemical grass and weed control methods came to the farm.

FIELD BREAKING is a springtime event at Knowlton Plantation

STEAM-POWERED COTTON GIN

STALK CUTTING in cottonfield before spring plowing

by the potent combination of slave labor, fertile western lands, and foreign demand, cotton culture in the antebellum era had been dynamic and expansive. In the postbellum era, the land and the demand were still there, but the end of slavery called forth new ways of ordering agricultural labor that proved crippling in much of the Old South. The preference of the former slaveholders was to replicate, as closely as possible, the antebellum plantation system but with wage labor. This meant employing former slaves as wage laborers and working them in closely supervised gangs – in return for ten to twelve dollars per month plus food, shelter, and the customary gardening, fishing, and hunting privileges from slavery days. Under slavery, the gang system had been highly efficient. So might it have been under freedom except for the problem that its resemblance to slavery made it unacceptable to the freedmen. The alternative was tenant farming. In the absence of federally instituted land reform that would have confiscated plantations and subdivided them into small farms to be given to the former slaves, some sort of rental arrangement between landlord and tenant offered blacks the semblance of release from the old regimented ways of slavery. Seldom, however, did it offer much more.

Crop lien laws, passed in the late 1860s, addressed the need for new credit arrangements. Although essentially a codification of customary procedures of the antebellum factorage system, in which the factor advanced the planter supplies on credit in return for the exclusive right to market his future crop, the postbellum crop lien regime was more severe. It operated in a fundamentally different economic context. Planters found themselves with increasingly *less* valuable property; they no longer owned slaves, and land values were low. One thing alone remained as security for the financing (or the "furnish") needed to make a crop: the crop itself. In addition and in contrast to the factorage system that had involved a relatively small number of people, the crop lien ensnared hundreds of thousands of former slaves-turned-tenants, each with responsibility (under the new order) for securing the furnish to make his own crop.

In the early twentieth century, "hoe and hand brigades" of peasant farmers and their animals broke the fields each spring for planting, "chopped" the cotton to control weeds in the summer, and picked the crop in the fall. Mule-drawn wagons hauled the seed cotton to steam-powered gins, which converted it to bales. In the Yazoo–Mississippi Delta, planters employed the same labor to build and maintain the levees that kept the river out. Ca. 1906–1915. (pp. 63 and 64)

Crossroads furnishing merchants multiplied across the New South land-scape to meet this demand for credit. With their only security in the form of the crop yet to be harvested, they took high risks and, not surprisingly, often charged high prices. The antebellum factor had served merely as the planter's agent in selling the crop, but the postbellum crossroads merchant, operating under the crop lien, often took legal possession of the mortgaged crop while it was still in the ground. This diminished the grower's freedom to shop for buyers, while the difficulty of obtaining other sources of credit made it hard to delay sale much beyond the time of ginning.[5] If the crop failed to cancel that season's debt, then the grower was tied over for another year to the same merchant and frequently (in a period of falling prices, as was the late nineteenth century) for another, and yet another after that.[6] Rational though it was in a capital-poor region where many growers lacked resources to get into production, the crop lien system – "debt peonage" – became one of the demons of southern history.[7]

In general, it was an arrangement stacked in favor of the owners, but variations in tenancy were numerous. The results on a given plot of land depended on locality, weather, the market, and the providence or improv-idence of the tenant. Some tenants prospered, but most lived in grinding poverty. A pure sharecropping farmer brought nothing to the bargain but

[5] Woodman, *King Cotton and His Retainers,* 293–302. A new pattern also emerged at the next steps in the marketing chain as cotton buying became "concentrated in the hands of a relatively few large European and American firms. These firms, known in the cotton trade as merchants, had representatives in virtually every market – often using the services of storekeepers and gin-ners – who bought cotton for them at given prices. The cotton was assembled in a number of given towns where merchants had huge warehouses to store it while they awaited orders from consumers all over the world. An order would send the proper grade on a through bill directly to the consumer. By the turn of the century, a small number of large firms, American and European, dominated this business. In 1904, Frank and Monroe Anderson, along with Will Clayton, organized Anderson, Clayton and Company, soon to become the largest cotton mer-chants in the world. By 1921, twenty-four firms with annual sales of 100,000 bales or more handled 60 percent of the American cotton crop" (pp. 288–9).

[6] The futures system, buying and selling contracts for crops to be delivered at a later date, also came to cotton, as it had to the Chicago grain trade in the 1850s. Speculation in "to arrive" cotton had boomed with the wartime cotton famine, and it quickly evolved into actual futures trading in which the contract was not based on particular batches but only on certain amounts of cotton of a certain grade. The reporting of both future and "spot" sales was common by the end of the 1860s. Rules regulating futures trading appeared in Liverpool in 1869, and estab-lishment in America of the New York Cotton Exchange in 1870 and the New Orleans Cotton Exchange a year later formally institutionalized it.

[7] In Mississippi, the state's crop lien law was actually called an "Act for Encouraging Agricul-ture." See C. Vann Woodward, *Origins of the New South, 1877–1913* (Baton Rouge: Louisiana State University Press, 1951), 180.

The crossroads country store, once a fixture of the cotton landscape, survives today in vine-covered ruins. Orangeburg County, South Carolina, 1999.

his and his family's labor and paid, as rental on a parcel of land, usually half of the crops it yielded. A share tenant who supplied (in addition to labor) capital goods in the form of his own farm implements and mules paid less rent, usually a third or a fourth of the crop. Cash tenants paid rent in an amount agreed to at the beginning of the growing season.[8] Along with use of the land, tenants who worked on yearly contracts commonly retained, as had their antebellum predecessors, rights to shelter and the freedom to gather firewood and to hunt and fish plantation woods and streams.

The growth of tenancy and the complexity of the system occurred in the context of concentration of land ownership throughout the cotton South. While census takers in 1880 mistook tenants' parcels as "small farms," it was the plantations – large landholdings worked by large labor forces – that reasserted themselves. They did so with labor no longer bound in ownership to the master but still very much bound to the land.[9] The key difference between the Old and the New South plantation was diminished landlord

---

[8] Aiken, *The Cotton Plantation South,* 29ff.
[9] Ibid., 68ff.; see also Woodward, *The Origins of the New South.*

supervision of this free labor force. Slavery had demanded aggressive plantation management and had yielded highly efficient production. Tenancy discouraged it. It dispersed responsibility for making the crop and diluted the concentration of labor under skilled oversight; under the strictures of the crop lien, it also shortened farmers' time horizons and limited their ability to sell freely. What had been "practically the factory system applied to agriculture," as U. B. Phillips characterized the antebellum cotton plantation, gave way in the decades after Reconstruction to "an industrial counterrevolution." The result was peasant farming.[10]

FIXERS

The late nineteenth century, so often associated with the rise of big business, also witnessed an increase in the public regulation of enterprise. Agriculture was no exception. The United States Department of Agriculture (USDA) had been established in 1862 to expand what had formerly been the functions of the agricultural division of the Patent Office. Abraham Lincoln called it "the people's department," and the "people" – more than half of whom still farmed for a living – needed good seed and good information to grow and market their crops. The USDA had chemical, entomological, statistical, and forestry functions, and its commissioner was raised to Cabinet rank in 1889. During the Progressive Era before World War I, the department was given oversight of the national forests, of the Pure Food and Drug Act (1906), of meat inspection, and of dairy products for export. Its functions spanned an array of agricultural industries, practices, and problems. Its purpose was to defend and advance the interests of farmers, then the nation's most powerful political constituency.

The relationship between the USDA and cotton was forged in the fight to stave off a particular natural pestilence. The Mexican boll weevil, *Anthonomus grandis,* crossed the Rio Grande into Texas near Corpus Christi probably in 1892 and spread relentlessly year by year, field by field, across the cotton South. Texas farmers were quick to spread the alarm about an invading boll-destroying insect, and the Department was equally quick to take up the banner of weevil control. Department experts closely monitored and mapped the pest's progress and developed techniques for dealing

---

[10] Ulrich B. Phillips, "The Decadence of the Plantation System," *Annals of the American Academy of Political Science* 35 (January–June, 1910), 37, cited in Aiken, *The Cotton Plantation Landscape,* 34.

The United States Department of Agriculture, established in 1862 and dubbed by Abraham Lincoln as "the people's department" (most Americans then were farmers), administers the country's farm programs, which historically have focused on managing supply and supporting farm income.

with it, typically several years before the weevil was expected to arrive in a particular cotton-growing region. The simplest solution, in theory at least, was to halt cotton planting in the path of infestation and thus starve out the insects. The Department recommended this approach to the Texas legislature as early as 1894 (in the equivalent of the sort of "cotton holiday" that appeared again in the 1930s when the enemy was not bugs but low prices).

However, control demanded more investment and more education than many farmers could (or cared to) muster. It was, for instance, important to plow under the cotton stalks as soon as possible after the fall harvest in order to deprive weevils of winter hibernation places. But this and other changes in agricultural practice that might have led to early defeat of the weevil represented putting more capital into the crop. Areas bordering infested fields needed to be burned and, during the growing season, weevil population had to be carefully monitored. If the population rose, the Department recommended dusting with calcium arsenate, which when mixed with molasses could also be applied with a mop. The longer the growing season, the more the weevil flourished. Some new varieties of cotton permitted earlier planting and helped the crop get a jump on the weevils, which matured later. More fertilizer, too, could increase the yield and make up for some of what the weevil had destroyed.[11] Agents from the USDA led by Seaman A. Knapp – and, after 1906, county demonstration agents working closely with land-grant colleges – spread across the South indoctrinating farmers on how to beat back the weevil. Their efforts, though, met with unintended consequences.

BUGS

A nemesis of plantation agriculture in the South, many of its critics had long argued, was the one-crop system. It depleted the soil and made farmers ever more vulnerable to capricious markets. "Scientific" farming, which emphasized the advantages of diversification, was standard USDA doctrine, and in one way the weevil advanced it. As county agents spread the warning of impending crop devastation, farmers – particularly in the more marginal growing areas – turned away from cotton to livestock and other crops.

Small grayish or brown beetles wintered in sheltered places (stubble left after the harvest was ideal), and the survivors emerged in spring and early summer to attack the young cotton bolls. They punctured the bolls for feeding and egg-laying. Eggs hatched in about three days, and though the life cycle was short (about three to four weeks) it was long enough for the grubs to destroy the cotton in the boll. It added up. By the 1920s, it is estimated that the boll weevil was destroying more than 2 million bales per year. Advancing relentlessly eastward, the boll weevil reached southeast Alabama in the summer of 1915, when cotton production stood at 35,000 bales. Two years later, production was down by two thirds, farm bankruptcies were up, and local bankers and merchants were left, in cotton vernacular, "holding the bag." Local farmers turned in desperation (and with ultimate success) to other crops: peanuts, poultry, and produce.

To some, this was a welcome development. A traveler can observe a literal monument to this phenomenon 90 miles south of Montgomery in Coffee County, Alabama, in a town with the ultimate New South name: Enterprise. It is, as the plaque says, "The Only Monument in the World Glorifying a Pest." The Enterprise statue – of a Grecian figure set amidst a

---

[11] Aiken, *The Cotton Plantation South,* 76ff.; Douglas Helms, "Just Lookin' for a Home: The Cotton Boll Weevil and the South" (Ph.D. dissertation, Florida State University, 1977).

fountain and holding aloft the bronze likeness of a boll weevil – was paid for entirely by local subscriptions and unveiled in 1919. It was a unique gesture that quickly became part of the lore of the Cotton Belt and, to outsiders, the butt of more than a few jokes. But to the locals who erected it, "in profound appreciation of the boll weevil and what it has done as the herald of prosperity," it was a beacon pointing toward the "saneness of diversified farming."[12]

Coffee County's experience notwithstanding, diversification was not the common response of southern cotton growers to the advancing pest. Many, while practicing some level of weevil control, also simply planted more cotton. By teaching farmers how to cope with the weevil, the Extension Service probably promoted results that were opposite to the official USDA line about the "scientific" and economic disadvantages of relying on a single cash crop.

The impact of the weevil varied in part with the attentiveness of landowners to their property. The problem of poorly supervised labor had arisen in the transition from slavery to freedom after the Civil War and, by the end of the New South era in the 1920s, poor agricultural management had become a widely noted phenomenon, especially in the older plantation regions. Success in agriculture depended on prudent decisions about allocating economic resources, which related in turn to landowners' willingness to live on the land and supervise those who worked it. Fewer and fewer were choosing to do so. Modest as they were, the New South's cities and industries beckoned many of the ambitious, and in the competition between nostalgic ties to the land and other opportunities for making money, agriculture lost out among the younger generation that inherited old estates. Absentee or passive ownership did not necessarily entail decline, but it was a signal that productive resources of land and labor were probably going to waste. "Absentee landlordism is most harmful to a community when it persists irrespective of the revenue received from the land," Arthur Raper observed in his landmark 1930s fable of agricultural decline, *Preface to Peasantry: A Tale of Two Black Belt Counties*; "that is, when large tracts are held for sentimental rather than economic reasons."[13] The combination of inept or uninterested leaders and isolated, uneducated tenants – who farmed year to

---

[12] Brochure: "Boll Weevil Monument," Enterprise Public Library, Enterprise, Alabama.

[13] Arthur F. Raper, *Preface to Peasantry* (Chapel Hill: University of North Carolina Press, 1936), 104. The book belonged to a genre of economic studies of the rural South produced during the Great Depression, including, most famously, Raper's and Ira Reid's *Sharecroppers All*.

The Mexican boll weevil (*Anthonomus grandis*) crossed the Rio Grande into Texas in the 1890s and over the next five decades scourged cotton in the Southeast. One response was to diversify into other crops. Enterprise, seat of Coffee County in southern Alabama, went so far as to erect a statue to the weevil in the middle of its main street – "the world's only monument to a pest" – in gratitude to the bug that broke local farmers' bondage to cotton. (p. 72)

year but lacked the means to plan much farther – was not a good formula for managing change.

Thus the weevil, for better or worse, symbolized change; in areas thus already in decline, the weevil triumphed. The Lower Georgia Piedmont, where negligence had led to soil erosion and declining fertility and where the USDA traced the root cause to a "great scarcity of real ability to manage large holdings of farm land," was a sad example.[14] Hugely prosperous in cotton before the Civil War, the region had declined steadily thereafter. The weevil arrived about 1912 and sealed the process.[15]

[14] O. M. Johnson and Howard A. Turner, "The Old Plantation Piedmont Cotton Belt" (Washington, DC: USDA, Bureau of Agricultural Economics, 1930), 6–7, 15, cited in Aiken, *The Cotton Plantation Landscape*, 68.

[15] The bug that visited such misery on southern farmers and precipitated huge changes in cotton agriculture also earned a lasting place in southern folklore and song. "The Ballad of the Boll Weevil" ran to a dozen verses and today brings a smile. Yesterday, it amounted to a lamentation for cotton:

The resulting radical fall in production, extending over several years, rippled backward through the financial structures that had, however precariously, supported the New South cotton culture. Growers in Hancock County, Georgia, who had produced 25,000 500-pound bales in 1914, produced only 710 in 1922. Greene County's 21,479 bales in 1919 shrank by 1922 to 326. The economic consequences were dire and not hard to predict. Tenants' credit dried up; merchants and other "furnishers" who supplied them faltered; local and regional banks failed. The phrase "boll weevil depression" entered cotton's vocabulary to describe this process of severe disinvestment. Witness to its consequences was a sullen landscape of abandoned gins, tumbledown warehouses and oil mills, and thousands of acres once blanketed with the South's "summer snow" gone back to scrub.[16] Elsewhere, the story could be different. In the Yazoo Delta, probably the richest cotton land anywhere in the world and still a developing agricultural region in the early twentieth century, generally high levels of farm management and heavier investment in good practices stymied the weevil and, after a few bad years, restored and even increased production. On the rich alluvial lands of the Delta, on both sides of the Mississippi between Memphis and

De boll weevil is a little black bug
F'um Mexico, dey say,
He come to try dis Texas soil
An' thought he'd better stay.

De fus' time I seen de boll weevil
He was settin' on de square;
De nex' time I saw de boll weevil
He had all his family dere –

De third time I seen de boll weevil
He was on the western plain;
Nex' time I seen de boll weevil,
He had hopped dat Memphis train.

De merchant got half de cotton,
De boll weevil got de rest;
Didn't leave de po' ol' farmer
But one old cotton dress.
[Chorus: An' it's full o' holes / O it's full o' holes]

De farmer say to de merchant,
I ain't made but one bale,
But befo' I'll give you dat one
I'll fight an' go to jail.

[Copyright 1947 by John A. and Alan Lomax]
[16] Raper, *Preface to Peasantry*, 216; Aiken, *The Cotton Plantation South*, 78–9.

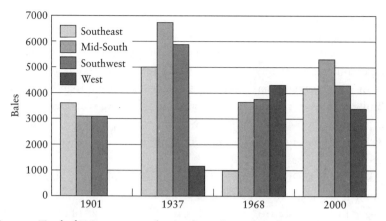

Figure 5. Total of U.S. cotton production by region, selected years. *Source:* U.S. Department of Agriculture, National Agricultural Statistics Service.

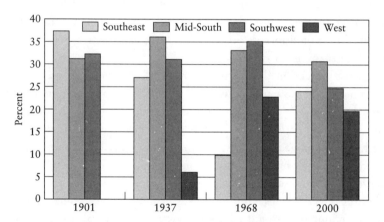

Figure 6. Percentage of U.S. cotton production by region, selected years. *Source:* U.S. Department of Agriculture, National Agricultural Statistics Service.

Vicksburg, cotton acreage expanded by more than 50 percent between 1909 and 1929, the years of the weevil's heaviest onslaught. A similar recovery occurred in north Alabama on the rich red lands of the Middle Tennessee Valley around Huntsville.[17]

As the weevil moved east, cotton moved decisively west, first from the Southeast to the Old Southwest, then to Texas and Oklahoma and finally to

[17] Aiken, *The Cotton Plantation South,* 78, map 3.3; Daniel, *Breaking the Land,* 9.

New Mexico, Arizona, and California. Controlling the weevil raised costs, and drier areas less susceptible to infestation enjoyed clear economic advantages. Between 1910 and 1930, acreage in the Carolinas, Georgia, and Alabama increased barely 5 percent, while Texas and Oklahoma doubled theirs. Texas, Oklahoma, New Mexico, and California together planted 23 million acres in 1925, up from 13 million only three years before. Texas was preeminent. With a crop that produced over 3.4 million bales in 1900, it boasted 34 percent of the national total and more than twice the production of any other state.[18]

As cotton shifted westward and simultaneously faltered in the lands left behind, it fostered the beginning of a human migration that ultimately changed forever the face of the rural South. The vast shoal of black tenants, slavery's living ghosts in a time of freedom, suffered – along with the poor whites locked into the same rickety agricultural system of high risks and pitiful prospects – acute vulnerability when anything went wrong. "Survivin' more than livin' was what they were doin'," as one Georgia grower described the condition of cotton's labor force as he remembered them, as late as the 1940s and 1950s.[19]

The well-intentioned government response to the boll weevil, while clearly helpful in more productive areas, turned out to be beyond the reach of much of cotton's peasantry and did little to save them. A "Black Exodus" from the cotton lands – to the South's towns and cities and to the North – accompanied the eastward march of the weevil. The out-migration reflected the larger problem of an economy that was beset with too many mouths to feed and that produced too few "goods" to spread around at the end of the day. Cotton's labor input was primitive (men, women, and children scratching the ground with hoes "frozen in time"[20]), its value linked to its numbers. When the numbers threatened to fall, as they began to in the 1920s, growers' worst fear (worse even than of the weevil) – of too little labor to plant, chop, and bring in the crop – threatened to become reality. County agents and the USDA hastened to promote better living conditions for sharecroppers and to spread extension work among black farmers, hoping (to little avail) to stem the tide.

---

[18] Helms, "Just Lookin' for a Home," 392–3; Simkins and Roland, *A History of the South*, 330.
[19] Wendell Dunaway interview, Hawkinsville, Georgia, April 15, 1999.
[20] Daniel, *Breaking the Land*, 155.

Table II. *Cotton heads West, 1880–1930*
(thousands of bales)

				State			
Year	NC	GA	TX	OK	NM	AZ	CA
1880	410	1,000	1,224	17			
1890	588	1,310	1,708	34			
1900	509	1,270	3,536	244			
1910	706	1,767	3,049	923			6
1920	923	1,415	4,345	1,336		102	67
1930	771	1,592	4,037	854	100	155	264

Source: United States Department of Agriculture, *Yearbook of Agriculture*, 1921, 1931.

TRACTORS AND HOES

Thus, by the time multiple crises converged on the industry in the 1930s, the fragile old cotton culture was poised for collapse. The black migration from the South in the first three decades of this century was largely the result of the "push" of this internal decline. It led blacks not only to the cities and the North but also laterally to agricultural areas of the South where cotton still prospered. (Between 1910 and 1930, the black population of the Delta increased substantially.) Blacks also responded to the "pull" of job opportunities in the North and to a system of racial segregation less onerous than the one dictated by the harsh "Jim Crow" laws and customs of the South. Most black cotton farmers abandoned the field for the city. Their exodus foreshadowed further collapse and transformation yet to come. It was the wholesale loss of labor that would spark the mechanization of cotton culture after the Depression and the Second World War – not, as a rule, the other way around. The "tractored-off-the-land" imagery of 1930s photographer Dorothea Lange and the enduring popularity of John Steinbeck's novel (and John Ford's film) *The Grapes of Wrath* are misleading on this crucial point. Indeed, cotton culture employed several millions of people well into the Great Depression. Modernizing what had been a highly labor-intensive process meant reducing the hours required for each of three distinct steps of production: preparing the land, planting, and cultivating; thinning and weeding; and harvesting. The machines and

In all the lore of agricultural labor, probably no task is remembered as more back-breaking than hand-picking cotton: the laborer bent 90 degrees at the waist, dragging the progressively heavier sack (made of cotton) down the rows, sun-up to sun-down, until the valuable and vulnerable bolls were gathered in.

chemicals necessary to accomplish all this would not be widely available until the 1950s.

Mechanization proceeded at an uneven pace, taking hold first in the new cotton territories of the West, where sharecropping and customary ways of doing things were less deeply entrenched. From there, mechanization followed the weevil eastward, where richer areas (like the Delta) moved quicker than declining ones (the Piedmont and the Black Belt). Nor did all stages of cotton production feel the impact of technology at the same time.

Mechanization came slowly and unevenly to cotton agriculture: tractors and a few trucks appeared (here, in the Delta) in the 1920s; mechanical pickers in the 1940s and 1950s. Wealthier areas, like the Delta, mechanized sooner; marginal lands, often not at all before going out of cotton forever.

The tractors came first. Although their presence on farms reached back to the late nineteenth century, cotton posed special problems for tractors. It was International Harvester's introduction of the all-purpose McCormick-Deering Farmall "tricycle" model in 1924 (competitors' models had names like "Row Crop," "All Crop," and "Universal") that brought tractor technology to the cotton fields. The Farmall was both agile enough for the more delicate cultivating tasks and powerful enough for breaking the land and general plowing, so it offered the prospect of extending the reach of mechanical power through the first stage of cotton production – where the mule and abundant, inexpensive, and patient human labor had formerly reigned supreme. East of the Mississippi, where innovative plantations in the Delta led the way in conversion to tractor power, implement manufacturers and dealers pushed their product relentlessly through the Extension Service and the Farm Bureau, some of them even to the point of taking mules as trade-ins toward credit on tractors. Old animals typically went first, and it was not unusual at the time to observe fields worked by machines and mules side by side, until the mules finally wore out.[21]

Mechanization came next to the harvest. A mechanical spindle picker had been patented as early as 1850, though it took decades to get the technology right and longer than that to find a market. International Harvester bet on the cotton market prematurely when in 1924 it bought key patents that led to a tractor-pulled picker ready for field trials five years later. In the meantime, the brothers John and Mack Rust demonstrated a model capable of picking five bales per day in 1933. There were few takers, however. Coincidence of improved picker technology with the Great Depression was bad luck for the manufacturers. The fear of displacing massive numbers of southern laborers at a time of already high unemployment rendered the potential market unreceptive. The breakthrough did not occur until after World War II, when International Harvester fitted a one-row picker onto the rear of a Farmall tricycle so that it could be driven down the rows in reverse and harvest approximately 4,000 pounds of seed cotton per day. Ginning technology, which lagged behind picking technology, also retarded conversion from the old ways of harvesting. Machine-picked cotton contained more trash and higher moisture than handpicked crops and presented special challenges for gins. Seed-drying attachments were common by the 1940s, but lint cleaning remained a stubborn problem.

The unevenness in technological development stalled forward progress. Just as it made little sense for generals to advance on one front until all battle lines were in optimal position, it made little sense for cotton farmers to invest in mechanization piecemeal until technology could be applied smoothly through all stages of cultivation.[22] Widespread adoption of mechanical pickers was constrained by the simple fact that the second stage of the cultivation sequence still resisted the machine. For thinning and weeding the young crop, that simplest tool of all – the hoe – was the only apparent

---

[21] Discussion based on Daniel, *Breaking the Land*, 155ff.; Aiken, *The Cotton Plantation Landscape*, 97ff.; James H. Street, *The New Revolution in the Cotton Economy: Mechanization and Its Consequences* (Chapel Hill: University of North Carolina Press, 1957); Gilbert C. Fite, "Mechanization of Cotton Production Since World War II," *Agricultural History* 54 (January 1980), 190–207; and Charles R. Sayre, "Cotton Mechanization Since World War II," *Agricultural History* 53 (January 1979), 105–24.

[22] The analogy is a popular one for historians of technology, who – following Thomas Hughes – note the occurrence of "reverse salients" in systems where developments are unevenly distributed across related technologies. See Hughes, *American Genesis: A Century of Invention and Technological Enthusiasm, 1870–1970* (New York: Viking, 1989), passim.

Table III. *Cotton acreage, production,*
and price, 1880–1931

Year	Acreage (thousands)	Bales (thousands)	Price (cents)
1880	15,475	6,605	11
1890	20,809	8,652	9
1900	23,403	10,383	9
1910	32,480	11,609	14
1920	35,872	13,429	16
1923[a]	37,000	10,140	29
1925[b]	45,968	16,105	20
1930	43,329	13,932	9
1931[c]	39,110	17,097	6

[a] Highest price.   [b] Highest acreage.
[c] Highest production and lowest price.
Source: C. Wayne Smith and J. Tom Cothren, eds.,
Cotton: Origin, History, Technology and Produc-
tion (New York: Wiley, 1999).

means of getting the job done, and it hung on to the very last. This was significant for the larger process of mechanization, because as long as any one stage of cultivation required retention of a large labor force, the incentive for continuing to apply those same backs and hands to cotton's other tasks remained high. Mechanical solutions to thinning and weeding came slowly, calling forth a remarkable range of technological responses.

Beginning in the 1920s, some types of mechanical planters had successfully reduced hand-thinning by spacing seeds out, rather than clumping them in hills. Reliance on this technique demanded fewer, better seeds with more dependable germination rates. In this, the weevil probably helped out again, as research in plant genetics aimed at higher-yielding cotton (to compensate for the pest's infestation) also produced better-germinating seed and earlier-maturing cotton. Weeds were another matter altogether. Machines to "chop cotton" had more colorful names – "Tillervator," "Kosik Crab Weeder," "Dixie Cotton Chopper" – than they had success in the field.

Some exotic alternatives suggested the urgency and the tenacity of the problem, which would not be solved until the 1950s. "Flaming" cotton was one such alternative that applied jets of propane fire to grass and weeds (but supposedly not to the cotton) with the aim of expanding the cells just enough to kill the unwanted plants. Or, if a farmer were willing to fence in his fields and endure the likely guffaws of his neighbors, he might turn "weeder geese" loose on his land. Hungry for grass but turned off by cotton (one brace of voracious birds to the acre was said to be the right formula), this environmentally correct approach was no doubt ahead of its time. But even though they did not eat the young cotton plants, big-footed geese were clumsy and so tended to trample them. Geese also proved vulnerable to the insecticides that farmers doused liberally over cotton and weeds alike to fend off the weevil.

The best answer to weeds would be neither mechanical nor natural, but chemical. The appearance of effective preemergent and postemergent herbicides in the 1950s changed everything. Preemergents were applied at planting and, if conditions were right, might retard weeds for the first month of the growing cycle. Postemergents were then applied as needed, and the better the chemistry the less frequent the need. Diuron, brought to market by DuPont in 1955, was key and signaled the end at last of the old hoe culture. In the progressive Delta that year, just five percent of cotton acreage received preemergent treatment. Ten years later, the figure was 80 percent for the entire Southeast.[23] Through chemistry, cotton farmers solved their most intractable labor problem, which then paved the way for full mechanization of their fields.

COTTON AWASH

The battle with the boll weevil, the resistance of the cotton culture to diversification, the migration of cotton westward and of labor off the land, and the sporadic evolution of mechanization constituted the text of cotton agriculture's story in the New South era, between Reconstruction and Great Depression. The uncertainty of what the world market would bring for a crop was the context. Next to fluctuations in price, the boll weevil looked like a modest problem. Nature, after all, was something that farmers claimed to understand or, at least, to have learned to live with. Bugs and bad weather could (within limits) be managed; not so the market. To cotton growers in these years, there was no more dire anxiety than the market — and no challenge they faced evoked a less effective response.

[23] Aiken, *The Cotton Plantation South*, 104–9.

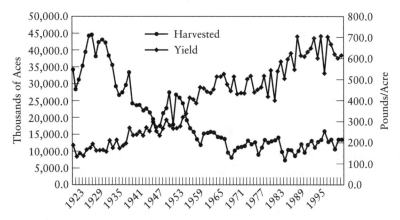

Figure 7. Harvested acreage and yield, 1920–1998. *Source:* U.S. Department of Agriculture, National Agricultural Statistics Service.

The outbreak in 1914 of war in Europe initially cut demand and prices, and planting fell back from 37 million to 31 million acres. But the war soon caused a boom, and acreage shot up. When the cycle turned again, in 1920, farmers the next spring planted 5 million fewer acres. During the mid-1920s, even as price slumped steadily, more and more acres came into production – chiefly west of the Mississippi (in Texas, Oklahoma, and Missouri), where production costs were lower. In 1926, from an all-time high of 44.6 million harvested acres came a record surplus guaranteed to keep the price moving down. This time, however, the price fell below, and stayed below, the cost of production. Farmers did not, as they had in the Populist Revolt of the 1890s, lash out politically at some real or imagined villain to the piece; nor, as would become their habit in the 1930s and afterward, did they turn first to the government for relief and solutions. Rather, they looked to themselves.

Seven hundred of them gathered in Memphis in mid-October, 1926, where Texans led the call for acreage restrictions. But the Cotton Belt was wide and reacted to price distress with different voices. The upper South, ravaged by the weevil and already raising less cotton than in 1914, opposed reduction. The voluntary reduction program agreed upon that year fell far short of the desired results. There was some gross reduction, but while many farmers dutifully held back, others took full advantage, hoping to reap the benefit of the higher prices that should have come with a smaller crop. And when prices stayed low anyway, some planted more in the hope of compensating (with more bales) for miserly merchants and markets. Cotton hit 20 cents a pound in 1927, but then fell as planting held fast at about 40 million acres. With the annual carryover equaling more than half the harvest of 15.5 million bales in 1926, prices looked certain to stay in the cellar.[24]

THE TROUBLE WITH SUCCESS

It was a deep, dark cellar, and a strange resting place for cotton after what had been a century-long success story since *Gossypium hirsutum* dramatically spread from the Carolinas to the fecund lands of the Old Southwest. Cotton had proved a "good" of great purity. Nature had endowed its fiber with innate advantages over the textile competitors then available (it was easily washable and didn't itch), and the addition of human inventiveness and financial capital had lowered the price of its manufactured end products to make it the world's first mass manufactured consumable. Supply had simply expanded to meet demand, as the growers of the American South fed first Britain's and then America's own mechanized mills.

For consumers, the product was good and the price was right, as manufactured cotton textiles rapidly displaced homemade products. For producers, though disorganized and thus incapable of conspiracy, monopoly psychology (if not monopoly itself) was the result. The market was easy to take for granted. Producers felt no pressure from the mills, which easily thrust their value-added products into a market that needed no persuasion. In the absence of competition, and when the weather was fair and the market returned them a good price, cotton growers did well. But the absence of competition also removed any comparative measure for what their returns really should be. Success dulled alertness. It was like that quiet time in the growing cycle – high summer, when the crop had been laid by and humans waited for nature to fill the bolls and bring forth her bounty – and cotton growers were lulled into a false sense of security. It was then that they became most vulnerable to enemies (other than the weevil) that ran to a different rhythm.

The situation in which cotton found itself at the end of the 1920s – huge surpluses, low prices, impoverished labor leaving the land for anything better – was emphatically new. This kind of distress was wrought not by the

---

[24] Gilbert C. Fite, "Voluntary Attempts to Reduce Cotton Acreage in the South, 1914–1933," *Journal of Southern History* 14 (November 1948), 484–99.

weevil, by the vagaries of rainfall and drought, or by the weaknesses of the credit system, but rather by progress itself. The weevil threatened but had not prevailed; what he destroyed in the East was more than replaced by expansion in the West. The "scientific" methods advocated by the USDA were only too successful, as insecticides, fertilizers, and (slowly) mechanization increased yields and saved cotton from every natural setback.

The mills, so it seemed, presented an entirely different problem. They wanted ever more of the stuff and wanted it ever more cheaply. After more than a century, the relationship between cotton supply and demand – first set dramatically off-kilter by the mechanization of spinning and weaving and then redressed by the coming of Whitney's gin and expansion of the South's Cotton Kingdom – was slipping out of balance once again. The boll weevil might have helped to keep the balance even had it not been for the habit of millions of American cotton farmers, backward and progressive alike, to continue planting cotton. No weevil was their match. "Progress" from primitive to scientific practices led only to overproduction, low prices, and poverty.

Cotton's distress on the eve of the Great Depression was hardly unique in the broader frame of agriculture, but it was illustrative of the conundrum bedeviling much of staple crop agriculture in modern times: its ability perennially to out-produce effective demand. It was a problem to which unorganized farmers typically responded by digging the hole deeper and further increasing the supply. It took nothing less than the economic catastrophe of the 1930s to drive home the truth that the old habits had taken cotton about as far as it could go. Cotton's success henceforth would depend on the willingness of growers to change their ways, to act before all that was left was to react. They acted first on the side of the balance they knew best. In large part they attempted, with ambiguous results, to manage supply. They resorted, as all farmers did, to using the political process to help control prices and output. Only gradually did they act more to stimulate (and then manage) demand through the mechanisms of the market.

3

ACTS OF GOD
AND GOVERNMENT
The Search for Political Solutions

Agriculture pits the farmer against nature and the market. With hard work, alertness, and luck, prosperity is possible. But failure is never far from hand. For cotton farmers in the South in the late 1920s, luck had run out as prosperity faded into memory. Nature alone would have disheartened the most determined. Atop the plague of the boll weevil, new disasters delivered fatal blows to a fragile system. In the Great Flood of 1927, the Mississippi River overflowed its banks from Illinois to Louisiana, covering 16 million acres, much of it the prime cotton lands of the Delta. The waters uprooted a million people and prompted an unprecedented Red Cross relief effort, with Secretary of Commerce Herbert Hoover himself in charge.[1] Then, in 1930 and 1931, drought visited the land. Mud turned to dust across the traditionally well-watered southeastern region, as rain refused to fall. For Bible readers, which southerners overwhelmingly were, it felt like the wrath of God had come down heavy upon them. Whether a message from the Almighty or not, cotton farmers took it seriously: the time had come to change their ways.

Hard times also carried a message from the market, for by the spring of 1933 cotton farmers were in desperate financial straits. Although cotton had suffered during the 1920s, its price had held up better than most other farm products. But in 1930, the price of lint cotton and cottonseed slipped below the parity level and stayed there. Between 1924 and 1929, the cotton crop on average had earned $1.5 billion annually; the 1932 crop brought in just $465 million. Such a decline in farm income cascaded across the financial structure of the Cotton Belt. Land values plummeted, farm foreclosures multiplied, and businesses dependent on cotton shuddered. USDA

---

[1] See John M. Barry, *Rising Tide: The Great Mississippi Flood of 1927 and How It Changed America* (New York: Simon & Schuster, 1997).

estimates of the 1933 crop, at 12.5 million bales, foretold a carry-over that exceeded any of the previous three years' annual consumption of American cotton worldwide. Continued high production – even as general economic depression shrank demand – drove cotton stockpiles to record highs. The price per pound fell to the neighborhood of 6 cents.[2] Toted up, it was an extraordinary challenge – the likes of which not even farmers who had lived through the crises of the 1890s could remember. It provoked an extraordinary response.

PLANNING PRODUCTION

President Franklin D. Roosevelt, who took office in March 1933, liked to fancy himself (among other things) a farmer. In addition to the family estate along the Hudson River at Hyde Park, New York, he also owned land in Meriwether County, Georgia, an old cotton-growing area near the polio spa at Warm Springs, which the crippled president's visits would make famous. He was known to have raised cattle and on occasion to have sipped moonshine with the locals, though he did not indulge in cotton.[3]

Roosevelt's administration visited greater change upon American agriculture, including cotton, than any since Abraham Lincoln's, which had seen the establishment of the USDA in 1862. Elected, he believed, to act boldly to promote recovery and bring relief to victims of the Depression, Roosevelt signed a torrent of legislation during his first hundred days in office: the "first New Deal." Among the most radical was the Agricultural Adjustment Act. "I tell you frankly that it is a new and untrod path," he said shortly after the enactment, "but I tell you with equal frankness that an unprecedented condition calls for the trial of new means to rescue agriculture."[4] Even this turned out to be something of an understatement. The federal government had been involved with agriculture for many years, and its actions had ranged widely: liberal homestead laws; appropriations for research, education, and extension work; high tariffs and marketing schemes to even out price cycles; and other indirect legislation to promote the farming interest. But never, before the Agricultural Adjustment Act, had the government attempted directly to control agricultural production.

---

[2] *Yearbook of Agriculture*, USDA, 1935, p. 672.

[3] Frank Friedel, *FDR and the South* (Baton Rouge: Louisiana State University Press, 1965), 10–14.

[4] *Congressional Record*, March 16, 1933, p. 488.

The Act responded to what the Congress and the President perceived as a national agricultural emergency, one created by the severe fall in farm prices relative to other prices. Its purpose was to redress this disparity; as Section 2(1) put it: "To establish and maintain such balance between the production and consumption of agricultural commodities and such marketing conditions therefor, as will re-establish prices to farmers at a level that will give agricultural commodities a purchasing power with respect to articles farmers buy, equivalent to the purchasing power of agricultural commodities in the base period ... August 1909 to July 1914." The Act gave Secretary of Agriculture Henry C. Wallace broad powers, and cotton, as a "basic crop," soon felt the full force of the new law.[5]

The Act also established a new federal agency under the USDA, the Agricultural Adjustment Administration (AAA), headed by Chester C. Davis, and under it the Cotton Section, headed by Cully A. Cobb, former editor of the Georgia–Alabama edition of the *Progressive Farmer*. The immediate objective of the Act, and the immediate strategy of the agency, was to increase the current income of farmers by enabling them to match production to effective demand. This was the meaning of "adjustment," and the concept was hardly new. Manufacturers practiced it more successfully than farmers, routinely reducing production when demand fell, largely at the expense of labor. In agriculture, quick downward adjustment of production was not so easy, and periodic past efforts at cooperation toward this goal (the "Cotton Holiday" movement of 1931 was the most recent attempt), while demonstrating farmers' understanding of the concept, also demonstrated their fundamental disorganization and consistently fell short of the desired results.[6]

The inherent problem with unsubsidized or noncompulsory schemes was that they enabled those who did not cooperate to profit at the expense of those who did. If enough farmers decreased production sufficiently to push prices up, then other farmers might simultaneously increase production

---

[5] In addition to cotton, other "basic commodities" named in the Act included wheat, corn, rice, dairy products, and hogs. Amendments later added sugar beets and cane, cattle, grain sorghums, rye, flax, barley, peanuts, and potatoes.

[6] On government policy focused on the supply side of the "farm problem," see David E. Hamilton, *From New Day to New Deal: American Farm Policy from Hoover to Roosevelt* (Chapel Hill: University of North Carolina Press, 1991); Victoria S. Woeste, *The Farmer's Benevolent Trust: Law and Agricultural Cooperation in Industrial America, 1865–1945* (Chapel Hill: University of North Carolina Press, 1998); and Sally H. Clarke, *Regulation and Revolution in U.S. Farm Productivity* (Cambridge University Press, 1994).

and so reap a windfall. The temptation of this "free-riding" was strong and could be countered, Roosevelt's team believed, only by "cooperative planning under federal guidance." With federal help, farmers would learn to work together to plan production in the hope of receiving more money for less output.[7]

The cotton program pursued this objective along several related lines of attack. It relied primarily on the subsidy principle. In return for a farmer's agreement to reduce his acreage or production by a specified amount (formalized in a contract between the individual cotton grower and the Cotton Section of the AAA), the government agreed to make direct rental or benefit payments. While the program was voluntary, the subsidy principle, as embodied in benefit payments, helped circumvent the free-rider problem by assuring cooperators (provided a high enough number signed up) equal or greater benefits than those accruing to growers who chose to stay outside. The Act stipulated that the AAA's programs be largely self-financing, and funds for the benefit payments were to derive from a tax on the processors of agricultural commodities – in the case of cotton, on the first domestic processing (ginning) and on the processing of cotton substitutes. The AAA also expanded the program of government loans to cotton growers in the spirit of the commodity marketing movement of the 1920s, capped by the Agricultural Marketing Act of 1929 and creation of the Federal Farm Board, which emphasized the desirability of "orderly marketing" and enabling growers to hold cotton off the market and push prices upward.

A bold stroke in the direction of a planned agricultural economy, the AAA encountered numerous practical problems and one fatal constitutional flaw. By the time the law took effect, much of the 1933 crop was already in the ground and reduction required a plow-up. Growers were offered cash for reducing acreage based on historic production, with higher payment going for more productive land. Cooperation was high, with all of the important southern cotton states signing up over 70 percent of their cotton acreage. In the South, Louisiana led with 80 percent and North Carolina trailed with 50 percent. Nationwide, California came last at 20 percent. Decisions about future plantings confronted the problem of achieving the largest possible reduction with limited compensating funds. It turned out that a reduction in acreage of somewhere between 25 and 50 percent was the upper limit beyond which few growers would agree to contract. It was

---

[7] *Yearbook of Agriculture*, 1935, p. 2.

also important to conduct the reduction program so as to minimize injury to related businesses – ginners, factors, brokers, exporters, and seed millers – and to individuals (chiefly tenants) whom reduction threatened to displace.[8]

None of these was a simple problem, and the AAA solved none of them definitively during its brief lifetime. What mattered for the long-term history of cotton, though, was that this first-ever comprehensive attempt at nationwide "adjustment" of agricultural supply and demand in fact tinkered with only half the equation. As an exercise in supply management, the AAA demonstrated impressive energy and not a little success. To the New Dealers, however, demand pretty much was what it was. When it was low, as it was during depression, farmers needed administrative means to reduce production to meet it and so maintain their income. When demand rose, as seemed reasonable to suppose would occur with the return of better times, the same means would enable coordinated adjustment of production upward. Thus, enlightened public policy would effect what the market alone had failed to: the ideal of stabilized farm income.

NAILING IT DOWN

Three subsequent pieces of legislation would fix income stabilization near the heart of the nation's farm program for the next fifty years. In 1934, the Bankhead Act supplemented the Agricultural Adjustment Act and signaled a sharp departure from its voluntary principle. Widely (and accurately) known as the Cotton Control Act, the law authorized compulsory limitation on the cotton crop and provided crop and marketing quotas for states, counties, and individuals. It operated through the mechanism of a large tax levy on the ginning of cotton and the issuance of tax exemption certificates for the desired national amount (10 million bales in 1934) to growers who signed contracts with the Cotton Section, in proportion to their production during a specified base period. The rate was fixed at 50 percent of the average central market price (determined in ten spot markets), but in no case

---

[8] Daniel, *Breaking the Land,* chapter 8, "The Southern Enclosure." Also, Neil Foley, *The White Scourge: Mexicans, Blacks and Poor Whites in the Cotton Culture of Central Texas* (Berkeley: University of California Press, 1997); Lee J. Alston and James P. Ferrie, *Southern Paternalism and the Rise of the American Welfare State: Economics, Politics and Institutions, 1865–1965* (Cambridge University Press, 1998).

lower than 5 cents a pound.[9] Cotton produced on any farm in excess of allotment was subject to the tax, which was expected to exceed any increase in price resulting from the crop reduction program. The idea was that the ginning tax would remove the price incentive for nonsigners to expand their acreage, effectively coercing them to join the program.

A more controversial provision of the program was aimed at preventing shifts in cotton consumption caused by the processing tax. Section 15(d) authorized the Secretary to recommend taxes on competing commodities. Such taxes were first levied in December 1933 on jute and paper used in the manufacture of bags, twine, and paper towels. Attempts by cotton textile manufacturers to levy a tax on other fibers, particularly rayon and silk, were supported by the USDA, but such levies were too politically sensitive to make it through Congress and so did not go into effect.

Government subsidies usually develop around economic and political fault lines, and the various aspects of the cotton crop reduction program were no different. While the southern-dominated American Cotton Manufacturers Association lined up in favor of the processing tax, for example, opposition came from New England textile interests, who were already expecting to pay higher prices for their inputs as a consequence of the overall reduction program. When the New Englanders, who themselves were under orders to reduce operations and cut inventories, called for an end to the cotton processing tax and for higher import barriers against cotton goods, Secretary Wallace (a midwesterner) forcefully defended the tax as the "farmers' tariff" which wouldn't be given up until the manufacturers gave up theirs, adding with a flourish that "the 'plowing out' of factory workers into the street by American industry in 1932 was a thousand times more unjustifiable than the 'plowing under' of cotton in 1933."[10]

The AAA and the Cotton Control Act went some way toward fulfilling their purpose of restoring cotton farmers' incomes through direct government payments and by enhancing prices, but their legal status was in doubt. Lawsuits were quickly cobbled together by their opponents,

---

[9] The tax rate reflected prevailing notions of "fair exchange" and was wound up in the concept of parity. Section 9(b) of the 1933 Act: "The processing tax shall be set at such a rate as equals the difference between the current average farm price for the commodity and the fair exchange value of the commodity." Fair exchange was determined by relative purchasing power at the time of parity (1909–1914).

[10] "Mr. Wallace Speaks Out," *Memphis Commercial Appeal,* April 19, 1935, cited in Henry I. Richards, *Cotton and the AAA* (Washington, DC, 1936), 251.

and in January 1936 the entire package proved too radical for a strict-constructionist Supreme Court, which ruled against both pieces of legislation. Regulation and control of agricultural production, said the Court, fell beyond the power of the federal government, and the processing tax was not really a tax but a "means to an unconstitutional end."[11] Yet the sail of policy had been set. A month later, Roosevelt signed the Soil Conservation and Domestic Allotment Act, which was more carefully crafted to continue acreage restrictions of the invalidated 1933 law while avoiding processing taxes. Instead, benefit payments would go to growers who practiced soil conservation by withdrawing from production soil-depleting crops (like cotton) and turning acreage over to soil-conserving ones. The economic downturn of 1937, however, made clear that the conservation approach alone was not up to the task of curbing production and supporting prices; and in February 1938, the second Agricultural Adjustment Act superseded the 1936 Act.

The new legislation reinvigorated the spirit of the pioneer 1933 Act and enhanced its scope. Safely shorn of processing taxes, the AAA of 1938 authorized the Secretary to fix marketing quotas in any export farm commodity, including cotton, when surpluses threatened the price. Further, it authorized acreage allotments when growers approved the marketing quotas by a two-thirds referendum. And it retained the subsidy principle (tied once again to the notion of parity payments) that was fundamental to the original legislation, but this time provided funding out of the general treasury. The Second AAA also brought to life an arrangement known as the "ever-normal granary," which was designed to stabilize agricultural prices through loans to farmers on surplus crops at slightly below the level of parity. The USDA would store the crops until lean years, when farmers would retrieve and sell them at prices at or above parity. Such sales would hold down big price rises in years of crop failure and so even out farm income. Finally, the second AAA established the Federal Crop Insurance Corporation as a USDA agency to insure (at first) wheat crops against losses from drought, hail, or disease, using the commodity itself as payment of the premium.

RISING INCOME?

For all its ingenuity, the cotton legislation of the 1930s was but a short-term political response to a chronic economic problem. Given the South's historic

---

[11] *United States v. Butler*, 297 U.S. 1.

suspicions of federal meddling, the initial strong support for the New Deal agricultural programs among cotton farmers signaled their sheer economic desperation as much as any ideological shift away from old habits. Many conservative farmers no doubt found the underlying principles of the cotton program to be discomfiting, if not repugnant – especially the provisions that encouraged them *not* to plant. But if the new-fangled government attempts to manage supply actually raised farm incomes, southern farmers could then be as practical as farmers anywhere; they would line up and collect their checks cheerfully.

The cotton program of the AAA met their expectations in part. From the low point of the spring of 1933, the program in its first three years successfully beat back disaster as cotton farm income recovered approximately 50 percent. Even so, cotton farmers in 1935 still earned 40 percent less than in 1925. And in terms of purchasing power – the restoration of which was a key aim of the whole concept of agricultural "adjustment" – cotton farmers still found themselves 25 percent poorer than a decade earlier. Moreover, that income did recover in the short term did not necessarily augur well for the long term. The difficulty was inherent in the very means that seemed to be successful: acreage reduction.

Through contracts with farmers, benefit payments, and ginning taxes as provided under the Bankhead Act, it was clear that a program of reduction, though administratively difficult, could be carried out. This required government coordination at the federal level, in the absence of which earlier efforts to manage supply had been futile. How successful such coordination could be (and for how long) depended on answering questions of how much cotton should be produced, and where.

The Bureau of Agricultural Economics routinely produced outlook reports that suggested the crop that farmers were likely to plant at certain prices (and the prices that would likely come from that crop), but actual decisions about how much to plant (and the comparative advantage of competing crops) remained with each farmer. Taken in the aggregate, the task became even more difficult. "Estimate upon estimate" was how one key study of the cotton program characterized the approach necessarily taken by New Deal planners. It was fairly conclusive after several years that the program had some desired impact on farm incomes, yet it remained unclear what the optimum percentage reduction in production might be. Ten percent, twenty percent, thirty percent? Instead, the reduction policy went forward opportunistically, responding to the level of funding available to support the program. And those benefit payments, more than any price rise caused by production control, are what led to any improvement in income.

In the longer run, it was plausible to suppose that with less to sell, American growers could also expect to experience losses to increased foreign production and falling foreign demand for American cotton brought on by the domestic reduction program. The program also left unanswered the question of where cotton should best be grown. It simply assumed that each cooperating farmer would cut back more or less the same percentage from the crop planted on that farm during the base period. It was a relatively inflexible approach that failed, for instance, to account for changes in the productive capacity of particular farms or for shifts in the comparative advantage of cotton and other crops across different regions.[12] Failure of the AAA to answer either of these basic problems in the government control of cotton production gradually led cotton growers to redirect their search for solutions inward.

DELTA DOUBTS

The Cotton Belt now spanned nineteen states from the Atlantic to the Pacific and comprised some 2.5 million cotton farms. Cotton set the pace in agriculture when it came to geographical, technological, and cultural diversity: small plots to huge plantations; mule and hoe operations to progressive pioneers in mechanization; Old Southerners, Texans, Far Westerners. By the time the Second AAA looked to become a permanent part of everyone's farming future, growers in one of cotton's historically most productive regions began to express doubts about the government's one-size-fits-all approach to cotton and about the adequacy of legislation that sought to stabilize farm income through supply management alone.

Restricting production on an acreage basis prevented some farmers from fully utilizing their basic productive resources of land and labor, and limiting acreage on the basis of pre-Depression years when output had been high meant including many low-yielding acres in the total used for current allocation. This meant that relatively inefficient farms received the same percentage allotment as the efficient ones.

Practical concerns about policy discrimination against the most productive areas reflected growing restiveness over the underlying philosophy of

---

[12] Richards, *Cotton and the AAA*, 316–37.

many New Deal agricultural reformers, which was to raise prices through government supports and then restrict production to the level justified by the higher prices. Such actions pointed to more and more restrictions and to redundancy in land, labor, and machinery; as American cotton thus dwindled, they opened the door to competition from foreign-grown cotton and man-made fibers.

Political considerations thus hobbled competition, which high-yielding farmers in the Yazoo–Mississippi Delta particularly resented. The record crop of 1937 – nearly 19 million bales, which dropped the pound price to 8.6 cents – brought the situation to a head, as industry leaders looked not just to Congress but also to themselves for answers. From a group of producers operating through a small organization in Stoneville, Mississippi, the Delta Council (founded in 1935 to represent business and agricultural interests in the eighteen-county alluvial area around Greenville), a new industrywide organization was about to spring. The idea for a national cotton council traces probably to a conversation between James Hand, a large planter in the southern Delta, and William Rhea Blake, secretary manager of the Delta Council.

James Hand was also a dealer for International Harvester, and he believed that cotton's basic problem lay as much with weak demand as with surplus supply. He was, on the one hand, a close follower of agronomic and cotton breeding research on improving quality and yields, but as a salesman for the leading farm machinery company he had developed a different perspective on the market than was common to cotton growers. He had learned how Harvester had become the leader in its industry through research to improve performance *and* promotion to stimulate demand. The same strategy, he reasoned, ought to be applicable to cotton: cut costs and improve quality through research, and then energetically promote the product. Rhea Blake had a promoter's instinct, too: he once worked for Virginia Power and Light, where his job was to travel around Virginia and West Virginia measuring levels of illumination (in factories, homes, and offices) and then putting the case that higher wattages made for happier, healthier customers. This was generic promotion; if it worked for electricity, it ought to work for cotton.

Hand and Blake broached the idea for a national organization for the entire cotton industry to the president of the Delta Council, W. T. "Billy" Wynn, a prominent lawyer, banker, and planter from Greenville, Mississippi. Wynn liked their ideas but cautioned that the challenge of bringing together an industry as diverse and contentious as cotton would require some high-caliber leadership. Wynn told them that he happened to know the only man with the ability, national stature, and Beltwide recognition to have any chance at pulling it off. His name was Oscar G. Johnston, and he lived just a few miles north of Greenville in the company town of Scott, Mississippi.

MR. OSCAR

The company was the 40,000-acre, British-owned Delta and Pine Land Company (D&PL) and the Delta and Pine Land Seed Company, located in Washington and Bolivar counties and then the largest cotton plantation in the world.[13] A lawyer by training, Oscar Johnston ("Mr. Oscar," as he

[13] Johnston had done the legal work for the development project that became Delta and Pine Land Company, originally the Mississippi Delta Planting Company, and their histories remained closely intertwined. Mississippi law then forbade any one entity from owning more than 10,000 acres, except for grandfathered timber companies chartered in the late 1880s. Johnston discovered one such dormant charter, "The Delta and Pine Land Company," which the developers bought to add to their landholdings in the state. In 1912, a group of fifty English cotton spinners, the Fine Cotton Spinners and Doublers Association, acquired Delta and Pine Land (D&PL) as part of a drive to assure continuing sources of supply and stimulate cotton production in various parts of the world. Similar projects to secure the supply particularly of long staple "Egyptian" cotton included the British Cotton Growing Association in the Indus River Valley in British India, the Empire Cotton Growing Corporation in Africa, and most successfully the Sudan Plantation Syndicate in the Anglo-Egyptian Sudan.

The Fine Spinners hired Johnston to run Delta and Pine Land in 1927, the year of the Great Mississippi Flood, which broke the levy at Mounds Landing at the northwestern corner of D&PL. Johnston's management turned D&PL into a model diversified operation, planting about 12,000 acres in cotton, 8,000 to forage crops, 9,000 in woodland and lakes, and the balance in pastures and garden. One thousand tenant families worked it, along with 1,000 mules, on a 50–50 share system. The plantation had a full-time doctor, a small clinic and hospital, and a school for tenant children. Mechanization did not come until after World War II. D&PL was the place to emulate, boasting during Johnston's administration a cotton yield of 638 pounds per acre when the national average was less than a third that. As neighboring farmers put it: "When they plowed, we plowed; when they planted, we planted; when they picked, we picked."

D&PL's high yields owed much to research, and it operated its own cotton breeding program, the Delta and Pine Land Seed Company, which sold seed worldwide. The company also ran its own gins and marketed its crop through the Delta Staple Cotton Cooperative (Greenwood, Mississippi), which Johnston had helped to found in 1921. Though no farmer himself, Johnston had the sure touch for managing a large and complex agricultural enterprise. He understood finance and during the 1927 flood staved off disaster through smart use of futures. Watching the waters rise, he bet on a crop shortfall and bought cotton futures at 14 cents per pound, which he then sold, with much of the Delta under water, for 22 cents. D&PL made a profit of $200,000, which went to rehabilitate the flooded plantation. Johnston also believed in engaging a highly competent professional staff under general plantation manager Jess Fox,

was commonly known) had returned home to run D&PL in 1934 after a highly successful and much-publicized stint inside the New Deal agricultural programs. Johnston had assisted Roosevelt and Henry Wallace in organizing the first AAA and had responsibility for liquidating the vast tonnage of "pool cotton" accumulated by the government under the Federal Farm Board during the Hoover administration. His performance there had brought him to the forefront of national agricultural policy deliberations. Johnston had served as director of finance of the AAA, as vice-president of the Commodity Credit Corporation, and as special trade representative to Europe in 1935 to promote U.S. agricultural commodities. He had been an enthusiastic New Dealer, at least at the start. But as Henry Wallace veered to the left during Roosevelt's second term, Johnston – who was a faithful Democrat but a southern conservative one – made no secret of his disillusionment with Washington planners ("social reformers, crackpots and starry-eyed do-gooders," in his own words), who seemed out of touch with real social and economic problems, particularly in the cotton South.[14]

Even so, when Johnston left Washington in 1937 it was with a record of accomplishment and a solid reputation as "Mr. U.S. Cotton," at home and abroad. Johnston was 57, looking forward to managing D&PL in addition to serving as a member of the Federal Reserve Bank of St. Louis and as a director of the Illinois Central Railroad. He did not need something else to do. Billy Wynn, who could never take no for an answer, took one sitting to persuade Johnston that he should take on a job that had no model: there was no precedent for a commodity organization engaging in promotion of a single agricultural product. He invited Johnston, along with Blake, to his home in Greenville late one spring afternoon, "poured a drink around and eased into his subject." As Wynn talked of the need and the responsibility and of how Johnston was the only man who could possibly make such a scheme work, Johnston – whose Washington experience predisposed him to a positive, demand-side approach for cotton rather than retrogressive plow-ups and endless restrictions – made up his mind then and there.[15]

He liked to think of the new challenge as his swan song for the South, which it happily turned out to be for Johnston personally. But the National

a former professor of mathematics and agriculture at Mississippi State. Under Fox, each of twelve unit managers ran and lived on his own unit, complete with its own barns, tools, and tenants. See Read P. Dunn, Jr., *Mr. Oscar* (Memphis, 1991).

[14] Ibid., 66–7.

[15] Albert Russell, *U.S. Cotton and the National Cotton Council, 1938–1987* (Memphis, 1987), 5.

Cotton Council (NCC) – which Johnston, Blake, and their helpers would bring to life in 1938 – marked an extended new beginning for the South's (and the West's) beleaguered white staple. Johnston had committed himself to a daunting task that demanded a combative frame of mind. Newspaperman Hodding Carter, editor of the Greenville *Delta Star,* captured Johnston's attitude in a piece (headlined "Cotton Fights Back") in which he recalled driving to Memphis with Johnston, Blake, and one or two others for a state agriculture commission meeting in September 1937, a few months after Johnston had taken on the job. With a little smile, Johnson told his fellow travelers how all this was really the fault of actor Paul Muni's recent movie on the life of Emile Zola, who gave up comfort and security to fight the good fight for a dying cause. "That picture got to me," he mused. "I'm not as old or I hope as fat as that Frenchman and somebody has to help cotton. The cotton people must be brought together to promote cotton and advertise it and fight for it and it's going to take someone with the time and a little money to start things. I'm no crusader and cotton's future can't worry me personally, but I think I'll try to start a cotton organization – a cotton council."[16]

Johnston understood the economics of cotton and the imperative to be competitive and always sell more. He also understood the politics of cotton, which meant that a national cotton council, if it were to succeed, would need participation and financial support not only from producers but from other cotton interests as well. Organizational planning began in earnest early in 1938, and on June 15 at the Delta Council's annual meeting in Cleveland, Mississippi, Johnston carefully laid out his ideas before a painstakingly inclusive audience of government officials and cotton leaders from all cotton interest organizations.

A master speechmaker, Johnston used this one to focus on the growing threat from synthetics, the importance of top-flight programs of research and promotion, and the need for cotton to speak with one voice if it were to speak effectively in the national and state capitols. His draft proposal for creation of the National Cotton Council of America – to be representative of all segments (originally five: producers, ginners, warehousemen, merchants, and cottonseed crushers), each working with the others to "increase the consumption of cotton and the products thereof" – met with unanimous support. The group established a committee on organization to reconvene in Memphis in November to finalize the structure, and they

---

[16] Cited in Read P. Dunn, Jr., *Mr. Oscar* (Memphis, 1991), 71.

appointed as temporary officers Johnston chairman, Wynn treasurer and Blake secretary. Whereas the goals seemed easy enough to agree upon, the matter of how exactly to enable each interest to speak with equal voice was trickier and indeed might well have scotched the whole project at the outset.

First there was the problem of the Farm Bureau, which had organized the Farm Bloc in Congress and whose policy positions, particularly on the tariff, often sat poorly with cotton's traditionally free-trading ways. The Farm Bureau was by far the largest farm organization in the country (others included the Grange and the more liberal Farmers Union), and Johnston realized the extreme difficulty of obtaining participation in the NCC of rank and file producers were the Bureau to be opposed. Led by national president Ed O'Neal from Chicago, the Bureau for its part was wary of separate commodity organizations (cotton would be the first) getting involved in Washington and state politics – organizations whose possibly divergent views might threaten the solidarity of the Farm Bloc.

Johnston was tempted to go it alone by establishing organizations of cotton farmers in the various states independent of the Bureau and actually succeeded in setting up the Mississippi Agricultural Council, which was composed exclusively of cotton growers. But other industry leaders persuaded him this approach was not practical and that it would be preferable to negotiate an agreement that would permit Bureau cooperation. Two key concessions, worked out with the help of Walter Randolph, president of the Alabama Farm Bureau, eventually mollified O'Neal. The first involved determining representation and provided that the Farm Bureau, in all states where it was organized, would appoint from its members the producer representatives to the new national cotton organization. The second concession concerned voting and invoked a highly restrictive procedure that further protected Bureau interests. Johnston agreed that no position would be taken by the NCC except by a two-thirds vote of each of the five interest groups, voting separately. Growers had a veto, and so did each of the other four interests. Such a veto provision obviously would limit what the proposed council might do. But it addressed head-on the historic industry divisiveness and the compelling need to close ranks and march to one step. The new council's actions might be narrow, but they would be powerful.[17]

---

[17] Dunn, *Mr. Oscar*, 81–2; see also Christiana M. Campbell, *The Farm Bureau and the New Deal: A Study in the Making of American Farm Policy, 1933–1940* (Urbana: University of Illinois Press, 1962).

Other interests came along with less difficulty, except for the merchants. Particularly strong feelings existed between producers and merchants (or shippers), and the veto provision was key to obtaining their support as well.

The counterpart to the Farm Bureau's O'Neal among the merchants was Will Clayton, a shrewd defender of his interests who had to be won over if a national cotton council was to work. Clayton was founder and president of Anderson Clayton Company of Houston, the largest cotton merchants in the world. To the intrinsic antagonism between merchants and growers (merchants wanted always to buy low, while producers wanted always to sell high), Clayton brought his own special antagonism for Roosevelt and the New Deal farm programs. Attacking the first AAA from the outset, he acted on the belief that it was always a grave error to tinker with market forces. He objected strenuously to what he saw as the New Deal's attempt to restore farm income through a supported market, and he preferred subsidies paid to farmers directly, if they were truly needed. He opposed artificial price fixing in commodities via above-market loans and, above all, the discrimination that the cotton-exporting South still suffered as a result of high U.S. tariff policies. Even though he opposed much that Roosevelt himself stood for, Clayton had the merchant's prejudice against protection and ardently supported one of Roosevelt's key men, Secretary of State Cordell Hull of Tennessee, in his efforts to negotiate tariff-lowering reciprocal trade agreements.[18]

Clayton and Johnston had first crossed paths when Johnston had consulted him regularly in the course of disposing of the cotton pool stocks early in the New Deal. While their views were not identical, common beliefs about basic economic principles brought them together. Johnston was himself disillusioned with the Second AAA and on that point, at least, the two men stood on common ground. Johnston was also a fervent supporter of reciprocal trade agreements to open world markets, and he was concerned that artificially engineered domestic prices would cripple cotton in those very markets. The two men could agree on those things, too. But Clayton regarded Johnston's new enterprise with a wary eye. As a merchant he was concerned that the high price objectives of farmers would make cotton noncompetitive in world markets. He was concerned that the high tariff convictions of groups like the Farm Bureau, which was dominated by grain farmers who did not then have significant export markets,

18 Dunn, *Mr. Oscar*, 43–5.

would influence the votes of cotton farmers against their own free-trading interests. Nor did he think much at first of Johnston's early close connection with the AAA and the acreage restrictions on cotton, which contradicted the merchants' own traditional freedom-to-choose views. Winning Clayton over took some long, tense meetings. Although the two men grew to get on well together, it was only the assurance of the veto provision that made Clayton and the merchants feel safe enough to finally sign on.

AT CREATION

Complex organizations grow slowly, and the National Cotton Council would be no exception. Even so, the speed with which Oscar Johnston brought together the NCC – the first industrywide, commodity-specific organization in the history of American agriculture – is remarkable. Not two years had elapsed between the meeting in Greenville, Mississippi, when Billy Wynn persuaded "Mr. Oscar" to step up to the plate one more time for cotton, and the meeting, just a few days before Thanksgiving 1938, when Johnston decisively persuaded cotton's leaders that the moment had come to take responsibility for their future for themselves.

As creation episodes go, the birthday of the NCC is memorable on several counts. One was the setting at the Peabody Hotel in Memphis. As the lore of southern history has it, the Delta begins in the lobby of the Peabody Hotel and rolls south to Vicksburg. If ever a crop had a capital city, cotton had Memphis, and the great red brick caravansary – built in 1925 and filling up much of a city block along Union Street – was its temple. In 1938, when everyone still came and went by train and when downtown marked the center of a community's life in every respect, the Peabody was what Memphians boasted about to the world, its public spaces air-conditioned against Delta summers, "circulating ice-water" in its guest rooms. There were swank restaurants and smoky bars, a rooftop terrace with a view of the river and Arkansas beyond, and of course the ritual daily parade of "the Peabody ducks."[19]

---

[19] To this day, ducks adorn everything at the Peabody, from the hotel stationery to the white sand in the ash trays. The tradition began in the 1930s, when general manager Frank Schutt and a friend, Chip Barwick, returned from a hunting trip in Arkansas, well-fortified with bourbon (colloquially, among southern hunters, "aiming oil") and taken with the idea of temporarily parking their live decoy ducks in the lobby fountain while the weary hunters retired to the hotel bar. Guests loved it and have ever since. Every day at 11:00 in the morning, hotel

There was also a grand ballroom where society belles "came out" at fancy cotillions and where, on weekends, hotel guests and locals alike jitterbugged to the hottest big bands of the era. But on November 21 of that year, the ballroom at the Peabody was given over to a nonmusical but equally high-energy event. Old photographs reveal political convention-style placards – "North Carolina," "Alabama," "New Mexico" – amid a crush of men in dark suits seated on old-fashioned bent-wood chairs with white dust covers, attention fixed squarely on the dais and Oscar Johnston. The room was quiet, but a newspaperman felt the anticipation as Johnston stepped up to address the Committee on Organization of the soon-to-be-born National Cotton Council. Delegates heard some fighting words.

"Cotton," Johnston said, "is sick." The cause of its malady was chronic, reaching back decades into southern history, and acute, tracing to the hodgepodge of New Deal agricultural programs. Johnston's purpose was to look ahead and identify the cure. It was seated right in front of him. "Is there any reason why representatives of each of the five interests should not come together, perfect an organization, and fight for the advancement of the industry?" The time had come to save themselves by their own united exertion: "Too often have cotton people looked to others to solve their ills. We have fought among ourselves." Too long had they had their eye on the wrong ball: "We have failed to see the importance of building demand, of removing restrictions on manufacture and sale of our products." And too late, unless they got down to work fast, to do much about it: "If major problems are to be resolved, it is something we do as an industry ourselves, and until we are prepared to do it, we are going to continue floundering."

If the industry were to cure the "sick King Cotton," it would have to learn to concentrate on a few basic objectives. To increase consumption of American cotton, all its players would have to learn how to advertise and promote. To compete with other textile fibers, they would have to learn to

---

staff unroll a 50-foot red carpet stretching from the fountain to the elevators. Meanwhile the Peabody's "duckmaster" calls for the ducks at their penthouse on the hotel's Plantation Roof, and in regal style the ducks march single file to the elevator, descend to the lobby, waddle down the carpet and splash into the Italian travertine marble fountain, all to the tune of John Philip Sousa's "King Cotton March." At 5:00 in the afternoon, the ritual reverses, and the ducks (usually four hens and a drake, the "lead duck") ceremoniously return to their Royal Duck Palace, "a fairyland birdcage with banners flying," an ornate fountain of its own, and a royal bedchamber. Today's mallards are raised by a local farmer and friend of the Peabody and live in the fountain only until they are full-grown, when they are "retired" and returned to the wild.

The Delta, it is said, starts in the lobby of the Peabody Hotel in Memphis and rolls south to Vicksburg. Built in 1925, The Peabody, "The South's Finest; One of America's Best," was a caravansary for the cotton culture. The National Cotton Council got started in its ballroom in 1938; "Maids of Cotton" were feted there. Menus in the hotel's rooftop restaurant – "The Skyway: The South's Most Beautiful Supper Club" – sported "Typical Cotton Scenes Down in Dixie."

Cotton has many uses. One, now sadly lost to time, was an arch celebrating Cotton Carnival in Memphis.

improve the quality of cotton through scientific research and endeavor to find new uses. To protect themselves politically from those with different economic interests, they would have to oppose legislation that discriminated against cotton and support legislation that benefited any branch of the industry. Well primed, the industry representatives that night at the Peabody responded to Johnston's war cry with a standing ovation. Unanimous resolutions quickly followed to go forth united under one banner of research, promotion, and political alertness.[20]

The National Cotton Council began operations in February 1939. In retrospect, the timing was symbolic. Like it or not, America was soon to find itself at the center of the second great war of the century, whose central lesson was the necessity always to turn outward and engage the larger world. For a hundred years, American cotton had looked outward geographically to world markets, and the new threat from synthetics would soon force it to

[20] Russell, *U.S. Cotton and the National Cotton Council,* 7–8; Memphis *Commercial Appeal,* November 22, 1938.

look outward in another sense and engage the competition as it had never done before. Cotton's job was only getting harder. Until the NCC, cotton lacked the organizational tools to unify its own diverse interests before the larger world. Left to run its course without the NCC, cotton's sickness, already dire by the late 1930s and largely impervious to the ministrations of "Dr. New Deal," might well have been terminal.

Oscar Johnston did not live to see the job through. He had not accepted the presidency of the new organization, he liked to say and say often, to preside over a "peanut stand."[21] He understood the shock value of big numbers and did not hesitate to tell the industry that the NCC's goal should be to spend $10 million per year. This was a long way off, and adequately financing the Council's ambitious programs would remain a wearying yearly challenge. The first annual budget was $250,000, raised by the states from a voluntary 2 percent (per bale) levy on production. (The second year, the budget fell to $150,000.) Office space was rented in Memphis and the first staff member recruited. Ed Lipscomb, a journalist who had headed up the Mississippi Advertising Commission, became the NCC's Director of Sales Promotion and Public Relations. He had $15,000 to spend.

---

[21] Johnston remained as president of the NCC until 1947, and a board member until 1953. He retired to Greenville and died in 1955 at age 75.

PART TWO
APPROACHING THE MARKET

4

SYNTHETIC SHOCK

Competition's Alarm

The promise of industry unity that came with birth of the National Cotton Council (referred to variously as the NCC, Cotton Council, or Council) in Memphis in 1938 put new spring into cotton's step. Unity depended on sticking to basics that everybody could agree upon. Profitability was the most basic goal of all, and the one to which government farm programs from the New Deal forward had claimed to hold the key in the form of various schemes of supply management and income support. Profitability was not, however, a matter of the right price alone. The Council's work evolved along a dual track. Lobbying – to ensure that cotton would have a strong voice in formation of national farm policy – was the first task at hand, and it would remain the ostensible purpose of the Council for its lifetime.[1] The more complex tasks of research and promotion, which were aimed at helping cotton compete in the market, became part of its mission more slowly.

RESEARCH AND PROMOTION

Agricultural research had a long history at the USDA and at the state experiment stations. This platform of well-established activity enabled the

---

[1] It did not take long for the Council to establish itself as a deft player along national corridors of power, where Oscar Johnston was no stranger. He established, as principles of effective lobbying, thoroughness and the importance of not hesitating. Hot on the Council's second annual meeting, he deployed the industry's troops to extend the Reciprocal Trade Agreements, due to expire in 1940, and used his friendship with Secretary of State Cordell Hull (from Tennessee, a cotton state) to good advantage. Hull welcomed the Council's ensuing campaign, which saw petitions mailed by the thousand across the Cotton Belt calling for signatures in support of renewal. Johnston saw that all the returns were carefully tabulated by state, county, and Congressional district and then submitted to the clerks of the House and Senate. It was the first of many legislative battles waged around the perennial issue of what price cotton farmers would receive for their cotton. See Albert Russell, *U.S. Cotton and the National Cotton Council, 1938–1987* (Memphis: National Cotton Council, 1987), 18.

Council to stretch its slim resources as it pursued its new research agenda. The Cotton Research Foundation, founded in 1936 with assistance of the Mellon Institute, had been one such early ally in research into cotton's needs and opportunities. Others followed. The Council established its own research division in 1944, with an offer from the University of Texas to use its laboratory and fiber-testing equipment in Austin. Help then came from Southern Methodist University, which shared its test-plot facility and weather station in Dallas.

The promise that mechanization would increase efficiency on the farm by lowering costs and raising yields became a particular NCC enthusiasm in the immediate postwar era. Together with private implement companies, the USDA, and several cotton states' extension services, the Council sponsored the first Beltwide Cotton Mechanization Conference in 1947 at the Delta Branch Experiment Station in Stoneville, Mississippi. That same year, the first Cotton Insect Control Conference convened in Columbia, South Carolina. Weed control was the last serious hurdle to reducing the enormous hand-labor input in raising cotton. The Council mounted its attack on this problem in conjunction with agricultural land-grant colleges and private industry. A highlight of the Beltwide Mechanization Conference in 1950 featured an experimental tractor that combined three operations in a single trip: cultivating, spraying for insects, and flaming for weed control. The challenges were wide-ranging. There was research on plant diseases conducted with the U.S. Weather Bureau, seed research into long staple varieties attractive to mills, the relatively new practice of defoliation, and work on bale size and packaging. (A third of the U.S. crop, the USDA estimated in 1947, went to market in misshapen bales and damaged by asphalt-coated ties.) In 1950, the Council participated in establishment of a cotton winter breeding nursery in Mexico to speed commercial development of new varieties.[2]

Early fibers research, which the Council organized into market and technical sections, addressed a range of qualities then central to cotton's competitive position, including fabric luster and crease and soil resistance. Cotton's flammability also became a focus for study after a series of hotel and

---

[2] On mechanization, see James H. Street, *The New Revolution in the Cotton Economy: Mechanization and Its Consequences* (Chapel Hill: University of North Carolina Press, 1957); Charles R. Sayre, "Cotton Mechanization Since World War II," *Agricultural History* 53 (January 1979), 105–24; and Gilbert C. Fite, "Mechanization of Cotton Production Since World War II," *Agricultural History* 54 (January 1980), 190–207.

apartment house fires in the mid-1940s. Attributed mainly to smoking in bed, these fires prompted legislative proposals to regulate the manufacture of fabrics easily set alight. The Council sought to turn this threat to cotton's reputation into an opportunity through its own research initiatives. Flammability studies yielded encouraging results, and there is a memorable photograph of several Camel-puffing Council members testing them out at a special exhibit mounted at the Memphis Cotton Exchange, which invited visitors to "Throw your lighted Matches & Cigarettes on the *FLAME-PROOF* COTTON INSULATION (It won't Burn)"! And it didn't.[3]

As with research, the Council's promotion programs relied on cooperative efforts across the industry. Yet while research promised tangible near-term results, promotion could promise dividends only over the longer run. An early example, from the Council's very first year, plugged "Cotton for Christmas" and consisted of a simple brochure – a long list of holiday gift suggestions – made available to retailers. An accompanying movie trailer slide added, "Santa Claus Picks Cotton in 1939." Advertising manager Ed Lipscomb also negotiated Council co-sponsorship (along with the Cotton Consumption Council, a chain-store group) of National Cotton Week, and he persuaded the Memphis Cotton Carnival to let the Council convert the local "Maid of Cotton" promotion into a nationwide merchandising symbol for the whole industry.[4]

America's entry into the Second World War presented cotton with an opportunity to promote itself as vital to the war effort and central to the nation's fundamental economic strength. The Council's claims for cotton in this context were anything but modest. In cooperation with the Quartermaster Corps, the Council's domestic consumption division mounted an information campaign, carried in nearly half the nation's newspapers every week, to demonstrate the connection between cotton and victory and to educate consumers on how to get the longest life out of every cotton product they bought. "Every U.S. Fighting Man Uses Cotton Every Day," the home front learned: second to steel, cotton was the most vital war materiel. Council posters depicted America's "Two Big Guns" side by side: one was a smoking big-bore naval cannon, the other a roll of "U.S. Quartermaster Corps Specification Cotton Cloth" essential to everything from

[3] Russell, *National Cotton Council*, 41–2.
[4] Ibid., 19, NCC archives. The Maid of Cotton remained a Cotton Council symbol and ambassador for the industry until 1993.

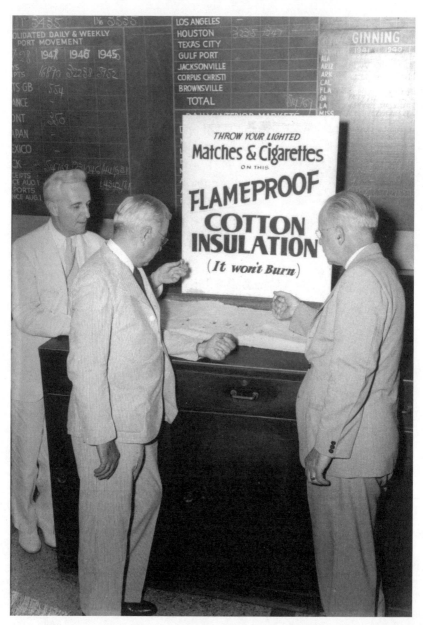

Cotton's flammability was an obstacle to overcome in the fiber's race for competitiveness. In the late 1940s, members of the Memphis Cotton Exchange were invited to test out, with their cigarettes, cotton insulation treated to resist the flame.

gun camouflage and mosquito netting to steel armament and munitions.[5] With America's entry into the war, cotton exports practically disappeared, and defense-driven consumption ate up the surplus. The USDA officially called upon the nation's 2.5 million growers to plant their full allotment of 27.5 million acres in an all-out production effort, while members of the Council's production efficiency committee went to Washington to see that the farm machinery and chemicals needed to do the job would be made available. The Maids of Cotton toured the Cotton Belt selling war bonds.

The demands of war hoisted America – and cotton along with it – out of its lengthy Depression. But fears that peace would see the return of bad times kept cotton's producers awake at night. The industry anticipated increased competition and overproduction. The NCC had attempted to put cotton on a figurative war footing, even before the real war came along, in its 1940–41 campaign to increase the assessment to 5 cents per bale and 3 cents per ton on cottonseed. A newspaper cartoon inspired by images of the previous Great War carried the message that cotton in war or peace faced dangerous enemies. Two American doughboys manned a machine-gun: the one at the trigger was the "National Cotton Council," the one feeding the ammunition (labeled "5 Cents a Bale") was the "Farmer." The Council gunner converted the farmers' ammo into "New Uses," "Foreign Trade," and "Advertising" and fired them off across no-man's land at a lineup of leering Huns labeled "Foreign Competition," "Discriminatory Legislation," "Surplus," "Underconsumption," and "Substitutes."[6] In reality, it would take many years and a great deal more than a nickel a bale to beat back the threat to cotton, but just understanding that a fight was unavoidable was the place to begin.

Publication in 1942 of the first edition of *Cotton Counts Its Customers* by the Council's market research division was a step toward more systematic analysis of changing markets. *Cotton Counts Its Customers,* which would appear annually thenceforth, took United States Department of Commerce data on cotton consumption – specifically, the volume of cotton going into hundreds of end uses – and statistically reorganized them to emphasize cotton's strengths and weaknesses. (The first edition counted 265 end uses for

[5] During the war, the Quartermaster Corps was the world's biggest buyer of textiles, and in one record order in 1942 called for 351 million yards of cotton cloth and 40 million yards of mosquito netting – enough, it was claimed, to make a barracks bag big enough to hold Honshu Island, "the largest part of Japan!!" [sic]. NCC Archives.

[6] Russell, *National Cotton Council,* 2; NCC Archives.

the immediate prewar years of 1938 and 1939.) As originally conceived, the publication provided a tool for detecting market change and, theoretically, for alerting the industry to areas needing more research and promotion. It was a catchy title, but it was also literal. The volume consisted of lists, which in an integrated sales and manufacturing company would have been raw information for the marketing department. But the cotton industry, with all its diverse segments (textile manufacturers would become the Council's sixth segment in 1941, marketing cooperatives the seventh in 1963), was the opposite of an integrated business, and the Cotton Council was not a business at all. Thus, although *Cotton Counts Its Customers* could provide useful information on cotton's markets, the Council itself had no direct power over what (if any) use was actually made of it.

Still, the postwar prospects for cotton clearly demanded some attention, and in 1944 the Council acted to improve them by attempting to identify cotton with high fashion. This was no small feat; cotton was widely regarded as a cheap workaday fabric. The vehicle for upgrading cotton's image was an advertising series that ran in *Mademoiselle, Vogue,* and *Harper's Bazaar,* in which "Governors' Ladies" became models for the work of top designers who were adapting their lines to cotton fabrics. The original idea was to feature the first ladies of the Cotton Belt governors, but as the project proved its popularity the wives of the midwestern and northeastern governors got in on the act as well. They included the aristocratic Mrs. Leverett Saltonstall from Massachusetts, whom the copywriter made sound as practical as she was fashion-conscious: "My family depends on cottons more than ever," she explained, "they're so serviceable for these strenuous days." The first postwar promotions continued with the message that cotton had style. The Council's "American Designer Series" of 1946 and 1947 targeted a fashion-starved public who now learned from designers like Adele Simpson that nothing could be better than "fine pure cotton": "Out of the kitchen, into the drawing room – that's cotton today."[7]

THE RIGHT ATTITUDE

The NCC's Ed Lipscomb held a philosophy about advertising that appeared to be fully in tune with the consumerist spirit of postwar America. Consumers, he said, bought benefits more than products. To women who cared

---

[7] Ibid., 29; NCC Archives.

about it, "fashion" was such a benefit, and it could be had in many products made of many materials. It was the Cotton Council's challenge, he believed, to convince the fashion-conscious that cotton equaled fashion.

While "fashion" could be tricky, subjective territory, the "benefits" principle applied across the entire product spectrum. At the more prosaic extreme, for example, it applied to the old market for awnings. The cotton awning manufacturers were not really in the awning business at all, but rather in the coolness business. "Look, you don't sell awnings," Lipscomb preached at them. "You sell more comfort, lower temperatures in the room because the sun isn't there." These were things that people wanted and were prepared to pay for. Unless they had some direct connection with the cotton business, Lipscomb thought that most people cared little about the identity of the particular fiber. It was best therefore to promote cotton "indirectly," concentrating on what it did.[8]

This was not the way the cotton industry had traditionally thought about the market, and with good reason. For more than a century before the 1950s, cotton had not simply found its way into the market – it had taken the market by storm and had done so without self-promotion. Compared with wool, silk, and linen, cotton was cheap, cool, washable, and abundant. Its fiber, cleansed of seeds by machine, adapted itself to the processes of mechanized manufacturing at each succeeding stage of production. Cotton clothed the world and found its way into scores of other uses, just as *Cotton Counts Its Customers* meticulously documented. Cotton's aura of invincibility survived well into the 1940s, thanks to the New Deal's promise to restore prices and keep cotton prosperous (albeit while employing fewer hands on fewer acres). In keeping that promise, however, the government performed a great disservice to those it attempted to help. Its relentless focus on the issues of supply and price nourished the growing deception that demand would always see to itself.

From the perspective of growers, it was easy not to see much beyond the crop itself – to miss the forest for the trees or, in this case, the market for the cotton. How many bales would their labor and nature's gift produce come November? How much would the market and the merchants give them for it? What kind of living would their investment in land, labor, machinery, and chemicals provide them and their families? It was easy to be lulled into

---

[8] Russell, *National Cotton Council*, 45; see also Ed Lipscomb, *Grass Roots Public Relations for Agriculture* (Memphis, 1950).

thinking that all that mattered was the cotton even though what really mattered were the benefits that cotton provided its customers. Of course, this
had always been so. But the time was quickly passing when consumers, just
like producers, found themselves surrounded by cotton and only by cotton.

What cotton producers should have worried about at the end of World
War II was not a depression but a changed market in which consumers
would enjoy other choices, many of them far more attractive than cotton.
The promotional programs of the NCC both battled this complacency and
fell victim to it. Later marketing successes of Cotton Incorporated would
vindicate Lipscomb's forward-looking advertising philosophy: that what
mattered was not the product per se but what the product did. In the late
1940s and 1950s, however, the timing was off. Cotton was not yet ready for
what would be claimed about it. In fact, it was falling badly behind in the
market for textiles.

COMPETITION'S ALARM

Cotton's problem resulted from several trends in the competitive arena that
had been building up for a number of years and that accelerated after World
War II. The first was a relative decline in the share of U.S.-produced cotton in the world market. America historically had dominated the world
cotton trade and continued to do so as late as the 1920s, when exports averaged over 7 million bales per year. In the peak year of 1926, exports totaled
almost 11 million bales, which accounted for 60 percent of all foreign mill
consumption. Thereafter, cotton's strength was eroded by the confluence of
expanding production in other countries, the disruptions of depression and
war, and the shortage of dollar exchange to buy American cotton after the
war. By the mid-1950s, American cotton farmers were producing no more
cotton than they had in 1920, about 13 million bales (but on half as many
acres), while foreign growers were producing 3-1/2 times as much, about
28 million bales.[9]

Domestically, American cotton had to confront a new enemy altogether
in the form of man-made textile fibers.[10] During the same 35-year period, as

---

[9] USDA, *Statistics on Cotton and Related Data, 1920–1956* (Washington, DC, 1958), 25.
[10] Rayon, introduced commercially in the 1920s, was the first "man-made" textile fiber. As a
cellulosic made from wood pulp, however, rayon was not a true "synthetic." The parade of
synthetics – which are derived from petroleum and include acrylics, polyesters, and Spandex –
began in the 1930s but burst upon the market only after World War II.

U.S. cotton production slipped relative to foreign cotton, U.S. production of man-made fibers rose from 32,000 to 5.5 million bale-equivalents. Consumption patterns shifted accordingly. Cotton, which had commanded an 88-percent share of the domestic apparel market in 1920, held only 66 percent in 1957. This difference was due to "man-mades," which rose from a 0.3-percent to a 28-percent share in the same period. (Silk and wool, cotton's traditional rivals, made up the remainder.) U.S. cotton consumption per capita, meanwhile, sank to two pounds lower (24 pounds) in 1957 than it had been in 1920. Failure of total fiber consumption to keep pace with the growth of the economy as a whole compounded cotton's decline relative to the competition. In 1930, Americans spent 9 percent of their disposable income for apparel; in 1956, they spent just over 6 percent. Cotton was consequently losing ground both in the battle against its direct fiber competitors and against the other goods and services competing for consumers' money.[11] The Cotton Council addressed this situation with research into three major factors affecting cotton's competitive strengths and weaknesses: price, promotion, and quality. The conclusions of the research ran sharply against the grain of the industry's conventional wisdom.

Ever since the New Deal, the federal government had supported cotton prices at levels generally considered higher than would have been the case in a market entirely subject to the cyclical fortunes of weather and commodity price fluctuations. The NCC's staff economists figured that, in over half of cotton's total end uses, price was a serious competitive consideration; hence, anything that inflated it worked to cotton's disadvantage. Moreover, price could also affect production of competing fibers. By the mid-1950s, for example, price was clearly an issue when it came to the oldest of the man-mades: rayon, a cellulosic fiber made from wood pulp. Relatively high cotton prices gave rayon producers maneuvering room to set their own prices high enough to be profitable but low enough to discourage cotton substitution for rayon. Higher profits from rayon were incentive, moreover, for expansion. With rayon costing 26 cents a pound to produce in the mid-1950s and cotton 32 cents, rayon enjoyed a 6–10-cent price advantage in a majority of broadwoven goods – incentive enough for mills to forsake cotton for the man-made substitute, provided the quality was equal or better. Although the price of the newer, true "synthetics" would remain

---

[11] Clifton B. Cox and Vernon W. Pherson, *The Competitive Potential of the U.S. Cotton Industry* (Boston, 1959), 21–3; *Cotton Situation* (November, 1957), 78–80.

well above cotton for some time, the situation with rayon was a warning of things to come.[12]

Compared to price, which was subject to competitive forces, promotion was something that the industry could control more directly. Cotton Council research indicated that sales promotion shaped consumer choices in over half of all end uses.[13] The NCC's early advertising program suggested the potential of promotion when resources could be found to pay for it and correct strategies could be agreed upon and implemented. This would not be easy, since cotton changed form so much between producer and consumer. Spreading promotional costs over the entire industry was especially problematic because cotton competed directly with man-made substitutes, which were available to end-product manufacturers of cotton as alternate raw materials. If end products made of rayon or synthetics carried the same manufacturer's brand as end products of cotton, where then was the incentive for the manufacturer to promote cotton as a commodity?

Those with the purest interest in promotion, producers and handlers, did not have the deepest pockets to pay for it. For this reason, cotton promotion as undertaken by the NCC relied heavily on help from groups interested in particular cotton products (major cooperative efforts focused on canvas awnings, cotton duck, automotive trim fabric, linen supplies, and cotton batting) and aimed to raise cotton fiber awareness by persuading advertisers that there was value in using the word "cotton" when talking about product characteristics – washability, versatility, and dependability – things that consumers cared most about. In addition to the Maid of Cotton and high fashion programs, a "freshness" campaign, partly paid for by the soap industry, touted the hygienic advantages of cotton clothing and bed and bath linens that could be laundered frequently. "National Cotton Week" meanwhile encouraged retailers to carry cotton in their stores. Radio stations received scripts for "Cotton Talk," aimed at women's program directors in metropolitan areas. Transit companies got "car cards" picturing happy women in cotton street dresses, happy men in cotton work

---

[12] NCC sponsored research into the price problem: M. K. Horne, Jr., Frank A. McCord, and George Townsend, *Price and the Future of U.S. Cotton* (Memphis, 1956); Robert B. Evans, "Price Factors in Competition between Cotton and Man-Made Fibers" (Memphis, unpublished, 1957).

[13] It was most important in women's apparel and least important in industrial products. NCC Market Research Division, "Some Factors Influencing Cotton's Competitive Position in Domestic Markets" (Memphis, unpublished, 1956).

clothes, happy children in back-to-school duds made of cotton.[14] The NCC could actually claim a few victories for its promotion campaign. Between 1948 and 1955, cotton clawed back some share in the markets for women's dresses and blouses and for men's sport shirts. In most end uses, however, such generic promotion probably served only to slow down cotton's loss of market share.

Competitiveness would never increase until the industry squarely faced a third factor determining cotton's competitive potential: quality. Quality related primarily to those characteristics that made a fiber desirable or undesirable for use. With respect to cotton, two distinct aspects were paramount. The first related to the production and processing of raw cotton: how clean or how long is it? The second related to the characteristics of a particular end product: does it have luster, or does it have to be ironed? Viewed as a raw material feeding a manufacturing process, cotton had to contribute to the manufacturers' operating efficiency and to help meet their end-product specifications. In the absence of explicit "cotton-specific" demand, mills and manufacturers based their decisions – concerning whether to use cotton alone, substitute something else for it entirely, or blend it with man-mades – on what they had to pay for it (plus the costs of processing) compared with the price they could charge for the end product that contained it. Therefore, it was essential that cotton have the inherent properties necessary to satisfy changing manufacturing technologies and specifications.

For growers whose families had been "in cotton" for many decades, it was hard not to think of cotton as a superior fiber, period. Yet in the new competitive context it was hard not to face the reality that quality was a relative virtue and lay not in the eye of the producer but of the customer. Intense competition among mills put a premium on technological innovation with regard to both speed and quality control, which further raised the quality bar for raw materials feeding into the manufacturing process. For example, mills keen on spinning efficiency looked for uniform staple length and strength of a fiber, areas where research into the breeding and production of new varieties was needed to help cotton even come close to the quality of man-mades. It was important that cotton arrive at the mill as clean as possible, which meant improving ginning technology and devising better means of storage and shipping. Compared with cotton, man-mades

[14] NCC Archives.

had relatively little waste and came to the mill in uniform, fully enclosed packaging. Traditional cotton bales left two sides exposed and were typically cut into at several places for sampling. Indeed, the USDA's techniques for sampling and grading raw cotton belonged to a bygone era, before the development of man-mades that could be engineered to meet stringent specifications for staple length, thickness, strength, and uniformity. If cotton could not measure up, then something else would.[15]

The quality question became even more complex when considering the range of characteristics required in end products. Drape, crease resistance, no ironing, quick drying, linting, coolness, and resistance to soil were only a few. The NCC's market research division calculated that such quality considerations explained shifts away from cotton to competing materials in markets representing close to 80 percent of end uses. Opportunities for quality improvement research at the manufacturing level were nearly countless and needed to be winnowed by careful market research into what exactly it was that consumers wanted most. This could change quickly. In the list of quality factors that could benefit from improvements, compiled for Congressional hearings in 1947, "no ironing" did not appear. By the mid-1950s, probably no single textile end-product characteristic loomed larger.[16]

Research, like promotion, cost money, and no one knew absolutely how much it might take to achieve the NCC's stated objective of cotton research: a better-quality product at lower cost that could expand the market for cotton. Yet anyone who compared research expenditures for cotton with research expenditures for cotton's competitors would have concluded that cotton needed help. In 1956, a total of $16.3 million was expended on cotton research in the United States, just under half of it funded publicly by the USDA and the state experiment stations. The balance came from a gaggle of private industry interests, led by agricultural chemical manufacturers ($2 million), textile mills ($1.5 million), and farm equipment manufacturers ($1.5 million). Man-made (by this point, largely synthetic) fibers research dwarfed cotton's effort. From a total estimated annual research expenditure of $74 million, just eight top companies accounted for $54 million, with the number-one company (DuPont) alone spending $25 million. When it is

[15] NCC Market Research Division, "Some Factors Influencing Cotton's Competitive Position."
[16] "The Competitive Position of Cotton by Major End-Use Markets," hearings before special subcommittee on cotton of the Committee on Agriculture, U.S. House of Representatives, July 7–8, 1947.

Through the 1950s, the National Cotton Council attempted to promote all sorts of uses for cotton in the hope of spurring demand – even sewing contests.

recalled that 2–3 times more cotton than synthetics was being produced during this period, some pessimism about cotton's future could be expected.[17]

THE COMPETITION'S ADVANTAGES

One pessimist was MacDonald "Mac" Horne, who came to the NCC from the University of Mississippi in 1950 and would become the country's leading cotton economist. Horne's work highlighted the huge disparity in research expenditures and was the catalyst for a fresh look at how cotton's leadership should confront the danger to cotton growers posed by synthetics. It was an all-out attack, in which large industrial corporations were systematically carving up the markets of textiles on every front. Farmers – "divided as they are by geography, by the nature of their production problems, by the quality of their products, by the size of their operations, by the coloration of their politics, and by the personalities of their leadership" – were

---

[17] NCC, "Cotton's Outlook in Research: Staff Report before Industry-Wide Committee on Cotton's Research Needs and Opportunities" (Memphis, 1957), 14–15.

too unorganized to respond effectively.[18] Never had such forces been arrayed against farmers as those arrayed against cotton; nor, he might have added, had any segment of American agriculture ever presented a fatter, more tempting, more unprepared target. For while the NCC had organized cotton politically, its nascent efforts in research and promotion were no match for the chemical companies, which could bring resources to bear on any problem in a more sustained and focused fashion. The advantages of coordinated corporate management seemed overpowering when arrayed against the sporadic efforts of the small and comparatively underfunded association that constituted the NCC.

In a competitive business where margins were thin, the factor of reliable supply made synthetics highly attractive. Cotton was an agricultural commodity produced once a year, and the amount of it produced from year to year depended on an array of natural and political factors not easily controlled. Synthetic fiber plants ran year-round, producing predictable quantities and controlled qualities of raw material, more easily calibrating supply to demand. This in turn made life easier for textile mill managers. To assure adequate supply, it might be necessary for mills to invest in a full year's supply of cotton (with all the attendant interest costs and price risks) compared with just a few days' supply of synthetics.

Advantages also flowed from the structure of the synthetic fibers industry: a small number of for-profit, industrial firms with the ability to channel resources – either from the capital markets or from their own retained earnings – into research and promotion. The disparity in financial muscle, which Horne first nailed to the mast in 1957, would not go away, he predicted. No matter how much cotton would spend in future years, the makers of synthetics could always spend vastly more.[19] And the disparity was not only in the quantity of their resources but also in the quality of their management. The synthetic fibers manufacturers were also synthetic fibers marketers and sales organizations. Such integration and coordination of production and distribution worked to enhance sales, lower costs, and increase shareholder value. Among the most sophisticated managers in American business, chemical company executives understood that particular products

---

[18] MacDonald Horne et al., "Finding a Future for the U.S. Cotton Producer" (Memphis, 1972), 27.

[19] In 1970, the year Cotton Incorporated was founded, some $42 million went for cotton research but $143 million for synthetics. Thirty years later, state and federal cotton research still totaled only $65 million (National Cotton Council).

or services were not ends in themselves but rather means to sustaining the competitive advantage and profitability of their firms.

DuPont, for example, which was the largest synthetic fibers company by the 1950s, had for most of its 150+-year history made its fortune as an explosives manufacturer. Matching up market demand with its own technological capabilities, it turned wholeheartedly to synthetic textile fibers only after World War II, where it concentrated enormous talent and resources. Building on pre-war beginnings with rayon and nylon, DuPont spawned an extended family of "miracle fiber" synthetics whose names – nylon, Orlon, Dacron, Lycra – had become part of the language. So did the qualities those products offered the consumer: "wash-and-wear," "drip-dry," "permanent-press." Such behavior demonstrated a healthy readiness to respond to the certainty of change in both technology and consumer tastes. For DuPont, as with its peer chemical companies, success presumed constant vigilance, attention to the market, and an ongoing sense of urgency that no business victory was permanent and no market position invulnerable.

GROWERS' RESPONSE: CPI

As the 1950s wore on, some growers realized that the Cotton Council might not be the best vehicle for responding to the synthetics challenge. Charles R. "Jerry" Sayre, president of Delta and Pine Land Company in Scott, Mississippi, was named chairman of an NCC committee in late 1956 to take a fresh look at the problem of financing cotton research. Sayre knew something about management. The British-owned Delta and Pine Land was then not only one of the largest cotton plantations in the world but also a major scientific cotton breeder whose seed business was known and respected all across the Cotton Belt. Sayre had run it for his owners (at a profit) since 1950, and he had brought to the mammoth operation – as to his subsequent involvement in other cotton organizations – the perspective not of a planter but of a scientist and a manager.[20] Nor was he a southerner; Sayre was from Illinois and held a Ph.D. in agricultural economics from Harvard. While still in his 30s, he had headed Mississippi State's prestigious Delta Branch Experiment Station in

---

[20] Sayre would serve as president of the NCC, head of the Delta Council, and also president of Staplcotn, largest of the cotton marketing cooperatives.

Stoneville, as well as the Cotton Division of the Bureau of Plant Industry at the USDA.

Sayre knew full well that cotton was outgunned by synthetics in quality, in costs, and potentially in price, and that without dedicated effort cotton faced a grim future. He saw that although the NCC had made itself the model for other commodity groups when it came to influencing government action, cotton's future depended on something more – a fresh organizational initiative. Sayre's committee called for growers to take greater responsibility and shoulder the financial burden that geared-up research and promotion would require. They advocated establishing a separate fund that – though under the Council's umbrella – would operate apart from other Council activities and would be financed exclusively by a voluntary assessment on producers of $1 per bale.

The idea became a reality in 1960 with formation of the "Cotton Producers Institute of the National Cotton Council" or, as it soon became known, "CPI" for short. CPI was incorporated separately as a Tennessee nonprofit corporation. It was an odd, halfway-house sort of organization, nothing like a business corporation but a step toward achieving more coordinated funding for research and promotion. CPI was to provide a mechanism for growers to give direct support to research and promotion over and above what was possible under the NCC's existing programs. Structurally, CPI was to be governed by a board of trustees made up of producers from each of cotton's four geographical areas (West, Southwest, Mid-South, and Southeast) in proportion to funds contributed: one trustee for each $150,000 collected. Their function was to authorize expenditures for research and promotion projects, which would be carried out through grants, contracts, or cooperative agreements. CPI was to have no staff of its own (and consequently, it was boasted, no overhead); it would tap NCC's own research and promotion personnel. Hopes were high that, within five years, the program would make available an additional $10 million for cotton research and promotion.

The voluntary principle on which CPI was based could not work without some sort of contracting mechanism. The process for making it work required signed agreements between CPI and individual producers for collection of the $1 per bale assessment at a designated point in the production process, usually the gin. With thousands of growers spread from coast to coast in 1960, this presented a huge logistical challenge that would consume three years' time of the NCC's Field Service staff, headed by Clifton

Kirkpatrick out of its Memphis headquarters. Kirkpatrick's burden was to orchestrate the most intense educational drive in the Council's history.[21]

It fell to a few recognized leaders in the cotton growing industry to sell the concept to enough farmers to make the program work. The voluntary nature of the program seemed key to its success. Sayre and his colleagues had looked at a number of alternatives to assure compliance, including a government-enforced check-off program – a kind of self-imposed "tax" to finance CPI's programs. But given the untested assumptions on which CPI was founded and the ambivalence of many growers toward existing federal farm programs, the NCC was reluctant to take that step. The conservative individualism that characterized cotton growers, embattled independent businessmen as they were, would be hard to challenge. These were people accustomed to making their own decisions and who liked to believe, even in the face of contrary evidence, that they were individually in charge of their own fates. Thus the NCC opted "to do it the American way – the voluntary way – to provide each farmer, on a voluntary basis, be given an opportunity to decide whether or not he desired to contribute to such a fund."[22]

If the fund had to be voluntary, it also had to be large. These two aims would ultimately prove to be incompatible, but in the early 1960s they made sense. Expectations were high that if CPI supporters campaigned hard enough, volunteers would materialize to get the job done. To get this message across, the producer committee that had recommended CPI to the NCC's directors also stipulated that all funds collected would be held in escrow until at least $1 million had been collected. If after two years it had not, then the money would be refunded and the concept abandoned. "This provision," explained NCC president and producer committee chairman Boswell Stevens, a grower from Macon, Mississippi, "is to insure that we are not just adding a little bit more money to the Council's present program, but that there will be sufficient funds to tackle some big opportunities."[23]

The producers for whom Boswell spoke included prominent farmers who were leaders in their communities from all across the Cotton Belt. From the Mid-South, Sayre (then head of the Staplcotn marketing cooperative in Greenwood, Mississippi) and Delta planter G. C. Cortright took the lead.

[21] "Resolution Implementing Recommendation on Development of Supplementary Research and Promotion Funds, Adopted by Special Producers Committee, May 18, 1960," NCC Archives.
[22] Press release, January 29, 1961, NCC Archives.
[23] Ibid.

The referendum that led to mandatory assessments on growers for support of a cotton research and promotion program took place in the summer and fall of 1965. Leaders of the Cotton Producers Institute painted a dire picture unless more money was forthcoming in the fight against synthetics. Headline writers agreed: "Cotton Doomed Unless All Growers Help Pay for Research and Promotion." Five years later, Cotton Producers Institute became Cotton Incorporated.

From the Southwest, Harold West, president of the Texas Farm Bureau, and Roy B. Davis, manager of the Plains Cooperative Oil Mill, spearheaded the sign-up effort. In the West, where the organizing campaign was launched, the names of Russell Giffen, a grower from the San Joaquin Valley, and Keith Walden, a prominent Arizona grower, quickly emerged as progressive spokesmen for the CPI cause.[24]

California, Arizona, New Mexico, and Texas growers raised more than $1 million the first year, which imparted essential early momentum to the campaign. Over the next three years, a host of steering committees in

---

[24] Committee membership also included: J. D. Hayes, Alabama; D. W. Brooks, Georgia; Harold Ohlendorf, Arkansas; Jess Stratton, Oklahoma; Clyde Wilson, Arizona; and Russell Kennedy and Earl Cecil, California.

thousands of meetings won over many, but far from all, growers elsewhere. With the rallying cry of "A Dollar a Bale," they sold CPI successfully to those growers who were prepared to believe that cotton was in a deep crisis. Confronting it effectively meant not only raising more funds but also learning to spend them in a different way.

FALSE STARTS

Russell Giffen became CPI's first chairman in 1961. He envisioned a cotton research and promotion program focused more on increasing U.S. cotton quality than quantity. The specific quality that mattered more than any other in the textile fibers business by the 1960s was "ease of care." Cotton had to perform better in this department or else be relegated to awnings and aspirin bottles.

Relieving housewives of the drudgery of ironing was the great promise of synthetic fibers promotion, but the Cotton Council's inflated reaction to it – bold claims for the virtues of "100 percent cotton" – had been the wrong response. Much was at stake, a 2-billion-square-yard market in the short term alone, and it was tempting to believe cotton was better than it was. NCC researchers, led by George Buck and Nelson Getchell in the late 1950s, had tried imparting "minimum care" characteristics to cotton, but with poor results. The NCC patented an early process for applying durable creases to all-cotton "wrinkle-resistants," but the chemistry was not yet as good as it seemed. When the much-touted "all-cotton durable press" garments fashioned from such fabric went on the market only to fray after a few washings, cotton suffered a public relations fiasco that set back its market position even further and must have caused some mirth at DuPont headquarters.[25]

The competition had a thing or two to teach cotton about product functionality and the importance of attending always to the character of consumer demand. If "ease of care with a modicum of comfort" was what the shirt market wanted, then that was what the shirt market should get, and not something else. DuPont understood this because it was good at both manufacturing and marketing synthetics. Moreover, DuPont had no need to sell "100 percent polyester" in order to give the market what it wanted. In fact, "100 percent polyester" would have been about as wide of the target

[25] Wrinkle Resistance Technical Reports, NCC Archives.

as "100 percent cotton" if it failed to deliver on quality. So the synthetics manufacturers embraced blended fabrics, while the Cotton Council, believing consumers preferred "all cotton," resisted it.

DuPont in particular played the blends game adroitly. Blended fabrics performed well in the judgment of easy-care–minded consumers. It was clearly advantageous to weight the balance of the blend as far toward the synthetics side as possible without forfeiting fabric performance. In the shirt and blouse market, for example, DuPont set the ratio at 65/35 polyester/cotton and stoutly defended its position – to the point of cutting off polyester supplies altogether for mills tempted to run higher proportions of cotton.[26]

Into this contest of content and quality, CPI entered with high hopes and best intentions. It also entered late and weighed-in light. In 1962, its first full year of operation, CPI collected from growers close to $1.5 million. One third of that was spent on eleven research projects, divided between (a) agricultural research aimed at easing the cost–price pressure on growers by reducing production costs and improving raw fiber quality and (b) end-use research aimed at improving cotton products. Like the NCC before it, CPI subcontracted its research to third parties and attempted to obtain matching funds to fatten total budgets. It selected projects primarily on the basis of their chances of success.

Getting the cotton plant to set more fruit was one key to higher yields, and CPI supported work at the University of Arizona to discover how plants used nitrogen to grow and produce fruit. At the University of California, Riverside, it funded research on systemic insecticides that would provide less costly, more dependable, and safer control of damaging insects. At New Mexico State University, researchers looked at verticillium wilt and why some cotton breeds resisted the disease and others did not. Texas A&M scientists examined the biochemistry of the cotton plant, and at the Stanford Research Institute others looked for better ways to measure the trash content of cotton lint, which bore directly on how much the grower received for a bale. The search for an accurate and automated means for measuring fiber strength and elongation, factors vital to determining cotton's spinning and end-use performance value, busied other Stanford researchers.[27]

[26] Russell, *Cotton Council,* 62, 86; Hervey Evans interview, February 17, 1999.
[27] In judging the merit of research projects on new or improved products, CPI's grower-trustees typically thought in terms of the number of bales at stake. For example, research into improving men's cotton trousers and suits by increasing wrinkle resistance and reducing seam pucker would allow cotton into markets previously held almost exclusively by wool and synthetic fiber

Two thirds of CPI's budget, however, went not to research but to promotion – in the beginning, chiefly to television advertising with a smaller amount to print. The primary effort was concentrated on the late-winter and spring season, when textile sales were at their peak; the opening campaign, which aired from September to December 1962, was timed to anticipate it. The ads targeted "the American housewife," seen (in that era of the male breadwinner) as chief decision maker in the market for household textiles. Research revealed that more than half of American women watched daytime broadcasts every day, and cotton's message was packaged accordingly for shows that were becoming icons of American popular culture: "I Love Lucy" and "The Verdict Is Yours" in the morning; "Secret Storm," "Queen for a Day," and "Art Linkletter's House Party" after lunch. The smaller audience of "working women" and "people who influence sales" (presumably men) got the same message at night on "Hawaiian Eye," "Gallant Men," and "The Flintstones."

Although the medium of television was new for cotton ("Today's leading mass medium of communication," boasted CPI's literature), the message conveyed there was not particularly new. Appearance, performance, comfort, and economy were the factors that research had shown mattered greatly to consumers in textile-buying decisions. All were claimed as timeless traits of cotton. One commercial touted the advantages of all-cotton fabrics in the wash-and-wear field. Another featured cotton's virtues as the number-one fiber for home furnishings. Scripts – "Washdays Are Happy Days with 100 Percent Cotton" – had not come all that far from the NCC's "freshness" print campaigns in the late 1940s and had a nostalgic old-fashioned ring to them. Cotton had always been there. As the CPI slogan put it, it was "The Fiber You Can Trust." [28]

The CPI television ads certainly were not bashful. Grower-trustees entirely new to the marketing world took pride in hard-sell commercials appearing hundreds of times across the country on stations of all three national

blends and would, they estimated, gain additional consumption of 255,000 bales. Successful "reversible crosslinks" in cotton, whereby chemically treated apparel and household fabrics would maintain unwrinkled appearance and require no ironing after laundering, coupled with "delay curing," whereby cotton fabrics would be presensitized for wash-and-wear qualities before a garment was cut, promised potential markets for another 1.3 million bales. Development of "lofty cotton products" with the appearance and durable warmth qualities of woolens would enable cotton to compete in markets for 1.5 million bales. Cotton Producers Institute report to members, 1962.

[28] Cotton Producers Institute television scripts, 1962–1964.

networks. But they were not all that effective, either. There were two problems: one of substance, the other of scale. The "cotton message" projected by CPI during the 1960s, for all its assertiveness, was never more than a trailer behind the competition's wagon. It was the synthetics manufacturers who had invented concepts like "wash-and-wear" and then conjured in the public an appetite for their products. It was the cotton growers who were stuck with finding ways to claim "me too." For all their chutzpah, CPI's ad men could not catch up, at least not until cotton research caught up and made credible the claim that cotton faced forward and stood for innovation, and not just over its shoulder, comfortably backward to grandma's time, when all the world wore cotton and was grateful.

The problem of scale made the lag worse. It sounded impressive, as CPI reported to growers year after year, that millions of Americans tuned in to cotton's message whenever they tuned in to their favorite television shows. Effectiveness surveys showed that housewives' awareness regarding cotton and wash-and-wear was greater after seeing the TV ads than before. However, the fact remained that, even as CPI organized progressively more growers willing to chip in a dollar per bale to the cause, tight budgets constrained cotton's television impact.[29] True, the map showed ABC, CBS, and NBC stations coast to coast and border to border that broadcast cotton's sales story, and on some very popular programs. But limited frequency, commonly just two or three times per week, diluted the message. Television had already become a notoriously "noisy" commercial medium, where the biggest players (tobacco, automobiles, and oil companies) relied on the saturation barrage principle: every day, every night, all day and all night. While the manufacturers of the synthetic "miracle" fibers did not play in quite that league, they played a much smarter and richer game than cotton could afford. In the 1960s, it was DuPont's progressive "Better Things for Better Living through Chemistry" and not CPI's "The Fiber You Can Trust" that best captured the convenience-fixated, push-button spirit of that era – and the dollars of millions of consumers along with it.

Not everyone that CPI needed to convince concurred with its approach. Sydney M. Cone, Jr., of Cone Mills Corporation spoke for mill owners generally when he complained that CPI's negative advertising about synthetics – "miracle fibers" washable only in lukewarm water came out only "dingy

---

[29] By 1965, CPI had signed up growers in twelve cotton states who accounted for close to 3 million bales and thus $3 million. CPI Sign-up Memorandum, March 30, 1965, NCC Archives.

Why Is Cotton So Comfortable?

Because:

Cotton Is Absorbent. It "breathes"; absorbs moisture; feels good next to your skin; is never sticky or clammy.

Cotton Is Soft. It feels gentle; quickly adjusts to the temperature of the body.

Cotton Is Static Free. No static electricity shocks from cotton. No annoying clinging either. Nor does it attract lint or dust as many other fabrics do.

Cotton Is Fresh. It smells fresh; feels fresh; looks fresh; *is* fresh because of its absolute washability.

Cotton Can Be Warm or Cool. Cotton can be made to keep you cool or to keep you warm. The light, sheer cottons cool you in summer; the corduroys and fish-net weaves that trap warm air, the laminates that give warmth without extra weight, keep you snug and warm in winter.

Extra comfort is just one of the many exclusive superiorities that make cotton easier and more profitable to sell. Men and women everywhere know from experience that fabrics made of cotton are cooler, lighter, fresher, more washable than any other fabrics they can buy. Cotton sells better because cotton *is* better! Feature it in all its rich variety!

COMFORTABLE. CAREFREE

100% COTTON
the fiber you can trust

Cotton Producers Institute/National Cotton Council, Box 12253, Memphis, Tenn. 38112.

Claiming that cotton was naturally comfortable, Cotton Producers Institute was onto something. It remained for Cotton Incorporated to make the case convincingly to consumers and begin to turn the market against the synthetics that weren't.

clean" – made textile manufacturers' lives more difficult.[30] Val Winkelman of Russell Mills, a man who claimed on principle "to want no truck with synthetics," complained that brave talk was no substitute for money. In the spring of 1965, Russell, then the largest domestic producer of seersucker fabrics, ran a few thousand yards of yarn-dyed textured all-cottons for their summer line but had difficulty moving even that modest stock. The reason, said Winkelman, was inability to support his cutter customers with advertising. As a consequence, Russell had little choice but to truck more heavily with Dacron/cotton blends, "certain that DuPont and other synthetic fibers producers would supply cutter support money on fabrics containing their fibers." As the synthetics producers grew increasingly able to dictate what mills would spin and weave, the textile industry found itself in an unenviable position, one where its hand was forced. "If you use synthetics," Winkelman told the NCC's field service manager, "your goods are pre-sold for you."[31]

A NEW DIMENSION: RECONSIDERING VOLUNTARISM

Russell Giffen, Keith Walden, Jerry Sayre, and CPI's other leaders were not the sort of people to kid themselves for long. In the spring of 1965, to appease the mills and reduce antagonism with the competition, they conceded on blends. Henceforth, CPI advertising headlines, logotype, print texts, and television scripts would no longer speak of "100 percent cotton," but just "cotton."[32] This concession presaged a deeper rethinking of cotton's prospects and how to improve them. For even as CPI gradually won over more and more growers to "$1 a bale" and attempted to woo consumers with TV spots two or three times per week, the stakes in the competitive game were going up fast. CPI chairman Giffen warned of a "new dimension in our battle for markets." Again, it was a question of how best to mobilize funds for research and promotion on an ever-increasing scale and on a more reliable schedule.

Despite some "solid hits" in CPI's research and promotion program, the competition had greatly expanded its own research and promotion in

---

[30] Sydney M. Cone, Jr., to William Rhea Blake, National Cotton Council, July 30, 1963, NCC Archives.

[31] Ernest Stewart, Field Service, to Ed Lipscomb, National Cotton Council, Memorandum, March 12, 1965, NCC Archives.

[32] Clifton Kirkpatrick, National Cotton Council, to R. Keith Walden, CPI Executive Committee, March 18, 1965, NCC Archives.

the years since CPI was created. This was because they had more products and better products to sell. New fibers, if not quite as "miraculous" as their promoters claimed, were certainly high-performance in many of the convenience-related qualities that consumers craved. Of the 4 million bale-equivalent increase in consumption of man-made fibers during the first half of the 1960s, the newer synthetics accounted for more than 70 percent. Consumption of synthetic fibers between the mid-1950s and mid-1960s more than doubled, and the manufacturers' research expenditures more than doubled to match – to $100 million in 1965. Research expenditures for cotton, on the other hand (counting all sources, including the raw cotton industry and public and private groups), totaled only $24 million. Promotion expenditures for synthetics had doubled in just six years (1959–1965) to $70 million, leaving raw cotton, with a paltry $4 million, to eat the dust.[33]

The widening gap between cotton and the competition, in Giffen's judgment, had finally forced the industry to sacrifice the sacred cow of voluntarism. Although grower support for CPI was increasing, sign-up from state to state and region to region was highly uneven, and total participation never reached 50 percent. Moreover, the voluntary nature of the $1 per bale assessment, and the manner of its collection at the first point of processing (gins and oil mills), had introduced a perverse competitive incentive that crippled the whole effort. Gins and oil mills vied with one another for growers' business, and those that chose not to collect the $1 CPI assessment could in effect offer their grower-customers a better price and so gain an advantage over their own competitors. While appealing philosophically, voluntarism had resulted in practical problems of too many free riders and too few dollars. It was this failure to secure positive sign-up and collection assistance at gins and oil mills that pushed CPI's leaders to seek a more radical solution.[34]

After months of study, CPI's trustees requested late in 1965 that the NCC's board of directors sponsor federal enabling legislation that would allow growers to hold a Beltwide referendum on the questions of research and promotion assessments and a uniform collection procedure. The trustees anticipated a system where all funds collected would continue to be grower

[33] CPI Report to Members, 1965–1966.

[34] By other measures of organizational success, CPI had done well enough: it had secured key leadership on basic committees driving producer unity and support; it had initiated organization in the most concentrated areas of production; and it had secured some measure of processor understanding and good will.

funds, control would continue to rest with grower-trustees, and funds would continue to be expended exclusively on research and promotion. The basic change was that the authority of government would be employed to establish, if approved by a two-thirds vote, that all growers would pay alike and that, at the point of collection, all processors would collect the same amount: at least $1 per bale.[35]

It was a plausible but risky step, one that touched a nerve with growers suspicious of using the instrument of government as a collecting agency for their own self-help programs. Even with those who pushed hardest for the change, there was a note of apology that only desperate circumstances had forced the issue. When he went to lobby Alabama Farm Bureau president James D. Hays, NCC's William Rhea Blake summarized CPI's position this way: "Large numbers of relatively small, independent agricultural producers cannot meet the competition of a handful of industrial giants in the fields of research and promotion unless a means can be devised for raising the huge sums of money to pay for such research and promotion. This is an unpleasant fact of life that faces us in 1965."[36]

The Alabama Farm Bureau was representative of smaller farmers who opposed the reform. For many of its members, the euphemism "uniform collection" looked like just one more lever of federal coercion. "The idea of a Federal check-off is personally obnoxious to me and I am not for it," wrote an aging but still colorful Walter L. Randolph, longtime Alabama Farm Bureau leader who had been instrumental in winning support for launch of the NCC thirty years before. "It is prismatically wrong, i.e., wrong any way one looks at it."[37] Others worried, with an eye on a current controversy, that a check-off for cotton would resemble a check-off for labor unions, which were an anathema to conservative, independent-minded farmers everywhere. "How," wondered James Hays, "could the Council be against one and for the other?"[38]

---

[35] CPI Report to Members, 1965–1966; Minutes, CPI Trustees, June 16, 1965 and November 30, 1965, NCC Archives.

[36] Blake to Hays, September 28, 1965, NCC Archives.

[37] Walter L. Randolph to William Rhea Blake, NCC, April 22, 1965, NCC Archives. A strong believer that federal intervention was the cause of most of the ills of the cotton industry, Randolph in a handwritten note to Blake two days later added: "You may recall what one of two persons said to the other as they were looking out of a window, across an alley, into the window of a room in another building, and observing certain actions on the part of a man and woman in such room. It was: 'It looks like this is where we came in.' " Randolph to Blake, April 24, 1965.

[38] Memorandum to CPI trustees, William Rhea Blake, NCC, June 28, 1965.

If points had been awarded for right premises and dedicated effort alone, CPI merited a long row of gold stars. The trouble was – and this was the message of the turn toward a new structure to enforce uniform assessment – that when measured against its central objective of holding and building markets for American cotton, its programs had not succeeded. At best, CPI had fought a delaying action while the synthetics producers had seized the initiative and gone on the attack. "Survival itself has been quite an accomplishment," explained Russell Giffen to the board of the Cotton Council as check-off legislation was being prepared. But just slowing up market losses only pushed back the precipice. Giffen spoke in the fall of 1965 and predicted CPI's collapse within a year if action was not taken "to raise the big money we need."[39]

How much? Uniform assessment, he guessed, would build up CPI funds to $12 or $15 million per year; when added to the NCC's own revenue, this would give the cotton industry $15 to $18 million annually. CPI had learned how to get a lot of mileage out of the little money it did have, and through cooperative advertising with department stores and other retailers it probably multiplied its own industry dollars by a factor of two or three. Thus $15 to $18 million became $30 to $36 million. If one added in the $20+ million spent annually on cotton research by nonindustry sources (the USDA, land-grant colleges, and businesses supplying and servicing the cotton industry) and funds that other cotton-exporting countries were applying to promote cotton, the numbers began to look impressive. It was also comforting to remember that it probably wasn't necessary to match the DuPonts dollar for dollar anyway – and certainly not in promotion. Synthetics producers, after all, strove not just against cotton but against one another as well, and they may have gone past the point of diminishing returns with their tactics of saturation advertising.

Times were desperate, but optimism was possible if only growers could overcome their fears of government encroachment. All cotton needed, its leaders tirelessly preached, was a fair chance to compete. All it asked from government was a mechanism under which producers could put up their own money to fight their own battle in a competitive marketplace. "We aren't asking for subsidies," Giffen asserted. "I don't think we are inviting controls."[40]

[39] Russell Giffen, CPI chairman, to National Cotton Council Board, September 9, 1965, NCC Archives.
[40] Ibid.

A NEW MANDATE

The legislative path toward achieving a uniform assessment and giving cotton a "fair chance to compete" began in August 1965 when the Senate passed a bill authorizing funds to be collected uniformly from producers of certain agricultural commodities under authority of the Agricultural Marketing Agreements Act of 1937.[41] The finished legislation, known as the Cotton Research and Promotion Act, was signed into law by President Lyndon Johnson in July 1966. The referendum it authorized took place, by mail, the first week in December. In between, CPI and the NCC conducted a nonstop get-out-the-vote campaign across the Cotton Belt. In addition to the general refrain about cotton's last chance to beat back the synthetics threat, it emphasized two operational points.

The first addressed the question of why cotton interest groups other than growers had not been asked to contribute to the program. The answer was that the program's purpose would be defeated by imposing an extra charge on textile mills for using cotton when DuPont was offering mills incentives for using synthetics. Moreover, asking other groups to share the assessment would be inviting them to share control. The second point addressed the issue of voluntarism. Were the referendum to stand any chance of passage, it was imperative to finesse the specter of coercion that (according to some growers) lurked behind the concept of any government-administered "uniform assessment." Once again, a compromise was sought and found: a modified form of "voluntarism." The answer was a refund provision that made "uniformity" seem voluntary. Although collections would be uniform in order to eliminate the competitive problem among processors and handlers, any grower who wished to do so could, upon application, get his money back. This opportunity to "opt out," by taking positive action to reclaim funds after they had been assessed, was unique to cotton. None of the federal marketing orders involving other commodities had a refund provision. It would prove an uneasy compromise in years to come. At the time, however, it helped accomplish what was possible, if not ideal.[42] The effort paid off in a vote from cotton growers that was 68 percent in favor of implementing a new marketing and promotion

[41] In addition to cotton, the original list included carrots, citrus fruits, onions, Tokay grapes, fresh pears, dates, plums, nectarines, celery, sweet corn, limes, olives, pecans, and avocados.
[42] CPI memoranda: "Main Questions Raised about Cotton Research and Promotion Bill during Congressional Consideration"; "How to Meet Synthetic Fiber Competition?" NCC Archives.

structure. If not resounding, this was a safe enough victory that effectively re-endorsed the concept of grower self-help while shoring up its institutional supports.[43]

Once the referendum had been approved by at least a two-thirds vote, the Secretary of Agriculture was authorized to appoint a "Cotton Board" from nominees submitted by approved producer organizations. Most states would have one board member, with a few more allocated to heavier producing states. The Cotton Board would recommend to the Secretary the rules and regulations for implementing the Research and Promotion Act, and it would have responsibility for collecting the assessments it authorized. However, the Cotton Board would not itself spend the money but would instead enter into agreement with a Beltwide producer organization equipped to carry out the research and promotion program. The governance of this organization in turn would be selected by approved statewide producer organizations in proportion to each state's production of cotton and its monetary contribution to the total program. This organization, it was anticipated, would be the Cotton Producers Institute, staffed and serviced just as before by the National Cotton Council.

They had the funding mechanism right, or largely so. Pockets of "refund resistance," though irritating, did not at first significantly hold back the program. By 1969, CPI's budget had risen to $10.3 million, of which two thirds went for promotion and one third for research.[44] But the numbers were somewhat misleading and encouraged false hopes that cotton had found the key to a comeback at last. For many growers, CPI's apparent revitalization made for stubbornness about further change. The problem was organizational as well as economic, and it was manifest in two ways.

First, there was widespread grower restlessness with their relationship to the National Cotton Council. The NCC was as diverse as the cotton industry itself, but growers alone were supplying approximately 60 percent of its funds. In 1968, a newly formed Producer Steering Committee composed of representatives of each of the cotton states met for the first time. While it did not overtly take a policy role – it functioned as a clearinghouse for ideas

---

[43] Returns revealed wide spreads in support from state to state, much as had been the case in CPI's original campaign to enlist growers in the cause of $1 per bale. States with the highest percentage in favor were Missouri (88.6), Louisiana (84.9), North Carolina (84.7), and Georgia (83.0); those with the lowest were Tennessee (37.9) and Alabama (39.6). Certified Referendum Returns, NCC Archives.

[44] CPI Research and Promotion Budget for 1969, NCC Archives.

on harmonizing relations among the interests – discontent lingered that the voice of producers still was not strong enough. What many growers really wanted was not a bigger say but a separate producer organization.[45]

The fundamental problem for the growers, of course, was the market. The relentless slide of cotton's market share continued, despite enhanced research and promotion budgets. Frustration never lay very far beneath the upbeat public rhetoric, and in 1969 it surfaced into yet another debate over CPI's purpose and mission.

BREAKING AWAY

Most men have but one profession, and most cotton growers were cotton growers, pure and simple. Yet circumstances had confronted them with competitors of vastly different experience: sophisticated corporate managers and marketers who imposed high performance standards that nonprofessionals could hardly be expected to meet. As cotton growers became more embroiled in this new competitive environment, many worried that the institutional response was inadequate or misconceived and that CPI was losing the confidence of its most important constituents.

What really was CPI, anyway? The very name, "Institute," suggested something almost academic, ivory-towered, and off on its own. CPI's research and promotion activities were tainted by CPI's political origins – arising from the Cotton Council, an entity devoted to balancing competing industry interests and negotiating complex legislation. CPI was charged to compete, on behalf of cotton growers, with bona fide fiber companies (e.g., DuPont). Yet was it really a business, or was it just a group of commodity producers rooted in a trade association? Asking these questions, a group of pro-CPI growers coalesced to coax the rest over the hurdle imposed by their own limited experience.

In 1969, Russell Giffen – perhaps the man most closely associated with CPI from the beginning and then still its chairman – brought together a small group willing to radically rethink means for moving forward. Like Giffen, they were all men of wider business experience than most growers, something that probably inclined them to the view that CPI's most critical challenge was not funding at all but rather management. Giffen himself

---

[45] Charles G. Bragg, "Organization, Structure and Functions of Producer Steering Committee," 1987, NCC Archives; Russell, *U.S. Cotton and the National Cotton Council*, 87–9.

owned and managed a large operation in California. Keith Walden was an accomplished agricultural entrepreneur who had made his fortune farming cotton in California and then moved on to growing cotton, lettuce, and pecans in Arizona. Howard Alford came from the Texas Panhandle near Lubbock, where he grew cotton and ran a large cattle ranch. Jerry Sayre was the Harvard Ph.D. from Illinois who had managed two of cotton's largest and most sophisticated businesses: Delta and Pine Land Company and Staplcotn marketing cooperative in Mississippi. Hervey Evans, who had an MBA from Harvard Business School and sat on the board of a New York Stock Exchange company (Cluett, Peabody & Company, makers of apparel including Arrow shirts), ran a diversified farming operation in southeastern North Carolina that included a cotton breeding and seed company.[46] Giffen, Walden, Alford, Sayre, and Evans were convinced that cotton's insiders were but innocents abroad in the world of marketing. They had run out of answers, and it was time to seek professional help. With the trustees' approval, they hired the management consulting firm of Booz, Allen & Hamilton to get it.

The job took the better part of a year to complete. It was headed up by James Pomeroy, a young Booz, Allen marketing specialist who had come to the consulting firm from Colgate Palmolive and Ralston Purina. Neither he nor any of his colleagues had any background in cotton. But that wasn't what Giffen's group of five needed. They needed a study focused on what made the market work and on the changes that cotton would have to make in order to survive and prosper in it. They needed validation of their belief that what the growers needed was more, not less, of what CPI had to offer. They needed a third-party, authoritative analysis that would give them ammunition to convince the rest of cotton's leadership that CPI, or whatever it might be called in the future, must finally be made to stand apart and run on its own. Giffen and company took pains to guide their consultants into what was a highly complex industry, and they built a strong relationship with Pomeroy in the course of the project. They set no conceptual boundaries, but they were likely not surprised by where Booz, Allen led them in the end.[47]

---

[46] Keith Walden interview, April 23, 1999; Jerry Sayre interview, April 20, 1999; Hervey Evans interview, February 17, 1999.

[47] Booz, Allen & Hamilton, "A Business Strategy for the Cotton Producers Institute, Phase I," September 1969; "Cotton: A Five Year Study, Phase II and III," December 1969, Cotton Incorporated Archives; hereafter BAH 1 and BAH 2. Booz, Allen's fee for the study was over $200,000, plus expenses.

The report recommended first that if CPI were to remain the organization exercising "full-time aggressive leadership" on behalf of cotton, then its relationship with the NCC would have to be broken. This, they said, implied no criticism of the Cotton Council but was meant rather to clarify different purposes. The Council had been built on compromises necessary to meet the objectives of its diverse member groups, which had diluted its ability to concentrate CPI's research and promotion activities most profitably on producers' needs. The Council was oriented toward industrywide coordination and legislation. It should not attempt to do more, nor should it attempt to keep under its wing a "subsidiary" that did.

CPI, on the other hand, would need to add skills in marketing, consumer and technical research, and industry planning – skills that were not available to it through the staff of the Council alone. Capabilities in both promotional and research areas would need to be securely established in-house, which would result in a more efficient and "self-sufficient posture" for the producer segment of the industry.

If an aggressive producer-directed program were to be successful, all cotton growers would need to commit to it and stay committed. Consolidated and sustained producer support was essential, because even the most effective market development programs would take time to "provide tangible benefits." Achievements that were not measurable or readily evident must not lead to member defections and consequent erosion of financial support. Large producers who accounted for the bulk of the cotton supply were particularly critical in this regard. Success would require CPI to make itself the single focus for directing industry efforts on behalf of cotton and would call for more explicit enumeration of how its policy and operating objectives would speak to producers' interests.

The report counseled reapportioning CPI's expenditures in favor of expanded research efforts to support marketing programs. Under the present budget of about $10 million per year, the ratio of research to marketing should be adjusted to half-and-half. The consultants' message was to resist the temptation to overpromote what one could not yet produce. In addition, around 5 percent of total budgets should be set aside and built up as "a war chest for contingencies." It was hard to know what DuPont might come up with next, and it would be prudent to have some resources reserved to combat "emergency competitive situations." In time – ideally, over the first five years of a new organization – total funding levels should be increased substantially to $30 million per year. Current levels were sufficient barely to cross the threshold of effective research, particularly fibers research, and promotion activity. Lack of funds severely handicapped cotton's ability to take the marketing initiative and to exploit future research discoveries.[48]

All these recommendations depended on one other indispensable requirement. CPI would need (and on this point Booz, Allen was unequivocal) strong and independent executive leadership. The dual roles of senior CPI managers within the NCC organization had limited their effectiveness. The complexity of cotton's marketing and technical environment demanded management skills of a high order and that a single chief executive be held directly responsible to producers for implementing their policies.[49]

CPI's full board of trustees, along with NCC representatives, received the Booz, Allen report in December 1969 at a meeting in Scottsdale, Arizona, where the ailing Russell Giffen gave over the CPI chairmanship to Texan Howard Alford. Early in the new year, the NCC's own board voted to implement Booz, Allen's fundamental recommendation for complete separation of the producer-financed research and promotion program from the Cotton Council.[50] Even before the formal vote, Giffen had set to work a search committee of Sayre, Walden, and Evans to find the right full-time executive whose job would be to set everything else in motion. The committee, impressed by what it had seen already, turned to Booz, Allen's Pomeroy to conduct the search. Pomeroy short-listed three names for interview.

They were looking, Hervey Evans said, for someone "who had keen marketing instincts and not someone who necessarily knew anything about cotton, who was bright enough and well-trained enough to direct a full-scale marketing and research organization." The search committee gathered at the Dallas Airport Hilton in April 1970 to meet the finalists. "We drew straws," Evans recalled. "Jerry took one of them. Keith took another. I drew Dukes Wooters."[51]

---

[48] BAH 2, pp. 64–79.

[49] Ibid., 70.

[50] Support was strong, though not universal. Opposition coalesced around G. C. "Cauley" Cortright, an aristocratic Delta planter who both feared further diminution of the NCC and failed to understand the marketing needs that drove the separation. "Grow cotton and shove it into the market," as Keith Walden remembered Cortright's attitude. "Eventually they got to have it and by God they'll pay us a price that we can live with. And we don't need to spend a dime." Keith Walden interview, April 23, 1999.

[51] Hervey Evans interview, February 17, 1999.

5

CREATING
COTTON INCORPORATED

The Cotton Producers Institute meeting with Dukes Wooters at the Dallas Airport was a turning point in the cotton industry's history. For years the self-appointed leaders among the cotton growers had been trying to achieve enough unity in the ranks so that collectively they could have a strong influence on national farm policy. In meeting this goal, the National Cotton Council had proven the ideal vehicle. A second goal had been to finance and manage a research and promotion program that would enable cotton to compete in the private marketplace. In this respect, the National Cotton Council and its offspring, CPI, had failed. Cotton's market share through the 1960s had continued to slide and forced growers to take a fresh approach.

Jim Pomeroy, the young Booz, Allen consultant who compiled the report for CPI, knew that the cotton industry was a house divided. In his view, the traditional leadership of the industry, centered in Memphis and heavily influenced by Delta interests, remained fixated on supply issues and mired in passivity. They seemed to believe that cotton, as "the best of all fibers," would somehow overcome the challenge from synthetics. In his interviews, Pomeroy again and again heard the old refrain about the virtues of "100 percent cotton" and that there was no room for blends. But he had also interviewed mill executives who told him something else. Mill owners were adamant that their customers were demanding the fiber performance that only blends could provide, and mills wanted all the help they could get in fashioning the best blends to meet that demand. The trouble was that the synthetics manufacturers were providing virtually all the help and cotton producers virtually none. A number of mill executives told him that they had been "sold" synthetics but had to "go buy" cotton.[1]

[1] BAH 1, p. 22.

Pomeroy was amazed at the stubbornness and lack of urgency among the Memphis-based leaders. The choice was clear, Pomeroy wrote in less than diplomatic tones: "Cotton could step back in the game and take a leadership role, stressing the benefits of high cotton blends; they could take advantage of the trend and move to the forefront of what was happening, rather than dragging their heels and fighting it."[2]

On the other side of cotton's house was Russell Giffen's CPI study committee (which included Hervey Evans, Jerry Sayre, Keith Walden, and Howard Alford), which had the advantage of understanding, probably even before the Booz, Allen report confirmed it, what needed to change if cotton were to reverse its sagging fortunes. Although the conclusions of the study were clear – set off CPI as an independent research and promotion entity with strong executive leadership and its own staff – and though implementation turned out to move with remarkable speed (December 1969 to April 1970), the politics of such a big change were sticky.

In the first of two add-on assignments, Pomeroy was retained to help with implementation; this was unusual for Booz, Allen, which usually did a study, issued a report, and then said good-bye. In fact, Pomeroy had to sell it to his own superiors, who were uncomfortable with such advocacy. But without it, he argued, the recommendations might not be implemented and then Booz, Allen would not have helped its client at all. So Pomeroy, himself trained in marketing, took to the road again. He became the point man in scores of one-on-one sessions with growers, small groups, and major association meetings "with a lot of personal selling, persuading, conjuring and what have you." Behind the scenes, quietly persuading on their own, were Evans, Sayre, and the others.[3]

GETTING THEIR MAN

Booz, Allen's second add-on assignment was to conduct the executive search for CPI's new leader. Three candidates came to Dallas in April 1970, the result of "an extremely top-level search" for a strong, independent, consumer-oriented manager.[4] The leading candidate was a vice-president

---

[2] James Pomeroy interview, October 13, 1999.

[3] Pomeroy interview, October 13, 1999. Pomeroy understood that he was part of "an extremely well-engineered, very cleverly designed process. Some of it evolved, as things always do, but a fair amount of it was planned or it wouldn't have evolved. A fair amount of it was planned."

[4] Ibid. The report could not have been more clear on this need: "Responsibility for overall direction of CPI's activities should be vested in a single executive capable of coordinating research

for consumer products and pharmaceuticals at Beechnut Squibb. Number two was a former Pepsi-Cola senior executive with international experience. Least likely, on paper at least, was an advertising salesman from *Reader's Digest*.

The upshot of the entire Booz, Allen report had been that cotton needed shock treatment, and Pomeroy and his colleagues decided early that their opportunity for administering the first jolt lay with selection of the new boss. Pomeroy himself knew nothing about cotton before starting the CPI project, which was one of the reasons that Giffen's study committee had been attracted to him. They saw the greatest credibility in a fresh view, based on fresh homework, done from the ground up. This of course did not go down well with some insiders, and tension between strategic correctness and political calculation was present from the beginning. One man in particular, G. C. "Cauley" Cortright (a Delta planter prominent in the Cotton Council and who would become head of the Cotton Board), was widely believed to have coveted the new post for himself.

As the CPI search committee made their rounds to different hotel rooms to interview each of the three candidates, their goal was more fixed than even Pomeroy had guessed. For that reason, their quick and unanimous choice fell to the man least qualified in terms of executive experience for the job. J. Dukes Wooters, a marketing vice-president at *Reader's Digest*, had been added to the list as a dark horse – but, for Pomeroy's money, a horse that could probably run. What Wooters lacked in broad-scale management experience he made up for with qualities that to Evans, Sayre, and Walden were irresistible. He was bright and quick, imaginative, high-energy, hard-driving, and possessed of a deep and arresting voice. Above all, he was a marketing man with great instincts for what would sell. "So," as Pomeroy remembered the encounter, "they fell in love with Dukes."[5]

Pomeroy and Wooters had a history of their own that went back to the early days of both of their careers. Pomeroy, a young assistant brand manager for Colgate Palmolive, and Wooters, advertising manager for *Reader's Digest*, had once teamed up and roomed together on a trip to the Pacific Northwest to sell a coupon promotion to A&P. They had not met in the

and market efforts to achieve realistic goals. The scope and complexity of cotton's marketing environment and technical alternatives require strong management skill to ensure optimum results. Producer representatives also need a single manager to be held directly responsible for effective planning and implementation of their policies." BAH 2, p. 70.

5 Pomeroy interview, October 13, 1999.

interim but, as was evident to Pomeroy even then, Wooters was clearly a man of parts. He was from New England with all the advantages that good upbringing and education confer: Taft School, Lehigh University, military service in World War II, Harvard Business School. He had a winning way with people and an inner-directed zest for life that would not fade with age. His was a personality made for sales.

Shortly out of business school, he had gone into publishing, selling advertising first with *Hearst,* then with *Good Housekeeping* and *LIFE.* Selling magazine advertising is an ultimate exercise in the art: nobody wants to buy it, and so everybody must be persuaded they can't live without it. In that heyday of glossy, mass-circulation general-interest books, Wooters mastered the techniques of presentation and sold a great many pages for his publishers. Success earned him a nice living (he and his wife and five daughters lived in New Canaan, Connecticut) and a reputation in New York advertising circles. When *Reader's Digest,* the publishing phenomenon founded and run by Dewitt Wallace, decided to forsake its historic all-editorial status for the lure of advertising dollars but got off to a shaky launch, they approached Wooters to set things right. It was a big break. The *Digest* then had twice the circulation of *LIFE,* and Wooters got to run the show.

No one told him what to do, so he just did what he knew: he built presentations. The first year he sold $6 million for the Wallaces. The *Digest,* he said, should obviously be turned into a woman's magazine, since most advertising was aimed at women. He hired a photographer and a model – "I wanted a lady who looked just like the girl next door" – and built a magnificent portfolio of pictures titled "Today's Mrs. America" that showed her in all the domestic roles (which, of course, correlated with product categories): chauffeur, shopper, cook, and companion. He bought a gatefold machine and instigated a 10-cent-off coupon campaign with a lucky number to move even more advertisers' merchandise. It was when the head of Colgate asked Wooters for its own *Digest* promotion that Wooters's path first crossed Pomeroy's. They would not meet again for many years.[6]

Pomeroy, like Wooters a Harvard MBA, meantime left Colgate for a consulting career at Booz, Allen, where from a distance he kept abreast of Wooters's subsequent successes. One of the things Booz, Allen did was to match business talent with business challenges, and over his years there

---

[6] J. Dukes Wooters interview, February 20, 1999.

Pomeroy had amassed a considerable file. In the spring of 1970, when Booz, Allen went shopping for talent to match the unique business challenge presented by the growers of American upland cotton, the name Dukes Wooters came back to mind.

"Dukes, do I have a deal for you," Pomeroy remembered his telephone opener to his old acquaintance. Over lunch Pomeroy pushed across the table his intimidating three-volume report to CPI, with an "I want you to read this; tell me what you think; I want your honest opinion." Wooters obliged, lugged it home on the train to Connecticut, and studied it for several nights. Then he called Pomeroy back: "I read your stuff. You've got a lot of guts. You told those guys the truth. They're in real trouble." Hearing the reaction he had hoped for, Pomeroy made his next request: "A week from Saturday we're going to have a selection committee meeting in Dallas, and we want some people to go down there. I want you to go." [7]

Wooters balked. He knew nothing about cotton. He had just returned from a stint in South America where he had turned around the *Digest*'s sagging operation in Brazil and was looking next to be posted either to West Germany or Argentina, probably on a similar "fix-it" mission. He had worked his way upward in a very good company. He had won a patron in Wallace, its famed patriarch, and looked forward to a secure future. He had a lovely home in an exclusive suburb, a nice salary, options, and prospects. With children in college and private schools, he had some big expenses and didn't need any big risks. He also loved a challenge.

Pomeroy knew his quarry; he guessed that with life and career in good order, Wooters was probably a bit bored. Wooters was then 53 and coveted one more success. The *Digest,* he suspected, had him pigeon-holed as a top-flight troubleshooter, and while he fit the hole he felt the hole confining. The *Digest* would likely have kept using his turnaround skills for fixing things up, and while the venues might have been exotic, the job no longer would be. "This was the only way we could really snare him," Pomeroy concluded, "by showing him that cotton was the kind of creative challenge that could really get his juices flowing." Thus the Booz, Allen consulting report, with its dire picture of cotton's situation, became the bait. Wooters rose to it and was hooked.

Against his better judgment, Wooters agreed to go down to Dallas. He did his homework. The meeting was scheduled for a Monday, so on the

[7] Pomeroy interview, October 13, 1999; Wooters interview, February 20, 1999.

morning of the preceding Saturday Wooters caught the commuter train to Manhattan and paid a visit to Macy's. He had read what Pomeroy had written, but he wanted to see for himself. Macy's was then still the largest department store in the world and a good place to learn a lot in a hurry. Wooters fancied himself as "purely a Brooks Brothers kid." Twice a year he bought his shirts (on sale) at that bastion of male traditionalism on the corner of 44th Street and Madison Avenue; needless to say, the shirts were all-cotton. What he discovered down at Macy's, where most people shopped, was that he would have a hard time indulging such an old-fashioned taste in fabrics. "I looked around," he said, recalling his surprise, "and there was hardly any cotton."[8]

Not content just to look, Wooters prowled men's wear, women's wear, and home furnishings, sought out section managers ("they wore white plastic carnations in their lapels"), and asked lots of questions. He took one manager "to some beer joint down on 34th Street" and in a couple of hours got solid street-level confirmation of all the careful analysis he had just read in Jim Pomeroy's report to the cotton growers. Neither Wooters nor his lunch partner had ever met a cotton grower or been anywhere near a cotton field. But they had been up and down the aisles of Macy's, which were a lot like the aisles of Gimbel's, Ward's, and Sears, all across America.

The experience made Wooters wonder just what cotton growers did with all their cotton, anyway. They certainly weren't selling much of it to the shirtmakers and dressmakers who sold to Macy's. Synthetics, especially polyesters, filled the racks. Yet it was not just the products themselves that worried him. It was evidence of the marketing muscle that lay behind them. Here were high (if not extravagant) claims – "no-iron," "easy-care," "permanent press" – that were stimulating the market for synthetics. No one, that he could see, was stimulating the market for cotton. As he had said in reaction to Pomeroy's report, cotton growers sure enough "were in real trouble." Heading home that night, he started thinking what he might do to help them.

On the plane to Dallas on Sunday, Wooters sketched out on a yellow legal pad the first business plan for the organization that would become Cotton Incorporated. It was in the form of notes to himself, as he prepared for conversation with the first four cotton growers he would ever meet. The notes do not survive, but their contents can be inferred from what was said

---

[8] Wooters interview, February 20, 1999.

and heard that day at the Airport Hilton. Four growers (Howard Alford, Hervey Evans, Keith Walden, and Jerry Sayre) interviewed three candidates, individually, each in his turn. A Booz, Allen representative came to Wooters's hotel room with the schedule for the next day. It began with breakfast with Hervey Evans at six o'clock.

They spent a couple of hours and then rotated. At the end of the day, the committee gathered to compare notes. Wooters had shown none of them his plan, though he had talked to them as if he had one.[9] He told them what Booz, Allen had told them already, but infused the message with his own special energy: growers needed to establish their own fibers company independent of cotton's other organizations, and they needed to hire an executive to run it who knew marketing, if not cotton, and they had to give that executive the freedom to hire his own team.

The committee's reaction to Wooters was uniformly positive. Evans was analytical. Realizing that Wooters didn't know anything about the cotton business, he asked what Wooters considered the single most important thing he needed to do to develop a strategy, an organization, and a program to carry it all out. Wooters's response was quick and direct: "The first and most important thing to do is to select the absolute best people you can to build your organization. That's where I think I need to initially concentrate." Evans liked that. Jerry Sayre was a practical man who thought that Wooters stood out, particularly in comparison with the "gray flannel suit" from Beechnut Squibb: "That fellow will get along with anybody in the industry. He'll ruffle nobody's feathers. He'll know how to smooth things out. We won't have any trouble with him. Wooters, on the other hand, is going to make some mistakes. He's going to plow through and really forcefully get things done. He's going to rub people a lot in the wrong way."[10] To Sayre, this was a good prospect. Howard Alford, less polished, thought that a long shot like Wooters would give cotton just the ventilation it needed: "You know what I liked about him? He's going to irritate a hell of a lot of people, but I think he's a get-things-done guy and that's what we need in the cotton industry. We don't need somebody that's going to be a kiss-ass." Keith Walden liked that Wooters had been off saving the bacon for

---

[9] He was anything but overconfident, however, and figured everybody had seen the same material as he had. He didn't really need the job, and though it looked exciting, he knew his qualifications for it seemed something of a stretch: "I thought that Pomeroy just wanted me to go down there and make the other guys look good." Ibid.

[10] Hervey Evans interview, February 17, 1999.

Dewitt Wallace and evidently was someone who knew how to get results. If Wooters could market the *Reader's Digest* in Brazil, then he could probably market cotton too. There had been enough words already: "We need somebody to go out there and do what we've been talking about."[11]

Wooters believed there were two exciting things in business: turn things around; start things up. Yet when Pomeroy telephoned him at home after the meeting in Dallas to say the selection committee had voted unanimously to offer him the job, he hesitated. After all, if he looked like a long shot to the committee, their proposed new fibers company was a long shot to match. He talked to his brother, who worked in the textile business with Berkshire Hathaway. He talked to his accountant to see whether, financially, there was any way he could give up what he had at the *Digest* and still live high, as he was accustomed.[12] The new company would be (and would always remain) a not-for-profit; there would be no stock, and salary would always be an issue. He would need $100,000, a lot for a small company in those days, to start. "You're a gambler," the accountant told him. "You're probably going to do it." And he did.[13]

He would do it because he wanted to create something without having to spend his own money, which he didn't have enough of anyway. He wanted to run, if not own, his own company, and the cotton growers appeared to be offering that opportunity. So he took it up, called Pomeroy, and paid his respects to Dewitt Wallace – who told him that if it didn't work out to come back and see him. To Pomeroy (one last time before he handed off the new man to his satisfied client) Wooters still expressed doubts, perhaps out of anxiety over the anticipated conflicts. "You're asking me to come into this thing and take something out of the National Cotton Council," he said. "That's what you're really asking me to do. That's a tough thing."

Pomeroy, Wooters, and Alford sealed the deal over lunch at the Greenwich Country Club later that month. There was a contract, of course, but Alford said that where he came from a man was as good as his handshake. So they shook. Greenwich was the kind of neighborhood Wooters was used to but not so Howard Alford, who was from the High Plains of Texas near

---

[11] Keith Walden interview, April 23, 1999.

[12] He had, or could have had, quite a lot. "In those days we were getting stock. We were still privately owned, but we had a beautiful plan. The dividends from the stock not only paid the interest and the principal, but there was a little residue left over, so I got a cash dividend and the stock was being paid for."

[13] Wooters interview, February 20, 1999.

Lubbock.[14] The gap between those two worlds bespoke the enormous risk that the selection committee had taken in offering the job to someone who was closer to Madison Avenue than to Main Street.

CLEARING THE GROUND

There were several ways of seeing the challenge that Wooters faced. Wooters himself viewed it as a personal dare that he could create a successful business organization virtually from scratch and then help turn an industry around. He had studied such challenges in business school cases, and cotton was the opportunity that happened across his path.

Thousands of cotton producers interpreted Wooters's challenge in personal terms of their own. Not long into the job, Wooters visited the Delta, where cotton had been both a business and a way of life for 150 years. The grower who was his host invited Wooters to meet his mother, who had heard a great deal about cotton's new head man and wanted to see for herself. "Mother's," Wooters remembered, "had big white columns, just like you saw in *Gone with the Wind*," and "Mother" was a haughty old steel magnolia who shook his hand at the front door and commanded: "Young man, come into my parlor. I want you to sit under the picture of the great one." She settled herself across from Wooters, under the likeness of Robert E. Lee, and looking him square in the eye, pronounced: "I would just like to hear you talk: I understand you are going to save our farm."[15]

Hervey Evans was a southerner, too, with some ancestral portraits of his own on the wall. He viewed Wooters's challenge on a more concrete level. Their intellectual affinity and practical working relationship would do much to assure the early success of the new organization. Evans accepted Wooters's longing to create and run something for himself, because

---

[14] In the years to follow, Wooters would invite key board members to his house in New Canaan for the weekend. Walden remembers asking Alford, who had just been there, how his weekend in Connecticut went:

Alford: "Oh, fine. We talked over quite a few things."

Walden: "Were you impressed with the house?"

Alford: "It's a very nice house."

"Howard," Walden added, "lived in a small house outside Lubbock. He could have put his house inside of Wooters's house three or four times. But the funny part about it was that didn't make any difference to Howard at all."

[15] Wooters interview, February 20, 1999.

he believed that such desire could be harnessed to cotton's need to learn to compete. He framed the challenge for Wooters and their new company as a challenge to "serve the industry," while leaving no doubt that it all came down, in the end, to rebuilding cotton's lost markets.[16]

Though from vastly different parts of the country and with careers hardly alike, the two men belonged to the same educated, cultured, and worldly class. Evans, like Wooters, was a product of elite schooling; he had gone to Woodberry Forest, Princeton, and Harvard Business School, class of 1948. New Mexico grower Morgan Nelson, contemporary and close friend of both, perceived an uncanny resemblance just beneath the surface. Wooters was "Old North." North Carolinian Evans was "Old South" and "New South" together: deep roots but, like the New Englander, eyes fixed dead ahead. They made a powerful pair.[17]

Thus briefed by Booz, Allen and blessed by the CPI board, Wooters came to work for cotton. It was "a dog's breakfast," he said. "They had a bunch of guys in research in Memphis at the National Cotton Council offices, and a group of people in a little cubbyhole in the Empire State Building." He rolled up his all-cotton Brooks Brothers sleeves, started cleaning out, and began planning.[18] A lot of the people he found in the New York office were transplanted from Memphis: half a dozen secretaries ("only one of them could take shorthand," he complained), some accountants, and advertising people whose job it appeared was to buy space in the trade press. He talked to each of them individually and not long afterward fired all but one, Libby Clark, an educated Mississipian whose family was "in cotton" back home. He also went to CPI headquarters at the offices of the Cotton Council, located on a broad boulevard in the old Midtown section of Memphis. It would take some time to sort this part out, but he came away with a critical first impression.

Memphis, in Wooters's mind, conveyed the wrong message. It was capital of the Delta and home of the "Cotton Carnival." Many of the comfortable houses in that same Midtown neighborhood were testimony to the wealth that, once upon a time, cotton had produced. Memphis was Mecca to wealthy growers and home to major merchants. Probably no one city was ever so closely identified with one agricultural commodity as Memphis was

---

[16] Hervey Evans conversation with author, March 17, 1999.
[17] Morgan Nelson interview, February 19, 1999.
[18] Wooters interview, February 20, 1999.

with cotton. But history had tied it to only one side of cotton's economy: supply. This was the fundamental problem for Wooters. He was hired for his marketing know-how, and, in marketing, image and substance traveled hand-in-hand. Memphis was fine for a cotton merchant but wrong for a fibers company.

With support from Evans and his circle, Wooters decided to move CPI's headquarters from Memphis to New York. This he saw as an integral part of his organizational mandate to take CPI's functions out of the National Cotton Council and, more generally, to give CPI a fresh start. With the decision to move formally voted by the CPI board and agreed to by the NCC, CPI successfully declared independence from cotton's complicated organizational past as represented by the Cotton Council. It was positioned to shake off the industry's old supply-side orientation and embrace the consumer-driven culture of marketing.

New York was, of course, the world that Wooters knew, and he realized that the key to cotton's comeback lay in changing what went on in New York. "All the big apparel people, all the big manufacturers had offices there," Evans recalled. "Everybody looked at fashion through New York eyes: the advertising business, the whole thing, and Dukes knew that."[19] CPI's existing advertising office in Manhattan was little more than a branch of Memphis and not at all what Wooters had in mind. One look at the tired old Empire State Building space told him the whole mind-set was wrong, and interviews with those who worked there confirmed it. Wooters's reasons for being in New York would call for a different setup entirely and, before long, a new address.

Taking the new company out of Memphis meant taking research out, too. But while marketing belonged by nature in New York, research did not. Hence Wooters and the board divided the company's locations geographically without a second thought. Memphis had a case to make with regard to keeping agricultural research based there, but its location by no means offered unique advantages – and none at all when it came to the customer-based fibers research that Wooters figured would command a growing share of the company's resources.

All Wooters knew about cotton research was what he had read in the Booz, Allen report just a month or two before; so, when it came to picking a home for the new company's research function, he deferred to Evans

---

[19] Evans interview, February 17, 1999.

and company. Evans told him there were only two possibilities: one was anywhere near Clemson University in the South Carolina Piedmont, the other near North Carolina State University in Raleigh. These were the best textile schools in the country, and they shared proximity to the country's major cotton textile manufacturers. The great mills of the southern Piedmont had been cotton's best customers since the turn of the century, and in 1970 the lion's share of all American textiles still came from the two Carolinas alone.

After some deliberation, Raleigh was chosen. It made sense to Wooters, because if his job was to market cotton then he needed cotton that worked for the mills, their customers, and their customers' customers. The problem with the industry's advertising strategy was that it had been pushing a product that, relative to the competition, performed poorly in the areas customers cared most about. They had claimed too much and delivered too little. It was a mistake that Wooters was determined not to repeat.[20]

Wooters also liked the move to Raleigh for a less tangible reason. It looked good. Appearances mattered. Relocating research – lock, stock, and barrel – to North Carolina's Research Triangle would miff some Memphians, but to wider audiences it would give the impression that the new company could act boldly, would not be crippled by old institutional ties, and would take actions henceforth of concern to customers.[21] The move certainly looked good to the mills, who had abrogated much of their technical research to the synthetics fiber companies and whom cotton meantime had serviced poorly, if at all. (Simultaneous with the move, a technical services department was added to the old CPI research division.) And to the entire textile industry it sent the message that this time cotton had come up with leadership that was prepared to support both farm and mill technology and was determined to get things right.

PUTTING A NAME TO IT

"Dukes Wooters had style. He had real style," said Morgan Nelson, who grew cotton near Roswell, New Mexico. Wooters was a man of high-toned

---

[20] Cotton Incorporated Annual Report, 1970.
[21] The move out of Memphis was the first instance of Wooters's characteristic readiness to incur a high political cost if what he deemed the right action called for it. Remembered Evans: "He was abrupt. He just realized that he wasn't going to win anybody over and he just had to get that change accomplished quickly. So he did. The board backed him 100 percent."

tastes. "Dukes didn't know how to do things the cheap farm way. He went first class." [22] Nelson thought that was probably a good thing.

In Wooters's view, "first class" made simple business sense. Wooters's title was at first only "Executive Vice-President and General Manager" (the wording came from the Booz, Allen report), yet he thought of himself as a true chief executive and carried himself so. It was essential that he and his company always look good and be perceived as prosperous, as sophisticated players in a sophisticated city working for a sophisticated industry. This was one reason why the old office space in the Empire State Building had to go. The new New York address on the Avenue of the Americas (where Wooters would move the company headquarters in 1973) cost, in refitting and decorating, over $1.2 million. It raised eyebrows at the Cotton Board, at the USDA, in Congress, and in the field, though the costs were modest by the princely standards of presidents and CEOs in the for-profit world. Wooters invested in a setting where he could welcome representatives of the fashion and textile industries and the media, from buyers to company presidents, without apology. [23]

For similar reasons, Wooters determined that the new company also needed a new name. Privately, he cringed at "Cotton Producers Institute," with its trade-association sound and historical baggage. Wooters searched for a phrase, a new name, that would evoke an image of a cotton fibers company. It would be a strange sort of "company," to be sure, a nonprofit corporation that until then had produced and sold nothing. It would have no shareholders and no property of its own. Wooters's chosen designation – "Cotton Incorporated" – suggested just the opposite. The new name became official on January 1, 1971. It was simple and direct and suggested a going, established concern. Its product would be *profit-supporting* services to the entire chain of cotton production and distribution.

Wooters intended to run Cotton Incorporated as if it were, in fact, "a real company" like *Reader's Digest* or, for that matter, DuPont. It could be managed with the same discipline and focus as if it were a for-profit corporation, as if it truly did have to create wealth for its "owners" or go out of business. In this case, the owners were the nation's cotton growers, a well-defined constituency, who paid their assessment to the Cotton Board

[22] Morgan Nelson interview, February 19, 1999.

[23] Wooters drove a company Mercedes and employed, for business lunches, an excellent Chinese chef. Despite rumors to the contrary, he never had a plane or a private elevator.

and for whom the stakes were high.[24] If Cotton Incorporated failed in its mission to market cotton, then their farming businesses might very well fail next. And if the growers should ever waver in their support for the research and promotion program, then that would spell the end of Cotton Incorporated. Changing the name broadcast this message loud and clear.

Wooters traveled widely from the very start, not just to Memphis but also far afield, across the Cotton Belt, presenting how he intended to reorganize and reinvigorate cotton. He had it outlined in his head and wanted to generate excitement fast, even before all the details were worked out and staff were in place to do the job. In the opening forays, he focused on the sales and marketing side, where the objectives seemed most transparent. He was a master at putting positive spin on negative fact. "They're in real trouble," he worried privately, but in public he was relentlessly upbeat. His theme was always the same: bright opportunities existed for cotton if key goals could be reached. Everything came down to servicing customers.

"Customers" was an inclusive noun. Cotton Incorporated would work to persuade textile mills to purchase more cotton. It would do this by presenting coordinated marketing plans linking mills, manufacturers, retailers, and consumers. It would convey back to those engaged in research and technical services ideas from the marketplace for new and improved fabrics and finishes. It would offer mills, manufacturers, and retailers new fashion ideas that could be interpreted in cotton and cotton blends. It would stimulate retail demand with advertising of cotton as a *brand*, not a commodity.[25]

None of this was complicated, just "pure marketing," the basics of which he had learned in business school and practiced for years in the publishing business. One Harvard case in particular came back to him as he plotted out the goals for Cotton Incorporated. "Andy Boy Broccoli," he remembered, had illustrated how an agricultural product could be branded and subsequently marketed with surprising success. Perdue was doing the same for chicken. Cotton Incorporated's challenge was the same as its strategy: to take an overabundant agricultural commodity called cotton – "that funny

---

[24] Wooters had come away from his first meetings in Memphis in disbelief at the lack of urgency evident in CPI. "It was one nonprofit organization talking to another and they'd bullshit each other and buy each other a lot of booze and food and that was it." Wooters interview, February 20, 1999.

[25] Wooters to Cotton Board meeting, August 20–21, 1970, Memphis; also see *Memphis Commercial Appeal*, August 23, 1970, and *El Paso Times*, August 21, 1970.

looking white stuff," Wooters liked to call it – brand it, foster broad consumer interest in the brand, and then sell it by the trainload.

AN ORGANIZATION TO MATCH

Back in New York, Wooters confronted the more mundane tasks of preparing a budget for the USDA and outlining an organizational structure to implement his strategy. Looking at everything up close confirmed his sense that he was engaged in a start-up situation. He pored again over the Booz, Allen report and everything else he could find on the synthetic fibers companies, including organizational charts. A less stouthearted soul might well have groaned at cotton's disadvantages and given up. Some were specific: the synthetics manufacturers were committing $150 million to research and $100 million to marketing (DuPont alone, he figured, was spending $19 million on advertising synthetics). He had less than $10 million to work with – for everything. Some were general: "I realized things they had and I didn't have and would never have. I would never be able to set my volume. I would never be able to set my price. I had to compete with guys who could." [26]

Wooters worked out a new organizational and operations plan designed to carry out his "total marketing concept" for cotton. Total marketing took into account the complexity of the industry, or actually four component industries: the fibers industry, including the larger chemical companies active in textile fibers; the textile industry, including the weaving and knitting mills, spinners, dyers, and finishers; the apparel and home furnishings manufacturers; and the retail industry, including department and chain stores. This meant a sharp reorientation from CPI's previous efforts at advertising and promotion. Those efforts were focused on behalf of consumer products made of 100 percent cotton. They were directed at manufacturers and retailers in an attempt to increase their promotional support for cotton fabrics and products they had already purchased. Cotton Incorporated would transform this communications and quasi-merchandising role into a strong fiber-marketing posture. Under Wooters's plan, the company would begin by exerting direct and sustained sales pressure on cotton's first customer, the textile mills.

Cotton Incorporated would turn the old CPI approach, which had advertising and public relations as its primary activity, on its head. A New

---

[26] Wooters interview, February 20, 1999.

York–based sales and marketing division was organized along three lines, paralleling the organization of the mills: one for men's and boys' wear, one for women's and children's wear, and one for home furnishings and industrial products. Each department was assigned its own marketing director who would report directly to Wooters. Their charge was simple and measurable. The objective for each department was to increase the number of bales consumed within its area. Total marketing for each of these departments meant, in turn, exerting maximum sales pressure at all three stages of value-added production and distribution: the mills (the primary target), the manufacturers, and the retailers. Four other departments, belonging to a marketing services group, would support the sales effort with market research, fabric development, fashion marketing, and advertising and public relations.

Under this regime, each sales department prepared its own annual marketing plan, the purpose of which was to focus staff energies and concentrate the company's limited financial resources along clear lines of attack. The marketing plans would also help avoid the traditional pitfall of responding opportunistically to promotional opportunities that were poor prospects for actually increasing the sale of cotton.

The desire of each department to win some early successes and then build momentum over time shaped specific strategies to meet achievable goals. In men's and boys' wear, for example, the marketing of men's dress shirts targeted the high-volume manufacturers Arrow, Van Heusen, and Manhattan (who were supplied by Dan River Mills, Lowenstein, and J. P. Stevens) and aimed to convert them to shirting fabrics with a high-cotton blend. With permanent press performance, the dominant factor in selection of fibers for men's shirts, Cotton Incorporated tried to direct attention of the "big three" shirtmakers toward a 65/35 cotton/polyester blend. When treated with the new "vapor phase" process, this blend effectively eliminated the need for ironing and performed favorably against blends that were much higher in synthetic content. At the upper end of the shirt market, the men's wear department also sought to anchor the all-cotton promotion positions of higher-priced shirtmakers like Gant, Hathaway, and Eagle. In men's underwear, a traditional cotton stronghold, a strong selling effort enabled cotton to block the blending of polyesters with cotton at Munsingwear, one of the biggest manufacturers. In the home furnishings department, early plans called for promoting 100 percent cotton sheets and pillowcases with Belk Stores. In women's and children's wear, the focus was on fabric and fashion innovation. A relationship was established with Pendleton Mills to increase the cotton fabric consumption in their sportswear division, a major departure for Pendleton in using fibers other than wool. By initiating contacts with the leadership of the top companies, sportswear generally was targeted as the key to broadening use of cotton fabric in women's wear.[27]

The marketing services group developed plans to support the three-pronged sales effort in several directions. One was market research, which positioned cotton products in the current competitive market by considering factors of price, distribution, performance, retailer and consumer preference, and the competitive advantages (or disadvantages) of synthetic blends. The goal was to help determine the most efficient course of sales action. Another was the fabric development department, which conducted short-term research projects relative to new fabric and product applications for cotton and also provided one of the most direct means for influencing mill decisions in cotton's favor. Improved dyeing methods, new fabric constructions, and special yarn treatments for the more efficient running of cotton on high-speed knitting machines would all help sharpen cotton's competitive edge. Organizationally, Wooters saw fabric development functioning as a liaison between research and sales. In business, everybody needs to make money, especially one's own customers, and Wooters wanted to make sure that the mills made money off cotton. It was part of his overall strategy of "translating a promotional relationship into a profit incentive. It is a more realistic motivation for the mills to take a stronger position on cotton."[28] Development of new products, either directly for the mills or indirectly through their fabric customers, would help cotton maintain sales pressure on the mills and at the same time increase sales and profits for the mills.

Fashion marketing, on the other hand, represented a new approach to the application of fashion trends and color forecasting to sales. Wooters revitalized three moribund fabric libraries (in New York, Dallas, and Los Angeles) and renamed them "The Cottonworks." These then served as up-to-date fabric workshops, promoting current cotton fabric lines to designers and manufacturers of apparel and home furnishings. In addition, fashion marketing kept abreast of changing fashions at home and abroad, analyzing them for potential cotton yarn applications and fabric constructions.

[27] Cotton Incorporated budget, 1970–1971.
[28] Annual Report, 1970.

Marketing services' final responsibility, advertising and public relations, was also refitted to serve the new total marketing approach by supporting specific products and forcing others to follow. Thus, while the sales departments were to concentrate on raising cotton input into the distribution system mainly at the mill level, advertising and public relations were aimed at accelerating the movement of fabrics and products through primarily retail channels. In addition to these consumer campaigns, advertising to the trade was designed to "pre-merchandise" the consumer programs to the textile industry; the intent was to secure retailers' commitment to cotton products that were already being promoted to the consumer. Public relations was to be accelerated, too, and the primary vehicle was the name change from CPI to Cotton Incorporated. Specific campaigns crafted to hammer home the new brand, such as "Cotton 365," touted cotton's year-round versatility. The "Cotton Clipsheet" distributed timely news about cotton products, all aimed at keeping cotton in public view.

One of the new Cotton Incorporated's most important goals was to develop a well-coordinated and "high-spirited" relationship between marketing and research. Wooters saw the 1970s as the decade when cotton would "leapfrog years of delay" in order to match the pace of technological innovation set by its competitors. Cotton Incorporated's investment in purpose-built laboratories in Raleigh was supposed to accelerate product development while cutting costs and quickening the commercial introduction of new products. Wooters wanted to link development work closely with commercial possibilities, and he offered to cooperate with mills and manufacturers in research at every opportunity. If they worked, such relationships would mean a faster return on Cotton Incorporated's research investment and lead to a reliable system for regenerating research funds through royalties and licensing agreements. Agricultural research would focus on practical matters of crop yield and fiber quality; insect, disease, and weed control; and processing and handling.

FRESH TALENT

The Wooters reforms came fast and were reflected in the hiring of new personnel. Wooters intended to motivate his staff in accordance with what he had learned at the knee of Dewitt Wallace. "Money motivates people. People won't admit it, but it does." It was as simple as that. It had been Wallace's theory that one hired the best people available and then paid them

a little more than the going rate. "Then," he had counseled, "they will produce twice as much." Although Cotton Incorporated would never have a lot
of money (by private-sector standards) to throw at salaries, it had enough
to tempt some high-powered talent ready for an unusual challenge.

As with his decision to exit Memphis abruptly and spend money getting
properly set up in New York, Wooters took some risks in "hiring high" and
drew criticism for it. Howard Alford, whose little farmhouse in Lubbock
was dwarfed by Wooters's residence in New Canaan, did his best to shield
him. Wooters phoned Alford every couple of weeks on Sunday nights to
talk about how things were going and how much he was spending. Alford
usually responded with a laconic: "You just keep doing what you're doing,
and we'll keep the flies off you." [29]

Wooters observed a second principle in staffing the new organization,
which would demand a range of specialized knowledge. "There's only room
for one person to learn in this company," he always said, "and that's me."
Employment at Cotton Incorporated was not to be an "on the job training" proposition for his staff. There was little time for that. Besides, the
jobs that cotton needed doing did not come with exotic new descriptions.
They were jobs that other companies, synthetics companies in particular,
had trained people to do for years. And that was where Wooters looked to
fill them.

Because he had organized the marketing side of Cotton Incorporated
into sales divisions – upon whose success everything depended – the men
he chose to lead them were to take no risks. The smartest bet, he figured,
would be to "borrow" from the competition. "I want to try to get a key guy
out of each of the major synthetics companies," and, adding with typical
directness, "I don't care what it costs. I want the guy to know the marketing
end of it." Wooters hired two such men, one each in 1970 and 1971. Richard
Abes, who became marketing director of home furnishings and industrial
products, was wooed away from Celanese Fibers Company, where he had
been home furnishings marketing manager for eleven years. (Abes then re-
cruited Allen Winch, another Celanese veteran and technology specialist,
to handle the industrial products side.) The women's and children's wear
slot was filled by Don S. Kleckner, formerly of DuPont. Other recruits came
not from the competition but from the customers: the mills. Mel Rahm
(who had worked for Greenwood Mills, Burlington Industries, and Deering

[29] Wooters interview, February 20, 1999.

Milliken) launched the men's and boy's wear division. His team, in turn, would include others from pools of talent at Allied Chemical and American Viscose.[30]

Wooters supported the three-pronged sales effort by hiring people into marketing services with similarly strong backgrounds in their fields. Sometimes he just got lucky. In July 1970, Lillian Rossilli – who had heard Wooters was starting a new fiber company – called about job possibilities. She had been out of work for a year but presented a dream resumé for the new post in fashion marketing. Rossilli had started her career as a fashion coordinator for the Newark retailer Bamberger's and had then moved up to fashion director of ready-to-wear at Macy's. She then worked five years at the Wool Bureau, another research and promotion program. When Wooters saw "Macy's" he was sold, and Rossilli came to work the next month. Advertising and public relations fell initially to Arthur C. Nigro, who had also worked at the Wool Bureau in addition to London Fog and Celanese Fibers. The only New York holdover from the old CPI regime was Libby Clark, who in October 1970 moved up from her clerical duties to become manager of retail promotions.

The research and technical service side benefited from greater continuity of personnel from the old regime. Here, Wooters inherited some good talent from the NCC. Harold L. "Hal" Lewis, a Ph.D. who had taught biology at Texas Tech, became Cotton Incorporated's first head of agricultural research. Joseph K. "Farmer" Jones, an agricultural engineer trained at Mississippi State, stayed on to oversee research on processing and handling. Wooters's first choice for the top job – director of the entire research and technical services division – came from the outside: S. Frank Moore, who had worked for Greenwood Mills and American Finishing Company. Moore stayed only two years, but his replacement, Hal E. Brockmann, went the distance. Brockmann had a textiles degree from Clemson and broad corporate and technical experience at Stonecutter Mills, Dow Chemical, and Prodesco, a contract fibers research company whose biggest customer happened to be DuPont Textile Fibers.

Two early hires supplied general management potential for the future. Robert J. "Bob" Boslet, from Avon Products, had spent much of his career in the advertising agencies of Ted Bates and J. Walter Thompson, and he had met Wooters there when Wooters was still selling space for *Reader's*

---

[30] Annual Reports, 1970, 1971.

Digest.[31] Wooters hired him away from Avon in January 1972 to head what was then called the communications department, although Boslet soon found himself involved with marketing research, where he had rich experience. A year and a half later, Wooters made him Vice-President for Administration and Assistant to the President (Wooters). J. Nicholas "Nick" Hahn arrived early in 1971, a young man in his 30s. Hahn, a cousin of Wooters's wife, Betty, was well-versed in textiles and had good instincts for marketing. He had followed a family tradition (his grandfather, father, and uncles had owned and operated a woolen business in Cleveland) when, fresh out of college, he had gone to work for Dan River Mills, a major cotton textile company. Dan River transferred him to their New York office in 1964, and six years later, toward the end of 1970, he and Wooters started talking. Wooters certainly needed specialists (like Kleckner), but in Hahn he saw an ambitious generalist and perhaps something of himself. Hahn came aboard early in 1971 to head up Cotton Incorporated's west-coast office in Los Angeles. Two years later, he would become vice-president for North American sales and marketing.[32]

COTTON'S SEAL

Wooters's plan coalesced steadily through the early 1970s, but something still was missing. In order to convert cotton from an agricultural commodity into a consumer brand, he needed a symbol. Muddled at first, he knew something of what he didn't want. A lot of people had told him about the "wool mark," but at lunch in 1971 with the head of the Wool Bureau he learned they had just spent $10 million in advertising to explain what the curly little thing meant. To Wooters this didn't sound right: if you had to advertise and give press conferences to explain what a logo meant, then it probably wasn't a very strong logo. Cotton had enough problems already without making that kind of mistake.

Yet Wooters's first instinct was that cotton's symbol, too, had to be modern and nontraditional. Cotton, he felt, had an image problem going back

---

[31] As Boslet remembered Wooters from that meeting at J. Walter Thompson: "He was by far the best, most buttoned-up, most effective sales representative for any media I had ever met. He really was interested in your business and how his product could help you, rather than just trying to sell space." Robert Boslet interview, October 6, 1999.

[32] J. Nicholas Hahn interview, October 6, 1999; Cotton Incorporated Executive Committee Minutes, June 29, 1973.

a lot farther than even the stodgy dungarees-and-faded-cotton-frock memories of rural America. Not only was cotton "old," it was the wrong kind of "old." "I needed," Wooters said, "to get rid of the image that cotton had of blacks in the field with a hoe." He asked Pomeroy who could help, and Pomeroy recommended graphic designer Walter Landor in San Francisco.

Wooters called on Landor just a few weeks into the job, while on a trip to visit Levi Strauss, one of cotton's biggest consumers. Landor's office was on a converted ferry boat in San Francisco harbor. Well-known in his own world, Landor was not initially much taken with Wooters or his pitch for cotton. He demurred. But Wooters was a hard man to intimidate. Leafing through Landor's portfolio, he shot back: "You haven't had a decent big success story. And I'm giving you the opportunity to change an industry." Then he stomped off the gangplank back to New York. Landor telephoned a few weeks later, but Wooters said that he wasn't ready yet and would call Landor when he was. A year went by before he returned, this time with Hahn from Los Angeles and with Boslet, who was then advertising director. He now knew what he wanted. He told Landor that cotton's mark could *not* be "contemporary and symbolic." It had to be, simply, cotton and nothing but cotton. Wooters kept in close and constant touch with Evans, who convinced the board that the resulting snazzy new emblem was worth the $50,000 price tag.

Three months later, they all went back for presentations. Landor had twelve versions to show, all rendered into slick ads and letterhead. Wooters hit on one in the middle of the stack: "That's it! I looked at the other two guys, and they were agreeing. Not follow-the-leader agreeing, but really agreeing." Landor knew it. He was himself a fair salesman. With the decision made, he noted that the sun was over the yardarm and that he had a nice wine account. He suggested they break open a bottle to close the deal. "Out came a guy with a silver tray, a bottle of wine," Wooters recalled, "and the cotton seal I'd just picked etched on each glass." [33]

The Cotton Incorporated seal (or Seal of Cotton, as it quickly would become) was actually the inspiration of Landor's daughter Susan, who worked beside her father in the firm. The Landors' design for the Seal of Cotton would become one of the most successful trademarks in the history of marketing. Unlike the wool mark, it was not a symbol but rather a picture and a

---

[33] "Boslet," Wooters remembered, "ran around the back to see if he had the other eleven with the seal there too – but he didn't."

REPRODUCTION ARTWORK FOR 100% COTTON®

INSTRUCTIONS FOR USE

Cotton boll must always print white.
Proper use in print advertising: Over 1200 lines – 2″ width; 1200 lines – 1.5″ width; less than 1200 lines – 1″ width.
IMPORTANT:
The SEAL OF COTTON is Cotton Incorporated's Registered Service Mark/Trademark for fabrics and end products made of 100% Upland Cotton.
Use of the SEAL OF COTTON trademark will not be permitted without written approval or a licensing agreement from: Cotton Incorporated, 488 Madison Ave., 20th Floor, New York, NY 10022 • 212-413-8300 • www.cottoninc.com

The Seal of Cotton, commissioned by Cotton Incorporated president J. Dukes Wooters in 1973 and designed by the studio of Walter Landor in San Francisco, marked an early milestone in the campaign to convert cotton, an overabundant agricultural commodity, into a sought-after consumer brand.

word – "cotton." It needed no other caption. The white cotton boll, rising up from the two tees of the word "cotton" and laid against a background of earth-tone brown, sent several positive messages at once. If nature was good, then cotton was good. With the farmer's help, cotton renewed itself year after year. Cotton had roots, but it also had bloom. Cotton was pure, soft, comforting, and natural. Cotton was something familiar that you wanted to have and keep around.

Creating the Seal of Cotton was but a first step on the long march to rescue cotton from its descent to obsolescence. In time, even without the word, the image would become instantly recognizable to millions around the world. In the hands of Cotton Incorporated's marketing teams and its advertising agency Ogilvy & Mather, the cotton seal would make possible the branded identification of apparel and home fabrics containing cotton. In the years ahead, the relationship between consumer awareness of the seal and cotton's recapturing market share was apparent. Market share bottomed out in 1973 at 33 percent. By the end of 1973, the year of its introduction, 18 percent of consumers could identify the seal. By the end of 1976, when awareness had jumped to 46 percent, market share was nudging back upward to 36 percent. It stayed there during most of the inflation-ridden 1970s and then resumed a steady rise. The seal led the way. More than half of American consumers recognized it by 1978. By 1980, 57 percent perceived it to connote "quality," "comfort," and "value."[34] By 1990, it had garnered 700 licensees.

DEPARTURE AND LEGACY

An archetypal start-up talent; a builder with boundless energy, a tightly focused vision, and fire in his eyes; a gatherer of other great talent and inspirer of great loyalty to himself and his cause – Wooters was unyielding. "I don't like to compromise," he said.[35] It was this characteristic that made him a lightning rod for Cotton Incorporated's critics and that otherwise wore people out, even his friends. Not even his greatest patrons – Hervey Evans, Jerry Sayre, Keith Walden, L. C. Unfred, Morgan Nelson – could "keep the flies off" forever. In 1982, his contract was not renewed.

In Nick Hahn, Wooters had prepared a successor who offered, in addition to top-flight skills as a marketer, political sensibilities that Wooters

[34] Wooters interview, February 20, 1999; Cotton Incorporated Annual Report, 1992.
[35] Wooters interview, February 20, 1999.

himself sorely lacked. Hahn consolidated the gains for cotton that had begun under his mentor, raised Cotton Incorporated's marketing to new levels
of sophistication, and conciliated its sometimes contentious stakeholders.
Wooters had left before he had planned to but Hahn left, just two years later,
before anyone expected him to. Tempted by another opportunity, he gave
short notice and caught Cotton Incorporated's board of directors (themselves cotton growers) off guard. With no succession plan, they turned to
insider Bob Boslet. Near retirement, Boslet presided during a difficult time
of constrained budgets and programs. When Hahn returned, quite by surprise, three years later, Boslet stepped aside. This time, Hahn stayed into
the mid-1990s; when he left again, the board was prepared with a well-
apprenticed successor, J. Berrye Worsham III.

In addition to their responsibility for research and promotion, all of these
leaders faced the ongoing task of managing Cotton Incorporated's unique
structure, and all needed enough political skills to deal with challenges
from both outside the company and within its own constituency. Tech-
nically "owned" by its private board, it was beholden for its funding to a
quasi-public entity (the Cotton Board), and through the Cotton Board was
responsible to a government department (the USDA), and through the USDA
to the Congress. Although all of the money (for the first twenty years) came
from growers' own pockets and so was in that sense "private" money, its
collection by authority of federal statute and through the agency of a quasi-
public entity colored it, to some degree, with the public interest. It was a
setup that institutionalized tension, inviting as it did conflicting interpreta-
tions of just how independent Cotton Incorporated could or should be and
how freely its management would be allowed to operate. Tension increased
when the original enabling legislation was amended in 1991 to provide for
equivalent assessment of cotton importers for support of research and promotion and, for the first time, to make the growers' own assessment truly
mandatory by eliminating the refund provision of the 1966 Act.

In the beginning, to operate the company as independently as possible,
Wooters took full advantage of the buffer that the Cotton Board represented between Cotton Incorporated and its would-be political masters at
the USDA. Independence was crucial to the company's early victories and
was an important part of the legacy that Wooters left his successors. But
it also set the stage for periodic episodes of encroachment by government
bodies seeking to assert greater control. Gradually, Cotton Incorporated
would evolve from Wooters's freewheeling start-up style to an organization

highly conscious of its reporting responsibilities to the USDA, and one that was more alert to managing all political interests that claimed a stake in it. Yet the more successful the company was, the more tempting a target it became for journalists, government investigators, and political opponents. That Cotton Incorporated survived was testimony to Wooters's strategy, which through years of unstable funding and shifting political fortunes worked to restore cotton to its historical leadership in the American textile market.

PART THREE
MANAGING THE MARKET

6

CREATING CONSUMPTION

Why should farmers across the cotton belt care what went on in the distant precincts of Manhattan? Dukes Wooters thought he had a reason why they should. As he said to one grower during a trip to the field, "you're not just raising a crop, you're selling fashion on Seventh Avenue." Wooters told every grower who would listen that "it was far more valuable to own a market than a crop."[1] The market for cotton, in Wooters's idealized conception, was a continuous loop that bound thousands of cotton farmers to millions of consumers through the good offices of textile mills, clothing manufacturers, and retailers. The relationships all along the loop were dynamic and interdependent, as consumers altered their preferences and as producers, mills, and manufacturers improved their products. To put it more simply, growing cotton and buying shirts were but two ends of the same big business.

This was the radical viewpoint that Wooters brought to Cotton Incorporated, whose mission was to give growers more "ownership" of the market by helping them manage the entire chain of relationships within it. Cotton Incorporated could do so by coordinating three critical "intermediate" functions – research, development, and promotion – that linked producers to consumers: from the field and laboratory to the mills, and on to Seventh Avenue. Only with concerted coordination of these intermediate functions would cotton sales increase and production be sustained. The results of the strategy are clear. Cotton's market share, which began to improve for the first time during the early 1980s, accelerated after 1985 to reach 60 percent by the end of the century.[2]

---

[1] "Letter to American Cotton Producers," Cotton Incorporated Annual Report, 1979.
[2] "An Evaluation of Cotton's Share Gains, 1975–1992," Cotton Incorporated.

PULL AND PUSH

The first step was to discern consumers' true desires for fabrics and then promote cotton to meet those desires. Advertising would be designed to "pull" cotton back into consumer consciousness. This looked to be the obvious part. Before Cotton Incorporated, both the National Cotton Council and the Cotton Producers Institute had tried their hands at it.[3] The trouble was, they had advertised the wrong things – largely 100 percent cottons – when consumers were beguiled by the synthetics' claims to no-iron convenience. The early cotton advertising efforts had no basis in any analysis of consumer needs. The effectiveness of any pull from advertising would depend directly upon the reality of an improved product, which in turn depended on applied fiber and fabric research. Without research and development, advertising could not claim much for long. And without product credibility to support subsequent building of a brand, no brand would ever be built.

It would also be necessary to "push" cotton onto the growers' first customer, the textile mills. Many mills had abandoned or drastically reduced their use of cotton in response to the sheer weight of advertising and merchandising campaigns mounted by the chemical companies for synthetics. In fact, advertising was the prerequisite for successful selling of cotton at the mill level. If it seemed that consumers were persuaded to buy synthetics, then that was the only signal mills needed. What mills could sell, mills would run, and advertising got their attention.[4]

When the Seal of Cotton symbol was created in 1973, there was not a great deal for it to symbolize nor much to advertise.[5] The Seal was an example of perception running ahead of reality, which was dangerous. Wooters did not want to leap precipitously into an advertising campaign until he could identify a market for cotton and convince himself that cotton, as a quality product, really had what it took to compete.

BOOMERS

The market research began with a close analysis of demographics. How did different groups of people clothe themselves and furnish their homes? The starchy prep-school crowd of Wooters's class and generation, who could

[3] See Chapter 4, "Synthetic Shock."
[4] Tom O'Gorman (formerly of Milliken, Burlington), Glenoit Mills, interview, May 22, 2000.
[5] See Chapter 5, "Creating Cotton Incorporated."

afford to buy their cotton shirts at Brooks Brothers and have them laundered professionally, were too small a segment to matter to mass-market producers. In contrast, the broad middle class of consumers from that same generation had largely forsaken cotton for the wash-and-wear convenience and economy of synthetics. By the 1970s, that generation was well into its early 50s – its families mostly raised and its biggest spending years behind it. But their children, the great population bulge of post–World War II "Baby Boomers" born between 1946 and 1964, were – as good luck would have it – already clad in cotton.

In marketing, when there is a choice, it is easier to pander than to proselytize, and for Cotton Incorporated the Baby Boomers presented a choice. Why bother trying to re-convert the parents, so set in their synthetics ways, back to cotton when the kids were in the tent already? It was so obvious as to be easy to miss. American youth of the sixties and early seventies, male and female alike, turned out for just about any occasion in T-shirts and blue jeans. In the name of nonconformity, they conformed to a dress code that had turned denim, that most homely and utilitarian of fabrics, into a fashion.

For cotton growers, denim represented an end-product stronghold that the synthetics at the height of their power had never significantly penetrated. Its history reached well back into the nineteenth century; though probably of European origin, denim – used in "dungarees" or "overalls" – became known as the quintessentially American fabric. Makers Loeb Strauss (later changed to "Levi," who first invented the copper rivets) and H. D. Lee made fortunes supplying the blue cotton pants to millions of America's farmers, miners, and factory workers. In the 1930s, the popularity of Hollywood westerns and denim-clad cowboy heroes like Gary Cooper, Gene Autry, and John Wayne made "authentic cowboy pants" something of a fashion rage for the first time. In 1935, Levi's even introduced a narrow-waisted, broad-hipped "Lady Levi's" product as part of its line, "Dude Ranch Duds." Katharine Hepburn fashioned sporty denim bottoms and daring halter-tops. In the 1939 film *The Women,* ladies killing time on a dude ranch while waiting for a Reno divorce all wore jeans.[6] Lee Jeans went on to become the predominant women's brand.

Yet the way the urban and suburban Baby Boomers that came of age in the 1960s adopted denim was something new. There is little evidence

---

[6] "The Story of Jeans: In the Beginning," *Women's Wear Daily,* May 2000.

that they took to jeans because clever marketers persuaded them to. Jeans looked unkempt, required little care, were comfortable, and – perhaps most important – projected an image that rebuked the buttoned-down fashion statements of the Boomers' parents' generation. For the budding "counterculture," jeans were an emblem of protest that were bound up with a range of rebellious acts – from recreational drug use and "sexual revolution" to civil rights and antiwar demonstrations.

To cotton's marketers, all this represented a gift without price. The danger was that it would be only a one-time gift if, as they aged, Boomers abandoned their youthful enthusiasm for denim in favor of some other clothing statement fashioned from some other ingredient. To forestall this fate, it was necessary to sell not just denim but also a reason for preferring it. How could fashion-conscious wearers of jeans be turned into fiber-conscious consumers of cotton?

Synthetics manufacturers had raised the art of selling fiber consciousness to a high level. They had already taught the textile industry how to become both consumer- and production-oriented. Until DuPont's intensive marketing of its polyester and acrylic fibers Dacron and Orlon starting in the 1950s, the textile industry and producers of natural fibers in particular had offered consumers (much like Henry Ford did with black Model Ts) "any textile you want as long as it's cotton, or wool, or silk."[7]

Cotton Incorporated's marketing staff studied DuPont's strategy closely and crafted an advertising approach that was centered on the performance characteristics of cotton garments. It was an artful exercise in reinforcing the obvious and the first to target the Baby Boomers, who had a lifetime of textile purchases still before them. It rested on the assumption that the consumer could be made to care about fiber content – that one could be made

---

[7] How the synthetics manufacturers had done it was no secret. Eastman Chemicals vice president Robert L. Churchill explained the steps in 1965: "A producer today has one group of marketing people who do personal selling to the mills ... he has another group who services the dyers and finishers to assist them in their work with fabrics containing his fibers ... still another group works with finished goods suppliers ... still another group concentrates on the manufacturers of garments and home furnishings ... and a last group carries the story of all that has gone on before to the retailers, using the promotional tools that will help the retailers move the goods off the shelves. All these advertising and promotional efforts have one prime objective: to help our customers sell our products to the eventual consumer and to make a profit. This is our real job – not only to sell fiber to mills, but to help the mills sell their customers, and help the garment manufacturers sell the retailers, and last, but far from least, help the retailer sell the public." Speech to International Federation of Cotton and Allied Textile Industries, San Francisco, October 18, 1965.

"fiber conscious" – so long as the fiber did something that seemed uniquely desirable.

Advertising's pull was essential in demonstrating the young company's worth to its constituents and in keeping its marketing program moving at all other levels. Its long-term impact is hard to overstate. With no product of its own to sell, Cotton Incorporated instead sold consciousness. Its advertising over three decades of campaigns was essentially consistent in this regard. From his vantage nearly thirty years later, Cotton Incorporated's fourth president, J. Berrye Worsham III, concluded that cotton had succeeded in rebuilding market share "largely because of our major long-term investment in consumer advertising."[8]

FIRST, THE SIGN

Ira Livingston came to Cotton Incorporated in 1975 after working for seven years at J. P. Stevens. He was, by training, a textile engineer who had never taken a formal course in marketing. Along with advertising professional Ric Hendee, who before coming to Cotton Incorporated had long experience at the J. Walter Thompson agency, Livingston in the 1990s oversaw the most recent iterations of Cotton Incorporated's well-established advertising program. He recalled the risk of that strategy in the early years: "We made a big leap to go directly to the consumer, because eventually if we could get the consumer buying more product, then the mills, manufacturers and retailers would have to respond."[9]

"Eventually" is a key word, for the risk in all advertising lies in the lag between money spent and subsequent benefit achieved in the shape of an uptick in demand for the product being advertised. The lag for cotton was not insignificant. Consumer advertising began in 1971, yet cotton's market share continued to decline for two more years – to its historic low of 33 percent in 1973. The following year it nudged up two percentage points, where it hovered through 1980 before commencing a gratifying uninterrupted rise to 60 percent in 1998. It took management consistency and owner patience to stay such a course.

It probably helped that the medium chosen to carry the message to consumers was almost exclusively network television. This set cotton apart

[8] J. Berrye Worsham, Cotton Incorporated, 1999.
[9] Ira Livingston, Cotton Incorporated, interview, November 16, 1998.

from other agricultural marketing programs and revealed its fundamentally different intent, generating consumer loyalty to an ingredient textile product and ultimately to a brand. The first television ads, created by the Jack Byrne Agency and overseen by Tom Akeson (first director of advertising at Cotton Incorporated), revolved around a budding cultural anxiety that had its origins in the Boomers' counterculture of the 1960s: if something was "natural" then it must, somehow, be better. This was not without irony. Cotton Incorporated was financed and directed by largely southern, church-going, culturally conservative cotton growers ideologically worlds away from the Woodstock Generation that had made denim and T-shirts fashionable. Yet there was an implicit common interest between them that good advertising might exploit. Few hippies stayed hippies forever and, as they grew up and turned in their T-shirts for button-downs, their youthful preference for clothing could be transformed into preference for cotton itself. The early ads thus strove to forge a link from adjectives to noun – from *natural* and *better* to *cotton*.

When Cotton Incorporated made its TV debut in 1971, the oldest Baby Boomers were just turning 25. The actors in the ads looked about 25, too. For the next twenty years, actors and advertising matured together. Tactics evolved to convince textile manufacturers, who themselves had been sold hard on synthetics, to make more cotton products. Under the tag line "Cotton: It's a Natural Wonder" (with "Brought to You by Cotton Incorporated and America's Cotton Growers" tucked in at the bottom of the screen), for example, viewers learned that the real reason for their attachment to those scruffy old blue jeans was that "Levi's still makes them that way: all 100 percent cotton." Levi's had for years been an enormously powerful retail brand, to the point of having entered the vernacular as a synonym for blue jeans: the trademark lawyer's worst nightmare but the honest marketer's dream. Here, "still" was the key word linking cotton to that rock-ribbed heritage. There was a romantic, nostalgic side of 1960s radicalism (as in "let's get back to 'simpler, better times'"), and Levi's appealed directly to it. "Come Home to Cotton," as the theme for cotton's home furnishings advertising put it, would become a summons that was hard to resist.[10]

While some early seventies clothing styles evoke shudders of embarrassment today, the Seal of Cotton trademark endures as a model of tasteful

---

[10] Cotton Incorporated advertising archive.

simplicity and enduring clarity.[11] From its conception in 1973, the seal gave cotton an identity of its own, separate from that of the brand names of manufactured cotton products. It quickly took off in public awareness and proved itself a rare masterpiece of design *cum* communication. No synthetics manufacturer had anything to approach it. The seal made it possible for consumers to identify cotton products more easily once they did get back into the marketplace, and no Cotton Incorporated advertising after 1973 would ever appear without it. The seal closed the loop of marketing perception and reality, where advertising image reinforced product qualities even as the product conjured the image.[12]

At first, television ads showed the seal identifying products of 100 percent cotton, whose performance story was self-evident and whose market strength had proven less vulnerable to synthetics. This was obviously true of denim – but also of towels and to some extent bedding: "You can count on all-cotton towels to be soft and thirsty," said the pretty model stepping out of the shower, primly wrapped in cotton terry. "You can count on cotton sheets to be fresh and comfortable," said the well-covered couple tucking into the king-size bed.[13]

To limit consumer advertising to "all cottons," however, was to surrender large swaths of the market that had been successfully staked out by blends. Therefore, the campaign to build fiber consciousness in consumers adapted to suit development of new blended products. In 1974, Cotton Incorporated had convinced Springs Mills to tip the balance back toward cotton in the blended fabrics it sold for shirting and bedding. Dubbed "Natural Blend," which carried the requirement of at least 60 percent cotton content (the seal was withheld from products carrying less), the fabric first appeared the next year at retail when Manhattan Shirts (then the country's largest branded shirt maker) introduced the first Natural Blend men's dress shirt. A parade of competitors followed, with Sears and J. C. Penney soon offering their own branded, cotton-rich shirts for both men and women. Cannon introduced "Comfortcale" cotton-rich sheets in 1977, with Montgomery Ward offering their own-label Natural Blend sheets and pillowcases

---

[11] On the origins of the cotton seal, see Chapter 5, "Creating Cotton Incorporated."

[12] The seal also gave Cotton Incorporated's producer-directors something to wear with pride. Each one, upon election to the board, was presented – in the trademark pale blue box from Tiffany's – a lapel pin bearing the seal. Retiring chairmen received a pin with one small diamond.

[13] Cotton Incorporated advertising archive.

the next season. In 1979, Fieldcrest introduced its Natural Blend sheet called "Dreamspun," with a corespun construction initiated by Cotton Incorporated that contained 65 percent cotton. Sears' similar Natural Blend sheeting product was not far behind.[14]

The phrase "The More Cotton, the Better You Feel" in television commercials touted this shift, aiming to convince manufacturers to add ever more cotton and to educate consumers to be more aware of fabric blend levels. The blue-jeaned Boomers of the 1960s were busy making a living and starting families in Natural Blend shirts and skirts a decade later. Cotton Incorporated advertising reflected their transition to a new stage of life. One particularly clever television spot played gently to the movement of more and more women out of the home and into the paid workforce. The scene was the bedroom and a couple packing for a business trip. The wife exclaims how she has bought the husband some new Natural Blend shirts for the occasion: "So comfortable, and with this new cotton-rich blend you won't even have to iron them!" The husband replies with a cheery "Thanks, honey," but then stands aside as she, not he, picks up the suitcase and briefcase and sets out for the road. Another, shorter take conveyed a similar message, the wife bursting onto the scene with a uncompromising "I'd do *anything* for James – except iron his shirts."[15]

ENTER O&M

The clarity of Cotton Incorporated's television advertising can be ascribed in no small measure to the company's long-running relationship with the advertising agency of Ogilvy & Mather (O&M). O&M came to cotton through the influence of Robert J. Boslet, Cotton Incorporated's third president, who had worked with O&M while vice-president for advertising at Avon Products.[16] O&M had a reputation in the industry for extremely high creative quality; though Cotton Incorporated would never pay fees comparable to O&M's bigger clients, the account offered the opportunity to do consistently top-quality work. Wooters knew Bill Phillips, who had worked for O&M in Brazil (where Wooters had worked for *Reader's Digest*) and who would soon become O&M's president. The two top men retained a good relationship for many years, which probably got little old Cotton

---

[14] Cotton Incorporated Annual Reports, 1975–1979.
[15] Cotton Incorporated advertising archive.
[16] Robert J. Boslet interview, October 6, 1999; J. Dukes Wooters interview, July 7, 2000.

Incorporated better treatment from a famous agency (with clients the likes of IBM) than might otherwise have been the case.

Because Cotton Incorporated had relatively little to spend, O&M faced a tricky creative, financial, and political challenge. Cotton could "never do it with tonnage alone," recalled Mike Vaughn, in charge of the account since the late 1980s. "We always needed ways to make them appear bigger players than they actually were."[17] It was also important, especially in the early years, that the cotton growers who paid for the program be brought along, too. This was one of the reasons that the early campaigns concentrated on the functional, performance aspects of cotton – no-nonsense matters that practical farmers and their wives readily appreciated. John Blaney, O&M's manager of the cotton account during the 1970s and 1980s, remembered how making the ads acceptable and understandable to growers in Greenville, Mississippi, and Lubbock, Texas – as well as to Cotton Incorporated's professional staff in New York City (not to mention officials at the Department of Agriculture) – was the "politically right and necessary thing to do."[18]

O&M soon added its own special flourishes. Walter Landor and his daughter had created the cotton seal in pen and ink. O&M animated the seal for the medium of television – making it appear to grow in a few seconds before the viewer's eyes, up from the good brown earth and into a full-blown, soft, white cotton boll. And it pioneered one of cotton's earliest major media tie-ins: its regular appearance, starting in 1977, on NBC's early morning "Today" show. "Farmers are up early," Blaney explained, "and could see for themselves what their advertising dollars were buying."[19]

Its association with "Today" vaulted Cotton Incorporated into the bigtime of consumer advertising. As more and more cotton products were selected for promotion, staff and O&M were able to turn to trusted and familiar television personalities to do live commercials right on the set. The approach yielded an immediacy and authenticity that was hard to achieve with slicker, more expensive ads. Viewers saw Barbara Walters in a bright Hawaiian shirt posed beside the seal in an outdoor tropical setting, expressing her confidence that cotton was "doing a lot to make *your* life more comfortable. I know it's making *my* life comfortable right now ...." The perpetually cheerful Gene Shalit, with his bushy signature mustache and

[17] Mike Vaughn, Ogilvy & Mather, interview, June 27, 2000.
[18] John Blaney, Ogilvy & Mather (retired), interview, June 27, 2000.
[19] Ibid.

Afro coiffure, plumped for cotton products available at Sears and other big retailers. Among O&M staff assigned to the cotton account, the "Today" engagement was "notorious." They were being facetious, of course, but without a doubt the gig was hard work. Live broadcast of "Today" began at 6 A.M. but preparation started at 4 A.M., and O&M people had to be on the set to be sure Barbara and Gene were properly coached and knew what was expected. Using the hosts themselves to make cotton's pitch beneficially blurred the lines between editorial content and advertising message and helped cotton ride the credibility of famous television personalities.

GETTING ATTENTION

Cotton Incorporated and O&M had more than the usual client–agency relationship. "Wooters and Cotton Incorporated were a dream to work with," remembered John Blaney. "They had imagination and drive and they knew what they wanted. Dukes always pushed, pushed, pushed."[20] It was a "SWAT team–like setup": there were close ties among a few key people at the client and the agency over many years, and the client felt they were getting high value for the modest sums they could spend while the agency felt that the fight for cotton was a good cause and worthy of one's best work – even if not the best fees. Stretching those limited dollars was never easy, and Wooters set the standard for being a tough advertising buyer and for husbanding scarce resources so that cotton's advertising could make a deceptively large splash.

One of the largest was at the 1976 Olympic Winter Games at Innsbruck, Austria. Cotton Incorporated was only seven years old and had a total budget that year of just over $17 million, but they became a television sponsor of this high-profile event.[21] Wooters had planned for this two years ahead, and he used the occasion to piggyback public relations and merchandising. As always, the seal was there and usually with a plug for the virtues of some cotton product: 100 percent cotton denim jeans or Natural Blend shirts. Cotton Incorporated's cost for the ads was $10 million, but Wooters leveraged that investment to pay returns long after the Olympics became history.

In the meantime, Wooters had approached Arrow Shirt company president Henry Henley with a deal. "Henry, we're going to put you on television

---

[20] Ibid.
[21] Cotton Incorporated Annual Report, 1977.

[Arrow had no TV budget], and we're going to do it at the Winter Games. Here's how it's going to go. You sew the Seal of Cotton onto the label of every cotton-rich shirt you make, and you let my people attend your sales meetings because your people have forgotten what cotton's all about, and they need to be told how cotton performs and why you're into 60/40 Natural Blend, anyway." Wooters successfully proposed a contest among Arrow salesmen: a "President's Award," and a check for $5,000, would go to whomever sold the most cotton merchandise over quota.[22] This arrangement thus leveraged an advertising opportunity into a merchandising package worth more than anything Cotton Incorporated itself could afford.

Wooters liked to "work the top" and had assigned to himself the job of making Cotton Incorporated known personally to major mill owners, manufacturers, and retailers. The Olympics were a golden opportunity to entice and reward these influential men. For the Games' two-week run, he turned Cotton Incorporated into a high-class tour operator for a select set of high-end clients. Nothing was left to chance. Don Kleckner, then vice-president for advertising and who later became vice-president for international operations, scouted the best mountainside hotel, lined up interpreters, and arranged for chauffeured Mercedes to ferry people around. Fancy invitations – embossed with the seal and festooned with red, white, and blue ribbons ("It looked like we were being invited to the White House or something," one executive's wife told her husband) – built anticipation. Wooters himself twisted arms at Pan American Airways headquarters in New York to get the carrier to add special through flights to Munich and to give him and his guests the entire first-class section.[23] He took ten guests the first week and another ten the second.

In those days, before the airlines felt the need to devote every square inch of a plane's interior to revenue space, Pan Am's 747s featured a first-class lounge with a stand-up cocktail bar, just up the spiral staircase on the top deck. It was a good spot for schmoozing, and Wooters wanted it for his guests. They included Walter Neppl, future president of J. C. Penney; Joe Lanier, president of West Point Pepperell; Willie Farah of Farah Slacks; and Whitey Lee, CEO of Lee Jeans. He wanted them to know him and each

---

[22] J. Dukes Wooters, Cotton Incorporated (retired), February 20, 1999.

[23] "I'm taking these top American executives to the Winter Games, and I would like to have a through flight to Munich," Wooters remembered telling the secretary of Pan Am's president, adding, "Lufthansa has offered me a fantastic deal. I'm not asking you to cut the rate, but I do want the whole first class." She called back three days later, everything arranged.

other better and, of course, to remember Cotton Incorporated. The truth was, most of them came because they already were impressed with the up-start marketing company unafraid to thumb its nose at DuPont and because they didn't want to be left behind just in case cotton proved itself. "Why did you come on this trip with us?" Wooters asked Whitey Lee at the air-port. "I'll tell you," Lee replied. "I wanted to see what you're all about. So I came."

Once aboard, Wooters had a captive audience and worked it shamelessly. He had made a special film showing all of Cotton Incorporated's advertising, which was screened after dinner, just before the movie. While at the Games, where athletes were the entertainment, Wooters played major domo, pump-ing for information and putting people in his debt. Neppl, from Penney's, spent an hour and a half explaining the differences between his operations and those of Sears.[24] Lanier, who had grown up around West Point Pep-perell, learned as much as his host. "There's Whitey Lee over there," he remarked to Wooters. "He's my biggest single customer, and I've never even met him before."[25]

The $10 million affair smacked of extravagance to some growers and offi-cials at the USDA, unaccustomed to the magnitude of promotional spending in the corporate world. Wooters was unapologetic, and some prestigious growers – including Hervey Evans from North Carolina, L. C. Unfred from Texas, and Morgan Nelson from New Mexico – backed him to the hilt. Such opportunities as the Olympics were rare, both to broadcast cotton's image to an enormous audience of TV-watching consumers and to influ-ence leaders of a textile industry, where cotton's competitors had for years spent lavishly and well.

TOUTING PERFORMANCE

The success of television advertising depended on connecting the fiber with something cotton actually did for consumers, thus differentiating cotton from other fibers that did not. This could mean appealing to a particular physical characteristic such as "comfort" or, as happened when synthetics

---

[24] Penney's had very strict rules: "You never drink at lunch and you never accept anything from anybody." But, as Neppl explained to Wooters: "We don't buy anything from you directly; that's why I came." Wooters remembered, however, that "the Sears guys didn't care ... we just had a ball. Everybody enjoyed it."

[25] Wooters interview.

threatened to invade cotton's greatest single stronghold, appealing to a particular memory. Such was the case with jeans.

In 1977 and 1978, Levi Strauss attempted something new and different in denim: a blend.[26] Although the mix was modest (never more than 15 percent polyester to 85 percent cotton) and although blending probably did yield a stronger cloth, the strategy turned into a memorable marketing blunder. Cotton Incorporated pounced hard and made Levi's strategy seem more radical than it really was. O&M's scripts reminded consumers that the denim they had known and loved since childhood was 100 percent cotton (more recently finished with processes like Sanforset that made for easier care) and *only* 100 percent cotton. In the style of the 1970s, when female modesty in the media started its long decline, the campaign featured pretty young women from the rear, clad in tight denims that were available – along with lawnmowers, washing machines, and power tools – at your friendly hometown Sears.

The sexy "girl next door" quality of those ads recalled the shifting social mores of the 1970s, which found the Boomer generation and their parents divided on so many issues. This was tricky territory for advertisers, but Cotton Incorporated, guided by O&M, managed to avoid major missteps and to find a voice for cotton that modulated credibly with the times. The central theme was this: in a world filled with fakery, cotton was real. It performed the way you wanted. Wearing it made you feel good – not just physically, but emotionally too. You could, with confidence, "come home to cotton."

O&M sniffed paydirt in emphasizing the perceived benefits of cotton over its substitutes, and it was not above a little synthetics bashing to make the point. It was important to get the clichés right. In one especially famous scene from the 1968 film *The Graduate,* a puzzled Boomer (played by Dustin Hoffman) is advised by a pudgy friend of his father that the future, his future, is "plastics."[27] The ridicule potential in such an atmosphere was too good to waste: "You know, even in a plastic world, some things should never change – like blue jeans." The actor in this late-1970s Cotton Incorporated ad portrayed a hip radio disc jockey whose hipness, however,

---

[26] Cotton Incorporated had first offered to work with Levi on a Sanforset jean, but Levi demurred. Cotton Incorporated then turned to Wrangler. Levi responded by coming out with a blend.

[27] The same scene, were it written today, would no doubt substitute "information" for "plastics" and would present promoters of things natural (like cotton) no such opportunity as fortuitously fell in their laps thirty years ago. Such is the power of timing.

called for cotton in his jeans just as it did for cool recording artists on his program. "There's nothing plastic or phony about them. Look at the label: 100 percent cotton denim. That's why jeans fit and feel natural and wash cotton clean." A tough, take-that ending gave no quarter: "If denim jeans aren't all cotton, they're not jeans at all." [28]

In the early 1980s, as cotton's market share began to edge upward, cotton's advertising voice grew more confident – as did the nation's mood after a decade that had been through the Vietnam War, two oil shocks, and rampant inflation. O&M hit upon an idea, long the preserve of the synthetics manufacturers, that fit well with the freshened spirit of the times and that, with technical improvements in cotton fabrics (made possible in part by better breeding programs), made its message believable. This was the portrayal of cotton as a "performance" fiber. [29] Television viewers were wowed as ballerina Heather Watts, in front of New York's Lincoln Center, proclaimed the wonders of her 100 percent cotton Ship'n'Shore shirts: "All cotton plus permanent press: now *that's* high performance." Out West, champion rodeo rider Marty Hinson extolled his Wrangler jeans – "no pucker, no shrink" – as the uniform of success in the ring and as the ticket to the pretty girl (in close-fitting Wranglers of her own) in the shiny pick-up after the show.

"Performance," as a fabric and fiber concept, awaited just the right phrase for expression in advertising form. "True Performance," originated at Cotton Incorporated and developed and executed by O&M in the early 1980s, evoked probably the most compelling image of cotton since coining of the phrase "King Cotton" in the 1850s. "True Performance" dominated Cotton Incorporated advertising through the decade, and a television viewer could tire out just watching all those cyclists, sailors, and pole-vaulters strenuously "performing" in their cotton duds. Physical fitness, jogging, and trimming down were all back "in" in the eighties. "True Performance" capitalized on that mood and broadcast the message that cotton was back in, too, and that indeed it was not just a fighter good for a round or two but a runner in shape to go the distance.

The "True Performance" campaigns were not limited to television; they were coordinated with an elaborate labeling effort at the retail level. Attractive "True Performance" hang-tags, depicting the slogan and the Seal of

---

[28] Cotton Incorporated advertising archive. Levi Strauss, in fact, soon gave up on polyester-blended denim and has stuck with cotton ever since.

[29] On the textile research that improved cotton's performance, see Chapter 7.

Cotton, appeared on millions of garments made of cotton and cotton-rich blends on the racks of the biggest retailers and smallest specialty shops. The television spots worked variations on the performance theme, with soft iterations like "Once you get a feel for cotton ... Abandon yourself to the feel of cotton ... Take comfort in cotton ...."

"True Performance" was a watershed campaign. But even after smart, consistent advertising and the introduction of improved products began to turn the tide for cotton, a problem remained. Demand for particular types of cotton apparel and home furnishings, like demand for many other consumer products, inevitably varied with fashion and the whim of consumer tastes. The challenge therefore was to even out these peaks and valleys by cultivating in the consumer's mind loyalty to cotton as a necessary component to a desired way of life, which transcended choices about any of the particular products that happened to contain it.

COTTON'S BRAND

"Take your product and turn it into a brand." This was article 1 in the gospel of advertising according to David Ogilvy. It was the necessary next step if cotton's comeback were to be made secure. Ads in the early campaigns had typically ended with such cooperative tags as "Look for the Seal of Cotton on 100 percent cotton Martex towels available at Bloomingdales," and O&M in fact produced them in a highly modular manner that permitted different retail partners to be easily slotted into the same creative material. In spirit, it was old-fashioned co-op advertising (sharing the billing in order to leverage resources), although in fact only Cotton Incorporated paid for it. They touted cotton's particular physical benefits – breatheability, washability, comfort – which were essential to tilting consumers' fiber consciousness away from synthetics. It was a message repeated again and again, for nearly twenty years, until consumer behavior could be observed to change. Once it did, as was evident through the 1980s when cotton's market share climbed from 36 to 50 percent and consumer recognition of the seal crested at 70 percent, the foundation was in place to enable implementation of David Ogilvy's belief about taking the product and conjuring from it the brand.

In 1987, Nick Hahn, who had returned to Cotton Incorporated for a second stint as president, changed the substance and the style of the company's advertising. "True Performance" and its variants, Hahn judged, had done their job well, establishing cotton's benefits in consumers' minds. It was now time to exploit their conversion back to cotton and to make sure it would stick.[30] He left little to chance. In focus groups and one-on-one interviews, O&M's research staff prompted people to talk about fiber, fabrics, garments, cotton, wool, polyester, and anything to do with clothing. For a student of body language, something interesting turned up. The researchers observed a curious physical dynamic whenever people started talking about cotton. Typically, they would caress their arms, and as they spoke their vocabulary became notably more tactile. Those present later recounted the story with a hint of embarrassment; it sounded silly. But it wasn't.

The contrasts were revealing. Talking about wool, interviewees would say wool was warm and scratchy. Talking about polyester, they would say polyester doesn't breathe so it's sticky and hot and sometimes pills. But when they got to cotton, they would start immediately saying there was "something about the feel of cotton." Simultaneously, they would start touching themselves, whether they had cotton on or not. "They would," remembered cotton's second manager at O&M, Mike Vaughn, "almost go into a fetal position."

Body and mind apparently worked together. While figuratively and to a degree literally "curling up," subjects talked about how they liked to have cotton close to their skin – about how little babies were bundled in cotton from the start of life and a whole array of emotion-laden images connecting cotton with stages of a person's life. No one used the words "cradle-to-grave," but the theme was unmistakable that cotton played a role in life from birth to death. The same emotional vocabulary was emphatically not present when people talked about any other fabric or fiber. Men, women, young people, old folks – it made no difference. When anyone started talking about cotton, emotions usurped the stage.[31] Out of this, O&M's creative team proposed the deceptively simple phrase that would be the basis for the new campaign to build cotton's brand: "The Fabric of Our Lives."

For Cotton Incorporated, the Fabric of Our Lives campaign was "revolutionary, unlike anything they had ever done before." It did not talk about performance features at all and did away with the mentions of manufacturers and retailers at the tail end. The first iterations were shot in a relatively avant-garde style directed by Leslie Dektor. This represented a strategic

[30] J. Nicholas Hahn interview, October 6, 1999.
[31] Mike Vaughn interview, June 27, 2000.

To establish the image of cotton as a desirable consumer brand, Cotton Incorporated relied heavily on television advertising. Early campaigns, like "Take Comfort in Cotton" (1986), touted cotton's superior qualities compared with synthetics and evolved into the more emotion-laden style of "The Fabric of Our Lives" (1992, 1996).

decision for Cotton Incorporated the company, as well as for cotton the brand. The thinking was that Cotton Incorporated had to be perceived within the industry as a major marketing force. It was an example of the principle, famously put by Marshall McLuhan, that the medium is the message. Thus while the advertising at one level was for cotton the brand, at a second level it was also the voice of Cotton Incorporated the company, which had to be heard as the voice of industry leadership. Cotton Incorporated and its advertising could never afford to look dated. This was why, historically, O&M had tried to renew cotton's campaigns every three years or so – even under the old scheme, when the message was not brand but product qualities.

"Violent agreement," as O&M chairman Shelly Lazarus liked to put it, captured the mood all around the table when the new approach was first laid out. Hahn liked it, as did his subordinates. The O&M people thought it would work but said it was risky. It lacked the precision of the earlier campaigns in one critical respect. The target audience had changed. No longer would Baby Boomers alone be in the crosshairs. While the Boomers would never be forgotten even as they aged, cotton "cradle to grave" commanded, right out of the gate, other targets: the Boomers' parents and, before long, the Boomers' children, too.

Old worries about money dictated a major change in the company's media strategy. In the late 1980s, the cotton check-off program was bedeviled by high levels of grower refunds and hence operating budgets were lower, when adjusted for inflation, than at the beginning of the decade.[32] With a new advertising concept to launch and not just a well-tried one to reiterate, and "without buckets full of money to spend," it was important to find the tactics ("stunts," recalled O&M's Vaughn, who authored some of them) that would make a little money look as if it were a lot. If only one could create the impression that consumers were seeing more advertising than they really were.

For launch of the initial Fabric of Our Lives campaign, they did this by laying down what was, for the time, a very big bet. Out of a $7 million advertising budget, Hahn authorized and O&M spent $2 million in one day: Thanksgiving, 1989. It was a bold strategy but justified, they hoped, by two facts. Thanksgiving Day was the day before the single largest retail shopping day of the year. It was also the day when the whole family from grandmother on down could be found watching television dawn to dusk, from the Macy's Parade in the morning, through half a dozen college football games during the afternoon, to the *Sound of Music* or *E.T.* family-type movie in the evening. Cotton commercials blanketed the day; it was impossible to watch TV that Thanksgiving without seeing the cotton seal and without hearing about the Fabric of Our Lives. One hundred fourteen million viewers saw and heard it.

For that day at least, Cotton Incorporated appeared as big an advertiser as many much larger companies, and the size of its expenditure helped O&M negotiate for reinforcing TV "billboard" space that only added to the illusion: "Macy's Thanksgiving Day Parade, brought to you [in part] by

---

[32] In 1981 the budget was $22.9 million; in 1985, $18.1 million; in 1989, $22.1 million.

Cotton Incorporated. Cotton: The Fabric of Our Lives."[33] This was on top of television spots every half hour through the parade and continued during the games, the early evening news, and the movie. It was the equivalent of the splash Wooters had bought by sponsoring the Innsbruck Winter Games a dozen years before. The message had shifted, from selling the qualities of cotton to selling the brand, but the means for getting it across were remarkably constant: spend big enough to be noticed and spend with style. Subsequently, O&M sought to sustain Cotton Incorporated's media "presence" with key franchise positions (twice a week with Willard Scott on "Today"; beside Peter Jennings on ABC News; with Johnny Carson) on high-rated shows on whose image cotton could once again piggyback its own message.

GETTING EMOTIONAL

"The Fabric of Our Lives" and the Seal of Cotton looked like a marketing match made in heaven. The seal was a rare masterpiece of visual design in service to a commercial goal. It flew in the face of that day's design fashion, which favored obscure abstractions (consider the "Woolmark") and offered instead a simple, representational picture that had instant resonance on Madison Avenue, Seventh Avenue, and Main Street. As with cotton farmers themselves, what you saw was what you got. Fabric of Our Lives was probably its equal as a masterpiece of the sloganeering art, one of those exceptional bits of advertising wordcraft (in a class with "Coke, It's the Real Thing") that would have lasting emotional traction across geographies and generations.

This is not to say everyone liked it. Long since retired from Cotton Incorporated, Dukes Wooters never approved: "What does it mean? It's not selling qualities. Product qualities are what you've got to sell."[34] In embracing a new style of unvarnished advertising reality, Cotton Incorporated was not alone, but some industry critics puzzled at just what was going on. "What, you may wonder, is this?" asked *Advertising Age* of a series of Cotton Incorporated spots featuring gang members at a funeral for a slain friend, elderly depositors at the locked doors of a failed savings and loan,

---

[33] The "in part" qualifier was something O&M was ethically obliged to insist upon: there were other sponsors. Nick Hahn, ever the attack dog for Cotton Incorporated, didn't like to share nevertheless. Remembered Mike Vaughn, with a laugh: "That 'in part' just made Nick Hahn crazy."

[34] Dukes Wooters interview, February 20, 1999.

and two boys in a fistfight. "A Cuban documentary of life in America? A preview for the next 'I-Witness Video'? An Oliver Stone retrospective? Nah. It's a TV commercial. For cotton."[35]

But advertising that was, as O&M explained it, "emotionally relevant" unquestionably worked. "The Touch, the Feel, the Fabric of Our Lives," mushy as it might have sounded to an old-school ad salesman, was an instant hit with 1990s consumers. It brought to the surface an emotional bond that had grown up between consumers and cotton products over the decade and a half since the debut of the seal and subsequent product breakthroughs, and it transformed preference for products made of an ingredient called "cotton" into loyalty to a brand.

By doing so, Cotton Incorporated negotiated a new turn in the evolving history of consumption. This was the rise of the informed, involved consumer of the prosperous late 1980s and 1990s, who had no experience of product scarcity but who suffered instead scarcities of time, attention, and trust and for whom the desire for "authenticity" would take on near-spiritual dimensions. The emotional linkage between liking a product and perceiving it as authentic accounted for some of the great brand successes of the era. A branded product or service that made its personality seem most like the consumer's own had enormous persuasive power. This was the secret of brands like Starbucks, The Body Shop, and Virgin Atlantic.[36] It was also the secret of cotton. Early evidence (after that first Thanksgiving extravaganza) that the concept worked was largely anecdotal but compelling. Consumers, the trade, and the growers all raved. Tracking studies subsequently showed continued lifts in awareness of the seal and positive attitudes toward cotton. It was more than enough to suggest that Cotton Incorporated and O&M had once again hit upon a winner.

---

[35] Bob Garfield, "Cynical Vérité: The Dark Side of Those de-Glammed, True-Life Ads," *Washington Post*, May 23, 1993. "In 'truth'," he went on, "there were some unfortunate consequences. The people at Cotton Inc. [sic] invoke funerals, shuttered S&Ls and other harsh images presumably to position their product as a sort of life's partner, for richer or poorer, in sickness and in health. But isn't it enough for TV commercials to remind us of how gorgeous and trim we all aren't, without rubbing our nose in violence and death? Granted there is a sense of quiet courage in the fabric of our lives, but couldn't they just tell us the cloth absorbs sweat and leave it at that?" There was still some mileage, it would seem, in "qualities."

[36] See David Lewis and Darren Bridger, *The Soul of the New Consumer: Authenticity – What We Buy and Why in the New Economy* (London: Nicholas Brealey, 2000). Lewis and Bridger cite AOL executive Bob Pittman to express the sometimes mystifying phenomenon: "I remind people all the time that Coca-Cola does not win the taste test. Microsoft is not the best operating system. Brand wins" (p. 33).

During the 1990s, Fabric of Our Lives adapted itself through enough subsequent iterations to confirm they were right. The ads ran the gamut of American popular culture, "diverse" in the means but unified in the end. There were images for, and of, everybody. An adolescent boy about to leave home for the first time bids farewell to mother, father, and sister on a rural railway platform. Is it Virginia, Illinois, or California? Cut to white sheets blowing in the wind on the clothesline, a small town anywhere. Cut to a baseball game. Cut to family reunions, to summer vacations at the beach, to children romping in the backyard.

The old association of cotton with everything that was "real," first tried out in the 1970s but then with a hard edge aimed to bash the "plastic" world of synthetics, blossomed in the mid-1990s in softer, more mature form. It was not a new insight in advertising that the personality of a brand speaks primarily through the stories that marketers spin around it. Foote, Cone & Belding's "Does she or doesn't she?" campaign for Clairol (1956) was one of the first to take a particular product (hair dye) and a particular transformation that it wrought ("Not even the man dancing with her can tell") and make it suggest a story that was part of the viewer's own experience.[37] The Clairol "Does she or doesn't she?" story was no doubt further enhanced by suggestive association with something else that nice girls back then emphatically did not do. Advertising was magic that used such power of suggestion to say it – without saying it.

The Clairol story, however, promoted what was essentially deception. New attitudes toward consumption called for the opposite. "Natural" cotton, which in the "Fabric of Our Lives" found its equivalent story, could hardly have matched up better with the new consumer's quest for authenticity. The new consumer did not wish to be magically transformed into something she was not; she wished rather to have her own self-perceived authenticity, well, authenticated. The scene is the master bedroom, where mom and dad are dressing up – a formal evening gown, a white tuxedo shirt – while children romp on the bed adoringly watching the show. At first glance, the take is hard to interpret, and the voice-over pushes the schmaltz limit. "Life moves pretty fast. So stop. Look around. This is the good stuff. This is the fabric of our lives. This is cotton."

Cotton and the good life went together, like parents and children in happy homes. That particular "family" was white. Another, carefully, was

<hr>

[37] Ibid., 37–8.

black. They sat around the dining room table in a 1990s reprise of the famous Norman Rockwell image of Thanksgiving dinner (back in the long lost days when attention was still on the turkey, not the TV). There are multiple generations, nattily turned out, nice up-market surroundings, lots of smiles. Knowing the value of one good cliché on top of another, O&M's copywriter interpreted the scene: "Joy is not like a pie. The more you share it, the more there is. This is cotton."

By the end of the 1990s, the Fabric of Our Lives campaign embraced in full the modish multicultural spirit of the times. "How different can we be," went the voice-over for one spot featuring a rainbow coalition of cotton-clad actors, "when we all love to wear the same thing?" "The same thing," in deference to diversity, could certainly no longer be the same style, but it certainly could be the same substance: cotton. Younger actors were used as research revealed that turn-of-the-millennium teens and young adults (the Boomers' offspring) sure enough liked cotton but displayed disturbingly low "fiber consciousness." The job of educating the market was never-ending, it seemed, and advertising's task undiminished. One particularly edgy series that aimed to reach this "Generation X" featured everyone – old men and women down to teens and small children – clad in just their underwear (some of which looked, admittedly, indistinguishable from what people then were wearing for outerwear). It was an unabashed, in-your-face, "I'll dress just the way I like thank you very much" theme, with a joke at the end: "Never be intimidated – just imagine what the other guy looks like in *his* underwear." The Maid of Cotton would have blushed.[38]

In the late 1990s came another cultural shift in fashion that was tailor-made, it would seem, for cotton: America turned casual. The wave toward more casual dress for all occasions had been building for many years (probably since the 1960s), as "restrictive" dress codes quietly disappeared from good restaurants and as men showed up in church sans coat and tie and with women in pants. The wave broke, thunderingly, in the last year or two of the century, as "corporate casual" became the reigning fashion orthodoxy. Once again, cotton apparel offered the correct alternative, as male corporate America doffed its woolen suits (and female corporate America

---

[38] But she was no longer around. The last young woman so honored (Anna Spiller from Eads, Tennessee, a small town near Memphis) retired in 1993. In 1995, Cotton Incorporated expanded its consumer research, aimed at providing timely information to cotton decision makers, with introduction of an ongoing behavioral study, *Lifestyle Monitor,* which charted America's changing tastes in apparel and home furnishings.

its linens and silks) for open-collared shirts and comfortable-fitting khakis made almost certainly of cotton. Insecurity as to what exactly constituted acceptable "corporate casual" spawned a new breed of fashion consultants and guideline writers (typically: no T-shirts, old jeans, or sneakers; but golf shirts, tidy Dockers, and loafers OK) who could all be counted upon to talk approvingly about sharp new cotton apparel that was just right for the office. Cotton Incorporated advertising promptly picked up the theme: "What would it be like," came the question as the screen filled with diverse hard-working Americans, "if we all dressed as if work were fun?"[39]

THE SYSTEM

In Dukes Wooters's time, the word "lifestyle" had not yet worked its way into the American vernacular. "Way of life" had once covered the same ground but then (probably during the 1980s) gave way to the newer term. Television ads featuring actors cavorting in their cotton underwear or going to work without neckties probably would have surprised Wooters. But the new "lifestyle" images were a logical outcome of his strategy of matching cotton's product to consumers' desires, and they conveyed an old but durable message: cotton is desirable.

Because cotton was used mostly for apparel and home products, it was ever a hostage to fashion.[40] The fashion for easy-care wash-and-wear garments rich in synthetic "miracle fibers" had pushed cotton to the wall in the 1960s and early 1970s. The parallel but more enduring fashion for denim

---

[39] The new rules could be confusing and amusing. The partners of one old-line Wall Street law firm agreed reluctantly to loosen up their dark-suit-and-conservative-tie dress code only after making precautionary arrangements with Brooks Brothers to counsel their younger colleagues, who might just be prone to take advantage, on what would do and what wouldn't. The Tavern Club in Chicago advised female guests that they must wear "full-shirts," males "full-shoes." The newsletter of the University Club of Washington, DC, ran pictures of "Acceptable Attire" (collared shirt, creased slacks) and "Not Acceptable" (T-shirts and jeans) and invited members "to give feedback." The Harvard Club of New York City (where Dukes Wooters is well-known to the waiters at lunch) tolerated "no ties" in the bar. A sign in the lobby of Cotton Incorporated's new headquarters building in Cary, North Carolina, notified staff and visitors that "Cotton Incorporated now observes a five-day-a-week corporate casual dress policy." However, Cotton Incorporated's board of directors, consisting only of cotton producers, bucked the tide with business meetings and evening functions still, at this writing, strictly "jacket and tie."

[40] "Fashion" is used here not in the sense of couture, or "high fashion," but in the sense simply of "taste" and "style." The clothing in this year's L.L.Bean or Lands' End catalogues looks somewhat different from that of ten years ago: styles of construction and preference for different fabrics change. Obviously, the "fashion content" in such everyday apparel was, and is, low.

jeans may well have saved it from commercial extinction. A new fashion for khaki certainly sustained its revival. Creation of the cotton brand depended on advertising that both pandered to fashion and transcended it. It required alertness to consumer preferences in apparel and home furnishings at the present moment, and it required crafting an advertising message that would flatter consumers for having made good choices already as well as enthuse them for making similar choices in the future. Fabric of Our Lives met this dual test.

Organizationally, Cotton Incorporated's marketing services division was the company's mediator of fashion. In addition to television advertising, which necessarily garnered the lion's share of the budget, it also engaged in print campaigns directed at the trade and key textile industry decision makers. The *Daily News Record, Women's Wear Daily, Home Textiles Today,* and *Home Furnishings Daily* were typical media. A striking example, from 1989, was a special insert produced for textile manufacturer Milliken & Co., which was printed directly on a swatch from Milliken's then-new 100 percent cotton fabric collection. The idea was to inform the industry of a new fabric development and actually place a sample in their hands. The same year was also notable for Levi's introduction of its all-cotton Dockers casual slacks, every pair of which sported, next to Levi's own mark, the Seal of Cotton. Levi's (denim jeans) were themselves a well-established brand already, and the company could never be persuaded to share its brand with the seal. With Dockers, however, Levi hoped to launch a new "lifestyle brand" and saw the Seal of Cotton as the means to establish fabric content without actually having to explain it, since the consumer was already familiar with the seal's meaning.

The company employed outside research services to measure its advertising reach in number of consumer impressions – which totaled, nationally, in the hundreds of millions. In local retail and merchandising efforts, the company partnered with retailers in key metropolitan markets to produce tailored television advertising that identified local stores carrying cotton products; in return, the retailers displayed the seal in their own newspaper ads and store catalogs. It was an arrangement that enabled cotton products to gain exposure both in consumer print and on local television and that, dollar for dollar, probably doubled the exposure of cotton's message. Promotions at shopping mall fashion shows corralled lookers and turned them into buyers. A public relations office pursued media placement of stories aimed at educating consumers on the benefits of cotton clothing. "Dressing for Hot Weather," for example, was picked up by Associated Press and found its way into 400 papers with total circulation of over 12 million.[41]

The company's fashion marketing department worked to maintain and build interest in cotton as a fashion fiber across numerous textile end-use categories. In-house researchers gathered trend and forecast information worldwide for distribution to textile manufacturers, designers, and retailers to help them identify new ways of incorporating cotton into their lines. Color, fabric, and silhouette directions were all charted and then packaged into seasonal presentations of "selling ideas." In New York, Dallas, and Los Angeles, Cottonworks Fabric Libraries were established as hands-on information centers where designers and manufacturers could view the latest collections of cotton fabrics from mills, knitters, and converters and also see marketing forecast presentations on fabric trends, color directions, print innovations, and new cotton yarn designs. Visited by thousands each year, these libraries became clearinghouses for market and technical information concerning every state of cotton fashion. The strategy was to identify and then track worldwide apparel and home fabric fashion directions, using that information to keep mills, manufacturers, and retailers on track with cotton.[42]

The objective of these efforts was to sustain demand on two fronts. Without the relentless pressure of advertising to persuade final consumers to buy cotton products, rekindling demand with intermediate customers in the textile industry was futile. The U.S. marketing division of Cotton Incorporated nurtured demand on the industry front. Informing the industry of new cotton developments and providing the business rationale for returning to (or, in the case of a few loyal mills, sticking with) cotton, it was the link between consumer promotion and the textile research that promised to feed the marketplace with competitive, high-performance products. The pull (to consumers), slightly ahead, and the push (to manufacturers), close behind, together created a marketing system that helped align production and consumption.

[41] Cotton Incorporated Annual Reports, 1988–1989.
[42] Cotton Incorporated Annual Reports, 1988, 1993, 1997.

7

MANAGING THE MILL

Textile mills have simple desires. All they want is cotton that is longer, stronger, finer, cleaner, and cheaper – and they want it all the time. Owners of textile mills generate profits when their machinery runs steady and full, which in turn requires conditions of continuous raw material supply and robust demand for finished output. Long in thrall to cotton, it is small surprise that many mill owners should have rejoiced at the coming of an alternative, in critical ways so superior to cotton. While some were men of traditional tastes who no doubt preferred and continued to buy cotton shirts, sheets, and towels for themselves, few had any illusions about the nature of the business they were in: the mass production of textiles for mass markets.

At both ends of the textile production process, synthetic fibers had huge advantages, "natural" and man-made, over cotton. As a raw material input, synthetics regularized the supply of raw fiber to the mill. DuPont, Celanese, and Eastman Kodak produced (respectively) Dacron, Fortrel, and Kodel polyester in plants that ran seven days a week, 365 days a year. Moreover, they were able to custom manufacture fiber to a mill's specifications and, within those specifications, to deliver fiber with highly uniform quality characteristics of length, strength, and color. Synthetics were clean, where cotton came with the trash included.[1] Synthetics made the mechanics of high-speed spinning, weaving, and knitting easier. (Extruded, continuous filament fibers did not even have to be spun at all.) They were an industrial product naturally suited to an industrial process.

---

[1] "Trash," which a mill paid for along with the cotton when it bought a bale, might constitute up to 10 percent of the gross weight of a 480-pound bale of cotton. Target weight for a bale is 480 pounds, plus the wrapping. See Appendix C.

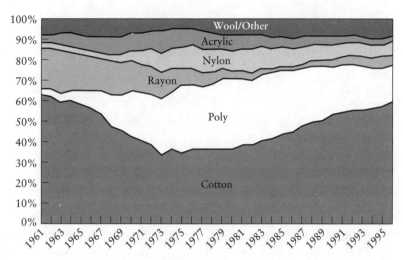

Figure 8. Fiber shares of U.S. mill fiber consumption, 1961–1997. *Source:* Based on data compiled by Cotton Incorporated from industry sources and the NPD group.

At the other end of the production process, synthetics had advantages both inherent in the product and "man-made" through marketing. The chemical companies dedicated top talent and large financial resources to creating and sustaining demand for the synthetics they supplied, promoting their advantages to users at every stage from mills to retail consumers. Their product generally justified their claims about it. The central theme of those claims was "performance," meaning convenience in care and durability in use. Thus did the advertising of that pre-feminist era bid the American housewife to put away her hot iron, switch on her tumble dryer, and clothe her family in fashionable man-made threads that did not shrink, fade, or easily wear out. The DuPonts and the others were not, of course, above throwing in some Madison Avenue flummery, too: the phrase "modern miracle fibers" was one example, best forgotten. But they need not have bothered. In convenience and durability, and with qualities like "wash-and-wear" and "permanent press," they were on to something good.

As far as cotton growers were concerned, they had to find ways to re-link themselves, as raw material suppliers, to their customers. The problem was that cotton by nature was more variable and temperamental than its substitutes. To make all the advertising about cotton's virtues credible, it was necessary to upgrade its performance characteristics through investment in research and development.

For those in the textile business, the prospects were not promising. Hal E. Brockmann, whom Dukes Wooters hired in 1973 as vice-president of textile research and development at Cotton Incorporated, had worked for Dow Chemical in acrylic fibers and plastics and later for Prodesco, a private textile research firm in Pennsylvania, developing yarns and fabrics on contract for synthetic fibers companies. At Prodesco, his biggest client for many years was none other than DuPont, and he had something of an insider's view of how DuPont and other synthetic fiber producers had pulled off their striking coup against cotton. By the time cotton growers agreed to pay for a research and promotion program in the late 1960s, the synthetics manufacturers had already usurped a key function of the mills that would make a comeback even harder.[2]

The synthetic fibers companies had sold themselves into a preferred position with the mills. Because synthetic fibers companies were spending handsomely to promote product development for the mills, the mills were only too happy to use their fibers, especially considering that the DuPonts of the world were also marketing those products to the mills' customers. The "sale" rested on two warranties: that synthetics were easier for mills to run, backed up with technical service to make sure that was so; and that synthetic-rich yarns and fabrics had the performance characteristics that consumers wanted, backed up with marketing dollars to sustain those preferences. In order to fight its way back in this newly competitive context, cotton would have to engage the competition simultaneously on two fronts: quality and spending.

NOT BY CONVENIENCE ALONE

In the early 1960s, textile "performance" referred to convenience and to ease of care. The Baby Boomer generation was not yet grown up, and the apparently secure affluent society created by their parents generated some memorable physical totems – from big cars to sprawling suburbs to color televisions. Consumerism was triumphant, and marketing and advertising rendered the idea of "push-button convenience" a basic cultural value. If "push-button driving" or electric can openers and carving knives seemed

---

[2] Hal Brockmann, Cotton Incorporated (retired), interview, October 11, 1999. Brockmann also had something of a personal interest in cotton. Starting out in the 1950s, he first had worked for a cotton textile mill in North Carolina. "My family also owned a cotton farm – or a farm on which we grew cotton, I should say – in South Carolina."

perhaps a trifle ephemeral, then remote-control garage doors, frozen food, "automatic" dishwashers, and (of course) home laundries became staples of modern middle-class life and, as Americans then were fond of boasting, "the envy of the world." In this context, old-time cotton looked faded indeed alongside the miracle fibers, and the synthetics manufacturers did everything they could to promote the contrast. For the mill operators, synthetics were convenient inputs to their production processes. Even more important to the final consumers of clothing, synthetics were convenient in their washday maintenance: easy to clean and easy (or unnecessary) to press. Yet clever as they were, the synthetics manufacturers and marketers had a product that was, by itself, a half-way technology. For people do not merely care for their clothing. They wear it.

Since antiquity, humans have clothed themselves for modesty, to stay warm, to fend off the sun, and to preen, show off, and be fashionable. In wearing their clothes – and this was the light bulb that switched on at Cotton Incorporated in the 1970s – people generally want to be comfortable. From the minimalist position that clothing which accomplished its practical purpose of warmth or coolness or fashionableness should not exact a price in discomfort, it was a short step to articulating comfort as a stand-alone, highly desirable virtue. The difference between the statement "I am comfortable in my [warm, etc.] clothes," and "I wear this particular clothing in order to be comfortable" was the marketing insight that gave cotton the point of entry it needed to counterattack the synthetics' claims to "convenience."

Webster's Dictionary gives us "comfort" as a state of contented well-being, satisfaction, or enjoyment, and in its verb form to cheer or strengthen. (Cotton in the 1970s needed all the strengthening it could get, and growers needed some cheering up.) "Comfort" could supply both – but not until it could be measured, since one person's comfort might easily be another's discomfort. It was a "soft" quality and highly subjective. To test for comfort in clothing was not original with Cotton Incorporated. To sell it was.

In the 1950s, the U.S. Army had commissioned the Harris Research Organization to develop a system for using human subjects to obtain numerical measurements of comfort for different sorts of uniforms. However, it was in metallurgy, not textiles, that "comfort studies" advanced the fastest. The Gillette Company, which made razors but which made its money selling razor blades, hired Harris to measure the comfort of a steel-edged razor sliding over a sleepy, soapy human face in support of its claims to "The

World's Most Comfortable Shave." Gillette eventually acquired Harris, re-named it the Gillette Research Institute, and moved it from Washington, DC, to Rockville, Maryland, where a researcher named Norman Hollies re-fined its techniques. At the behest of Cotton Incorporated, Hollies applied these techniques to cotton with positive results.

Thenceforth, cotton marketing drove the idea of comfort, and "comfort studies" (which continued through the 1970s) supplied the supporting hard data in accordance with strict protocols. Human subjects were sorted by age, weight, and sex; they were screened for health problems that might skew their responses. They were put on exercise bicycles in a temperature-and humidity-controlled atmospheric chamber and then told to pedal long enough (usually fifteen or twenty minutes) to work up a mild sweat. The "weather" in the chamber rotated through a series of changes: Chicago in winter, New Orleans in summer, New York in June. As they went, sub-jects responded to researchers' questions – "Do you feel blah?"; "Do you feel clammy?"; "Do you feel cool?" – using a carefully worked-out list of descriptors aimed at pinning down the essence of comfort.

Cotton comfort researchers tested different articles of clothing – dresses and blouses, dress shirts, sport shirts, slacks, and jeans – made from dif-ferent fabrics and constructions: some all cotton, some blends, some all synthetic. Most tests were conducted using 25 subjects, though in some there were 50 or 100. The results confirmed "scientifically" what believers in cotton had long held by faith and known by anecdotal experience. Peo-ple were simply more comfortable when clothed in cotton.[3]

The systematic and rigorous underpinnings of the comfort studies de-fended Cotton Incorporated from the claims of false advertising that were part of the game competitors play. The company's television ads in the 1970s – "The more cotton, the better you feel" – prompted a complaint from DuPont to the Federal Trade Commission. Prove it! DuPont had learned to back up its claims for "performance" with mountains of research data. "I helped generate some of that data," Hal Brockmann recalled. Nor-man Hollies presented the case for cotton's claims, and the complaint was dismissed. "That probably was one of the most important things that the

---

[3] Cotton Incorporated comfort studies, Annual Report, 1980; Technical Bulletin 4007, "The Measurement of Cotton's Comfort"; Brockmann interview. The company also commissioned a series of "back of the closet" studies to discern what clothes people actually wore and what clothes they didn't. Synthetics, it turned out, were typically found relegated to the neglected back of the closet; natural fibers were typically found near the front.

cotton growers ever spent money on," Brockmann said, "to demonstrate once and for all that there was a difference in comfort perceived by human beings wearing cotton."[4]

The successful equation of cotton with clothing comfort laid the platform for cotton's future recovery. The validated perception of "comfortable cotton" gave the fiber a potential competitive advantage at the margin, but that alone was not enough. Cotton Incorporated's marketers wanted to challenge synthetics on their own turf. If only comfort could be added to convenience and performance. This would call for more than affirmative research; it would require new technology.

LEARNING FROM THE ENEMY

"Performance," though, was a steep hill for cotton to climb. In order for the cotton marketing strategy to work in the long run, some "push" was required to educate mills in the efficient uses of cotton in textile production.

The obstacles to more efficient cotton textile production began at the very start, with the nature of the cotton bale itself: the unit of raw material that a mill purchased, stored, opened, "laid down," blended, cleaned, carded, drew, spun, and (if that mill were vertically integrated) wove or knitted. Synthetic fibers were generally uniform when they arrived at the mill, but the fiber in a cotton bale originated on any one of thousands of farms stretching from Virginia to California, produced under wide-ranging conditions of climate, soil, agricultural practice, and methods of harvesting and ginning. Wise decisions about the price to be paid for it, and the most efficient uses to which it might be put, depended on making the correct judgment about the quality of any given shipment.

Measuring quality has a long history of inexact judgment. In England in the late eighteenth century, cotton was identified only by place of origin (Indian, West Indian, or American). Invention of the cotton gin and explosive growth of the cotton textile industry in the nineteenth century called forth more detailed standards of classification, for cotton could vary enormously within any one growing area in terms of color, fineness or coarseness, length of fiber, and amount and type of foreign matter. For the purpose of making commercial transactions, merchants and textile manufacturers (mills) needed a uniform way to describe quality factors, at first

---

[4] Brockmann interview.

discerned merely by "look and feel." In countries that imported and exported, cotton exchanges developed terms for classifying cotton that soon entered the language.

In the nineteenth century, mills came to rely on a loose system of classification for judging a number of cotton fiber's physical attributes, a method that might be charitably described as an art. (French impressionist Edgar Degas captured the art in his own depiction of the cotton exchange in New Orleans, prints of which still enjoy great popularity in the homes and offices of growers, merchants, and mill operators a century later.) The term for average quality cotton, "Middling," appeared in Liverpool in 1800, and the Liverpool Cotton Association first developed standards specifically for American cotton in the 1840s. These were adopted by the New York Exchange in 1853, and all United States exchanges agreed to New York's nomenclature for grades in 1874. However, what the grades actually meant still varied widely from one exchange to the other.[5]

Early in the twentieth century, the USDA attempted to rationalize the grading system (thirteen standards were then in use – from "Fair" to "Ordinary" – with "Middling," at #7, in the middle), but uniform grade standards for upland cotton became compulsory only in the context of federal regulation of cotton futures trading with passage in 1916 of the Cotton Futures Act. Under its authority, the Secretary of Agriculture mandated use of nine grades from "Middling Fair" to "Good Ordinary" as well as standards for color grades. The Cotton Standards Act of 1923 extended the compulsory principle from cotton traded in the futures market to all cotton moved via interstate commerce.[6] Also in 1923, the most important foreign exchanges (then, all in Europe) agreed to adopt the official U.S. standards for grade and color, thus making them "universal" (The Universal Cotton Standards Agreement). Since then, "Universal Cotton Standards Conferences" have met at three-year intervals to reexamine and sometimes revise the classification standards, which would eventually include determination of staple length, fiber length uniformity, strength, micronaire (fiber fineness and maturity), color, leaf, and extraneous matter content.[7]

[5] H. H. Perkins, et al., "Fiber," in R. J. Kohel and C. F. Lewis, eds., *Cotton* (Madison: American Society of Agronomy, 1984), 437–509; H. H. Ramey, Jr., "Classing of Fiber," in Wayne C. Smith and J. Tom Cothren, eds., *Cotton* (New York: Wiley, 1999), 709–27.

[6] USDA, *Compilation of Statutes Relating to the Agricultural Marketing Service and Closely Related Activities,* Handbook no. 665 (Washington, DC, 1990).

[7] USDA, *The Classification of Cotton,* Handbook no. 566 (Washington, DC, 1995).

For decades, the entire classification process was accomplished manually by USDA-licensed "samplers" and "classers" at official classing facilities located across the Cotton Belt. Seasoned in the "look and feel" of raw cotton as these experts certainly were, the process – particularly with regard to color and extraneous matter – remained highly subjective. Manual classification was a concentrated exercise in comparing this to that under, it should be noted, just the right environmental conditions. With color grading, for example, lighting was crucial; a north skylight from over the shoulder was best, given room surroundings of off-white to light gray. For measuring staple length, calibrated in thirty-seconds of an inch, it was important that the sample "pull" (a tuft of fibers worked parallel by lapping and pulling) be drawn from two opposite sides of the bale and tested at a relative humidity of 65 percent at 70 degrees Fahrenheit.[8]

The "standard" never varied, but the classification of any two particular bales derived from that standard might vary simply because different individuals were doing the classing, or even because the same individual was doing the classing but at different times under slightly different conditions. Each year, the USDA made up fresh examples of the standards for color grade and leaf content ("practical forms" as they were known), which were examined by representatives of the industry (including growers) and then dispatched to the classing offices for reference by classers and growers. The master set resided in a bank vault in Memphis.

The need to objectify the judgment of cotton fiber quality – and thus improve the quality of information on which cotton markets and cotton use alike depended – pointed toward the substitution of mechanical measurement techniques for human "look and feel." This movement had a history of its own, reaching back to experimental work sponsored by the Fine Goods' Spinners Association in the early twentieth century in England, and at the Shirley Institute, established in 1919 also in England, that aimed to systematize cotton properties measurement.[9] Across the Atlantic, USDA scientists commenced their own work about the same time, achieving some landmark results in the 1920s. Working with the USDA, Clemson University (South Carolina) professor E. E. Chandler developed a technique for bundling fibers for strength tests. USDA scientist Robert Webb developed

---

[8] USDA, *The Classification of Cotton*, Publication no. 310 (Washington, DC, 1956).

[9] W. L. Balls, *The Development and Properties of Raw Cotton* (London: A. C. Black, 1915); A. W. Palmer, *The Growth of Cotton Fiber Science in the United States* (Washington, DC: Smithsonian Institution Publication 4452, 1961).

a fiber sorter and a method for measuring length and length distribution. The cotton color meter or "colorimeter," which made possible the description of cotton fiber color by instrument, was the work of USDA scientist Dorothy Nickerson. K. L. Hertel, at the University of Tennessee, developed the fibrograph, which measured length, and the arealometer to test for fineness and maturity. At the University of Arizona, E. H. Pressley refined a new strength tester. Instrument testing research also reached into the mills, in the 1930s and 1940s still largely wedded to cotton. In 1947, W. S. Smith (working at West Point Manufacturing Company) demonstrated a mechanized test for "micronaire," or fiber fineness, which had the significant advantage of running at a high enough speed to make it potentially useful in the cotton marketing system.[10]

Discoveries at the bench proved, in principle, that machines could do the job of classing cotton. It took many years, however, to move them out of the laboratory and into the industry. For example, micronaire as a quality measurement was not incorporated into the official classification system until 1965. The reasons that the industry moved so slowly in this direction were both political and technological. Merchants were cautious, fearing the potential of mechanization to undercut the role of the middleman.[11] Automation also awaited machines that were not only accurate but fast. Speed required dependable integration, assembly-line fashion, of tests developed separately over forty years.

By comparison, the synthetic fibers producers arrived on the scene with such quality assessment issues more or less resolved from the start. One of the greatest claims and most persuasive arguments to the mills, and

---

[10] E. E. Chandler, "A New Method for Determining the Strength of Cotton," USDA Bureau of Agricultural Economics Preliminary Report, 1926; D. Nickerson, "Cotton Classing by Artificial Light," *Illumination Engineering* 47 (1952), 135–42; G. W. Pfeiffenberger, "Development of Cotton Fiber Technology in the United States," *Cotton Trade Journal International Year Book,* 1955, 1956.

[11] "Cotton buyers saw these instruments as a means of just wiping them out," observed Jim Parker, head of the Textile Research Center at Texas Tech. "If you're going to measure the cotton in instruments, why do you need a cotton buyer?" Cited in Jack Lichtenstein, *Field to Fabric: The Story of American Cotton Growers* (Lubbock: Texas Tech University Press, 1990), 41. Nor were many classers happy at the prospect of change. Preston Sasser remembered the skepticism of classers in the Raleigh, North Carolina, classing office: "A lot of classers would come into that room where the instrument was and look at it and they would pull on the cotton and they would say: 'This instrument measures this cotton too long.' I can still see those people standing around the conveyor and saying: 'North Carolina cotton is not this staple length. You've got this thing calibrated wrong.' But just the fact that those instruments were there testing all that cotton, and the classers themselves began to inch up."

especially to vertically integrated clothing manufacturers, was the reliability of synthetics as a raw fiber input: it was clean, of uniform strength and
fineness, and just the right color. The mill that bought Dacron knew exactly what would be the spinning, weaving, and dyeing characteristics of a
particular "lay-down" of fiber.[12] Synthetics enabled mills to know the fiber
properties going into their machines better than they could know the properties of cotton. Synthetics promised improved spinning efficiency, better
yarns, and improved weaving and knitting. Instrument testing of cotton,
which would enable mills to select raw cotton fiber of comparable uniformity and dependability, might erode (if not erase) one of the synthetics' key
competitive advantages. Testing for micronaire in particular was crucial to
cotton: fiber fineness related directly to how cotton would spin, and fiber
maturity related to how well it would dye in the fabric form.

The chronology of cotton's response to this challenge reveals involvement
of a variety of grower organizations, private industry, and the USDA (chiefly
the Cotton Division of the Agricultural Marketing Service, the federal entity responsible for classing cotton). It also reveals a series of incremental
developments on several fronts that would take decades to bring together
into a commonly accepted system for improving the quality and speed of
cotton textile production.

Automation of basic fiber measurement techniques began in the 1950s at
a small firm in Dallas called Motion Control, Inc. Its founder, Glenn Witts,
had a knack for hydraulics and electronics and had fashioned a highly reliable and fast instrument called the "Fibronaire" to measure micronaire.
That instrument was incorporated into the first conveyor-style system for
measuring micronaire, installed at the Dallas cotton merchant, Volkart
Brothers, in 1959. There the system attracted the attention of the Plains
Cotton Cooperative Association in Lubbock, whose manager, Dan Davis,
saw potential in integrating other fiber testing instruments along a line that
could measure several properties smoothly and rapidly in one operation.[13]

---

[12] Bales of raw fiber, whether natural or synthetic, upon entering the mill and being opened are
literally spread out and laid down on the floor before moving into the spinning process. Thus:
"lay-down."

[13] West Texas growers had an interest because they had a problem. "Cotton from our area had
a horrible reputation in the textile industry," explained Dan Davis, head of Plains Cotton
Cooperative, "and unfortunately most of it was accurately perceived. We had absolutely horrible cotton. It was short and the fiber was weak. It was lousy cotton, and it was very difficult
to get a handle on how to improve it." Instrument evaluation promised to help: "The classing system and marketing system was so poor that, if a producer raised better quality than

Davis and Witts collaborated so that, in time for the 1960 harvest season, three fiber testing lines went into operation at Plains Cotton in Lubbock, with tests for micronaire (by Fibronaire), color (by Nickerson–Hunter colorimeters), and trash content (still judged by the human eye). The lines ran for just over one month and tested 435,000 bales. Responding to grower support, the USDA incorporated machine-read micronaire into the classing system in 1963. That same year, the USDA and the instrument manufacturers began discussions exploring the possibility of instruments fast enough to measure the important fiber qualities of the entire U.S. crop, which, it was agreed, would require a testing cycle time of no more than ten seconds per specimen. However, this awaited development of high-speed instruments for determination of the remaining key fiber qualities: length and strength. Motion Control, Inc. and Plains Cotton developed a high-speed length tester in 1965; Cotton Incorporated's predecessor, the Cotton Producers Institute, funded research at the Stanford Research Institute that led to a high-speed strength tester.

Preston Sasser, in 1964 a young Ph.D. in agricultural engineering from North Carolina State University, got his first job as "ginning engineer" at the National Cotton Council in Memphis; there he met Glenn Witts, who was working with CPI on a strength tester. The USDA soon installed a prototype of that instrument at its Clemson, South Carolina testing laboratory. It was an ungainly device, five feet by five feet by six feet high, but it had promise; the government pursued discussions with Witts, which led to a contract with Motion Control in Dallas to refine and commercialize the concept. Sasser left the Cotton Council to go to work with Witts in Dallas, a partnership that produced a machine capable of 300 tests per hour and that incorporated much of the basic technology that would still be in use decades later. This included the use of tapered length specimens for strength testing; automated combing, brushing, and micronaire correction of specimens; and use of spring-loaded jaw clamps to hold fibers during strength testing.[14]

At this point, all the instruments were still separate and required dedicated operators working at separate stations. "We made a conveyor," remembered Sasser of the next step, "so that the samples went along and

his neighbors, then he didn't get any more money for it. The classification system [most of which was still done by hand] was not sensitive enough to detect the fact that he produced fiber that was deserving of a better price." See Lichtenstein, *Field to Fabric*, 37ff.

[14] Preston Sasser and J. F. Moore, "Historical Perspective of High Volume Instrument Developments in the U.S.," 1991; Preston Sasser interview, Cotton Incorporated, April 7, 2000.

stopped here and a lady did micronaire; then the conveyor indexed and the sample went to the next station and the lady measured length, and so on." The first complete system to incorporate all the tests was installed at the Textile Research Center at Texas Tech in January 1969: "Motion Control Serial Number 1," which was soon purchased by 75 West Texas ginners, organized as Quality Fiber Control, Inc. Plains Cotton installed their own fiber testing line later that year and embarked on a length–strength–micronaire program to market 230,000 bales of High Plains cotton. The USDA began testing the full system, first with a unit in Memphis and then in its classing office in Raleigh. The USDA also jiggered the original terminology: "high-speed testing" became "high-volume testing or instrumentation" (HVI for short). In 1969, Burlington Industries (Greenville, South Carolina) became the first mill to install an HVI line – and bought a second one within a few months – for its cotton purchasing department. Burlington was a vertically integrated textile manufacturer and thus was positioned to see immediately the benefits from better fiber information. Sasser helped install that first system: "They quickly figured out that by gaining better control of the fiber properties going into their mixes, they could make better yarns."[15]

USDA evaluation continued in the 1970s at multiyear field trials centered in Lubbock; beginning in 1980, instrument-measured length (instead of the classer's staple length) was reported as the official staple length determination. It still remained to combine the conveyors and individual instruments into one space-efficient console, an improvement that came in the late 1970s. At that point, the Lamesa (Texas) Cotton Growers Association offered to cooperate with the Agricultural Marketing Service in a large-scale evaluation of the entire system and, in 1980, contributed $500,000 toward purchase and installation of twelve HVI systems in the new government classing facility in Lamesa. Over 300,000 bales were classed the first year, and thenceforth the crop in the Lamesa classing territory was judged, except for grade, by instruments alone.

High-speed instrumentation came just in time to ward off another threat to cotton's business. In the 1980s, regulatory and market pressures accelerated spread of the system in the industry in order to address the problem of cotton dust in textile mills. A hazard posed to workers in the form of *byssinosis* disease became a target of the U.S. Occupational Safety and Health Administration (OSHA), which handed down strict regulations mandating

---

[15] Sasser interview.

drastic dust reduction.[16] Compliance typically required installation of high-speed automated processing equipment, which in turn required much closer control of fiber input characteristics. HVI systems went far to control those inputs. Similarly, the introduction of open-end (or rotor) spinning systems to compete with traditional ring spinning put a premium on the accurate measurement of fiber quality. These systems produced cheaper, coarser yarns, but at much higher speeds and with far less labor. Fiber strength was the most important fiber property for making strong yarns with this system, yet fiber strength could be determined only by HVI measurements – not by the traditional classer's judgment of grade and staple.

During the 1980s, many U.S. manufacturers – including Dan River, Avondale, Graniteville, J. P. Stevens, Cone, Parkdale, and West Point Pepperell – joined Burlington in installing HVI systems. The USDA meanwhile continued to introduce the system in more and more classing offices, and it gave growers the choice of having their crop graded the traditional manual way or by HVI. The government also conducted studies to improve the reliability and repeatability of HVI-generated information. In 1987, the industry passed a major milestone when the National Cotton Council officially endorsed the HVI classification system. With this support, the Agricultural Marketing Service moved toward implementing an all-HVI classification system. In 1991, for the first time the entire U.S. crop was classified using high-volume instrumentation.[17]

PROCURE, MANAGE, MIX

Automation of instrument classing of cotton served the interests of growers, who hoped it would add value to their crop. It served the interests of the

---

[16] Research on cotton dust began in 1970, following identification of cotton dust as a target health hazard and OSHA's adoption of a permissible exposure level for cotton dust. Cotton Incorporated focused on solving the problem of byssinosis, the disease related to dust, particularly as it threatened the health of workers in textile mills. Between 1970 and 1986, the company spent $12 million on the problem. As if cotton needed yet another competitive blow (synthetics were dust-free), the dust problem for a time threatened any possibility of cotton's comeback. See "Cotton Dust/Byssinosis Research Program of the Industry/Government/Union Taskforce for Byssinosis Prevention: Objectives and Plan," 1984; "Research on Cotton Dust," 1983, Appendix C, Cotton Incorporated; Robert R. Jacobs, "Strategies for Prevention of Byssinosis," *American Journal of Industrial Medicine* 12 (1987), 717–28.

[17] Sasser, "Historical Perspective," 5. The final step, measurement for color, became part of the HVI testing protocol in 2000.

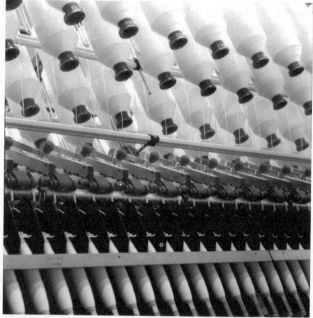

Largely a matter of subjective sight and "feel" until the 1970s, the classing of raw cotton fiber is today a highly automated process that enables mills to procure cotton with the same confidence in fiber quality and consistency as they could expect when procuring synthetics. Modern textile mills are tough customers who demand cotton fiber that is longer, stronger, finer, and (of course) cheaper than the synthetics alternatives. Cotton Incorporated spinning machinery in Cary, North Carolina, simulates those requirements.

Agricultural Marketing Service of the USDA, who saw it as a way of delivering a more uniform classing service (and, incidentally, as a way of reducing its need for a large seasonal labor pool of qualified classers). It also served the interest of the mills, which had ample alternatives and so needed ways to run cotton at high speeds if they were to run it at all. The mills made by far the most sophisticated demands on the system.

Charles Chewning had worked at Burlington Industries for over ten years when Hal Brockmann hired him at Cotton Incorporated in November 1973. His job was to help build up cotton's technical credibility with the mills in order to match its marketing credibility then being advanced by Dukes Wooters and his staff in New York. The synthetic fibers companies at this point had a ten-year head start, deploying skilled technical people to the mills to teach the ins and outs of running chiefly staple polyester fiber. In addition, Brockmann gave Chewning the job of evaluating uses that might be found for HVI testing equipment, which Chewning had come into contact with at Burlington. "Charlie," Brockmann said within a week of hiring him, "we're going to change the way cotton is used in the textile mill. I don't know how, but it's going to use this instrument testing and it's going to use a computer."[18]

Cotton Incorporated–sponsored tests ensued at Texas Tech, Cone Mills, and Burlington to evaluate the applicability for mills of HVI-generated data on length, strength, micronaire, elongation, and color. The early USDA tests of the system had shown that the data was indeed good data: it was accurate and precise. What became clear in the tests, which lasted four years, was that HVI-generated information could actually be used to make commercial decisions about cotton that were not otherwise easy to make. "You could make some money," it seemed clear to Chewning, "if you better understood the properties of cotton."[19]

In 1977, Chewning acquired for Cotton Incorporated its own HVI line, which permitted intensive work on what became a years-long project in information technology. This was before the terms "software" or "IT" became part of everyday business vocabulary, and it was fortuitous that cotton's needs for managing information generated by HVI met promptly with fast-developing computer technologies that would make such management possible and affordable. The HVI system itself, as Chewning foresaw it, was

[18] Brockmann interview.
[19] Charles Chewning interview, Cotton Incorporated, April 7, 2000.

a service to the mills; it was the hardware that drove the software needed to manipulate data into forms that were commercially useful and easy to use.

Initially, the output of an HVI line was confined to printed paper. If you tested a thousand bales, you got a thousand lines of data on paper. "Up to our eyeballs in data," remembered Preston Sasser of the output of the early systems he worked with, which had been hooked up to an old-fashioned teletype punch tape from which the data were entered into a mainframe computer.[20] Chewning's team needed a computer interface; the first, a stand-alone Techtronics 4051, enabled the data at least to be put into electronic files instead of on rolls of paper. But there still wasn't much that could be done with it. Experimental work followed, developing software programs to massage the data. Precisely what was needed was not left to scientists at the bench, for at this point the market spoke.

Rising competition from lower-cost foreign textile manufacturers in the 1970s had pushed the U.S. industry to take up the technology of rotor (open-end) spinning. Because the technique increased spinning speeds and decreased labor costs, it was a valuable weapon in the mills' own battle to stay profitable. However, the new technique had drawbacks that affected quality. In traditionally ring-spun yarn, the fibers are drawn nearly parallel to one another, which resulted in increased yarn strength. In open-end spinning, the fiber was far less well aligned within the yarn structure. What might appear a smooth and even yarn on the outside could be seen in cross-section to contain fibers that were highly tangled. This meant that the length of the individual raw fibers was not available to add its full amount of strength to the resulting yarn, because tangling had (in effect) rendered the fibers shorter than they actually were. Consequently, open-end yarn – however efficiently it might be spun – was lower in strength, and its performance in weaving (the next stage in the production process) was in fact less efficient than that of the ring-spun alternative. The fabric made from open-end yarns tended to lower tensile and tear properties, and this caused problems with garment manufacturers farther down the line.

Even at its lowest ebb, in the mid-1970s, cotton had two reliable strongholds: absorbent terry fabric for toweling and tough denim for jeans. Levi Strauss & Company of San Francisco consumed more denim than any other manufacturer and had built its brand, Levi's, on this fabric. One subjective measure of the power of that brand was its entry into the American

[20] Sasser interview.

vernacular, whatever the trademark lawyers might say, as a synonym for denim jeans. The tough, durable work clothes of rural America were transmuted into the uniform of urban and suburban youth, who had never been close to a tractor or a plow (or a cotton field). "Levi's" meant quality. They lasted forever, and they got more comfortable the more you washed and the longer you wore them. It was a reputation to protect jealously.

But these jeans were only as good as the threads they were made of, and the trend to open-end yarns soon caused consternation in San Francisco.[21] It was not that Levi executives had strong preferences about how yarn was spun – provided that the fabric made from it, whether open-end or ring-spun, met the same specifications that for years they (and in turn their customers) had come to expect. "We don't care which one you use," one Levi official put it, "but you better turn out the same product." Responding to complaints that jeans made from open-end yarn lacked Levi's' accustomed toughness, the company established strict and explicit strength standards, which put new pressure on mills somehow to balance the advantages (to them) of open-end spinning with the unyielding quality demands of their customers.[22]

This was no easy assignment, and it led in 1981 to a telephone call to Charles Chewning at Cotton Incorporated. The caller was the plant manager of a Burlington Industries yarn mill in Smithfield, North Carolina, desperate that their own denim mill just down the road in Erwin was returning yarn and complaining that Smithfield's open-end yarn didn't weave efficiently and had failed to meet Levi's' tensile and tear standards: "What can you do to help me?"[23]

Chewning thought that HVI data might be of use and visited the troubled mill for samples of all the cotton in their inventory. He then ran them through Cotton Incorporated's own HVI line and analyzed the results for signs of weak fiber: what came out could be no stronger than what went in. From an inventory of some 2000 bales, he identified those with too short a fiber length and suspicious micronaire and eliminated all weak bales. Then he went back to Burlington with a schedule detailing which bales to run and in what order. The trial run succeeded the first time, and over the next few months the Erwin denim mill accepted every shipment of yarn from

---

[21] See Chapter 6, "Creating Consumption," on the role of denim in Cotton Incorporated advertising.

[22] As reported to Charles Chewning, Chewning interview.

[23] Chewning interview.

Smithfield. It was at that point, Chewning concluded, that "we had commercial confirmation that High Volume Instrument data was in fact useful to mills."[24] Interestingly, within a few months, Burlington's management took the decision to reactivate their in-house HVI lines, which had been mothballed in the mid-1970s after mill managers opted out of the program because of cost considerations.

With the principle proven, Chewning moved on to the next challenge. If the information to be gleaned from HVI data could be packaged so that mills could use it – not just to troubleshoot problems, but indeed routinely to prevent problems from occurring in the first place – then cotton would have taken a large step to overcoming one of its historically crippling disadvantages relative to synthetics: that it was a highly variable and thus unreliable input. During the rest of 1981 and 1982, Chewning's team worked on developing software for personal computers that would enable the user to discern at a glance what could never have been mimicked by hand at any cost. Cotton Incorporated leased the first system to Graniteville Mills late in 1982, as much of a milestone as the earlier encounter with Burlington. "That brought enormous recognition," remembered Chewning, "as people saw that the software would run, not only be helpful, but actually run. There's a difference."

Sasser and his associates at Motion Control developed the hardware that made it possible for Chewning, his engineers, and the software program(s) they developed on behalf of Cotton Incorporated to analyze the fiber characteristics of a bale of cotton using HVI data; this came to be known and marketed to the industry as the "Engineered Fiber Selection System" (or EFS for short). The name aimed right at the heart of the competitive issue, for nothing was more "engineered" than Dacron. For years, Sasser and Chewning kept up a friendly chicken-or-egg banter about which mattered most: "Charlie claims from his viewpoint that, without EFS, HVI would never have made it. I argue that if you didn't have HVI, then you wouldn't need EFS."[25] Both were essential. Together, they integrated the ability to originate data (using high-speed instrumented measurement of key raw fiber qualities) with the ability to manipulate that data easily and economically. It was the tool the mills needed in order to know what they needed to know

[24] Ibid. West Texas growers, whose cooperative had built their own large denim mill, also learned through hard experience how demanding customers could be. See Lichtenstein, *Field to Fabric*, 139ff: "The 'Denim Dream' Becomes a Nightmare."

[25] Sasser interview.

about every bale of cotton they handled. The more they knew, the better decisions they could make about whether to buy it in the first place and then how precisely to lay it down and use it – for what product and on what machinery. Such knowledge was as good as money.

The EFS system employed regression equations to estimate product parameters that allowed laydowns that were consistent with end-product quality specifications. It controlled for variance not only within particular mixes of fiber but also over long periods of time. This feature was the crux, for it helped overcome the single greatest difference between a raw material input that was manufactured and one that was fashioned afresh each year by nature (by many different natures actually, given the size of the Cotton Belt and the fact that no one growing season was ever quite like the next) and with a bit of help from growers. It meant that the EFS program, when fed HVI data, could assure that the mix of cotton a mill laid down today would be just like (have the same specifications as) the one it had laid down a month ago and would lay down a month from now.

Starting in 1982, when Cotton Incorporated first licensed EFS to Graniteville, the technology evolved through increasingly sophisticated management applications. At first it was designed to acquire HVI data and select mixes. Within a year of the first program, Chewning's men had added a warehouse management program to help mills understand and control just where the cotton was that they had bought. The enhanced program generated all the paperwork required to bring a bale of cotton into a mill's warehouse, store it, retrieve it, and consume it. Later, a contract-monitoring function was added. Once a contract was created, EFS could keep track of how many bales had been bought and when they were being delivered; it could calculate the amount due on a bale upon delivery and it eventually could even track the various "fixations" and options that are a normal part of managing a cotton contract. Ever-fancier software applications would keep the EFS system, and the HVI data that backed it up, current with mills' needs for reliable, smooth-running raw material best suited for specified end products.

EFS represented a more comprehensive raw material management program than the synthetic fibers companies themselves had ever placed in a mill. Smoothing the information linkages up and down the production system, from grower to spinner, EFS enabled users to correlate the unique natural properties of various types of cotton with their growing, ginning, spinning, and processing techniques. Mills optimized production equipment and met customer specifications at lower material cost. In time, merchants could apply EFS to preselect mixes using USDA HVI data by bar-coded bale number for direct shipment and consumption by the mill without further testing.

Better knowledge of bale location also increased the efficiency of the merchant's warehouse. Producers and ginners, meanwhile, sharpened their ability to supply cotton that best met a mill's technical requirements. Ginners could evaluate and improve their output quality by comparing selected cotton fiber properties with growing conditions among different producers, farms, and even fields. It conferred on Cotton Incorporated (and, through Cotton Incorporated, on its grower–owners) a unique position as supplier of the analytical tool that managed the product that the mills bought from the same people who supplied the tool.[26]

RESEARCH TO TRAINLOADS

Hal Brockmann recalls how, shortly after coming to work at Cotton Incorporated, he decorated his office with artifacts from other jobs. One was a plaque from NASA honoring their previous employee for developing flame-retardant fabrics worn by the Apollo astronauts who landed on the moon in 1969: "It was real gee-whiz, high-tech stuff!" Dukes Wooters soon spotted it but wasn't particularly impressed: "I know you've done some exotic stuff up to now, but what we do here isn't exotic and it's not rocket science," he told the nonplussed Brockmann. "So take it down; wrong message. We sell cotton here – and we sell it by the trainload."[27]

It wasn't really the wrong message; Wooters, a marketer by instinct and not trained as a researcher, had missed the connection. The sort of research that had suited-up the astronauts could be applied to cause of selling cotton "by the trainload" – indeed, it was essential to that cause. Trainloads "in" depended on the mills' ability to sell trainloads "out," which depended on fiber processing technologies that were responsive to consumer demands. Brockmann and the people he hired in textile research knew something about fiber processing. Their experience had taught them that the reputation of Cotton Incorporated depended on product credibility, and that product credibility depended on textile research.

---

[26] EFS technical literature, Cotton Incorporated.
[27] Brockmann interview.

The realization that research was key came at just the time when synthetics producers were brimming with confidence. Their stunning market successes had probably surprised even the most optimistic among them. Product success cemented brand power, but the temptation was to rely too heavily on the power of their names. Thus, when the public thought of "DuPont" they associated it with the textile fibers (nylon, Orlon, Dacron, and Lycra) as much as with anything else the huge chemical company made. By the time cotton producers organized their counterattack, they had the advantage of having no brand to start with and of having to think hard about product.

The striking correlation between the Seal of Cotton's rise to recognition and cotton's winning back of market share was no accident. It occurred within a context of technological innovation and product improvement. Yet gains from engineering better raw fiber and better yarn with the help of EFS/HVI technology would be squandered unless ways could also be found to engineer better fabrics made from cotton. Three problems pressed hardest – namely, that cotton wrinkles, shrinks, and fades.

In 1971, Don Bailey was a senior majoring in textiles at North Carolina State University in Raleigh. He had fallen in love, wanted to get married, and needed extra work to afford it. A professor there told him about a new company in town, Cotton Incorporated's research laboratory, that was looking for someone who could come in at night to run washing machines and tumble dryers. Bailey promptly showed up and was hired by Glenn Morton, an Auburn University–trained chemist who had worked for manufacturer West Point Pepperell Company and who was in charge of Cotton Incorporated's first physical testing laboratory. "We're running trials out in the mills to improve performance characteristics of cotton products," Morton explained to the young man. "It takes about six to eight hours to wash a fabric five times and tumble dry it in between so we can test it. Because we only have one shift, all we want you to do is come to work and make sure those dryers run!"[28]

Bailey still works for Cotton Incorporated, and what he witnessed in those early days prepared him to do a lot more than look after the Kenmores. Then, however, he was the distinctly junior member of the team of textile fibers research talent assembled by Wooters, Frank Moore, and

---

[28] Glenn Morton interview, Cotton Incorporated (retired), April 6, 2000; Don Bailey interview, Cotton Incorporated, April 6, 2000.

then Hal Brockmann – a team whose work would give to cotton the product credibility necessary to support the brand in the marketplace. Glenn Morton came from Auburn and West Point. Wallace Blanton, who headed up technical services to the mills, came from the National Cotton Council. Brian Jones, an English-born textile chemist and wool expert who had immigrated to the United States and joined the Cotton Producers Institute, came to Raleigh when Wooters moved the textile research function there from Memphis in 1971. Jones took charge of textile chemistry research and soon hired John Turner, a Ph.D. in chemistry from Duke, who had worked for Burlington Industries in nearby Greensboro, North Carolina. Rob Stone came from Springs Mills and the American Association of Textile Chemists and Colorists to add expertise in testing. Mike Tyndall, Bob Cleaver, Doug Fain, and Phillip Dabbs – trained experts all – came aboard soon afterward, and Wolfgang Strahl arrived in 1974 to head up fabric development. "I was just the grunt, in the beginning," remembers Bailey of this fast-growing group, who together would solve cotton's toughest performance problems.[29]

TUMBLING OUT THE WRINKLES

One of the greatest technical feats in the whole history of textile fibers was the synthetics' creation, both in physical reality and in marketing imagery, of wrinkle resistance. Synthetics, particularly polyesters, had advantages of wrinkle resistance and strength that were inherent in their molecular structure and that were near impossible for cellulosic fibers, whether natural (cotton) or man-made (rayon), to match. Synthetics manufacturers spared nothing to promote the convenience that such fibers promised to deliver to apparel consumers. By the early 1960s, durable press textiles (fabrics that required little or no ironing after home laundering and had wrinkle-resistant properties during wear) had changed the way Americans dressed and the way they thought about value in apparel.

Of course, polyester was not perfect. It absorbed moisture poorly (low "hydrophilicity" was the mellifluous technical term) and, as Cotton Incorporated's comfort studies demonstrated, in too high a concentration it was uncomfortable to wear. It was hot in hot weather, cold in cold. It generated annoying static electricity. Its soil-release characteristics left much to

[29] Bailey interview.

be desired, especially when it came to oily soils. Depending on the fabric construction, it was prone to snags and pills. Its "hand," the way the fabric felt to the touch, was not the friendliest.[30] That polyester very nearly triumphed, despite such disadvantages, lay in the coincidence of the high value Americans had come to place on convenience and the "natural" neatness of polyester.

Before World War II, most middle-class American households had washing machines, virtually all of which were "wringers." Wringers did the washing much the way a modern "automatic" does it, by churning clothes back and forth in a water-filled tub with a motorized mechanical agitator. However, it was then necessary to feed the laundered clothes manually, one article at a time, between two rotating rubber cylinders that wrung them out to damp-dry condition. Wringing left the laundry flattened, misshapen, and far from ready to wear.[31] Wrung-out laundry fell into a wicker basket for the journey to the clothesline outside – if it was a sunny day. Shirts and trousers then headed for "sprinkling" and the ironing board. The fully automatic clothes washer, which replaced the wringer, took middle-class America by storm in the 1950s and automated the wash, rinse, and damp-drying operations. Automatics relied on two technological innovations: use of an electric timer to manage the stages of the laundry process; and substitution of the old wringer with a powerful centrifuge spinning action, which occurred in the same tub that only a few minutes before had done the washing. "Automatically" washed clothes emerged spun-out, not wrung-out, and ready for the line.

Many, however, never saw a clothesline again, thanks to simultaneous introduction of the electric tumble dryer. An appliance typically the same size as the automatic washer and set beside it, the dryer tumbled spun-dry laundry in a rotating drum through which was forced electrically heated air, which was then vented outside the machine. Clothes emerged dried and "fluffed," but still (if they were made from cotton) as much in need of a press as ever. The dryer's tumbling action, which left cottons wrinkled, left an opportunity for the synthetics to jump on.

---

[30] John D. Turner, "Durable Press Garments," Cotton Incorporated, no date; John B. Price, Timothy A. Calamari, and Wei Ying Tao, "Yarn Preparation, Fabric Formation and Finishing," in Wayne C. Smith, *Cotton* (New York: Wiley, 1999), 751ff.

[31] The procedure "wrung" the laundry with a vigor unknown in earlier manual devices and no doubt gave new life to the old phrase "all wrung out" to describe the condition of being sapped of vitality and urgently in need of a lift.

The molecular structure of polyester fiber imparted to it an inherent "memory," which predisposed it to a microscopically flat configuration and, to the eye, a smooth surface appearance. The same memory also meant that if the fabric had been creased and cured, it tended to retain the crease line through many launderings. The tumbling action of the new electric dryers enhanced this characteristic, liberating the fiber from the distortions wrought by the abuse of washing and spin-drying and permitting it to return to its "natural" flat configuration. The correlation was direct: the higher the polyester content, the greater a fabric's memory and its wrinkle resistance.[32] By comparison, cotton fiber was amnesiac. And though petroleum-based synthetics did not absorb water (reducing their comfort), they were strong – and strength along with wrinkle resistance made for a potent marketing advantage. Wear life and laundering convenience seemed to justify some sacrifice in comfort, and they added new dimensions to the perception of value in apparel.

These dimensions did not exclude cotton entirely. Synthetics manufacturers were alert to the quality shortcomings of their product, some of which they knew could be finessed by blending with cotton. In woven fabric for shirting or trousers, for example, the presence of cotton enhanced fabric "hand," reduced pilling, and improved soil release. The landmark technical breakthrough with blends came with the "Koratron Process," patented in 1963 by Korata Mills of Korata, California. In this process, fabric woven from a blend of polyester and cotton was impregnated with a wrinkle-resistant chemistry, dried, and shipped to the cutter. There it was made into garments, pressed (and with trousers, creased), and placed into a curing oven to induce a chemical reaction. The result was apparel soon marketed as "durable press," which represented an important performance step up from mere wrinkle resistance and which involved the whole textile production chain – from fiber manufacturers to spinners, finishers, dyers, and cutters.[33]

---

[32] Total (or extremely high) synthetic content could, under certain processes, produce fabric that would return, after laundering, to its natural flatness with line-drying alone, a characteristic described by another term that soon entered the vernacular: "drip-dry." Tumble dryers remained for many years largely an American phenomenon, however. In Europe, where interest in line-drying remained keen, special chemistries were developed that gave excellent wrinkle resistance, in particular Milliken's "Belfast Process," which originated "drip-dry." As long as you did not wring it out, you could hang up your shirt in the shower the night before and wear it next morning with never the touch of an iron.

[33] John D. Turner interview, Cotton Incorporated, April 18, 2000.

The optimum blend, from the perspective of the synthetics manufacturers, was that which achieved the desired fabric characteristics with the smallest amount of cotton. Their primary interest, to maximize the mills' consumption of polyester, dictated an effort to identify and guard that threshold. DuPont chemists concluded that no more than 30–35 percent cotton would impart the qualities expected by the market, and it became a company policy to drive hard bargains with mills not to exceed that level if they wished to keep a reliable supply of Dacron from DuPont.

Cotton, whose own inherent natural qualities were not yet in fashion, took what it could get in such a situation. And what it could get was not enough to turn around its falling market share. In the early 1970s, yet another synthetics innovation came on line. The introduction of 100 percent polyester double-knits and textured wovens will not be remembered as a high point in the history of American fashion. At the time, however, polyester double-knits were the latest in a line of "new and different" textile products that appealed to consumers and marketers alike. There was just enough substance to sell the sizzle, for a while: double-knits would not shrink; they had "stretch" with recovery, giving some garments a novel wear sensation; they had bold colors that did not fade; and, of course, they never needed pressing. Unfortunately, they also picked and snagged with distressing ease, fairly lit up with static, and exaggerated the wearer's every temperature-related discomfort.

The physical shortcomings were slight compared with the smirk these products evoked as symbols of bad taste. Its ultimate fashion expression was probably the "leisure suit," which few who wore would later admit to. Accented with white patent leather belt and shoes to match, "full Cleveland" became a running fashion gag. The *Wall Street Journal* (among whose readers, it is safe to say, probably numbered the most stubborn holdouts for cotton) captured the mood with a cartoon in which the maître d' of a toney restaurant announces, down his nose, to a would-be diner dressed in the wrong threads: "I'm sorry, sir, but you've set off our polyester alarm."

Before cotton could profit from the cultural backlash against polyester, it was an urgent matter to upgrade its own wrinkle resistance. The technical foundation for wrinkle-resistant cotton dated back to the 1920s, when textile chemists in England demonstrated in principle that cotton could be chemically treated to impart stability and some degree of wrinkle resistant "memory." But the chemistry was still far from fully worked out, and there was then little competitive pressure to drive the technology forward. By the 1950s and 1960s, bench techniques advanced to commercial processes, as mill-based researchers focused on "cross-linking" to keep the wrinkles out. Cross-linking entailed treating fabric with reactant resins, which acted like chemical springs and gave cotton a measure of the "memory" that was polyester's by nature. Obtaining the proper formulation was important. Too much cross-linking reduced the fabric's strength and abrasion resistance, and early attempts at wrinkle-resistant all-cotton fabrics failed for inadequate wear life.

Koratron and Koratron-like blends had fudged the issue for cotton, as its strength problems were covered by the polyester, just as polyester's comfort problems were covered by the cotton. As it happened, consumers would move toward blends higher in cotton and then to all-cottons, which could be seen in the chart of cotton's market share (level at 36 percent between 1975 and 1980, then rising from 38 percent in 1981 to 43 percent in 1985 and to 50 percent in 1990). Cotton-specific solutions to the fiber's traditional shortcomings proved preferable to blends.[34] The synthetics, in this regard, did cotton a backhanded service by raising the performance bar as high as they had. Competition worked, stimulating innovation.

COTTON ALONE

Beginning in the 1980s, cotton researchers and engineers turned out a steady stream of fiber and fabric processing improvements that gave "performance" new meaning. Chemist John Turner, who led wrinkle-resistance research at Cotton Incorporated, recalled the market shift away from synthetics in the 1980s and the technical challenges it posed: "We were going back to natural – all the way back to natural, all the way back to 100 percent cotton."

It was the work of Wolfgang Strahl's division, headed by John Turner's department, that opened the door for cotton's return to important markets and its strengthening in others. The combination of the right product (100 percent cotton with no-iron convenience) and Cotton Incorporated's marketing and promotional support prompted manufacturers once dedicated to synthetics to offer new cotton choices. All-cotton shirts with no-iron performance appeared in 1979 and were snatched off the store shelves. Arrow, then the country's largest men's shirt manufacturer, had worked with

---

[34] Cotton Incorporated Annual Report, 1990.

Cotton Incorporated to introduce the "Natural Blend" (minimum 60 percent cotton content) shirt in 1975, and it was now leading the way to bring out the first 100 percent cotton no-irons for both men and women. Other branded shirt makers soon followed. All-cotton no-iron shirts soon appeared on the shelves at Sears, then the nation's largest retailer: "The shirt's a best seller ... they're walking out of the stores."[35] The major towel producers restored 100 percent cotton towels to their lines. One hundred percent cotton also returned to bedsheets, cotton's second largest home textiles market after towels, with the appearance of J. P. Stevens's Utica "Cottoncale" and Dan River's "Criterion " brands.[36] In 1985, Cotton Incorporated launched a take-that advertising campaign and retail product identification system – "True Performance" – to trumpet its comeback specifically in terms of fabric qualities at the synthetics' expense. Thus reinterpreted, "performance" left little out. Cotton, and cotton alone, offered consumers fabric that was "comfortable, easy-care, washable, durable, pill-free and breathable."[37]

Cross-linking to improve wrinkle resistance of all cottons traditionally had been achieved through "pre-cure" or "post-cure" processes. Pre-cure, which was especially suitable for fabrics that did not require pleats or creases and were meant to remain flat, afforded good chemical process control and was performed at the mill level. Post-cure, also performed at the mill level, entailed low-temperature controlled drying following the chemical application. This "sensitized" the fabric to take creases after being constructed into garments, which were then cured at high temperature to fix the press. The same curing process also set the seams to give less puckering when laundered. One of the first cross-linking agents to be used on cotton was formaldehyde (and its derivatives), which had the advantages of low cost and little or no effect on the "hand" of the fabric. The most widely used formula was a reaction product (urea and glyoxal) of formaldehyde with the forbidding name "dimethyloldihydroxyethyeneurea" or the not much better DMDHEU. The disadvantage of formaldehyde's alleged toxicity led to development of formaldehyde-free durable-press agents; one of the most effective was DMUG, short for "dihydroxydimethylimidazolidinone."[38]

---

[35] Cotton Incorporated Annual Report, 1979.
[36] Cotton Incorporated Annual Report, 1980.
[37] Cotton Incorporated Annual Report, 1985.
[38] John D. Turner, "Chemistry and Mechanism of Durable Press Cotton Products," Cotton Incorporated, no date. The toxicity of formaldehyde to humans in concentrations common in

The new popularity of all-cotton slacks was signaled by the triumph of Levi's Dockers, introduced in 1987. By the early 1990s, Dockers would be produced at a rate of 25 million pairs per year, and subsequent styles – varying from the most casual look to the most neatly creased items – prompted search for a more refined and environmentally friendly process. Cotton Incorporated approached Farah, a manufacturer, with the idea that wrinkle-resistant performance might be imparted not only before but also after a fabric had been formed into garments. The technology did not differ chemically from the conventional post-cure process, but it moved all of the fabric finishing one step farther down the line of production. After garments were constructed from non–cross-linked fabric, they were then impregnated with the appropriate chemical finish, dried, pressed, and cured. There were two techniques, each of which required sophisticated controls. Garments might be dipped in a chemical bath and thoroughly saturated with the finish solution, which contained a wetting agent, a cross-linking resin, a catalyst, and a softener. The solution would then be extracted to a level of about 50 percent. An alternative approach was to place the garments into a tumbling apparatus, where the finishing chemicals could be precisely metered on in a fine spray and then tumbled until spread evenly throughout all the garments. Conventional pressing and oven curing then followed. The metering and tumbling approach, which became known formally in 1995 as the "metered garment addition process," allocated the finish more precisely, thus cutting chemical costs. Better still, it left behind no effluent and thus had no disposal problems.[39]

The most recognizable physical benefit when compared with post-cured fabrics was much softer fabric "hand," a natural advantage of cotton that had previously lost out in the trade-off to get better wrinkle-resistant performance. Another benefit was lower shrinkage. It was also possible to control for the loss of strength and abrasion resistance (occasioned by the use of ring-spun yarns) by precisely managing the temperature and length of the cure, carefully measuring the concentration of resin, and other techniques.[40] Garment makers also gained manufacturing flexibility and enhanced ability to

the textile industry is highly problematic. The chemical is a natural part of human metabolism and occurs in the bloodstream at one part per million. Apples contain it at about two parts per million.

[39] "Wrinkle-resistant Finishing of Garments with Controlled Metering of Chemicals," Cotton Incorporated, 1997.

[40] Turner, "Chemistry and Mechanism of Durable Press," 8.

customize their lines and better control their inventory. ("Stone-washing," for example, a technique popular in the 1980s to yield a "distressed" already-worn look, could be achieved before the durable press treatment was applied, the worn look thus rendered as durable as the press itself.) The "garment addition" process also removed chemistry from the cut-and-sew rooms once heavy with the scent of formaldehyde, a boon to garment workers.[41]

SHORT PANTS

Don Bailey, the college student who first came to Cotton Incorporated to tend the washers and dryers, eventually became head of textile research and implementation. His powers of observation must have helped his career. He had two brothers (one older and one younger), a father who farmed in addition to working as superintendent of a prison camp, and a mother who was a nurse. "My father felt bad about not being able to help my mother out very much around the house, so he bought her a tumble dryer." Bailey soon began to notice something strange happening with his and his brothers' wardrobes. "I can remember, before I got out of high school, that cotton shirts and pants that had always fit back when they had been line-dried, now went to my little brother, and I got my older brother's stuff."[42] Though he did not know it then, it dawned on Bailey soon after coming to work at Cotton Incorporated that the new dryer had been the culprit. While saving his mother some work, it caused havoc with the proper fit of his clothes and condemned him to an embarrassing adolescence of hand-me-downs.

The dryer made things worse for the boy, but for the man it was an opportunity. In 1972, Cotton Incorporated moved to new rented space on Creedmoor Road in the Crabtree Valley section of Raleigh's north side and installed, under Glenn Morton, its first benchtop physical testing laboratory. It was nothing fancy, and shrinkage was one of the first problems they tackled. Shrinkage went hand-in-hand with wrinkle resistance and was related to it in terms of fabric finishing. And, like wrinkle resistance, it was a problem where chemistry gave polyester a natural advantage, which the tumble dryer accentuated. Toss the stuff into the dryer and, unlike cotton, it did not shrink.

---

[41] John D. Turner, "Durable Press Garments," Cotton Incorporated Textile Research and Implementation, no date.

[42] Bailey interview.

Although high levels of shrinkage of 100 percent cotton fabrics (particularly knits) had long been known, not until the competitive threat from polyester was there much incentive to do anything about it. So, it had remained a mystery. Fabric department head Wolfgang Strahl brought with him a fresh approach to the old problem of shrinkage. Trained as an engineer, he thought in engineering terms of achieving a desired result by linking a series of processes into a system and then managing the system to meet a particular set of design criteria. The best strategy for textile product development, he believed, was not to concentrate on designing exotic new fabrics but rather to take basic products and make them better. Rather than selling cotton by the trainload based on clever or fancy things that only a few mills could make, what was needed was to help the mills make basic products better and then "throw in some innovative things as you go along." [43] It was tempting and fun to tinker, for instance, with new equipment design and how it might improve knitting to reduce shrinkage. However, the more practical approach was to start with the basic machines (that mills were already full of) and try to improve those machines so they would produce fabric that was stronger, looked better, and shrank less.

Shrinkage, formally speaking, is a change in the dimensions of a fabric or garment resulting from some application of force, energy, or change in environment that allows a fabric to "relax" – or causes it to move in a certain direction, which can be negative (contraction) or positive (growth). Cotton fabrics are unique among textiles for their extreme dimensional instability. There are different types of shrinkage: construction shrinkage (the amount of shrinkage inherent in the yarn as a function of the machine and construction variables used to create it), elastic shrinkage (how much a fabric tends to "relax" from the tensions imposed during construction), and drying shrinkage (caused when a fabric "de-swells" and contracts upon itself as a result of drying). Cotton's natural hydrophilicity, which made it comfortable to wear, proved to be its downfall when it came to shrinkage. As the fabric becomes wet, swelling of the fibers and subsequently the yarns and fabric results. Upon swelling, the loops in the knitted structure become more round, which is their lowest energy state and which results in a change in fabric dimension. During swelling (wetting) and de-swelling (drying), the water tends to lubricate movement within the structure of the fabric, and when energy is applied in the form of mechanical action (as in

---

[43] Ibid.

a tumble dryer), shrinkage can be severe. Combating shrinkage requires mechanical or chemical approaches to help stabilize an inherently unstable material.[44]

A number of factors can have an impact on shrinkage: the fiber itself, size and type of the yarn, finishing processes used, manufacturing techniques, and care methods practiced. Such multiplicity of causes, and their overlapping character, made shrinkage a challenge well-suited to an engineering response. In the mid-1970s there was no "silver bullet" – just some good practices that, when added up, would help cotton perform better.

Strahl's team set out to examine the performance characteristics of cotton knits and to build that knowledge into a practical program that would allow a manufacturer to control the whole process – from selection of the yarn and knitting machinery through dyeing, finishing, and garment processing. They were convinced that the processing of a knitted cotton – through the textile dye house, manufacturing steps, and ultimately consumer laundering – was no different from any other engineering process that could be measured for critical dimensions and performance criteria during its use. Once measured, it could then be matched to any standards desired.

The principle was the same as that behind Chewning's Engineered Fiber Selection (EFS) process, though a step or two farther down the line. The innate (and detrimental) variableness of the "natural" fiber input, here with regard to another of its weaknesses, would be "engineered" into submission and placed into the service of consumers who wanted clothes that combined cotton's comfort characteristics with the shrinkage-resistant characteristics of synthetics. This particular bit of engineering depended on working out the fundamental relationships between the fully "relaxed" fabric as it was wet-processed and the construction parameters of knitting. It promised to answer why cottons shrank to different levels when produced at different weights and widths.[45]

Experiments in the Raleigh lab looked at hundreds of different combinations of fabric constructions, yarns, knitting machine settings, and dye house finishing processes. Thousands of fabric tests were performed and tens of thousands of data points recorded, measuring fabric variables in its

---

[44] Donald L. Bailey, "A Guide to Improved Shrinkage Performance of Cotton Knitted Fabrics," Cotton Incorporated, 1998.

[45] Donald L. Bailey, "Engineered Knitting Systems – Fiber to Garments," Cotton Incorporated, 1999.

"reference state."[46] From analysis of the empirical data, researchers derived a series of "K-factors" ("K" representing the mathematical constant that related fabric structure to its processing) to predict fabric performance. There were K-factors describing stitch density, width per inch, length per inch, ratio of width to length, and yield (measured in ounces per yard).

K-factors had been used in the industry since the 1960s for undyed goods only, but missing was the calibration necessary to relate them to particular sequences of dye house techniques. Cotton Incorporated optimized service to the mill by showing how each plant could calculate K-factors for each of their own processing lines. Once the K-factors had been established for a particular processing sequence, a computer program could be written to predict the performance of any fabric processed through that sequence. The program could be customized to each manufacturing facility and allow each product line to be engineered to achieve its customer's desired weights and widths with low shrinkage. If the manufacturer wished, the same program could incorporate other data as well, such as costs or production rates at different efficiencies.

The goal was to take large amounts of data that otherwise served only as physical descriptors and put it to analytical use (as EFS had done for HVI data), enabling manufacturers to determine if they could meet customer specifications without having to knit, dye, finish, and test every candidate. The output was a spreadsheet that summarized a particular set of calculations and told the manufacturer what that process would yield against the product specifications for shrinkage. The program first accounted for the fabric's construction parameters: cut, diameter, number of needles, yarn count, and stitch length. From this data, the computer then calculated the fabric's reference (relaxed) state. Once the target shrinkage values were entered, the computer then calculated the delivered dimensions needed to achieve the desired shrinkage.

"Engineering Cotton Knits for Performance," as Cotton Incorporated described the process, made cotton – that is, the fabric characteristics that could be derived from it – more predictable. It quantified how low shrinkage could be achieved in cotton by thoroughly engineering the product from fiber selection through all subsequent processing steps. Thus it benefited

---

[46] The "reference" or "relaxed" state of a fabric refers to its dimensions when it will shrink no further (which is, ideally, the state in which the consumer receives it). This state is achieved on most cotton fabrics after five cycles of washing and tumble drying.

textile mills, whose managers hated surprises. As the market turned from synthetics back to "naturals," the mills needed all the help they could get in meeting the fabric demands of apparel manufacturers. Mills needed help to develop specific products for manufacturers; to fine-tune their processing equipment; and to reduce the time taken to test fabrics for shrinkage. Cotton engineering, though it could not banish cotton shrinkage entirely, could at least help the mills manage its consequences.

FAREWELL FADED COTTON

Don Bailey tells another story about how fabric development work proceeded in the early days, before Cotton Incorporated had its own dye house: they begged, borrowed, and stole time from mills' processing floors. "We'll be glad to pay for it, but we need to use it to develop some fabrics," went the well-worn company line. A sympathetic mill typically responded with a date of its choosing and never with quite all the time that was needed. Bailey – along with Rob Stone, Mike Tyndall, Wallace Blanton, and others – made many road trips around the Carolinas, sometimes sleeping on a sofa in plant offices to monitor 24-hour-a-day tests. "My first child was born in 1975 and I probably would have changed careers," Bailey remembered, "if our dye house hadn't been put in." [47]

In 1976, Dukes Wooters scavenged money from a budget heavy on marketing and tight on everything else in order to add a dye house. It was located next to the railroad tracks in an unused grocery warehouse in Raleigh near North Carolina State University. The place soon was transformed into a first-rate textile processing facility. It was here that some of the answers to another of cotton's inherent disadvantages were worked out.

One of the things that consumers had noticed, and had liked most, about polyester products was their affinity for color. Something purchased bright red or Kelly green was still bright red or Kelly green fifty or a hundred launderings later. It might be full of snags and pills, but the color was as good as ever. Cotton, by contrast, faded after half as many times through the wash. Just as with wrinkling and shrinking, so it was with color; the synthetics had this, too, among their chemical advantages.

The polyester molecule took to dye like cotton took to water, or better. Dyeing Dacron had about it a simple elegance. First, the fibers were softened

---

[47] Bailey interview.

and made porous under high temperature and pressure. Once soft, a dye-stuff was diffused and the temperature then reduced. As the fiber cooled and contracted, the color was effectively trapped on the inside, never again to escape. Nature, by contrast, worked against cotton, a highly morphous and reactive fiber. Its molecules were filled with carbon and chemically re-active side chains, all sites for troublesome reactions to take place and for color to seep away. The thickness of cotton's cell wall, determined by the fineness and maturity of the fiber and measured by the micronaire value, could alter the shade of the dyed fiber. Cotton's irregular reflectance and degrees of yellowness, also measured at the very start of the production process, made preparation and dyeing a challenge. Mills were known to lay down as many as forty bales to achieve needed consistency and to be sure that the product from each successive processing machine was mixed again at the next stage. Neps – pesky knotlike entanglements of fine fibers – took dye less readily than other fibers and so further hampered even coloring. Fuzzy surfaces reflected light less well than smooth and gave cottons an un-welcome dull and faded look.[48]

In 1974, Hal Brockmann hired Rob Stone away from Springs Mills. Before that, Stone had managed laboratories at the nearby American Associa-tion of Textile Chemists and Colorists, the organization that set world-wide standards for colorfastness, shrinkage control, and other textile char-acteristics. Experienced with the mill's perspective and testing regimens, Stone, Bailey, and others started to look for ways to dye cotton better. Cotton Incorporated was not alone in this – the chemical and dyeing ma-chinery companies also worked on the problem – but it had the credibility to demonstrate what worked and to promote its implementation in the industry.

In equipment designed for dyeing polyester, cotton fabrics performed poorly; hence cotton promoters had to overcome mill owners' resistance to switching. Cotton Incorporated addressed the problem by taking the prin-ciple of reactive dyeing: using time and buffered chemistry (instead of just elevated temperature) to dye goods. The result, first applied commercially in 1978, was the system of pad-batch dyeing and beam washing of reactive dyestuffs for 100 percent cotton knits and wovens, a technique that worked without the use of common salt and required many times less water than conventional jet dyeing. The result was a dyeing system for cotton that

---

[48] John B. Price et al., "Yarn Preparation, Fabric Formulation, and Finishing," 778–9.

significantly reduced processing costs while improving the color and appearance of the fabric.[49]

Well-dyed cotton without wrinkles, creases, or fuzz was at first hard for some people in the mills to believe. To demonstrate that their new approach would actually work, the Cotton Incorporated researchers went so far as to set up bleacher seats overlooking the dyeing machinery in the Neil Street lab and invite an audience of mill experts to watch demonstration trials. "It felt like we were on live TV: if something goes wrong, you look real bad," Don Bailey remembered. "It's a fairly complicated process, but we were able to show them we could do it."[50]

FINAL JUDGE

The consumer is the last chemist to touch the cloth, to wash it and dry it, to judge whether or not it has faded, and to decide whether to repurchase a product like it or instead something else. As much as fashion, the technology of home laundering changed the way consumers viewed cotton and its competition, at first to the advantage of the synthetics. Cotton caught up through focused research, much of it via the agency of Cotton Incorporated. Improvements in fiber selection, wrinkle resistance, fabric stability, and color enabled mills and manufacturers to engineer a natural product to specifications comparable – if not in all ways equal – to what synthetics had to offer. Retaining all the while its own "natural" advantage of superior comfort, cotton thus rehabilitated itself in a skeptical marketplace.

The marketing partnership forged between Cotton Incorporated and Procter & Gamble in 1993 to display the Seal of Cotton on millions of boxes of Cheer, Tide, and Ivory Snow came at the exact intersection of textile research and consumer marketing. Technology supported and validated

---

[49] "Open-width Pad-batch Dyeing of Cotton Fabrics," Cotton Incorporated Technical Bulletin.

[50] "Pad batch" itself was not new. Cotton Incorporated changed a key step in the reactive process. Ordinarily, dyed material went through a steamer, or a drying and curing oven, which reacted and fixed the dyestuff with temperature. Cotton Incorporated instead padded dyestuff onto the fabric at a 1:1 ratio (one pound of dye liquor to one pound of fabric), rolled the fabric up to 2000 yards onto a perforated beam, wrapped it air-tight in plastic, and rotated it at room temperature for between 4 and 24 hours, depending on the type of dyestuff and shading desired. Time, not temperature, reacted the dye. The beam then went to a wash-off station where the plastic was removed and water, first cold and then hot, was pumped from the inside of the beam through the perforations and out through the fabric. The result was a clean fabric with very little fuzz on it, and brilliantly dyed.

such advertising coups. It also factored into larger societal concerns. Cotton's recovery of market share corresponded with environmental worries about the presence of chlorine and phosphates in home laundry chemicals. Soap makers refashioned their products to meet new government standards and still deliver clean clothes. In doing so, they added new activators to detergent chemistry that also had potential to alter color. Mike Tyndall and Norma Keyes at Cotton Incorporated and researchers at Procter & Gamble uncovered enzymes that addressed the fading problem. If a fabric got fuzzy in laundering, as cotton tended to when washed in the new formulas, its color looked washed-out. The enzymes removed the surface hairs that refracted the light to a disadvantage, and the color got richer again. Procter & Gamble's subsequent advertising campaigns drove home to the consumer – the final judge in the testing chain – that cottons washed with their products would retain their color, load after load. So, in the ultimate marketing triumph, soap sold cotton.[51]

The incessant claims of advertising and the demands of consumers pressed ultimately backward through the entire chain of production to cotton's first supplier, the grower. The mill's output, and the output of each subsequent processor in the chain, depended on the grower's initial input. No effort could be spared, therefore, in improving his capabilities for supplying high-quality raw cotton and supplying it profitably. As a competitive market had stimulated innovations in textile processing that produced better yarns and fabrics, so competition would press cotton growers to practice better agriculture.

---

[51] The Procter & Gamble partnership, forged by Cotton Incorporated's Ira Livingston, also marked the first time the Seal of Cotton was applied to a nontextile product.

8

THE NECESSARY ILLUSION
OF CONTROL

By the 1970s, it was do or die. Independent businessmen all, growers knew they were all in the same peril. In coffee shops in a thousand Cotton Belt towns – wherever they gathered to talk about the weather, the government, the crop – they expanded their business and technological horizons. Ruminations about making a living turned to "how good" and "how profitable" their cotton had to be, no longer simply how plentiful. Their hopes for concerted action now turned not simply to government but to a more private-sector mode of action in the new Cotton Incorporated. And though many of them may have had a poor grasp of just what it was Dukes Wooters and his New York marketing staff were up to, growers everywhere knew that, for better or worse, this new organization might be the best shot they had for putting the brakes on cotton's steady market decline. They hoped so, at least, since they had agreed to ante up one dollar a bale to support it.

It is important to recognize that even as cotton growers looked forward to saving their farms, they harbored few illusions about their livelihoods. They never did. As farmers, cotton growers tend to be stoic idealists, at peace with the change of the seasons and firmly attached to the soil. But rarely are they romantic about it. They are the scions of uncertainty, constantly and pragmatically aware of the shifting fortunes of both nature and market, never knowing whether they are dealing with friends or adversaries. Like all people engaged in business, they crave a stable prosperity, the market to oneself, the price that will never fall, the product that will not grow obsolete – while at the same time secretly knowing that all of that is fleeting. Throw nature into the mix, and the very idea of stability becomes an utter illusion.

Yet some measure of illusion is vital to the cotton grower's survival. Simply to accept the inevitable vicissitudes of both market and nature would be more than discouraging, it would be psychologically paralyzing. "Why grow cotton at all? We don't need cotton to eat. There are other ways to clothe ourselves." Instead, the grower strives to cope with nature as best he can and respond to the market, as he must. He manages. And as science and technology have displaced traditional sources of know-how, the grower has learned there is more and more that can be managed, if not altogether made certain.

As for market forces, just what was needed to improve the grower's ability to meet demands for higher quality at lower prices – higher yields? Cost-reducing handling methods? Better cotton fibers? As for nature, what was needed to improve the grower's chances of bringing a good crop to market – fewer bugs? Bigger machinery? Better resistance to weather? In the modern world, such questions are impossible for the individual grower to address alone, and it is impractical even for groups of growers to seek solutions on a local or regional basis – at least without considering the impact of their actions on the larger interests of cotton growers everywhere.

The agricultural research division of Cotton Incorporated was organized as a cooperative effort to search for some of the answers on a nationwide basis. Over the years, it produced or encouraged the development of a line of research products that changed the way growers – in Georgia, Missouri, and Texas alike – grew cotton in response to natural threats and more stringent market demands. It has also established a process for performing research that linked the grass roots to the ivory tower and brought focus to disparate calls for help from growers stretched out from the Carolinas to California. It has contributed substantially to the progress researchers around the country have made on the fundamental biological reality of the industry: that cotton growers are in the business of producing cellulose.

No one yet knows all the chemical pathways by which that cellulose is produced; if researchers do eventually discover all the steps in the process, then growers might or might not be better off. The problem, which is no tautology but just the messy part of science, is that there is no way to know until you find out. Still, scientific research transformed into well-disseminated new knowledge makes the illusion of control marginally easier to hold, and it has helped the more progressive cotton growers remain profitably in the business.

THE PROCESS OF RESEARCH

Cotton growers had some experience relying on technical help provided by the agricultural schools of the land grant universities, the state experiment stations, and the USDA, all of which courted growers as a major constituency. And so too, for a price, did the seed, chemical, and implement companies. But now the pace of technological innovation would quicken as Cotton Incorporated entered the picture. Its focus, by law, was upland cotton and upland cotton alone, and its only constituency was the people who grew it.

Growers had several channels for communicating what problems they wanted solved, and there was never any shortage of candidates in the queue. Cotton Incorporated was set up as a representative organization. Growers alone sat on its board, working farmers to a man, each with a network back home of friends and neighbors on whose behalf he spoke. Its professional agricultural research staff, on the other hand, were paid to listen. Starting with the first director Harold L. "Hal" Lewis, they were an itinerant crew, logging thousands of miles each year on little airplanes and in rental cars and countless nights in not-so-fancy small-town motels. It was no job for desk jockeys or lab hounds. "Field work" meant just that: long dusty days under a blazing southern sun.

To what they learned in the field, however, Cotton Incorporated's staff added all the analytical skills implied by their advanced scientific degrees. These degrees came mainly from land grant universities, which from the time of the Civil War had elevated the study of agriculture to a science.[1] Science for its own sake was left to those same universities; the company's mission was to bring workable technology to bear on growers' manifold problems, natural and economic alike. "We do very little science for its own sake," explained William F. Lalor, the company's fourth and current head of agricultural research. "We find solutions to problems."[2]

Cotton Incorporated would find it relatively easy to position itself at the center of a network of scientific and technological knowledge that growers could use. The cotton scientific community was relatively small and, because nongreenhouse field work could be conducted nowhere else, with few exceptions was located within the Cotton Belt. The company's staff knew what most everyone was up to and served, on the basis of relationships going back as far as their own graduate-school days, as a bridge linking grower

---

[1] Four men have headed the agricultural research program: Harold L. Lewis, George Slater, J. K. Jones, and William F. Lalor. Of the company's seven-member (in 2000) professional agricultural research staff, six are trained to the Ph.D. level in engineering, physiology, agronomy, entomology, economics, and systems engineering. The seventh holds an MS and an MBA.

[2] William F. Lalor, Cotton Incorporated, interview, February 15, 2000.

problems to the best academic talent at hand to solve them. As needs were identified – whether to make cotton fiber longer, improve cottonseed, make cotton plants more tolerant of cool temperatures, or banish white flies or boll weevils – the staff went back to the university and USDA researchers working in those specialties in order to fashion plans of action and project proposals. The research format that resulted came to be known as the "co-operative agreement."

In general, it would be hard to conceive of a less self-aggrandizing approach to a research and development function that, in the for-profit world, would be expected to yield a concrete return on investment. But Cotton Incorporated had an ambiguous attitude toward profit. It was not itself a for-profit business entity but rather was charged to increase the profit-making potential of the private individuals who funded it. This was an important distinction. The circumstances of shifting budgets, for instance, circumscribed its ability to patent and thus potentially to profit from many of the research discoveries and technological innovations that it subsidized under co-operative agreements. It did better in this regard in the early years than later.

The agricultural research budgets of the first half of the 1970s, which came from grower check-off funds and were augmented (after 1973) by federal "610" funds, were large enough to command respect at universities for whom Cotton Incorporated dollars represented a valuable subsidy for faculty researchers.[3] Never before had such concentrated slugs of money been devoted to cotton research, and in the company's early cooperative agreements it had no difficulty stipulating that researchers filing patents would assign them back (except for patents from 610 funds). However, the attitude among cooperating institutions of "take the money and let Cotton Incorporated have the patents" was shortsighted and did not last.

The size of the company's agricultural research budget depended, as did the promotional budget, on the size of the total dollar-a-bale assessment in any given year, which depended in turn on the number of bales growers

---

[3] The Farm Bill of 1970 granted, through the Commodity Credit Corporation (CCC), direct federal subsidy to the Cotton Board for research and promotion: "Section 610 Funds." In August 1971, the CCC, the Cotton Board, Cotton Incorporated, and the Secretary of Agriculture signed a contract governing distribution of these funds that was virtually identical to the one concluded earlier between Cotton Incorporated and the Cotton Board, which made Cotton Incorporated sole contractor for the expenditure of check-off funds. The new contract made it sole contractor for expenditure of cotton 610 funds as well, only with a stipulation providing that the Secretary was to hold and dispose of any patents resulting from research conducted with 610 funds.

took to market and on the level of refunds they requested. It also depended on what share of the total budget agricultural research could command relative to promotion. Beginning in 1977, when cotton's 610 funding ended, these numbers dropped precipitously from over $5 million (24 percent of Cotton Incorporated's total budget) to just over $1 million (less than 7 percent). They hovered at that level for fifteen years. As agricultural research lost dollars, it lost the leverage it once had with its university cooperators, who were now recognizing the income potential of patents filed by their faculty – and whose lawyers typically rejected the company's research contracts unless the universities retained the patent rights. By the time the agricultural research budget reached its nadir of just over $800,000 (4.4 percent of the total budget) in 1986, patent rights had vanished from the company's cooperative research agreements.

With the coming of uniform (mandatory) assessment and importer contributions in the early 1990s, the picture changed. Agricultural research budgets reversed their decline and rose steadily to over $7 million in 1998 (11 percent of the total), circumstances that emboldened Cotton Incorporated once again to reassert itself on the patent issue. It was not an issue of money per se; the company's total "earned revenue" from patents and royalties had never amounted to much. In negotiations conducted with various state experiment stations in the late 1990s, the aim was not to secure patent rights in cooperative research but to influence, in the growers' interest, to whom and under what conditions patents might be licensed to others. (Cotton Incorporated also negotiated provision of royalties enough to cover twice the amount of its own subsidy.) The point was to try to protect growers from paying twice for the fruits of company-subsidized research: once in form of their mandatory assessment to the Cotton Board and once again, for example, in the form of a license fee required to plant advanced forms of cotton seed and paid to the companies that sold it.[4]

---

4 Lalor interview. On discoveries resulting from the relatively small amount of research conducted exclusively in-house (that is, with Cotton Incorporated's own staff and with no outside cooperator assistance), Cotton Incorporated did continue to seek patent protection. "Easiflo" cottonseed was one example. Renewed effort to influence the licensing of patents by others was consistent with the spirit of the company's original patent policy as established for CPI in 1968, which put the grower's interest always first: "The basic policy of [Cotton Incorporated] in the acquisition and use of patents and trademarks and in the establishment and use of licenses and royalties is to secure maximum utilization of U.S. cotton in domestic and foreign markets and to serve the best interests of the U.S. cotton producer." Board Minutes, July 11, 1968.

Budget vicissitudes under the original voluntary assessment program (in addition to constraining patent policy under cooperative research agreements) led to the creation of the other primary vehicle for agricultural research at Cotton Incorporated: the State Support Program. As great an improvement as Cotton Incorporated was over CPI when it came to funding mechanisms, the growers' right to receive an unconditional refund of their assessments bedeviled the company for two decades. Year after year, the board and professional staff rode the refund rollercoaster, which made long-term planning difficult on both the research and promotion sides of the company. Moreover, leakage through refunds of precious assessment dollars from the research and promotion program meant that the company's war chest, not large to begin with when compared with the synthetics competition, was very hard to augment.

Making matters worse, refunds went up when cotton prices went down. To combat this penny-wise temptation of growers to compensate for lower profits at the expense of longer-term cost-saving science and technology, the company devised a means to persuade skittish growers to stick with the program by making it more "local." Under the State Support Program, if any state managed to contribute at least 80 percent of its assessment under the voluntary check-off program (i.e., to limit its refunds to 20 percent or less), then everything contributed above 80 percent would be returned to the same state for agricultural research of its own choosing. States like North Carolina, which typically paid at close to 100 percent, collected some large sums under the scheme. The program could not ultimately solve the refund problem, but it did create a large second stage of funding that had the added political benefit of making growers feel in closer touch with their research program.

The clever solution would become a new problem with the coming of mandatory assessment in 1991, which removed the need for a give-back incentive to keep growers in the program but also threatened suddenly to inundate the State Support Program with an embarrassment of riches (that is, 20 percent of the company's entire annual budget). The board deemed such a windfall simply too high and worried that too heavy a focus on local research interests could erode one of Cotton Incorporated's key strengths: its ability to coordinate research efforts across state lines and disseminate results for the benefit of all cotton growers.[5] Thus they revised the program

[5] Cotton Incorporated Board Minutes; Chairman's Reports, 1991, 1992.

downward to 5 percent, though not without a fight from some of the historically best performers – Arizona, New Mexico, Oklahoma, and North Carolina – who were "grandfathered" in for five years at the 20 percent level so as "not to be cut off at the knees."[6]

From the outset, the State Support Program work tended to focus on production-related research with short-term time horizons rather than long-term work in basic research and development. Proposals reflected growers' concerns at the moment. If a region had suffered drought one year, it was not unusual to see State Support proposals heavy on irrigation projects the next year. The role of Cotton Incorporated's staff, which sat on the committees that dispersed State Support funds, was to lend detached scientific judgment and to evaluate proposals for co-funding from the core agricultural research budget. But it was also to temper the tendency toward short-term projects and to keep alive such work – on molecular genetics, for example – that might prove promising only after years of study. Even the simplest field projects took at least three years to get good data meriting publication and were sometimes subject to uncontrollable delays, often the result of bad weather. Good science took patience, and useable results could not be rushed.

Since the natural tendency of the State Support Program was to speak to immediate concerns of local interest, Cotton Incorporated's agricultural research effort provided a countervailing force to parochialism. Since its constituency (growers of upland cotton) was unified in its economic interests but diverse in its geographic and cultural characteristics, the company had to develop the capacity to work across state lines and from region to region when coordinating complex research efforts on problems that affected, though not necessarily equally or simultaneously, cotton growers who labored thousands of miles apart.

The key point is that, until the coming of Cotton Incorporated, there had been no true clearinghouse for scientific information devoted to upland cotton. Nor had there been an adequate clearinghouse for disseminating practical know-how to growers nationally. Previously, a grower might attend the occasional USDA or experiment station meeting in his state, read the extension service bulletins, and (with luck) piece some things together.

---

[6] Lalor interview. Fortuitously, by the time the five years was up, states like North Carolina had so increased their crop (and thus their assessment) as a result of boll weevil eradication that 5 percent turned out to produce more money than 20 percent had.

But as in the challenge of marketing, so in the challenge of research: the grower's natural instincts for independence were at odds with his need to cooperate beyond his own neighborhood on problems that threatened cotton generally.

An early example was the resurgence of cotton bollworm infestation in the early 1970s. The problem began in the lower Rio Grande Valley of south Texas and, like the boll weevil blight before it, spread with the prevailing winds eastward across the Mississippi. Chemical means to manage the pest had long been available, but Cotton Incorporated added a new capability of superior information. Bad news had always spread, but now growers had the means of more nimble response. Organizing meetings of researchers across Texas and the mid-South, the company was able to inform growers about what to expect. Texas had serious worm infestation one year, and studies that indicated the building up of populations in Louisiana and Mississippi foretold they were next. Texas' previous experience with treatment helped growers to the east to calibrate the timing and level of their own spraying and supplied reliable recommendations about which insecticides worked best. Forewarned was forearmed.

The cotton module builder and the boll weevil eradication program were other examples, from the 1970s and 1980s respectively, of Cotton Incorporated's facility for interstate and cross-regional applied research. More recently, work in defoliation (cotton must be defoliated before it is harvested, but there are huge variations in the conditions across the Cotton Belt for accomplishing this economically), in "bronze wilt" and "seed rot" (as-yet unexplained diseases of cotton, caused perhaps by ubiquitous organisms awaiting just the right climatic conditions to emerge and do their damage), and in conservation tillage (a tillage and planting system that maintains at least 30 percent of the soil surface covered by residue after planting to reduce erosion) carried on in that tradition.[7]

MECHANIZATION'S FINALE

Cotton is not the easiest of field crops to handle, and the history of its mechanization was long and halting. This had less to do with the lack of

---

[7] Thomas Valco, Cotton Incorporated, et al., eds., *Conservation-Tillage Systems for Cotton: A Review of Research and Demonstrations Results from across the Cotton Belt* (Fayetteville: Arkansas Agricultural Experiment Station, 1995).

technological innovation (a workable mechanical picker was available in the 1930s) than with its unevenness across the different stages of cotton's cultivation – and with the persistent availability of cheap labor well past the time when many good-enough mechanical alternatives were available.[8] The popular image of cotton agriculture mechanization is dominated by a single device, the mechanical picker. This is probably because another image dominates popular understanding of cotton agriculture before machines: broad fields of mature cotton dotted with scores of human pickers dragging long white sacks, gathering in the "snow of southern summers." The harvest, it would seem, was all.

The imagery conveyed a certain truth. For the grower, ever at risk from the moment of planting, the harvest was the last hurdle over which he exercised direct control. The harvest concludes each year's timeless ritual of planting, chopping, cultivating, and praying. It is the final moment when a farmer's ignorance or negligence or misjudgment can bring all to naught, or when smart practice and good timing can win success. One way or another, the harvest ends a farmer's contest with nature for that year and launches him into the subsequent perils of the market.

Timing is everything. The longer the mature crop stands on the stalk exposed to the elements, the more it deteriorates both in quantity and quality. Orchestrating its timely harvest is a function of the grower's instinct, experience, and access to the mechanical or human resources needed to do the picking. Once picked, however, other variables enter the equation as the picked but unginned cotton, known as "seed cotton," enters the long chain of production. Traditionally, seed cotton entered that chain at the gin; in covering the distance from field to gin – measured out in space and time – a perennial problem arose.

Because unharvested cotton is perishable, the grower reduces his risk the most who harvests his crop with the greatest dispatch. Gin operators possessed fixed capital investment in highly specialized machinery, good for nothing else than ginning cotton, and which needed to earn a return while operating only a relatively small numbers of days per year.[9] Ginners,

---

[8] See Chapter 2, "Nature and Know-How." James H. Street, *The New Revolution in the Cotton Economy: Mechanization and Its Consequences* (Chapel Hill: University of North Carolina Press, 1957); Charles R. Sayre, "Cotton Mechanization Since World War II," *Agricultural History* 53 (January 1979), 105–24.

[9] Before the module system, many gins ran only 400–500 hours per year; now most run 1,400–1,500 hours.

Cotton is ready for picking anywhere from July to November in different parts of the Cotton Belt. Once mature, it is vulnerable to weather and deterioration of quality. Speedy handling from field to gin is essential.

who therefore made the most by running their machinery constantly, and growers, who needed to gin their cotton (and get paid for it) as quickly as possible, had congruent but not identical interests in this first nonfarm stage of cotton processing. Supply of and demand for ginning capacity proved devilishly difficult to match up.

On the demand side was the crop, which needed to be harvested quickly. On the supply side was the gin, often overwhelmed with but sometimes hungry for seed cotton. One of two things might occur. If the harvesting capacity in terms of bales per day in a particular locality was higher than the ginning capacity, then either the harvesting came to a halt (increasing the grower's risk of crop damage or loss) or the seed cotton had to be stored. Ginning capacity much in excess of harvesting capacity was by definition uneconomic for the gin owner. It was the natural tendency of growers to increase picking capacity (more hands in the field working longer hours or more mechanical pickers) to match any increase in gin capacity, but too much gin capacity was still a risky business. When the weather was inclement and growers could not get into the field to harvest, the gin was left standing idle with nothing to do but with a crew still on the payroll. Unequal capacities created inefficiencies and raised costs in labor, energy, equipment, and capital along the line from getting cotton off the stalk and into the packaged bale.

If only there were a way to establish a reservoir between field and gin. The principle had been long understood, but traditional approaches never worked smoothly enough to bring the urgency of the harvest and the capacity of the gins into balance. The oldest, dating from the earliest days of cotton's first revival before the Civil War and practiced by smaller growers well into the 1960s, was simply to use the means of transport from field to gin as the reservoir. At first this was a mule-drawn wagon (later on a pick-up towing a trailer or a flat-bed truck hauling custom-made baskets), filled with seed cotton in the field and then driven to the gin and lined up in the gin yard to wait its turn for processing. The labor that drove the wagons (and then the trucks) obviously could not do anything else at the same time. And nobody ever had enough trailers to create a big enough reservoir and still keep the flow of cotton coming from the field and the harvesters moving.

Beginning in the 1950s, a different technology began to make some progress toward solving the reservoir problem. The ricker was a bottomless and topless three-sided rectangular steel box into which seed cotton was deposited directly from the picker. Next into the box were human stompers, farm workers who compressed the cotton with their boots. When the box was full, the stompers got out and a tractor pulled the ricker forward just enough to make room for some more cotton, and the process was repeated. The result were ricks sometimes 200–300 feet long at the ends of the fields: great loaves of cotton, covered with tarps against the weather and packed just tightly enough to keep their shape for a time. Ricks were easier to make, however, than they were to move, and thus fell short of creating a comprehensive field-to-gin handling system. Their low density made them hard to pick up, which was typically accomplished with a front-end loading tractor that dumped chunks of the rick (and, not unusually, chunks of soil along with it) into a trailer for the journey to the gin. Half-way technology that it was, rickers were popular – particularly in West Texas and California, where dry conditions mitigated against persistent worries about the safety of storing seed cotton.[10] Near Lubbock, there were even some efforts to mechanize the "lift" part of the process.[11]

The ricking system helped relieve the bottleneck between field and gin, but it fell short of achieving greater efficiencies that depended on removing more labor from the process and on finding a smoother means of delivering the stored seed cotton to the gin. The answer lay with patents granted to J. K. "Farmer" Jones, formerly with the National Cotton Council and Cotton Incorporated's specialist in cotton picking and handling, and Lambert H. Wilkes, an agricultural engineer at Texas A&M University and author of a widely used textbook on farm mechanization. The patents were assigned by them directly to the company.[12]

Patent 3807950, for a "seed cotton handling apparatus," had a history that began at the University of Arkansas in the 1960s. Arkansas cotton belonged to the Delta, famous among other things for the Stoneville Experiment Station across the river in Mississippi and a world-famous center of cotton agricultural research. This particular innovation, however, belonged squarely to Arkansas. The inspiration of Zinn McNeil, an agricultural engineer at the University of Arkansas, the device was a steel box open at the top and with a pallet that formed a false bottom. Into it was compressed seed cotton equivalent to about three bales, tramped down by foot. It was called the "Arkansas Cotton Caddy." The Caddy formed a module, or package of cotton, and thus minimized the amount of energy required for reloading the cotton for the journey to the gin. It suffered from the disadvantage that the stack-forming device and the transport unit were one and the same, which potentially slowed down the harvesting rate.

Jones saw huge potential in the idea if it could be refined and brought to market, so he tried to persuade the Arkansas researchers to advance from

---

[10] See J. W. Sorensen, Jr., and Lambert H. Wilkes, "Seed Quality and Moisture Relationships in Harvesting and Storing Seed Cotton," Final Report Cooperative Agreement no. 73–630 between Cotton Incorporated and Texas Agricultural Experiment Station, Texas A&M University, August 1973.

[11] William Lalor, Cotton Incorporated, interview, February 25, 2000; L. C. Unfred interview, July 2000.

[12] Lambert H. Wilkes, Harrison P. Smith, et al., *Farm Machinery and Equipment* (New York: McGraw-Hill, 1937 and later editions).

their bench model to something larger, more mechanized, and more powerful. He approved small grants to the University of Arkansas to move the concept along, but ultimately teamed up with Wilkes at Texas A&M, whom he met at a Western Cotton Producers Conference in 1971. It became a highly productive partnership.[13] "Farmer's way of operating was to sit down on a concrete floor with a piece of chalk and sketch out what he wanted to do," remembered Gay Jividen, a young Cotton Incorporated researcher who knew them both. "Lambert Wilkes was one of those guys who could interpret that."[14] The result of Wilkes's interpretation of Jones's idea was the Arkansas Caddy grown-up and powered-up into the cotton module builder. The module builder typically appears on the list of the three most important technological innovations in cotton agriculture, alongside the mechanical picker (available in the 1930s but not widely used until the 1950s) and the cotton gin (1793). Like them, it changed the cotton landscape profoundly and, with associated innovations, filled in the last piece of the mechanization puzzle.

"Module" referred both to the shape of the compressed seed cotton that the machine left at the end of a turnrow and to the mechanized handling system that it finally made possible. Wilkes had done work on the storage of seed cotton and demonstrated that it could be done without damage to seed or fiber. This was crucial in winning acceptance of the module system among growers and gins.[15] Working cooperatively with Texas A&M, Cotton Incorporated moved ahead with a prototype, which was first tried out during the 1971 harvest at the farm of grower Jack Funk in Sebastian, Texas, in the lower Rio Grande Valley.

The module builder was a rectangular steel box tapered in at the top and with a door at one end. Its key advance over the ricker was the capability, through use of a mechanical and later a hydraulic transverse ram, to compact the seed cotton to a density of 11–12 pounds per cubic foot so that it created a self-standing brick of cotton (the first modules contained 500 cubic feet of seed cotton and were increased gradually as field tests

---

[13] Lambert H. Wilkes, Texas A&M (retired), interview, March 15, 2000.

[14] Gay Jividen, Cotton Incorporated, interview, February 25, 2000. Jones's curious nickname, "Farmer," came from his parents, who thought their son's habit of rising early fit him for a life in agriculture. Wilkes interview.

[15] Lambert H. Wilkes et al., "Design, Development and Evaluation of Seed Cotton Storage and Handling System from Stalk to Package," Final Report Cooperative Agreement between Cotton Incorporated and Department of Agricultural Engineering, Texas Agricultural Experiment Station, Texas A&M University, 1974.

increased confidence in the durability and thus transportability of the compressed cotton). This was important for two reasons. First, it took the labor
out of the compaction process and greatly improved it. Second, it opened
the way to effective mechanization of the movement of cotton from the field
to the gin. Like its Arkansas Caddy predecessor, the first module builder
systems were designed to rest not directly on the ground but on steel or
wooden pallets. This conformed to the wisdom of the time, which believed
it not possible to store seed cotton directly on the ground and still protect it
from damaging moisture. But the pallet also provided the means to grasp
the module and winch it mechanically onto a lowboy trailer.

Confident that the device would perform in the field after the Funk trials,
Jones next sought out a firm that Cotton Incorporated could license for commercial production. An agricultural equipment builder in Lubbock (who
had specialized in the cotton trailers that the module builder would replace),
"G. A." Huskey, had an entrepreneurial streak and jumped at the chance to
be the first. "Huskey Module Builders" soon appeared in Texas and then
spread across the Cotton Belt. Other early manufacturers were the John
Blue Company in Huntsville, Alabama, and FMC Corporation in Santa
Clara, California.[16]

Cotton Incorporated added its own field staff (headed by Fred Abel) dedicated to promoting the module builder, baby-sitting its early operations,
and making sure that growers' suggestions for its improvement were noticed.
At first the Texas High Plains and California (with their dry climates) were
the biggest takers, although these were also the areas where large growers with already big investments in ricking systems were sometimes hard to
convert.[17] Gradually, however, the module system spread eastward, across
the Delta and on to the Southeast.

Technical refinements followed. One of them aimed to eliminate the
need for pallets, since pallets cost money. If it was possible to pick up
stacks of hay off the ground, as was common practice, then why not a far
more tightly packed cotton module? Another Lubbock entrepreneur, Barry
Reynolds, took the lead; with a license from a midwestern manufacturer of
the self-loading hay wagon, Reynolds applied the concept to cotton. He designed a simple but ingenious mechanized trailer bed specifically for picking

[16] Ibid., 4.
[17] Despite Dukes Wooters's strenuous efforts to bring them around early, J. G. Boswell, California's largest grower, was one persistent "ricker."

up modules directly off the ground. The speed of the conveyor chains in the trailer bed was synchronized with the speed of the trailer over the ground; thus, as the trailer was backed up under the module, the module rose vertically onto the trailer in one smooth uninterrupted motion. A single operator controlled the whole operation, and later there were even module builders run entirely by computer.[18]

Yet one piece was still needed to make the separate module-based innovations into a seamless field-to-gin system. Ever since steam power (and later electricity) had been applied to ginning technology, seed cotton had been raised to the gin intake by means of a suction pipe. These pipes had increased in size and power over the years to 16-inch versions with unloading fans driven by 150-horsepower motors typical of the 1970s. Until the module, this basic technology had seemed adequate. With the module, however, gin operators noticed a problem: the tendency of the vacuum to pick up chunks of cotton that were too large and so stopped up the pipe and interrupted the flow of cotton into the gin.[19] It was a problem that careful operators learned to deal with, but it suggested the need for fundamental rethinking. Another problem was that the suction pipes at many older gins, because they were 2–2-1/2 feet short of the ground, were just not long enough to reach the bottom level of a module. Consequently, it proved impossible at first for many gins to unload a module completely – whether on a pallet or on the ground. Longer pipes were obviously needed, but there was resistance in many areas to even this change.

For a time, pallet and palletless forms of the module system coexisted. The trucks needed for the palletless approach cost in the neighborhood of $25,000 each, compared with $6,000–$7,000 for the trailer and rig that would handle a module on a pallet. Either way, the module eventually forced gins to innovate and supplement the old suction approach with a new gin-feeding mechanism. The new approach, borrowed from the mining industry, consisted of a conveyor table that carried the module forward into a fixed bank of rotating cylinders that literally tore the cotton out of

---

[18] Wilkes, ibid., 34–43. The lifting motion did tend slightly to bend the modules in the middle, and there was a limit on the number of times a module could be loaded and unloaded before it started to break apart. Second and third lifts were sometimes necessary, depending on whether or not interim storage was required before ginning.

[19] "Gin stand" refers to the machines in the cotton gin that actually separate the fiber from the seed. The larger ginning system includes feeding mechanisms as well as drying, cleaning, and packaging processes.

the module. The loose seed cotton then fell downward into an air stream that blew it through a circular duct into the gin. The technique had the advantage of eliminating the large chunks of cotton that had stopped up the suction system as well as the labor that had been necessary to keep it

The cotton module system eliminated the bottleneck between field and gin at harvest time with an efficient means of storage in the field and a technology for transporting seed cotton to the gin, which eliminated the need for trailers.

going. The suction system typically required a crew of three, in addition to a tractor driver and helper to pull the trailer to the suction pipe; the approach using a conveyor table module feeder required a crew of only two. At first, many gins had to maintain two-lane intakes to accommodate the old-fashioned trailers and the new-fangled modules, but advantages of the automated module feeder would prove compelling. More and more growers converted (or left the business), while new gins were delivered with module feeders as original equipment.[20]

The original module builders cost about $12,000. Big growers embraced the technology first, with early studies suggesting a grower needed to be producing at least 600–700 bales per year to justify investment in the module system. Cotton Incorporated sponsored elaborate research into the engineering and economics of the module builder, including time-and-motion studies led by Texas Tech industrial engineer Milton Smith, who had also worked on the ricking system. The drive for innovation was soon evident from both ends, with some ginners – who saw great advantage in the

Cotton modules are fed into the gin on a conveyor system, which eliminated the old suction pipes and reduced labor requirements at the gin.

system – providing module builders to smaller growers. As an inducement to lure growers, early-adopting ginners typically offered a $5-per-bale ($60-per-module) discount on the price of ginning if the grower delivered his cotton in modules. This worked out to the equivalent of a premium on price of about 1 cent per pound.[21] Efficiencies to the gins were real and could be read most powerfully in what they charged growers for their services. After introduction of the module builder, ginning charges held remarkably steady and even, for a time, came down. Moreover, the module gave growers greater flexibility in timing the sale of their crop, since it cost less to store seed cotton as a module than to have it ginned and then stored as a bale.

The module builder quickly took its place as a central instrument in sustaining the profitability of cotton agriculture and is a striking example of cost effectiveness in agricultural research. Including antecedent research on the ricker and research on the gin module feeder, Cotton Incorporated spent $532,000 on the seed cotton storage and handling system between 1970 and 1974. William Lalor calculated consequent savings in cotton handling (in 1999 dollars) to have been $10 per bale. With 180 million bales "moduled"

[21] Lalor interview.

since introduction in 1972, this makes for savings of $1.8 billion on investment of half a million.[22]

To the student of agricultural history, the module system represents a final link in the chain of mechanical replacements for field tasks – reaching back to the tractor – that made it possible to continue raising cotton with a tiny fraction of the hands (and none of the animals) once required to do the job. Moreover, it reduced the grower's risks in several important ways. It broke the yearly picking-to-ginning bottleneck. It hastened the crop from the field and provided means for its safe storage and efficient handling en route to the gin. It helped keep low the charges paid for ginning. But before growers might reap any such benefits, they first had to make a crop. This sounds obvious but the irony was that, by the time the module handling system was promising to round out the mechanization process in the early 1970s, there were more and more growers (particularly in cotton's oldest regions) who had no crop to make. Cotton Incorporated, while successfully promoting the module, also found itself in the thick of the fight against one of cotton's oldest natural enemies.

FEAR NO WEEVIL

It was the company's bedrock strategy to increase the demand for cotton, which was the mainspring that drove the modern response to the old plague of the boll weevil. It is conventional wisdom in postbellum southern history that the boll weevil did the South a favor by forcing farmers to forsake, better late than never, old King Cotton and take up the progressive banner of diversification. Such was the message of countless *Progressive Farmer* editorials over the decades and of that famous seventeen-pound bronze likeness of *Anthonomus grandis* that adorned the main square of Enterprise, Alabama: "The World's Only Monument to a Pest."

The time came, however, when the greater enterprise meant turning back to cotton in order to get ahead. If growers could make more money in cotton than in corn or soybeans or poultry, then no mere bug was going to stand in the way. It took some politicking and organization and some practiced

---

[22] William F. Lalor memorandum to author, May 26, 2000. "Savings are probably higher," Lalor adds, "but have not been estimated recently and probably never again will be estimated in comparison to the alternative: cotton trailers, which have been virtually eliminated by the module system."

instruments for furthering the common goal; it took a raised consciousness of cooperative possibilities.

The cotton boll weevil arrived in southeast Texas from Mexico in 1892, and within thirty years it had migrated east and north to infest every state of the old Cotton Belt, 85 percent of the area that produced 95 percent of the cotton. The pest may have done more harm to American agriculture than any other insect and, as if in conspiracy with other human and natural forces, helped bring cotton and many cotton growers to their knees. Weevil infestation notoriously slashed yields and precipitated staggering losses. The severe outbreak between 1921 and 1923 probably cost in excess of $400 million; 1950, the worst weevil year on record, saw losses of $750 million.[23]

The onslaught triggered a range of responses: just plain giving up (the weevil was the last straw for thousands of marginal growers who simply left the land and, often as not, the South as well); picking up stakes and starting over in weevil-free West Texas or the Far West; diversifying into other crops; or, as far as was possible, holding one's ground and fighting back.

Fighting back meant finding ways to kill the bugs. This occurred, it should be noted, before the rise of environmentalism. Fierce regimens that today would be condemned for causing all sorts of collateral damage (to beneficial insects, wildlife, and groundwater) were considered – fifty years ago – to be the best scientific practice by universities, the government, and growers alike. The first major breakthrough in chemical control came in 1916 with the introduction of calcium arsenate, which would hold sway for thirty years. After World War II, a new arsenal of organic pesticides – including DDT and benzene hexachloride (BHC), an array of chlorinated hydrocarbons (toxaphene, endrin, aldrin, dieldrin), and then organo-phosphates (methyl parathion, malathion, and EPN) – was liberally applied as growers learned to spray early and often in hope of maximum control. While much of the research into control substances was done under the auspices of the USDA, land-grant agricultural schools, and state experiment stations, weevil control ultimately remained a responsibility of the individual grower, who also bore its cost.

The strategy of control foundered, however, as the weevil developed resistance to organochlorine insecticides starting in the 1950s and as the growing environmental movement resulted in 1970s regulations that banned, one after another, many of the most effective chemicals. The weevil's depredations

---

[23] USDA; National Cotton Council; *Progressive Farmer* (October 1992).

came at the same time, moreover, as the competitive attack on cotton's market position by synthetic fibers. Relative to synthetics, demand for cotton from the 1950s through the mid-1970s was falling sharply. Had it continued to fall, there would have been less incentive to move beyond half-way attempts at merely controlling the weevil to a means for eradicating the pest once and for all.

As it was, the total marketing strategy of Cotton Incorporated to rebuild demand at the consumer and the mill level halted cotton's free-fall in 1973 at 33 percent of the U.S. textile market. Thenceforth, as demand steadily rose, it looked as if cotton had a future after all. Better prices in the 1970s and 1980s encouraged growers to expand acreage, and the federal cotton program responded by rescinding allotments in favor of a base acreage system. As the freshening wind of opportunity blew across the Cotton Belt, conditions were right to launch a final assault on the weevil.

An increasing market for cotton justified increased research efforts into just how this might be done. At its 1958 annual meeting, the National Cotton Council had voted a resolution (drafted by South Carolina grower Robert Coker) to find the funds to eliminate the boll weevil as a threat to U.S. cotton "at the earliest possible time." Although it would take more than twenty years to begin to implement Coker's vision, the USDA-ARS Boll Weevil Research Laboratory was established at Mississippi State University in Starkville, and promising work got underway in 1962.[24]

Starting in the early 1970s, Cotton Incorporated agricultural entomology researcher George Slater subsidized the equipping of a special laboratory in Starkville. Refined technologies such as "grandlure" (a synthetic sex and aggregation pheromone) and dependable weevil traps soon set the stage for experimental field trials. The new techniques aimed at suppressing and then eradicating the boll weevil population in a specific, geographically isolated cotton-growing area. The first test was made in southern Mississippi and adjacent areas of Alabama and Louisiana between 1971 and 1973. Some experts were left unsatisfied, but the test demonstrated how – through careful mapping of fields and a combination of removing the weevils or their overwintering habitats, the use of pheromone traps (a sex lure) and human "scouts" to monitor them, insecticide treatments at the pinhead square stage of the plant's growth, and diapause spraying at the end of the season – it was

---

[24] See J. H. Perkins, *Insects, Experts and the Insecticide Crisis: The Quest for New Pest Management Strategies* (New York: Plenum, 1982).

The boll weevil ravaged much of the Southeast and virtually eliminated cotton there in the 1950s. Boll weevil eradication, a comprehensive approach to pest management that eliminated the bug where insecticides alone had failed, brought about cotton's return in the 1980s.

possible to keep weevils from propagating and thus sweep an area clean.[25] Keeping it clean, however, proved as much a political as a scientific challenge.

Cotton Incorporated, along with USDA's Animal and Plant Health Inspection Service (APHIS), disseminated technical information in support of the feasibility of eradication, as distinct from control, and looked for a place to test it definitively. First thoughts were to begin broad-scale tests in the Brownsville area of southeast Texas. This had a certain historical resonance (Texas was where the weevil had first arrived in the United States) but also the practical attraction of a peninsula-like topography that would permit the isolation necessary for starting and sustaining a successful eradication

[25] J. R. Brazzel et al., "Boll Weevil Eradication," in E. G. King, J. R. Phillips, and R. J. Coleman, eds., *Cotton Insects and Mites: Characterization and Management* (Memphis: Cotton Foundation, 1996), 625–52.

program. Texas was the country's largest cotton producer, and if eradication could be established there then the economic benefits would be highly visible and the momentum for moving forward would be strong.

Boll weevil eradication demanded, however, strong political consensus. This did not exist among Texas' diversity of cotton cultures, some of which (in the High Plains, for example) had no weevil problem at all. Eradication was conceived as a public–private partnership between APHIS and the state departments of agriculture (on the one hand) and growers themselves (on the other). Growers had to want it enough to agree to tax themselves much of the money to pay for it. This required effective lobbying and state legislation that authorized binding referenda and uniform assessment of growers across the proposed eradication zone. In Texas, this was not forthcoming.

Far to the east, in North and South Carolina where the weevil had virtually wiped out the cotton culture, strong political leadership and presence of a geographical "edge" from which to start eradication set the stage for success. North Carolina growers had planted over 2 million acres of cotton in the 1930s, which had fallen to a low of 16,000 acres in 1978; in South Carolina, only 69,000 acres were planted in 1983. But among those who had remained, like Marshall Grant in North Carolina and Robert Coker in South Carolina, the lure of cotton's impending market comeback fired a determination to win back the ground that the weevil had eaten away.

"It was a disaster," as Grant looked back on cotton's plight. With his son David, Grant still farms in Northampton and Halifax counties on land with a family history of cotton going back to the late eighteenth century. He was a staunch believer in the early scientific "proof-of-principle" results from Mississippi and was convinced, too, that North Carolina (and the small adjacent cotton-growing area just over the state line in Virginia) was the place to roll out the program. North Carolina had a natural climatic buffer on the north, the buffer of the Atlantic Ocean on the east, and also the unique advantage of two relatively isolated cotton-growing areas that were separated by a buffer zone – in the middle of the state – dominated by tobacco and diversified field crops. This effectively closed off the first proposed eradication zone in the northeast, some 42,000 acres, from reinfestation. North Carolina also had enough political cohesion among growers to persuade the USDA that this was the place to start.[26] The program that Grant and his neighbors pioneered became the model for weevil eradication all across the Cotton Belt.

[26] Marshall Grant interview, March 16, 1999.

The North Carolina legislature enacted the Uniform Boll Weevil Eradication Act in 1976, which authorized a grower referendum (held that December) that would give legal status to the Boll Weevil Eradication Trial (BWET). Though the program was only statewide and restricted to the single purpose of weevil eradication, the procedure followed was analogous to the one that had created Cotton Incorporated, and it produced a parallel self-help organization. In this case, the costs were shared among producers on a per-acre basis, with producers paying 50 percent of the total and with the USDA and the North Carolina and Virginia departments of agriculture paying 25 percent each.[27]

The National Academy of Sciences judged the eradication trial a success in 1980, and a year later growers further assessed themselves to pay for a containment program to prevent reinfestation. South Carolina growers then moved promptly to expand the program there, which began in earnest in 1982. Both states organized permanent boll weevil eradication "foundations," not-for-profit organizations governed by grower boards and supervised by USDA-APHIS operations officers. In 1983, the two states cooperated in formation of the Southeastern Boll Weevil Eradication Foundation (SEBWEF), with offices in Raleigh and with Marshall Grant as chairman and South Carolinian Robert Lee Scarborough as vice-chairman. SEBWEF was an important organizational step because it allowed for operational and financial coordination among the growing number of state foundations and for the eradication program to be conducted on an areawide basis without regard to state boundaries.[28] Referenda followed in Georgia, Florida, and parts of Alabama in 1987, and the headquarters was eventually moved to Montgomery. By 1985, eradication campaigns had begun in northern New Mexico, Arizona, and California, where weevils sought a foothold; in the 1990s they commenced in the mid-South states of Louisiana, Mississippi, (parts of) Arkansas and Tennessee, as well as in Texas.[29]

[27] King et al., eds., *Cotton Insects and Mites: Characterization and Management*, 1–13; Robert Lee Scarborough, *Twentieth Century Cotton Experiences: The Boll Weevil Story, 1920–1990* (Sumter, South Carolina: Sumter Printing Company, 1999); Philip Haney, ed., *A History of the Boll Weevil Eradication Program in the United States* (Memphis: National Cotton Council, 2001).

[28] Bill Dickerson, "History of the Boll Weevil Eradication Program in North Carolina, 1978–1987."

[29] B. Grefenstette, "Boll Weevil Eradication: Status and Future Plans," *Proceedings Beltwide Cotton Conference, 1996.*

Because cotton is the only plant that will host the weevil, 100 percent grower participation was crucial. The program could spread no faster than the biology of eradication itself, and typically it took 2–3 years to do the job in a given area. Still, tension was common between growers who had been hurt most by weevils (and thus who stood to profit most from the assessment) and those less bothered; as the program moved south and west, it called for ceaseless political management. But cotton returned – and much more quickly than it had been driven out. In 1995, North Carolina growers planted 810,000 acres; their South Carolina brethren, 348,000. The level of the self-assessment fell dramatically as the program succeeded in eliminating the pest. Routine containment, which continued indefinitely, cost less than the initial eradication process and far less than endless efforts at uncoordinated chemical control. In 1983, both North and South Carolina growers assessed themselves $25 per acre, an amount that dropped in 1990 to $8.40 in North Carolina and to $10 in South Carolina; in 1998, the assessment in North Carolina was only $3.95 per acre and in South Carolina just $5.75.[30]

The benefits seem obvious now, but at the time it was not always easy to convince even the most vulnerable growers that eradication would save them money through reduced need for insecticides. In part, the problem was due to a lag in behavioral adjustment to the success of the program. Even as weevil populations dwindled, old habits – developed over years of battling the pest – died hard and so retarded the rate of financial savings that some growers realized. "Even after eradication was accomplished here," explained Marshall Grant, "our North Carolina growers still sprayed five to eight times a year, because they perceived the boll worm [another troublesome pest] was going to be there anyway." What they couldn't yet quite believe was that, with the weevil eradicated and insecticide use radically reduced, beneficial insects would return to take care of pests like the boll worm. ("It took us five years to convince them they didn't have to spray those five to eight times," said Grant.) But the savings, grasped at first or not, were real. In Grant's part of the state, insecticide applications went from 14 to 1 per acre per year.[31] Thanks to the return of beneficial insects,

---

[30] Scarborough, *Twentieth Century Cotton*, 61.

[31] Other areas were hard to convince because growers did not see they had a problem when in fact they did. In the Delta region of the Midsouth, for instance, it was common to spray heavily for boll worm, which also suppressed the weevil. Eradication promised both to finish off the weevil and then let the beneficial bugs take care of the worms. It was not the easiest promise to believe when, historically, not spraying had invited disaster.

the use of sprays to control all insects across the entire Southeast fell some 75 percent by the early 1990s.[32]

Good science and methodical application stood up over many years, and all of the original arguments in favor of eradication are still firmly in place. Beltwide, the USDA calculates that eradication saves growers $36 per acre per year in insecticide costs and adds $42 per acre in increased yield. The National Cotton Council figures the overall cost/benefit ratio of the program at 12/1, and in some states it is said to be as high as 40/1.[33] In Missouri, where an eradication program would not commence until early in the twenty-first century, past successes in the Southeast were trumpeted as proof of the gains to be had in return for a modest (compared with what North Carolinians had paid two decades before) $10 per acre per year assessment. "Georgia growers," the Missourians were told, "decreased their overall insect control costs from $125 to $66 per acre and managed to increase yields from 482 to 733 pounds per acre." Not to eradicate would be to forfeit such gains ahead of time and would put Missourians, relative to growers in states already weevil-free, at a competitive disadvantage.[34]

But these Missourians, assuming they voted for a referendum and entered the program, would only be protecting what they had: broad acres of well-watered cotton and a sophisticated ginning infrastructure. When it came to the weevil, they were history's beneficiaries. Without a doubt, Cotton Incorporated's direct contributions to the success of boll weevil eradication must be accounted in concert with the contributions of other agents: APHIS, the National Cotton Council, the experiment stations, and land-grant universities. What the company contributed uniquely was breadth of grower participation and common commitment among growers that cut across deep historical and geographical divides.

NOTHING TO WASTE

The cotton plant produces seed as well as fiber, and it was the seed that for centuries had been the chief obstacle to economic production of the fiber.

---

[32] G. A. Carlson et al., *Economic Returns to Boll Weevil Eradication,* USDA Agricultural Economics Report 621, 1989; "Economic Evaluation of Insect Eradication: The Case of Boll Weevils in the Southeast," in King et al., *Cotton Insects and Mites.*

[33] Lalor to author, May 26, 2000.

[34] Cotton Producers of Missouri, "Boll Weevil Eradication Program Questions and Answers," February 2000.

With the invention of the gin and the corresponding mechanization of the textile industry at the turn of the nineteenth century, the production of cotton fiber soared, and with it the production of cottonseed.[35] Unlike the fiber, the seed for many decades had no market other than to plant next year's crop. But after the Civil War, with the development of seed crushing and delinting technologies, cottonseed emerged as a profitable byproduct that found its way into diverse markets. Crushed seed yielded vegetable oil suitable for cooking, margarine, and soap. Cottonseed meal or "cake" was used for fertilizer and animal feed. Even "linters," the small bits of fiber that clung to the seed after ginning, could be removed and used in high-quality papers, including currency; when subjected to new chemical treatments, linters became ingredients in rayon, paint, and smokeless gunpowder.[36]

The lean times of the early 1970s, when the competitive fortunes of cotton fiber hit bottom, brought home to growers the importance not only of constantly cutting costs but also of increasing the value of everything they produced. This inspired an array of research on cottonseed, especially on its uses for feeding livestock and planting new cotton. The latter was particularly important.

Because cotton-planting seed is the foundation for all subsequent crop development, seed quality has an impact on desired yield and fiber-quality outcomes.[37] Mechanization of the planting process placed upon it an additional requirement. The fuzzy linters that remained on the seed after ginning had to be removed if the seed were to be used in precision mechanical planters.[38] This was a challenging process, because planting seed called for careful handling; nothing could be done that might crack the seeds or predispose them in any way to invasion by microorganisms once they were put in the soil. If a cold spell came after planting, for example, damaged seeds would continue to absorb water but refuse to germinate; microbes, with lower temperature thresholds, invaded and killed the seeds. The process

---

[35] See Chapter 2, "Nature and Know-How."

[36] Luther A. Ransom, *The Great Cottonseed Industry of the South* (New York, 1911); Alton E. Bailey, ed., *Cottonseed and Cottonseed Products: Their Chemistry and Chemical Technology* (New York: 1948), especially "History of Cotton and the United States Cottonseed Industry," 17–23. See also Herman Clarence Nixon, "The Rise of the American Cottonseed Oil Industry," *Journal of Political Economy* 38 (February 1930), 73–85.

[37] Wayne C. Smith, ed., *Cotton: Origin, History, Technology and Production* (New York: Wiley, 1999), 793ff.

[38] In places less mechanized than the United States, much of the crop is still planted "fuzzy." Ibid., 817.

Once deemed waste, cottonseed became a major business by the twentieth century, finding a wide variety of markets from cooking oil to cattle feed.

of "delinting" therefore called for a high level of technological refinement. The earliest attempts to solve the problem were mechanical and essentially entailed ginning a second time. But ginning, even once, is highly abusive to both fiber and seed, and a second run-through could result in physical damage to the seeds' outer coating. Flame zipping (sometimes used in conjunction with second ginning), whereby fire burned off remaining fuzz, only heightened the same risk.

Chemical processes gradually came to dominate. "Acid delinting" was the subject of experimentation in the 1920s and 1930s. This involved immersing seed in a bath of concentrated sulfuric acid and stirring it up until the acid ate its way through the residual cellulose fibers, leaving nothing but smooth black seed. There were dangers, however. If left in the bath too long and the acid penetrated the seed coat, the seed could be fatally damaged. It was not unusual at all for the seed coat to be etched, which had no ill effect if planting conditions were ideal. But if conditions were not ideal and the soil became cold and damp after planting, then the etched seed would be predisposed to absorb moisture before it was warm enough to use the moisture and germinate.

To the scientific problems, government regulation in the 1970s added others. The sulfuric acid effluent from the delinting process typically ended up in open storage lagoons – hazardous to groundwater, wildlife, and humans alike – a practice that naturally provoked environmentalists. With ever-tightening EPA and OSHA restrictions governing the handling and disposal of such substances, Cotton Incorporated researchers set about to find a more acceptable alternative.

Building on early work done by an outside consulting company, J. K. "Farmer" Jones – along with scientists Gay M. Jividen, William F. Lalor, and George A. Slater – developed a dilute acid process that employed a 10 percent sulfuric acid concentration instead of 98–100 percent. The process reduced to zero the hazardous effluent and cleaned the seed as well as (if not better than) the old method, with the added benefit that there was less etching of the seed coat, which left the seed better equipped to deal with adverse germinating conditions. The old method probably had entailed a fair amount of overkill, but what enabled the dramatically reduced concentration to perform even better was a refined "scalper/drier" technique of first spraying the acid solution onto the seed and then drying it. The high temperatures in the drier concentrated the acid just on the linters, not the seed coat, and accelerated the desired reaction between the cellulose of the linters and the acid. Tumbling action of the seed against itself in the scalper/drier abraded away the lint and finished the job.[39]

---

[39] J. K. Jones, G. M. Jividen, W. F. Lalor, and G. A. Slater, "Dilute Sulfuric Acid Process for Delinting Cotton Planting Seed," Paper 7603009, American Society of Agricultural Engineers,

Again, Jones worked with Lambert Wilkes at Texas A&M and committed Cotton Incorporated to build a pilot delinting plant in concert with Flowers Brothers Mississippi Seed Company in Tunica, in the Delta. Results were not perfect at first, but refinements back in the lab led to a second, more successful plant in Hollandale several years later. The payoff for the grower was better germinating seed, and for a time this helped keep small seed companies viable. It meant that a grower could still catch and use his own seed, which journeyed first as seed cotton to the gin, then on to the delinting plant, and then, come next planting season, back into the field. Through the 1980s, many growers continued in this time-honored use of what was known as "brown bag seed," though they would also use new varieties every year.[40]

For whole seed not destined for planting, there were two other possible routes: crushing for oil or processing for livestock feed. Cotton Incorporated sponsored early work with growers in California to develop cottonseed with increased oil content, but primary attention focused on the feed market. In the early 1970s, Hal Lewis pursued work through Stanford Research Institute; they indicated that, if it could safely be fed to cattle on a large enough scale, then whole seed would be worth far more to the feed market than crushed seed in the oil market. The sight of cattle grazing in a harvested cotton field, picking up "leftovers," was not uncommon in less fastidious olden times, but there was a large obstacle in the path of commercialization. This was the compound "gossypol," a pigment in cottonseed, which in high enough quantities was toxic to nonruminant animals.

Gay Jividen and Lee Warner conducted five years of feeding studies to determine how much seed livestock producers (chiefly dairy farmers) could safely feed their cattle. Different cotton varieties contained different amounts and isomer types of gossypol, and the studies aimed to find the chemical mechanisms that would optimize the positive isomer.[41] Pressure

1976; J. K. Jones, G. M. Jividen, and G. A. Slater, *Batch Delinting with Dilute Sulfuric Acid,* Agro-Industrial Report PSP1, vol. 4, no. 1, Cotton Incorporated, 1977.

[40] This practice would end, however, in the 1990s with the coming of patented, genetically modified seed and with the licensing of growers for its one-time use. Cotton Incorporated also did work with cold-testing of seed, which was especially important when planting large acreages where seed that went in early needed to have cool vigor. Lalor, Jividen interviews.

[41] J. P. Cherry and H. R. Leffler, "Seed," in R. J. Kohel and C. Lewis, eds., *Cotton* (Madison: American Society of Agronomy, 1984), 511–69; M. C. Calhoun and C. Holmberg, "Safe Use of Cotton By-products as Feed Ingredients for Ruminants," in L. A. Jones et al., eds., *Cattle Research with Gossypol-containing Feeds* (Memphis: National Cottonseed Products Association, 1991). See also comments on biotechnology in the next section.

from the cottonseed oil industry periodically threatened Cotton Incorporated's cottonseed research program, but when the price of seed fell so low in the early 1990s that it would no longer pay the cost of ginning – and growers consequently could no longer, in the time-honored pattern, "gin for seed" – incentive rose to expand the markets for seed.

In 1991, a special grower committee within Cotton Incorporated instructed the agricultural research division to accelerate seed research and promotion. Later that year, the division hired Thomas C. Wedegaertner, who had a degree in animal science along with an MBA and experience working for some of the large crushing companies. His job was to head a new effort in cottonseed marketing, research, and animal nutrition. He did so by working trade shows and industry meetings across the country and by sponsoring experiments to enhance "seed as feed" in every way possible. Seed began to appear in pelletized form and as blocks of feed supplement that dairymen could handle easily.

After gossypol, ease of handling was the key issue. Seed destined for crushing was delinted only mechanically, which left it quite clean but not as stark naked as seed processed with acid for planting purposes. Seed destined for feed was often not delinted at all and – with all its linters and even longer "tags" still in place – had a surface not unlike Velcro (and flowed about as easily), making it impossible to handle in the same conveyor systems that handled corn and wheat (and, indeed, very difficult to handle at all). Experiments had been done at the University of California with the coating of seeds other than cotton, with the purpose of adding nutrients or protective fungicides to yield a ready-made, sure-fire package to put in the ground at planting time.

It was William Lalor who first made the connection to cotton's different need, which was to make "flowable" seed not destined for the ground but for the stomachs of cattle. Until that happened, cottonseed had been shut out of a substantial part of the cattle feed market. Few stockmen, except the very largest, were prepared or could afford to bother with something that could not be handled by the same equipment used for corn or soybeans. Many things were tried. The pharmaceutical companies had long experience with coatings to make pills easier to swallow, but costs that may have been justified in the prescription drug market hardly computed when the product was cattle feed. John Turner, a textile chemist who worked in Cotton Incorporated's fiber research division and not in agricultural research at all, came up with the answer: starch. Cooked starch was put on yarn to make sizing, as with cotton shirts that come back stiff from the laundry. Turner's idea was to cook starch, apply it to the seed, and then thoroughly mix it up. The linters would adhere (essentially be glued down) to the surface of the seed, which when dried would have a smooth surface almost as if it had been more expensively delinted. Tom Wedegaertner carried forth these ideas to develop a mechanical process that would be called "Easiflo."[42]

The starch coating worked except for the problem of longer tags, which caused the starched seeds to clump together and impede flowability. A modification of the traditional gin stand was developed to remove tags, and by the end of the 1990s this research had spun off results to improve traditional ginning technology as developed under cooperative research conducted with the federal ginning laboratory in Lubbock, Texas. The new techniques raised the return on the cotton fiber that the tags contained. Instead of being priced alongside linters and worth perhaps 25 cents a pound, the longer length of the tags would make them worth almost twice as much when baled separately. Moreover, they would increase by over 10 pounds the amount of cotton fiber captured from the harvested material that went into a bale. The new machine produced more fiber turnout and ginned faster than the old-fashioned models.[43]

One development, often as not, leads to another. Cottonseed research illustrates the interrelatedness that has characterized much of Cotton Incorporated's agricultural research. Historically, cotton breeders had tried to come up with varieties that produced ever-smaller seeds and therefore more fiber. The motivation lay in the biology. It takes approximately three times the amount of photosynthetic activity to produce one pound of cottonseed oil as it does to produce one pound of cotton fiber. Therefore, that cotton plant produces most efficiently that puts greatest productive effort into fiber relative to seed. As this trend continued over the years, the seeds in some of the highest fiber-yielding varieties became quite small, so that the industry went from an average of 800 pounds of seed per bale of fiber down to 680 pounds for some modern varieties. This in turn had implications for growers, who had less seed to pay for ginning, as well as for gins, most of which had been designed to process large-seeded cotton. When fed small-seed varieties, gin stands tended to break the seeds, putting fragments of the seed

---

[42] Easiflo cottonseed became available to feed formulators in 1998.
[43] Lalor interview.

coat into the fiber. These then went on to the mills and caused problems there, because there was no way to remove seed coat fragments from fiber in the textile process.

There was a time when powerful bleaches would have destroyed such unwanted matter, but more recent (environmentally friendly) hydroperoxide bleaching solutions left them untouched. This prompted a closer look at what was actually happening in the saw, combs, and ribs that composed the gin stand. Cooperative work between Cotton Incorporated and the national ginning laboratory at Mesilla Park (New Mexico) revealed that the spacing between the ribs in gins all over the country was designed for bigger seed. Smaller seed tended to jam between the sawblades and ribs and to push the blades to one side, which then tore chips off the seeds. Researchers experimented with inserting Teflon spacers between the gin ribs. These spacers stabilized the saws and practically eliminated seed coat fragments from the fiber. Serendipitously, the solution to the seed problem also improved general fiber quality: testing at the USDA Cotton Quality Research Laboratory showed greater fiber length and reduced nep content, both characteristics coveted by the textile industry.[44]

ORIGINS AND VARIATIONS

To meet the industry's rising expectations for fiber and seed quality, cotton growers supported research into how cotton was planted and cultivated, how it was handled at harvest and at the gin, and how it was protected from predators. The quest for optimum efficiencies led back to the very beginning of the chain of production and the cotton plant itself. The experience of Cotton Incorporated (and its predecessor, Cotton Producers Institute) in this endeavor illustrates the haphazardness that often attends scientific advance, and how even the most disciplined of applied research efforts necessarily involve a good deal of "fishing."

By the time growers had effectively organized themselves for research and promotion in the 1970s, genetic manipulation of *Gossypium hirsutum* and the three other species that provide the world's cotton fiber already had a long history.[45] Indeed, some growers like Robert Coker in

---

[44] Lalor interview.

[45] In addition to *G. hirsutum*: *G. barbadense, G. herbaceum,* and *G. arboreum*. Among earliest work, see W. L. Balls, "Studies in Egyptian Cotton," in *Yearbook Khediv Agricultural Society* (Cairo, 1906).

South Carolina and Hervey Evans in North Carolina, wearing their "cotton-breeder" hats, had played their own parts in it. "Classical cotton breeding" applied Mendelian principles of genetic segregation and assortment through in-breeding techniques to the goal of enhancing useful plant characteristics. Over the years, selective breeding had resulted in the steady improvement of long-term yields and in substantial genetic mapping.[46] The next step, which involved the biochemical genetics of cotton and centered on the study of proteins and nucleic acids, was of more recent vintage and reached back only to the 1970s. In addition to biochemistry, an early objective was to achieve a repeatable plant regeneration system from cell culture, which could then serve as a basis for *in vitro* manipulation.[47]

Groundwork in cotton biotechnology began under CPI in the late 1960s. A weed scientist at the University of California, Davis, C. A. "Bud" Beasley was able to take cotton ovules and, supplying all the right nutrition, grow fairly normal fibers. Beasley worked with Irving Ting, and the nutrient material they developed became known as the "Beasley–Ting media," which would long remain the basic media for regeneration work in cotton. In the early 1970s, Gay Jividen, a young plant physiologist and geneticist, took charge of keeping the cooperative work moving forward. The next step was to see if haploid cotton plants (plants with half the normal number of chromosomes) could be coaxed from the ovules or from tissue. Jividen ran through a series of university-based plant physiologists. He found a man at Texas Tech who had done earlier promising work at Cornell, only to fail at cotton. Subsequent efforts at the University of Georgia met with no more success. At Penn State, however, he found a young postdoctoral scientist, Gail Davidonis, who had had some success with other organisms and was interested in working on cotton. Shortly thereafter, Davidonis was able to regenerate cotton, although she was not quite sure how. She had tossed some dirty petri dishes, still coated with Beasley–Ting media, into a box; returning later to wash up, she noticed that they had sprouted little plantlets of cotton.[48]

---

[46] W. R. Meredith and R. R. Bridge, "Genetic Contributions to Yield Changes in Upland Cotton," in W. R. Fehr, ed., *Genetic Contributions to Yield Gains of Five Major Crop Plants* (Madison: Crop Science Society of America, 1984), 75–86; P. A. Fryxell, *The Natural History of the Cotton Tribe* (College Station: Texas A&M Press, 1979).

[47] Andrew H. Paterson and Robert H. Smith, "Future Horizons: Biotechnology for Cotton Development," in Smith, ed., *Cotton: Origin, History, Technology and Production*, 415–32.

[48] Shortly after, she did succeed in regenerating cotton, but Penn State did not renew her postdoctoral fellowship. Perhaps it was too far north. As Jividen later speculated: "They just

Cotton Incorporated also supported work done at Texas A&M, where in 1986 M. H. Renfroe, Jean Gould, and Roberta Smith successfully regenerated cotton from the shoot meristem areas (small growth points at the base of the cotton bud) of *Gossypium hirsutum* seedlings. This method of regeneration became part of the foundation for later experiments by the same researchers in cotton's genetic transformation.[49] A second approach emerged from Cotton Incorporated–sponsored research by Norma L. Trolinder of Texas Tech and later of the USDA. Trolinder discovered that not all cotton varieties regenerate easily. (This had been one of the reasons others had failed: they had tended to experiment only with the predominant variety in their areas.) Only one cotton, it turned out, worked well: a Coker variety, "Coker 312," developed by a southeastern seed company but for use on the Texas High Plains. Trolinder went on from there to develop reliable and commercially viable regeneration techniques using a callus medium (an undifferentiated tumorlike tissue material), which was what the Penn State researcher had happened upon by accident in her unwashed petri dishes.[50]

Cotton's genetic transformation followed. The genetic material (DNA) could be introduced into a "soup" of target cells in two ways. The first was an "agrobacterium" approach, in which *Agrobacterium tumefaciens* bacteria was used to carry foreign DNA into the cells of the host plant where a new trait was desired. Introduction of the first agronomically significant gene into cotton ("Coker 312") occurred in 1990, with the aim of increased insect resistance, and field trials confirmed that the progeny of the transformants effectively repelled bollworms.[51] The second, "biolistic" technique employed a particle gun literally to bombard the target plant with DNA-laden projectiles.[52]

didn't want somebody working on cotton in Pennsylvania." Penn State had also refused to accept the cooperative research contract proffered by Cotton Incorporated, perhaps for the same reason.

[49] M. H. Renfroe and R. H. Smith, "Cotton Shoot Tip Culture," *Beltwide Cotton Producers Resource Conference Proceedings,* 1986; J. Gould, O. Hasegawa, M. Fahima, and R. H. Smith, "Regeneration of *G. hirsutum* and *G. barbadense* from Shoot Apex Tissues for Transformation," *Plant Cell Reports* 10 (1991), 12–16.

[50] R. H. Smith et al., "Defined Conditions for the Initiation and Growth of Cotton Callus *in vitro,*" *In Vitro* 13 (1977), 329–34; N. L. Trolinder and J. R. Goodwin, "Somatic Embryogenesis and Plant Regeneration of Cotton," *Plant Cell Reports* 6 (1987), 231–4.

[51] F. J. Perlak et al., "Insect Resistant Cotton Plants," *Biotechnology* 8 (1990), 939–43; J. J. Estruch et al., "Transgenic Plants: An Emerging Approach to Pest Control," *Nature Biotechnology* 15 (1997), 137–41.

[52] J. J. Finer et al., "Transformation of Cotton via Particle Bombardment," *Plant Cell Reports* 7 (1990), 399–402.

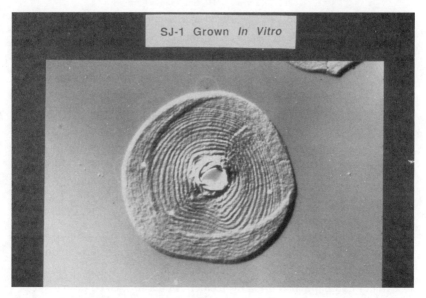

SJ-1 Grown *In Vitro*

Cross-section of a fully mature cotton fiber demonstrates definitive "rings" of cellulose. The high thickness of this particular example indicates that it was grown under controlled conditions, with warm days and cool nights, and would be graded as high micronaire.

The results of Cotton Incorporated's cooperator-based research belonged to the researchers and their universities, which fit with the company's role as a promoter of knowledge that would redound to the benefit of cotton growers. However, as chemical companies patented more and more genes (Monsanto, for instance, had control of the bollworm gene, which it patented as "Bollguard"; other chemical giants, spying big growth opportunities, quickly became major players), it became evident that Cotton Incorporated would have to get into the gene business, too. In the 1990s, Cotton Incorporated invested steadily in research aimed at modification of the cotton plant through genetic transformation – except in such areas as pest and herbicide resistance, where the chemical companies were most active. The company's main concern was with quality and yield factors and the persistent problem of gossypol.

One fruitful idea was to impart greater hardiness to cotton, which meant making it more tolerant of low temperatures. Among all the growing areas, the Texas High Plains experienced late cool springtimes and early cool autumns that interfered with growth. Cotton Incorporated first looked at

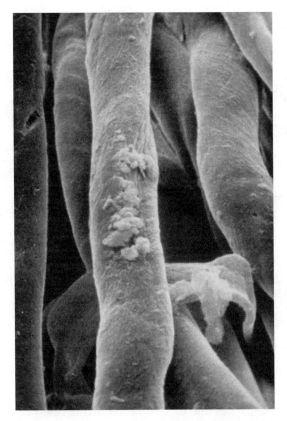

Mature cotton fiber before the opening of the boll and subsequent drying. After drying, the waxy surface clumps will disappear, and the fibers will assume their typical twisted-ribbon configuration.

other cotton strains from as far away as Uzbekistan but with little success; it then turned to genes from other, colder-weather plants that might be used to transform cotton. One was spinach. Field tests in 1999 under both university and commercial conditions produced results that, empirically, were highly promising: total yields increased significantly. With insertion of the spinach gene, the cotton plant produced more seed and more fiber as carbohydrate synthesis went up.

Cotton Incorporated's longest-running effort in biotechnology began in 1993 and focused not on the quantity but on one particular aspect of the quality of *Gossypium hirsutum*. Gossypol was both bane and boon. In cottonseed, when fed above certain levels, it was toxic to nonruminants; in

Two to three days after blooming, cottonseed is covered with emerging fiber cells, composed of primary-wall cellulose.

the cotton plant, it imparted a natural insect resistance that was much desired. The challenge was thus to develop cotton that banished the substance from seed but retained it elsewhere in the plant. Two of the most promising methods involved looking for micro-organisms that could break down gossypol with its own enzyme system. The identity of such bacteria was, it was thought, already known. Upon closer examination, however, they turned out not actually to break down gossypol but only to bind it into its own cell wall. The search continued through thousands of bacteria, with Cotton Incorporated issuing a worldwide call for exotic cotton plants that might harbor the right bacterial weapon.

A cotton rootball from a field in Pakistan (that allegedly had been cultivated in cotton for centuries) at last yielded a bacterium that could destroy gossypol. With Cotton Incorporated support, researchers at the USDA Plant Genetics Laboratory in Albany, California, laboriously worked out the genetic construct, which was then expressed through the whole cotton plant. They then added a seed promoter to restrict its action to the seed alone and are presently awaiting seed production from the transformed plants. The second approach, by Chan Benedict, was to follow the genetic and chemical pathway along which the plant produced gossypol. At the last step in this path, a key enzyme for gossypol synthesis, Deltakatanine, was isolated. Researchers then sequenced the gene for Deltakatanine and assembled a construct with the gene reversed. Jean Gould at Texas A&M, who had done the work on meristem regeneration and transformation, aided in this work as well, which in tests resulted in an 80-percent reduction of gossypol in seed but with normal retention in the plant. The work, when commercialized, promised once and for all to solve the gossypol dilemma.

The history of scientific discovery strongly suggests that key breakthroughs in concept or technique often occur in several places at more or less the same time: if Scientist A didn't think of it, then Scientist B was surely just about to, anyway. Science works best when at its most transparent; when it is transparent, ideas migrate quickly. It helps, too, when there exists a central clearinghouse or institutional focal point for making ideas useful. Over the years, Cotton Incorporated sponsored several cotton breeding programs but none designed to produce a ready-for-market variety. Yet it would probably not be claiming too much to say that, without the company's research and support, cotton would not have been the first field crop to undergo successful genetic modification and commercialization. Even though the names of "life sciences" companies like Monsanto, DuPont, and Aventis are more publicly identified with the commercialization of biotechnology in agriculture, it was Cotton Incorporated's task to help such companies, along with academic researchers, to bring their work on cotton to fruition.

Cotton Incorporated did not compete with cotton breeders whose job is to create new plant varieties, and it did not seek patents except where deemed advisable in order to forestall others from trying to "patent away" new knowledge. When it occasionally applied for a patent it was simply to protect growers, who had paid for the research once, from being forced to pay for it again.[53]

SCIENCE AND CONTROL

In their effort to put science to work for cotton, the agricultural research staff at Cotton Incorporated and their cooperating colleagues in academia

[53] Lalor, Jividen interviews.

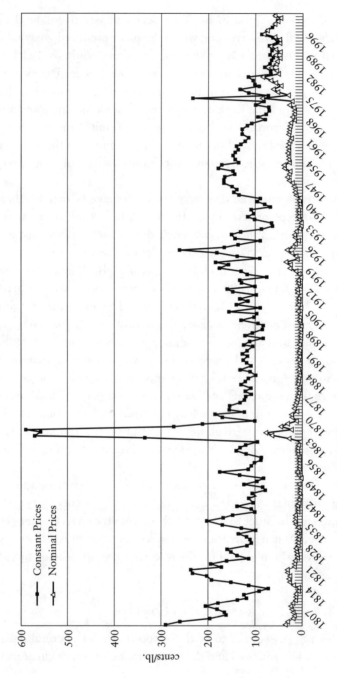

Figure 9. Cotton spot market prices over time, 1800–2000. *Source:* Time series data provided by David Fraser, Cotton Board.

shared kinship with researchers in many other fields. To link science and service (service to the sick, as in medical research; service to the customer and the stockholder, as in for-profit corporate R&D) depends always on achieving some practical outcome. It is never enough merely to know. There were a few areas where Cotton Incorporated could be said to have sought knowledge for its own sake, as in some genetic modification work and electron microscopy studies exploring how the cotton fiber actually forms. It could be very basic work. "You can't look at it and say 'here's what we hope to get out of it, other than knowledge.'" But, added one veteran Cotton Incorporated scientist, "without that knowledge, we can't take that next step toward control." [54]

Economics impels the quest for control through science and technology. Despite the uptick in demand for cotton since the mid-1970s, the price of cotton in constant dollars since the Civil War has only gone down. It has done so in the company of many other commodities: gasoline today is far cheaper than when Henry Ford first started peddling Model Ts, as are soybeans and aluminum, for that matter. Over time, prices decline for desirable products as a function of competition and efficiency. Cotton is no exception. While marketing has stimulated cotton demand and won back share from competing fibers, it has offered no escape from the need to continue to sustain competitiveness, which means keeping efficiency high and the relative price of cotton low. In other words, the individual grower's ability to stay in the cotton business depends on his ability to increase yield and productivity, which leaves agricultural research with plenty of work still to do, particularly in the area of genetic research.

Just as the module builder lowered risks and increased productivity at a key juncture in the farm-to-mill process, and just as boll weevil eradication drastically reduced the costs of managing with insecticides alone, genetic research may hold the greatest promise yet for enabling growers to profit from cotton, even as prices fall. Current research on short fibers is an example. Cotton's short fibers or "linters" represent the second wave of growth on the cotton ovule that for some reason never reaches full length. Linters fill up with cellulose and form solid fibers – unlike longer, fully grown fibers that are hollow, like straws. If research can discover the genetic control mechanism that cuts off this second-wave growth prematurely and manipulate it to maintain growth long enough to turn short fibers into long ones, then

[54] Jividen interview.

growers might capture from 10 to 15 percent more fiber yield from cellulose that is already there anyway.

Genetic research into cotton's tolerance for cold weather also holds good potential and illustrates the economic dilemma in which growers find themselves. Cotton altered to the hardiness characteristics of spinach would enable growers to plant sooner, with predicted results of as much as a 20-percent increase in yield. But if such cotton were planted on 15 million acres across the Cotton Belt, to say nothing of the prospect of seeing it planted in Uzbekistan and China, it is not unreasonable to suppose that prices would crash as supply soared.

The challenge to agricultural research is to enable growers to make money at the price the market gives. The grower who grows tomorrow the same amount of cotton on 400 acres that yesterday he raised on 500 acres will thus have produced it at a lower cost per pound and will therefore be more competitive in the market. Profit per pound is a narrow measure, however. A broader measure is the amount of profit a grower can make for a year's work, whether on 10 acres or 10,000. A grower will do what makes the most money. And like growers of grains or livestock, cotton growers attempt to do so within a model of intensive agriculture – the goal of which is to produce ever more abundant, ever higher quality, and ever less expensive food and fiber. To the extent that agricultural research can make upland cotton serve that end and enable the grower to coax more output from the productive assets (chiefly land and water) under his control, upland cotton will flourish.

There is considerable irony (a virtue, from society's standpoint) in the way markets treat the improvements that applied research makes possible. Agricultural research is a means by which growers hope to winnow advantage, but they do so only for a time. Growers who innovate early typically profit from premiums paid for cotton with these attractive but still scarce characteristics. But followers then inevitably spoil the party. As soon as use of the improved varieties spreads and supply increases, the premium disappears and in time even begins to look like a discount, as mills take a "what have you done for me lately" attitude and raise expectations further. They can do so, of course, because of competitive alternatives, which include the next-generation relatives of the synthetics that nearly drove cotton to the wall in the 1960s and early 1970s as well as cotton from abroad, some of which (from Australia and Israel) approximates U.S. standards.

A steady state in farming is never achievable, and science is one of the reasons. Nature remains insistently unpredictable. New technical challenges surface; price pressures never go away. Control of all these factors remains an illusion on even the best-run cotton farms, and increasingly so as cotton's markets become broader, freer, and more global.

9

COMPETITIVE MARKETS
IN A GLOBAL ECONOMY

The young American republic was a trading nation, and cotton its international currency. When South Carolina Senator James Henry Hammond dared the world to make war on King Cotton in 1857, the United States exported 90 percent of its cotton crop and dominated the world's cotton trade. Square-riggers loaded cargo from cotton-clogged wharves in Galveston, New Orleans, Savannah, and Charleston, and the crop moved east and north, mostly to Great Britain and (to a lesser extent) to the European continent. Cotton's export earnings in 1850 offset the cost of two thirds of all America's imports.[1]

Exports remain a large factor in the yearly "disappearance" of the U.S. cotton crop,[2] though the proportion that is exported has decreased to between 35 and 45 percent. Between 1986 and 1996, exports averaged 7.1 million bales, or 43 percent of the crop. At the end of the twentieth century, pictures of immense (usually foreign-flagged) container ships taking on cargo of top-quality California, Arizona, and New Mexico cotton in San Francisco and Long Beach, bound for Japan and Southeast Asia, and pictures of cotton-laden tractor-trailers queued up at Laredo, Texas, waiting to cross the border into Mexico, reveal the new pattern of an old trade. Originating in a Cotton Belt widened westward from cotton's original kingdom in the Old South, U.S. exported cotton today moves to consumers farther west and south still. Conditions in world markets are never far from the minds of American growers.

---

[1] Irving R. Starbird et al., *The U.S. Cotton Industry* (Washington, DC: USDA Economic Research Service, 1987), 114.

[2] "Disappearance" is the term commonly used in the cotton industry to describe what happens to each year's crop: domestic consumption by U.S. mills, plus exports. Anything in excess is "carryover."

THE SHIFT IN COMPARATIVE ADVANTAGE

In the antebellum years, the lion's share of cotton was exported because the demand of Britain's mechanized mills for cotton far exceeded the demand of America's own relatively small textile industry. In 1860, the U.S. supplied close to 90 percent of Britain's and continental Europe's cotton needs. The shift came about quickly with the outbreak of hostilities between the North and the South in 1861 and the U.S. naval blockade of southern ports, which caused a dire cotton famine in Britain and a severe shortage in France. Any expectation on the part of the Confederacy that the loss of southern cotton would result in diplomatic recognition and military help from those countries failed to materialize. The Cotton Kingdom was doomed to fight on, alone, to defeat.[3]

After the war was over, population growth and economic development in the industrializing nations of Europe restoked demand for American cotton. Britain, however, had been developing alternate sources of supply, a sign of change to come. In 1862, Egypt, then under British suzerainty, produced about 150,000 bales of cotton; only two years later 400,000 bales were produced, mostly for export to Britain and France. By the 1890s, Egyptian producers grew over 1 million bales; by the 1930s, over 2 million bales. Moreover, Egyptian cotton boasted a long staple well suited to the spinning of fine, strong yarns and so commanded a price premium over the shorter American product.[4] The Civil War had prompted other countries, too, to establish domestic cotton production. The Sudan, India, and later China, Russia, Brazil, and Argentina improved their cotton cultivation techniques in order to service their own emerging textile industries and export markets.[5] Thus, a long-term shift in the balance of world cotton power was underway. Even though United States production recovered steadily from the 4.3–4.5-million-bale level of the 1860s to 6.6 million bales in 1880, 10 million in 1900, and 14 million in 1930, and even though exports continued

---

[3] J. Scherer, *Cotton as a World Power* (New York: Frederick A. Stokes Co., 1916); Francis Butler Simkins and Charles P. Roland, *A History of the South,* 4th ed. (New York: Knopf, 1972), 206ff.

[4] In 1900, Egyptian long staple brought 15 cents per pound in Alexandria, American upland 9.5 cents in Boston. In 1907, the spread was 21.4 cents to 11.8. T. H. Kearney and W. A. Peterson, *Egyptian Cotton,* Washington DC, USDA Bureau of Planting Industry Bulletin 128, 1908.

[5] J. O. Ware, "Plant Breeding and the Cotton Industry," Washington DC, USDA Yearbook of Agriculture, 1936, 657ff.

to account for over half the crop,[6] other countries were eating into America's domination of the world market for raw cotton fiber.

Decline in the relative quality of American cotton contributed to this shift. Well into the late 1860s, upland cotton had enjoyed an excellent reputation with the British textile industry, and cottons denoted (after the locale of its origins) "Deltas," "Red Rivers," or "Benders" were much sought-after for their superior spinning qualities. This reputation, which had taken years to build, was gradually eroded by improved competition and then, in the first decades of the twentieth century, collided with the boll weevil. The problem was not so much the pest itself as the response to it. As yields tumbled, the available insecticides and manual techniques proved unable to cope. Growers turned to science and developed breeds of cotton that matured more quickly and could be harvested before the weevil could do his worst. Early-maturing cottons, however, tended to produce shorter staple fiber than the later-maturing varieties. The declining quality of American cotton in turn stimulated more competition – in yield and fiber quality – from abroad.[7]

Wherever cotton grew, industry usually followed. The development of textile factories in virtually all fiber-producing countries further challenged American cotton's competitiveness. Following the example of Britain and New England, other countries fostered textile firms in the early stages of their own industrial development. So did the American South, albeit slowly. Even though textile production seemed a logical step toward economic (if not political) independence for the erstwhile Confederacy, the "cotton mill crusade" to bring the factory to the field would eventually alter the geography of the domestic cotton industry. The process took decades and failed to make the South rich, as its proponents had hoped, but it was relentless nonetheless.[8] At the end of the first decade of the twentieth century, northern mills still produced over 70 percent of the yarn spun in the United

---

[6] By the 1890s, the United States still produced three times the crop of the rest of the world combined. In the 1910s, three fifths of the world's cotton was still American. Only in the early 1930s did the American crop for the first time slip below the total for the rest of the world (13 million bales to 13.8 million in 1934).

[7] Another problem contributing to declining fiber quality and thus to lessened competitiveness of the U.S. crop was "mongrelization of cultivars," caused by indiscriminate mixing of seed by gins that ginned several different types of cotton together. J. O. Ware, *Opportunities for Improving the Quality of Cotton*, Washington DC, USDA Bureau of Planting Industry Bulletin 224, 1935. The problem of "short season" cottons producing shorter staple persists today.

[8] Henry W. Grady, editor of the *Atlanta Constitution* in the 1870s and 1880s, is remembered as chief spokesman for the "New South" movement, an attitude toward repairing the postbellum

States, but they could not withstand forever the two key advantages the South possessed: proximity to the source of supply and cheaper labor. By 1920, more than half of domestically traded cotton was spun in the South. Weaving moved accordingly so that South Carolina was finally turning out more cloth than Massachusetts.[9]

Such has been the story ever since of the movement of textile factories from "rich" to "poor" regions. By the turn of the twentieth century, textile factories had moved to the fields in many countries, where local growers attended first to the quality needs of local textile industries. These grew vigorously in countries where Europe and the United States had once taken export markets for granted. Japan, for example, built more than a hundred new spinning mills between 1910 and 1924 and quadrupled the number of its power looms. In so doing, it became the world's third largest importer of raw cotton, which came largely from India, the United States, and China. Japan's production increasingly met its own textile needs and made it a powerful exporter to regional neighbors, China, and the Dutch East Indies, where Britain once held sway.

After 1895, when the Chinese government encouraged the introduction of foreign capital and technology, that sleeping giant would become an exporter of finished cotton goods. Even in India, where British colonial control and the tradition of hand manufacturing held back the mechanization of textiles, a modern industry began to emerge that by the 1920s consumed 3 million bales of domestically produced cotton. Contemporary

South's backwardness and restoring material prosperity through a combination of political reconciliation with the North and industrial and commercial development of the region on a Northern model. Grady was also a thorough romantic about cotton:

"Not the fleeces that Jason sought can rival the richness of this plant as it unfurls its banners in our fields. It is gold from the instant it puts forth its tiny shoot. The shower that whispers to it is heard around the world. The trespass of a worm on its green leaf means more to England than the advance of the Russians on her Asiatic outposts ....

"The uttermost missionary woos the heathen with a cotton shirt in one hand and a Bible in the other, and no savage, I believe, has ever been converted to one without adopting the other .... And it peeps from the satchel of every business and religious evangelist that trots the globe ....

"The Dominion of our king is established, this princely revenue assured, not for a year, but for all time. It is the heritage that God gave us when He arched our skies, established our mountains, girt us about with the ocean, tempered the sunshine, and measured the rain – ours and our children's forever."

[9] Broadus Mitchell, *Cotton Mill Crusade* (Baltimore: Johns Hopkins University Press, 1919); M. D. Crawford, *The Heritage of Cotton* (New York: Putnam's, 1924); Paul M. Gaston, *The New South Creed* (New York: Knopf, 1979); C. Wayne Smith and J. Tom Cothren, *Cotton: Origin, History, Technology and Production* (New York: Wiley, 1999), 92ff.

developments in Latin America further eroded markets previously serviced by the United States and Britain. When World War I disrupted imported supplies of cotton goods, Brazil spawned a textile industry that by 1918 was large enough to begin exporting cloth to other countries in the region and by the 1930s was large enough to meet 90 percent of domestic demand for textile products. Brazil also produced raw cotton fiber and ever more of it (500,000 bales in 1933, 3 million in 1937), which disappeared into its own mills and in export to Britain, Germany, and Japan. Smaller Latin American countries – Argentina, Colombia, Guatemala, and Mexico – also took to textiles to one degree or another. On the eve of World War II, Peru exported 90 percent of its crop, mostly to Britain.[10]

The increase in competition for the world's cotton markets was an inevitable consequence of the dynamics of "comparative advantage" that drive world trade. When David Ricardo first enunciated the principle late in the eighteenth century, cotton grown for export in the American South and manufactured for export in Great Britain would soon be a dramatic case in point of how it was supposed to work: countries should produce what they produced best and trade for what they needed with countries who produced other things better but who also must trade with others for what *they* needed, and so on. Countries had learned that trade was predicated on the status quo; people – entrepreneurs, investors, even governments – could act to create comparative advantages. That being the case, industry leaders could not afford to rest on their laurels.

RECOVERY RESCUES DEMAND

The 1930s marked a maturing of the domestic cotton market. As the quantity of world production rose, domestic consumption now rose only with the increase of population and no faster. Americans in 1940 used no more cotton apparel per capita than had their grandparents, although some marginal increases in demand came from industrial uses such as automobile tire cord.[11]

As cotton's world grew more crowded and competitive at home and abroad, U.S. producers were beset by excess production capacity, overages,

[10] Smith and Cothren, *Cotton*, 92–5; L. Bader, *World Developments in the Cotton Industry* (New York: New York University Press, 1925); H. B. Brown, *Cotton* (New York: McGraw-Hill, 1938); *'Round the World with Cotton* (Washington DC: USDA, 1941).
[11] USDA, *'Round the World with Cotton.*

and low prices – hardly a formula for long-term profitability. The political response was expressed in government programs that attempted to protect producers through various schemes of supply management and income adjustment.[12] Such an approach turned out to be a palliative only. Even as the New Deal cotton programs were just getting started, there were rumblings that the real problem lay elsewhere.

The authors of a 1941 USDA study of cotton at home and abroad raised the question of whether, in a market that would "not take up at even the low prices of the 1930s any more cotton than is being purchased," per-capita consumption could be increased. "It could" was the answer, if more consumers could be found, if their income increased, or if new uses could be discovered for cotton lint and seed. But these were big "ifs," and it was not unduly negative to suppose that cotton's glory days were already behind it: "Perhaps the conditions limiting the sale of cotton may be changed so that larger quantities may be sold, but until such additional outlets are available the United States will not be able to use all of its cotton-producing facilities profitably."[13] Oscar Johnston, founder of the National Cotton Council, also knew that the issue was consumption, which lay largely beyond the reach of the government programs he so fiercely lobbied for – unless, perhaps, more consumers could be found abroad.[14]

A strong supporter of the efforts of Franklin Roosevelt's Secretary of State Cordell Hull to lower tariffs through reciprocal trade agreements in the 1930s, Johnston believed that the biggest opportunity to expand demand for U.S. cotton was through exports. But the era's high tariffs discouraged imports, thus lowering incomes of foreigners who might otherwise buy more U.S. primary goods, such as cotton. This problem had deep historical roots in the American politics of trade. The cotton South, with a commodity largely sold abroad, had generally favored open markets, while the industrial North, with industrial investments to "protect," favored high tariffs. The NCC's first major legislative campaign was for renewal of the Reciprocal Trade Agreement Program, scheduled to expire in 1940. With strong support, especially from merchants, the Council soon followed up with creation of its own foreign trade committee as an advocacy vehicle for

---

[12] See Chapter 3, "Acts of God and Government."

[13] USDA, 'Round the World with Cotton, 140–2.

[14] Read P. Dunn, Jr., Mr. Oscar: A Story of the Early Years in the Life and Times of Oscar Johnston and the National Cotton Council (Memphis: National Cotton Council, 1991).

expanding cotton exports.[15] But the Great Depression of the 1930s was not an auspicious time for advocating free trade, and German U-boats effectively shut down what remained of cotton exports early in the 1940s. Only after World War II, with American industry and agriculture returning with surprising quickness to peak production levels, did the issue of revitalizing foreign markets move to the forefront of American foreign policy – and with it, free trade. Cotton figured prominently in these discussions from the beginning.

In October 1945, in a speech at the Army War College in Washington, DC, Johnston argued that surplus U.S. agricultural commodities (like cotton) be used for humanitarian relief in Europe and to help jump-start the process of European recovery. Europeans needed clothes, and Americans had the fiber. Johnston's close friend from before the war, cotton merchant and Undersecretary of State Will Clayton, outlined a plan for subsidizing European recovery. History would know the plan by the name of Clayton's boss, Secretary of State George C. Marshall. The plan called for direct U.S. assistance to Europe with no obligation to repay. As he prepared to announce separate aid plans to forestall communist takeovers in Turkey and Greece, President Harry Truman was primed for a far larger effort. In May 1947, Johnston and Clayton arranged for Undersecretary Dean Acheson to unveil the comprehensive "European Economic Recovery Program." His venue, a month before Marshall would announce the plan to great fanfare at Harvard University, was the annual meeting of the Delta Cotton Council in Cleveland, Mississippi.

The Delta cotton growers, who were the first to hear about the Marshall Plan, were invited to participate in a quest to save Europe with U.S. dollars and trade. The margin of survival for war-battered Europe was exceedingly narrow, Acheson said, and it was America's challenge – and in America's interest – to apply its financial and economic resources to widening that margin. (Clayton also arranged for Marshall to be principal speaker, and to detail the recovery program, at the NCC's tenth anniversary meeting in Atlanta.)

Cotton Belt votes would be crucial in winning the Marshall Plan's acceptance in Congress, and given Americans' weariness at everything to do with the recent war, its success was not a foregone conclusion. The staff of

---

[15] Read P. Dunn, Jr., *Remembering: An Account of the Cotton Council International and the International Institute for Cotton* (Memphis: National Cotton Council, 1992), 48–9.

Secretary of State George C. Marshall promoted a plan for European recovery to the tenth anniversary meeting of the National Cotton Council in Atlanta in 1948. The meeting was arranged by cotton merchant and Undersecretary of State Will Clayton, a close friend of Cotton Council founder Oscar Johnston. Europeans needed clothes; Americans had the fiber.

the NCC's foreign trade division, which had been established late in 1945, campaigned hard to win over the cotton states. Economic more than humanitarian arguments carried the day. American cotton and other products needed the markets that only a rehabilitated Europe and Japan could provide. The textile industries of those countries, when running full, accounted for three quarters of the world's raw cotton imports and most of America's exports. The plan passed the Congress with the support of the South and – under the agency of the Economic Recovery Administration, which administered the program – reinvigorated Europe's mills and America's cotton exports.[16]

[16] Ibid., 50–1; Albert R. Russell, *U.S. Cotton and the National Cotton Council, 1938–1987* (Memphis: National Cotton Council, 1988), 37–8. When George Marshall died, in October 1959, the head of the French Cotton Textile Institute cabled the NCC's foreign trade division to offer sympathy and a personal tribute for Will Clayton: "We just want to tell you who the American was with whom we had the closest contact, and how deeply appreciative we are of what he did. He [Clayton] saved our industry." Read Dunn, Cotton Council International (retired), interview, April 4, 1999.

ORGANIZING ABROAD

In 1945, Read Dunn mustered out of the Navy and returned home to Mississippi, where he had been a manager for the Delta Council. He hired on with the NCC to organize its foreign trade division and then made two trips to Germany (in 1945 and 1946) to assess the destruction of German textile mills and develop programs to reestablish exports. One early result was an agreement with the Export–Import Bank of Washington for a $100 million line of credit to countries needing assistance to restore their mills. In 1947, a special mission of government and industry leaders went to Japan to study the needs of the cotton industry there and to assess the ability of Japanese mills to finance their imports of raw materials.

The question of how to regularize trade of American cotton and foreign mills (after the Marshall Plan had done its work) occupied Dunn and the foreign trade division for many years. The need to export was rendered even more urgent when competition from synthetic fibers became apparent at home. The foreign textile landscape was also changing quickly as the postwar boom took off and old enemies recovered surprisingly fast. One symptom was Britain's call in 1952 for an international meeting of cotton textile countries to discuss what already looked (to the British, anyway, with their outdated industrial plant) like excess capacity. The meeting was held at Buxton, a seaside resort near Manchester in England's textiles heartland. Dunn sailed from New York on the *Queen Mary* with a blue-ribbon delegation of American textile executives headed by Robert T. Stevens, chairman of J. P. Stevens and Co. Also aboard were the NCC's advertising and promotion man, Ed Lipscomb, and W. Howard Stovall, a prominent Delta producer. The conference did not turn out quite as its British hosts had hoped.

Britain's relative decline from industrial preeminence had begun even before the end of the nineteenth century in the face of energetic competition from Germany and the United States. Victory in 1945 put Britain at an added disadvantage. Though the conflict had taken its toll on British industry, it was nothing compared to the wholesale destruction that was visited on the Germans and Japanese. In those countries, propped up by American aid, recovery advanced more rapidly than predicted. The vanquished rebuilt afresh from the ground up, while the victors were left with the burdensome remains of older plants, older technology, low investment, and complacent management. This was especially true of textiles in Britain.

The typical response to decline, as distinct from desperation, is to run for protection. While Germans and Japanese rebuilt and looked outward to export, the British agenda at Buxton in 1952 was to establish some sort of quota system on textile machinery, or on production and exports, that would bring relief – particularly from Japanese and other Asian competition. The key to such a policy was the United States, the world's largest producer and exporter. Not yet feeling the pressure of foreign competition as keenly as the British, and looking for exports themselves, the Americans refused to go along. United States representatives at the Buxton conference asked participants to consider the problem the other way around, to look for ways to "make the whole pie bigger."

To the British, expanding cotton consumption through some mechanism other than lower prices seemed a nice idea, but something of a stretch. To others – particularly among the French, the Dutch, and the Japanese – the idea of promoting consumption looked like the sensible way to move forward.[17] Buxton produced nothing concrete, but it was a watershed. The new focus on consumption became the central theme for all subsequent cotton market development programs outside the United States, up to and including the international program of Cotton Incorporated after 1970.

Agricultural market development through exports was boosted with the passage of the Agricultural Trade Development and Assistance Act of 1954. Known as PL 480, the law addressed the problem of trying to market America's agricultural surplus to still-recovering foreign countries strapped for the dollars to pay for it. The law permitted sales for local currencies and was administered through the Foreign Agricultural Service (FAS) of the USDA. It sought to establish private trade channels for dollar sales when the program was ended, and it designated part of the proceeds earned from converted currencies to programs for expanding markets for U.S. farm products. Between 1955 and 1963, the program accounted for the disappearance of over 8 million bales of U.S. cotton – chiefly to India, Korea, Poland, and Spain.[18]

---

[17] Dunn, *Remembering*, 55.

[18] When the idea was first proposed, responsibility for U.S. agriculture overseas fell to an agency of the State Department, the Office of Foreign Agricultural Relations. Concerned that State would not promote market development aggressively enough, farm organizations lobbied to have responsibility shifted to the USDA and an assistant secretary appointed to oversee it. The result was the Foreign Agricultural Service (FAS). Soon after passage of PL 480, other export-oriented commodity organizations formed and joined the bandwagon: American Soybean Association and the Soybean Council (1956), Great Plains Wheat Market Development

Public Law 480's provision for international market development required cooperation from the agricultural organizations who would carry out the work. The NCC proposed a series of cooperative agreements with textile industry associations in Western Europe and Japan, who were to conduct cotton market research and promotion programs under the NCC's technical direction. The NCC, which would cover its own administrative expenses, would also reimburse the industry associations for half of their costs before seeking recovery of those reimbursements from the FAS. Within fifteen months of acceptance of its proposal by the FAS, the NCC negotiated agreements with most of the countries of Western Europe and Japan, markets that together accounted for three quarters of the world's cotton imports.[19]

In 1956, before the programs ever went into operation, the NCC spun off international market development to a subsidiary corporation, the Cotton Council International (CCI). (This was done to shield the NCC from tax liabilities in foreign countries arising from agreements with local industry associations.) Henceforth, CCI would be the official "cooperator" with the FAS. Though legally separate, the NCC and CCI were one in spirit and administration. The NCC would pay CCI staff and expenses, and it was agreed that the executive vice-president of the NCC would also serve simultaneously as executive vice-president of CCI. CCI's Rhea Blake was the first to fill the dual roles. Read Dunn became CCI's executive director, with offices first in Paris and then in Brussels.[20]

Association (1958), and Western Wheat Associates (1959). The Dairy Society International, Millers International Federation, and the Tobacco Associates were involved, along with the NCC, from the beginning.

[19] Read Dunn, "The Story of Cotton Market Development"; James O. Howard et al., "Partners in Developing Farm Markets Overseas" (Washington, DC: U.S. Agricultural Export Development Council, 1989).

[20] Cooperating industry organizations described the range of cotton's world in the late 1950s, still heavily concentrated in Europe: Verein der Baumwollspinner und Weber Osterreichs (Austria); Nationaal Katoeninstituut (Belgium); Canadian Cotton Council; Instituto de Fomento Algodonera Carrera (Colombia); Textilfabricantforeningen (Denmark); Puuvillatehtaitten Myyntikontorri (Finland); Piraiki-Patraiki (Greece); Syndicat Général de l'Industrie Cottonière Française (France); Institut der Deutschen Baumwollindustrie Frankfurt (West Germany); Cotton Textile Fund Committee (India); Associazione Cotonniera Italiana (Italy); Spinners and Weavers Association (Korea); Japan Cotton Promotion Institute; Nederlands Katoen Instituut (The Netherlands); Tekstilabrikkens Konsulent-og Opplysingskontor (Norway); Textile Mill Association of the Philippines; Servicio Comercia de la Industria Textil Algodonera (Spain); Svenska Bomullsfabrikantforeningen (Sweden); Piblizitatsstelle der Scheizerischen Baumwoll-und Stickerei-Industrie (Switzerland); Thai Textile Manufacturing Association; and The Cotton Board (England). For details of particular country agreements, see Dunn, *Remembering*, 70ff.

The cooperative agreements provided that the various industry associations would carry out programs of market research, sales promotion, and publicity modeled on NCC programs in the United States. Market research work included quantitative and qualitative studies of fiber trends in the major end uses, studies of merchandising practices and price relationships between cotton and competing fibers, and studies of consumer preferences about the qualities and prices expected with cotton products. In sales promotion, there were fashion campaigns to stimulate interest in cotton apparel, educational programs to help wholesalers and retailers better meet consumer expectations, and sales training at the retail level to teach personnel the advantages of cotton. America's Maid of Cotton traveled to cooperating countries every year with a tour manager and secretary provided by the NCC and, as part of the training programs, foreign country directors and specialists traveled to the United States to meet their NCC counterparts. In 1961, CCI created and registered its own cotton emblem (a stylized white cotton boll in a black oval), which it licensed to manufacturers and distributors to unify the promotion programs and enable customers to identify cotton products more easily.[21]

The expansion of world cotton production continued to erode the relative position of U.S. producers, but the CCI turned its attention to what seemed to be an even more potent threat from man-made fibers. If cotton's share of the world's total fiber market could be increased, then it was assumed that all countries producing cotton – including the United States – would stand to benefit. As the NCC slogan of the time put the strategy: Bake a bigger pie to get a bigger slice.[22]

In its first full year of program operation in 1959, CCI had a total budget of just over $1.3 million. Over the next thirty years, as Congress increased market development funds through the FAS, this number would rise substantially. However, it became apparent that, even as the program grew, its resources were grossly mismatched to the promotion expenditures of the synthetic fibers industry worldwide. It seemed unreasonable to expect that a program funded largely by the U.S. cotton industry (with some help from the USDA) would shoulder a generic promotion effort from which other cotton-producing countries reaped advantage while paying nothing. Efforts to develop internationally funded collaboration in cotton promotion

[21] CCI quarterly and annual reports.
[22] Dunn, "Story of Cotton Market Development."

led in 1966 to the formation of the International Institute for Cotton (IIC). NCC leaders Keith Walden, Elkan Hohenberg, and Hervey Evans pushed hard to expand the international promotion effort in the belief that collective action that increased consumption of cotton in the importing countries was in the best interest of U.S. cotton growers. Competition from man-made substitutes, not other countries' cotton, was the biggest danger to U.S. exports.[23] The IIC added a technical research function to support its promotions regarding the "easy care" properties of cotton products,[24] but keeping U.S. cotton qualitatively competitive with cottons grown elsewhere was generally considered as a separate problem, to be dealt with through largely political means.

The mechanism for obtaining international funding proved hard to achieve. Collecting funds from cotton growers to support the program (a notion popular with the Americans) would be too difficult without some sort of government involvement. In most cotton-growing countries, there were no private organizations in a position to collect and remit funds for such a purpose. What was needed was a treaty relationship along the United Nations pattern. The document that created the IIC was agreed to in December 1965 and became operative with the signatures of the United States, Mexico, Egypt, Sudan, India, and Spain – which together accounted for just over the 60 percent of world cotton exports required to make the agreement operational. It invited into membership any cotton-exporting country and fixed as the required levy one dollar (U.S.) per bale of cotton exports of that country to Western Europe and Japan. Initially, this was expected to raise approximately $4 million.

Europe and Japan accounted for the majority of the world's raw cotton imports and, outside the United States, were the center of fashion trends that shaped consumption throughout the world. The program soon encountered trouble, however, as cotton textile manufacturing (first of yarns, but then of fabrics and garments) shifted more and more to developing

---

[23] NCC board resolution, October 1964.

[24] International Institute for Cotton annual activity reports, 1975, 1988, 1989. The IIC also published a newsletter, "Cotton Times," in Brussels recounting its activities. As officially stated, IIC's purpose was to strengthen demand for cotton by: "Research to improve the quality of cotton products; Promotion to stimulate consumer demand; Service to trade and industry to encourage them to produce more and better cotton products." IIC efforts were concentrated in the apparel markets, where the needs and opportunities were deemed the greatest. CCI's cotton emblem evolved into IIC's, with the addition of the word "cotton" in four languages (English, French, Italian, and German) bordering the cotton boll.

countries with new and modern equipment and cheap labor. Unable to meet the price competition, the older textile countries experienced falling consumption in their local mills, and so the old roles reversed: one-time exporters of cotton products became importers. The decline in Europe was the most marked. Britain's consumption fell from over 6 million bales at the turn of the nineteenth century to 2 million bales in 1950 to less than 100,000 in 1990. France consumed 1.5 million bales in 1950 but only one third that much in 1990. In the Netherlands, the numbers in the same period dropped from 300,000 to 20,000; in Scandinavia, from 400,000 to 60,000. In less developed countries the pattern was the same. Brazil, once the largest-paying member after the United States, shifted in a relatively short number of years to become the largest importer of raw cotton in the world and a significant exporter of manufactured cotton products, especially yarns. Mexico had been the third-largest cotton exporter at the time of the formation of the IIC, but by the 1990s it was a net importer and a growing manufacturer.

It was not unusual to find one-time exporters like Greece, India, and Uganda using much of their own cotton right at home. Before the fall of the Soviet Union and economic liberalization in China, these large producers were ideologically hostile to advertising and sales promotion of any sort. Volatile internal politics rendered Pakistan, a large fiber producer and exporter of cotton products, also generally uncooperative. In general, increases in mill cotton consumption were occurring in countries that were not members of the IIC. This turnabout doomed the organization, which found it harder to explain to member countries what their contributions bought. By the middle 1990s, when signatories had dwindled to three small African countries, the IIC shut down.[25]

SELLING U.S.

The fate of IIC and the limitations imposed on CCI were symptoms of the difficulty of nation states administering markets amidst increasing globalization of trade. For U.S. cotton growers, competition – whether from raw fiber or synthetics – made the problem doubly complex. The "bigger pie" rationale for international cooperation had seemed both noble and logical, but it had proven too hard to accomplish. A more frankly national strategy turned out to work better. It required a different structure to accomplish the narrower goal of increasing consumption of U.S. cotton worldwide.

[25] Dunn, "Story of Cotton Market Development"; IIC reports.

Cotton Incorporated set up an international division in 1973, staffed out of the New York headquarters. On the surface it did so for reasons similar to those that impelled much larger American firms to venture abroad to enlarge markets for their products. At first it was a small commitment, representing only about 3 percent of the company's annual budget and with minimal staff (headed first by John McNutt and Don Kleckner, followed by Ira Livingston and Dean Turner) at the New York headquarters. They began by replicating abroad practices first applied at home, specifically the push–pull strategy of mill and (to a far lesser extent, overseas) consumer marketing, combined with research to improve product performance. Of course, Cotton Incorporated had no product of its own to sell abroad, any more than it did at home. Rather, it sold *advantage* and, as it looked for ways to increase consumption of U.S. cotton, it discovered that quality, not price, was the key competitive advantage for U.S. cotton growers. It also learned that synthetics manufacturers had provided the mills with less technical assistance, and retailers with less advertising, than they had at home.

In 1978, Cotton Incorporated reached a milestone in its international program when it sponsored a Western European Marketing Forum at the company's research center in Raleigh, North Carolina. The logistics of the meeting were significant. European mill executives representing the buying power of more than 800,000 bales per year came to meet with American textile industry leaders, researchers, and cotton producers. They came with their own laundry lists of requirements for the kind of cotton fiber that went into their mills and to learn what the Americans had on offer to meet their needs. They spoke frankly about why U.S. cotton was not always as desirable as cotton from other sources.

To some of the Americans in attendance, for whom the visit was a significant on-site "sell" opportunity, the forum was also an eye-opener. "I found out that cooperatives and merchants can't sell cotton in sophisticated markets such as Europe," remarked James Hansen – a grower from California's San Joaquin Valley, where some of the best-quality U.S. cotton was grown – "unless we can supply the fiber properties those spinners want. Nor can we sell cotton for top dollar if it's improperly ginned and packaged." The Europeans, many of whom were converting to new open-end spinning machines, emphasized their need for fiber performance and quality control and talked less urgently about price. They wanted strong and mature cotton with uniform staple length of 1 to 1-1/32 inch with uniform color and low trash content. Irregular fiber quality caused manufacturing problems and cost money, sending buyers like them to other sources of supply.[26] So successful was the event that it was followed up by a series of annual international mill gatherings held in New York, Raleigh, and grower locations across the Cotton Belt.

Cotton Incorporated responded to the visiting mill operators' concerns with increased technical assistance to those who used U.S. cotton, dispatching staff from Raleigh to study the needs unique to particular spinning, weaving, knitting, and finishing operations. As in the United States, the technical assistance was provided free of charge, smoothing the way for foreign mills to choose U.S. cotton over synthetics and cotton from other sources.[27] Whatever was learned in the process was transmitted back to U.S. growers.

Cotton Incorporated's Engineered Fiber Selection (EFS) system became a powerful weapon in the company's marketing arsenal, abroad as well as at home, beginning in the late 1980s.[28] EFS enabled textile mills to regulate the quality of the cotton they purchased to a degree never before possible, just as it enabled growers, selling through the regular merchandising channels, to tailor their supply to the needs of the market. Moreover, EFS was unique and opened to American growers the potential for significant quality advantage. Intensive analysis of proper growth areas in the United States that tied in to a particular mill's equipment and products gradually yielded favorable European response. By the end of the 1970s, eighteen European mills had started using EFS and U.S. cotton. One Italian mill returned to the U.S. fold after buying nothing for ten years. Another in West Germany, in return for technical assistance in finishing and marketing, turned away from other suppliers and came back to America.

ADDING FASHION

Getting it right with foreign mills was critically important because growth in the U.S. textile industry had stalled. Importer–retailers dealt increasingly with smaller mills overseas to serve U.S. consumers, and in doing so they

---

[26] Cotton Incorporated Annual Report, 1978.

[27] In accounting terms, Cotton Incorporated's service to customers can be thought of as a component in the "cost of goods sold" on the grower's income statement, a cost included in the assessment growers paid to keep Cotton Incorporated in business. Although Cotton Incorporated never literally charged for its services, those services nevertheless came with a price, which was the use of U.S. cotton.

[28] See Chapter 7, "Managing the Mill."

took advantage of Cotton Incorporated's promotional programs. This was fortunate because, through the mid-1980s, as U.S. mill consumption limped along at less than 5 million bales per year (today it is 10–11 million), imports of all-cotton or mostly cotton textile products surged.

There were two reasons for the increase in imported textiles. First, the appeal in Europe of natural fibers remained strong, synthetics marketers faced a harder sell than at home, and European mills, responsive to local tastes, had not made so massive an investment in synthetic fiber processing and production as had their U.S. counterparts. Moreover, rare was the European household in the 1950s and 1960s that boasted an automatic washing machine and a tumble dryer, the two prerequisites of home laundry technology that together made the synthetics' claims to "no-iron convenience" such a great success in the United States. The second reason was that the foreign mills patronized by U.S. importers tended to be more flexible in their production runs. As the U.S. industry consolidated in the 1970s, per-plant output scaled up so that production minimums became very high. For example, while it was easy to get delivery of 50,000 yards of synthetic fiber, 500 yards of cotton was another matter.

The economics of such scale reflected a set of factors, including the sheer size of the American market, the relative homogeneity of its tastes, and the advantage of one language and one set of laws (more or less) spread across a whole continent, making trade easy. Textiles were something of an exception to the popular image of America as the land of planned obsolescence and of Americans as blinkered believers in the wonders of "next year's model." Because America was big, it took longer for fashions to percolate through it than in Europe. "A style might start out in New York or Los Angeles, appear next in Chicago or Dallas, and finally wind up in Des Moines," as Ira Livingston, Cotton Incorporated's director of international marketing in the early 1980s, put it. "And that's going to be a three-year run." With that kind of fashion lifetime, a mill could indeed make 50,000 yards of something or other and have a good chance of selling it. Thus the huge production runs that reduced costs and made U.S. mills more efficient created a problem for cotton. Their high capital investment requirements made big mills reluctant to switch and experiment. "They're great jeans makers and sheet makers," Livingston observed, even in the late 1990s. "But couture? Forget about it." [29]

[29] Ira Livingston, Cotton Incorporated, interview, November 9, 1998.

In this context, Cotton Incorporated supplemented its technical and information services with a fashion marketing service, the second pillar of its international marketing program. Technical services had helped foreign mills with how to run U.S. cotton and with buying precisely the kind of U.S. cotton they desired. Style and fashion could also determine profitability, however, and the fashion marketing office offered overseas mills ideas about fabric, apparel, and interior design – with important intelligence about what would sell in the United States, the largest single consumer market of all. This service commenced in late 1979, just as U.S. cotton exports were surging to a 50-year high of 9.2 million bales, or 63 percent of the total crop. Fashion marketing services finished out, in the international arena, a structure that supported the field-to-final-product strategy that the company had first applied domestically. Innovative products and new technical systems meant more profits for intermediate cotton customers and ultimately for American growers. Cotton Incorporated developed for mills an annual series of international trend presentations on interior design and apparel. These presentations emphasized Dukes Wooters's "total marketing" approach and related to all levels of textile production, from raw fiber to finished garment or home product. Color and style forecasts reflected dominant trends in the U.S. market and became a particularly important component of the international marketing mix.[30]

"WEST" TO "EAST" TO "SOUTH"

Gradually, the international marketing effort carried programs to the most important cotton-consuming countries in Western Europe – in the late 1970s, to Belgium, France, Italy, Portugal, Spain, the United Kingdom, and West Germany. In 1980, the company also turned its attention to four major markets in the Far East: Hong Kong, Japan, South Korea, and Taiwan, soon followed by forays into Thailand, China, Indonesia, and the Philippines. It kept company executives and technical staff airborne and soon reached a level of activity where a less transient foreign presence seemed justified. Even as a strong U.S. dollar hampered exports generally, cotton exports in 1982 continued at over half the U.S. crop for the fourth year running.

Was this evidence of market resilience or rather of overproduction, weak domestic demand, and thus dependence on foreign trade? It was a situation

[30] Cotton Incorporated Annual Reports, 1979, 1980.

that certainly demanded attention. Cotton Incorporated's managers decided that world markets were too important to be administered from New York, and so it opened two "headquarters" overseas, one in England and another in Japan.

There was a picture in the 1982 annual report of Cotton Incorporated's president, Nick Hahn, striding not past the Houses of Parliament and Big Ben but through the textile district in Osaka, site of the company's first Asian office. It was a portent of the shifting geography of the cotton trade and a test of how U.S. producers would respond to it. American growers in the early 1980s shipped 10 to 15 percent of their exports to Western Europe, where total mill consumption had been in decline (as it had in the U.S.) since 1960.[31]

It is not that Europe mattered less. It was very important, but for reasons other than just tonnage. Many of the most advanced textile machinery manufacturers were located in Europe (the U.S. had largely walked away from that business after World War II), and it was crucial to assure that they continue to provide mills with equipment suitable for processing cotton. The major equipment manufacturers became regular calls for Cotton Incorporated staff in London, and they were serviced with information about U.S. cotton's comeback in the market and the improvements in fiber quality that were making it once again attractive for mills to run. A Cotton Incorporated–sponsored seminar on how U.S. cotton could be efficiently and profitably run on existing spinning machinery became a feature at meetings of the International Textile Machinery Association, where spinners, weavers, and suppliers gathered to review technology and purchase new equipment. Europe also boasted – in London, Paris, and Milan – three of the world's leading fashion and apparel retail centers, where trends were set that mattered worldwide.

The Far East, however, now accounted for a whopping 80 percent of U.S. cotton exports, with the majority of the crop shipped to Japan, South Korea, China, and Taiwan. The new office in Osaka facilitated stepped-up servicing of mills, machinery manufacturers, and cotton trade associations in Asia. For the new overseas offices, the mills that used U.S. cotton were the primary focus of activity and were treated in all respects (except for the absence of financial consideration) as sales accounts whose business the company would go the extra mile to protect. The offices were lean; technical

---

[31] Starbird et al., *The U.S. Cotton Industry,* 110–11.

experts continued to journey out from Raleigh to provide the complete package of textile engineering consultation services, covering spinning, weaving, knitting, dyeing, finishing, fabric development, styling, and product manufacture. As special problems and opportunities arose, technicians were dispatched to recommend preventive or corrective programs. In 1982, they achieved a breakthrough "sale" of their own, convincing Japanese spinning machine manufacturer Murata (the leading maker of air-jet spinning frames designed for most synthetic fibers) to provide replacement parts to enable the processing of cotton and cotton-rich blends on the new high-speed machines.[32]

The international marketing effort required steadfastness in the face of uncontrollable forces. Market and currency fluctuations were impossible to manage. United States exports in 1984–85, for example, while more than a million bales higher than the five-year running average since 1945, dropped off sharply. This was due to the threat to U.S. mills from growing levels of textile imports and the high value of the U.S. dollar. By the end of the year, U.S. cotton was on average 10 cents more expensive than competing growths, which left foreign mills hard pressed to "buy American." What *could* be managed were the long-term relationships established between U.S. growers and foreign mills. Cotton Incorporated's year-in, year-out international presence ensured that international mill accounts were kept constantly aware of U.S. cotton. Throughout the 1985–86 downturn, Cotton Incorporated's international activities were not scaled back but actually increased.

The Food Security Act of 1985 gave the Secretary of Agriculture greater discretionary authority in administering commodity programs and also provided more flexibility to promote market competitiveness. This helped cotton exports to rebound, up 2 million bales, from the unusual low of the 1985–86 crop year. In such an improved climate, Cotton Incorporated increased mill visits and dissemination of marketing services and demonstrations. With an eye to availability, *U.S. Cotton Market Updates* provided market overviews to mill executives and raw material purchasers. With another eye to fiber quality, a sampling program was launched to gather competitive nations' cotton samples for evaluation and comparison with U.S. growths. Cotton Incorporated then collected information on foreign cotton quality to guide U.S. growers as they planned their own crops and to

---

[32] Cotton Incorporated Annual Reports, 1980, 1984.

document for buyers the competitive advantages of U.S. cotton, which was shown to be consistently stronger than similar types of foreign growths.

It was Cotton Incorporated's technical assistance that remained the most visible part of its international effort. High-volume instrumentation (HVI) was becoming more commonplace overseas, and the company's proprietary EFS computer software was for the first time licensed to Asian mills in the late 1980s and tied to their purchase of U.S. cotton. In cooperation with CCI, the U.S. Cotton Seminar helped bolster relations with European spinners. In 1985, CCI and Cotton Incorporated directly coordinated their marketing efforts, the latter providing technical, marketing, fashion, and product development up to the point of retail. Meanwhile, CCI worked directly with retailers to promote cotton products to local consumers in foreign markets. The two organizations also worked together on the government-sponsored Targeted Export Assistance Program to increase U.S. cotton usage in Europe and the Far East.[33]

By the end of the 1980s, a new pattern of world cotton consumption was becoming clear. Europe, now, meant fashion. Asia meant fiber. Cotton Incorporated's market focus on the ASEAN countries sharpened, and in 1989 the company opened its third overseas office, in Singapore, to service Thailand, Indonesia, the Philippines, and Malaysia. Technical and fashion service experts staffed it, and a Cottonworks Fabric Library was established there. To increase the visibility of U.S. cotton downstream, Cotton Incorporated worked manufacturers as well as mills, sponsoring fashion shows and seminars in Asian cities. When Singapore hosted Asia's first international fashion conference, "Fashion Forum '94," Cotton Incorporated was a major participant. ("Première Vision," the largest fabric trade show in Europe and held twice each year in Paris, did the same job in that older market.) In these ways, the well-established "total marketing" was replicated in new markets.

Expansion into Asia underscored the role of international marketing at Cotton Incorporated, which had in effect become a global communications

---

[33] Cotton Incorporated Annual Report, 1985, 1988; CCI reports; Allen Terhaar (Cotton Council International), interview, October 16, 2000. Cotton Incorporated first provided seed money to support CCI's promotion efforts in foreign markets in 1989. Cooperation between the two organizations henceforth was close, emphasizing Cotton Incorporated's technical and fashion expertise and CCI's consumer promotion and trade servicing activities. In order to maintain a consistent message in core home markets, it was agreed in the mid-1990s that the Seal of Cotton would replace CCI's Cotton USA mark for promotional purposes in Central America and the Caribbean.

network. Anchored in New York and Raleigh, the network allowed efficient transfer of economic data, fashion information, and textile technology to consumers of U.S. cotton in major markets of the world. Better-informed customers, the premise went, would buy American cotton for reasons of fiber quality, reliable supply, and (not incidentally) America's reputation for respecting contracts. Price always mattered at the margin, but fiber quality and reliability of supply were vital if the U.S. were to maintain a leading position in the world's cotton markets. Both were factors over which growers exercised more control than they had over their relative costs of production. By 1992, exports to ASEAN markets topped 1.5 million bales, which suggested the message was getting through.[34]

In the 1990s, surprises were in store for even the nimblest marketers. The sudden break-up of the Soviet Union was a two-edged sword for American producers. In the newly free-standing nations of central Asia, huge crops previously bartered within the Soviet Bloc suddenly found their way onto world markets, dampening especially the demand for U.S. fiber in Europe. The silver lining was that with the opening of the old Soviet empire to the global market economy, it was possible to think about how these areas might become export markets themselves. In 1991, Cotton Incorporated relocated its European office from London to Basel, closer both to longstanding textile and equipment manufacturers and to potentially emerging markets in central and Eastern Europe. Soon enough, Russian textile experts arrived in Raleigh to inspect Cotton Incorporated's research facilities.[35]

After years of laboring to stay competitive in world markets, U.S. cotton exports soared in 1994 from 5.2 to over 9.4 million bales. The sudden increase was due in part to crop difficulties in India and China, but it served to reinforce the opportunity U.S. growers had in the export markets. Overseas cotton production was likely to be uncertain from year to year, while demand for textiles – synthetic or cotton – was likely to increase. As traditional end markets in the United States matured and levels of domestic synthetic fiber production rose, the pressure to open new export avenues for cotton usage increased. Chief of these would be close to home, in Mexico.

Overuse of insecticides and reduction of government subsidy programs were major factors in explaining the drop in Mexico's cotton production in the early 1990s, with the effect that Mexican imports of raw cotton jumped

---

[34] Cotton Incorporated Annual Report, 1992.
[35] Ibid.; Dean Turner, Cotton Incorporated, interview, November 1998.

Auténtico algodón.

With the coming of the North American Free Trade Agreement in the 1990s, Mexico became a major export target for U.S. cotton and a primary focus of Cotton Incorporated's international marketing efforts.

from 142,000 bales in 1990 to over 700,000 bales in 1993. More than two thirds of that came from the United States, whose proximity and logistical advantage held out great promise for long-term dominance of the Mexican market. Cotton Incorporated hired its first Spanish-speaking textile engineer and geared up to provide technical and information services south of the border. In 1994, as Mexico's imports from the United States surged upward, the company hired a Mexican national as director of international marketing for Latin America to work with existing and potential mill customers. A year later, the company's fourth office officially opened in Mexico City.

In 1994, the North American Free Trade Agreement (NAFTA) entrenched the American advantage in the Mexican cotton market. The political debate over NAFTA had spawned some memorable political soundbites, 1996 presidential candidate Ross Perot's "great sucking sound" among them. Contemporary opinion depended a good deal on which side of the border you stood on and what you hoped to move across it: "It works great," *The Economist* noted, "if you are inanimate and moving south; not so great if you are animate and hoping to move north." For U.S. cotton growers keen to export, NAFTA indubitably "worked great," and early. Tractor-trailers laden with bales of cotton lined up to cross the Rio Grande at Laredo, bound for Mexican mills. In 1998, Mexico consumed 2.3 million bales, of which 1.6 was imported from the United States; this level of usage bought a high level of service from Cotton Incorporated.

Starting in 1995, Cotton Incorporated licensed the Seal of Cotton to Mexico-based mills, manufacturers, and retailers for domestic use on 100 percent cotton products. Consumer advertising built awareness of cotton's performance benefits and "lifestyle" fashion appeal. Billboard and magazine campaigns focused on distinct product categories, from the traditional standbys – denim, sheets, and towels – to women's wear, casual apparel, and underwear. Every version carried the seal and the tagline *Auténtico algodón*. Under Cotton Incorporated's master agreement with Procter & Gamble, the Seal of Cotton appeared on the popular laundry detergent, Ariel. By the end of the decade, more than 100 Mexican mills and retailers had been licensed to display the seal, and recognition among Mexican consumers of the white cotton boll approached 60 percent. Mexico had become the number-one market for U.S. raw cotton, fabric, and yarn.[36]

[36] Cotton Incorporated Annual Reports, 1997, 1998; *Cotton Reports* (Cotton Incorporated). "Globalization" became a management mantra in the 1990s, and one founded on the hard facts of communism's sudden demise as an alternative to free-market capitalism and of the increasingly (though far from perfect) free movement of goods, services, and capital (but seldom labor) across national borders in search of lucrative markets and optimum returns. Most firms wished at least to appear to be intently "globalizing" their operations and philosophies, and Cotton Incorporated – whose annual reports for 1991, 1992, 1993, 1994, and 1997 all featured global motifs – joined the bandwagon. "Building a Future for World Cotton" was something of a company theme for the decade, though hardly a new concern for American growers. Also see John Micklethwait and Adrian Wooldridge, *A Future Perfect: The Essentials of Globalization* (New York: Crown Business, 2000).

Globalization presented marketers with both opportunities and risks, however. By the late 1990s, the economic forces driving free trade had spawned intense political and ideological opposition. Anti-globalization and anti-capitalism activists frequently targeted global brands – Nike, Shell, Microsoft – which became metaphors for a global economic system deemed run amok and somehow to the disadvantage of the poor. One anti-corporate manifesto of the day said it all in the title: *No Logo*. Levi's, a big consumer of cotton, came in for difficulties when it attempted to restrain the British discount chain Tesco from selling its famous jeans for far less than they went for at authorized outlets. "This presents brand owners with a dilemma," mused Richard Tomkins in the *Financial Times*. "The whole purpose of brands is to enable them to maintain their profit margins. But when profit-making is perceived as profiteering, the brand owners run the risk of being demonized and seeing years of patient brand-building destroyed" (April 25, 2001). The economic consequences could be real. Since protesters disrupted the World Trade Organization summit in Seattle in 1999, the stock of the world's most famous brand, Coca-Cola, has fallen 30 percent and global pharmaceutical companies have backed off defending key patents in South Africa.

Close to home or far away, Cotton Incorporated always employed the same basic tools of promotion and technical assistance that had restored cotton's fortunes in the domestic market. This strategy proved able to transcend regional and local market idiosyncrasies. However, one market that had been difficult to penetrate was the world's largest.

For any business wanting to export, China was as vexing as it was alluring. It was impossible to travel to China on business in the 1990s and not breathe in something of the gold-rush atmosphere of the place and time. The promise, if not reality, of economic liberalization coupled with the prospect of access to millions of Chinese consumers sent Western firms stumbling over themselves to get in and establish relationships. Most soon discovered, however, that there was considerably more "rush" than gold in the Middle Kingdom, and that China demanded more patience than probably any other market.

China's history of cotton production, as in most other things, extends back to ancient times. Sealed off from the world since 1949, China emerged as a first-rank player in the world cotton economy between 1960 and 1985, when world raw cotton production increased from an average of 48 million bales to 73 million bales. While U.S. production during that period remained flat at 13–14 million bales, China's rose from 4 million to 19 million bales. On the demand side, Chinese mills consumed 5.2 million bales in 1960 and 17.5 million in 1985; over the same period, U.S. mill consumption fell from 8.3 million to 6.4 million bales and in no year exceeded the 1965 high of 9.6 million. Moreover, China's share of the world's cotton trade (rising during these years less than half as fast as production) tended to fall, on the import side, to less than 1 percent of world imports in 1985 (as domestic acreage and mill capacity were added) but to rise, on the export side – so that by the late 1980s China was a net exporter of raw cotton.[37] Why then, one might well ask, did Cotton Incorporated open (in 1997) its fifth overseas office in Shanghai?

Given the potential size of the market and the dependence of U.S. producers on exports, a China that was opening up to the world was too big a plum to ignore, even if far from ripe. In the mid-1990s China was in an import spurt to the tune of approximately 1.5 million bales, not a small number. It was more than enough to trigger the opening "sell-in." This involved mastering complicated steps in an intricate dance with Chinese procurement

---

[37] USDA, Foreign Agricultural Service, "Foreign Agriculture Circular: Cotton," November 1986.

If economic growth and consumption can be sustained, Asian markets promise large opportunities for U.S. cotton.

officials, where *guanxi* – relationship building through personal and political connections – counted far more than economic rationality. These were the meetings where Cotton Incorporated staff laid out the reasons Chinese mills should think about using U.S. cotton and the array of technical, fashion, and fiber economics services that accompanied that usage.

Just when talks seemed to be progressing, the decision came down that the country had more of its own cotton in inventory than it needed. Import quotas continued, and exports of cotton to China fell precipitously. The company retrenched, focusing on those mills that were allowed an import quota and hence were still potential customers of U.S. cotton on the open market. If, for instance, Shanghai Textile Mill Number Three had a quota of 10,000 tons (40,000 bales), then Cotton Incorporated tried hard to get even that much-reduced order for U.S. growers. Though Cotton Incorporated never involved itself in the actual sale – the inviolate territory of government-sanctioned cooperatives and merchants – it pre-sold the package of advantages that led to it. This effort was, if nothing more, an opportunity to remind the Chinese that Cotton Incorporated services came with a price, which was buying U.S. cotton. Soon thereafter, when much of Asia tumbled into severe economic downturn, there was little that Cotton Incorporated or many other foreign companies could do but wait for the recovery. When it came, it would be important to be set up and ready to go.

TO IMPORT – AND TO EXPORT

The competitive strength of the United States as exporter of raw cotton remained formidable through the 1990s, which came at the price of a relentless marketing effort. But there was no price that U.S. textile producers could pay to forestall the relentless erosion of their position to the comparative advantage of "offshore" competition. At the close of the twentieth century, imported cotton yarns, fabrics, and finished goods accounted for close to 60 percent of total U.S. consumption.

Though hard to quantify, the marketing drumbeat of Cotton Incorporated on behalf of cotton's "natural" advantages also had an impact. From the mills all the way to the final consumer, the cotton promotion program stoked demand for cotton. Such retailer/importers as J. C. Penney and Wal-Mart, who sold foreign-made cotton shirts by the millions, benefited from reinvigorated demand for cotton as much as (if not more than) the farmers who grew it. So, too, did brand manufacturers like Calvin Klein and Tommy Hilfiger. It was estimated that, for each 1-percent increase in cotton's retail market share, retail sales of cotton products rose some $1.5 billion. Between 1973 and 1998, as cotton's share rose from 33 percent to 60 percent of the market, retailers of cotton products enjoyed a seller's market and profited commensurately.[38]

It was this logic that had led to revision in 1991 of the Cotton Research and Promotion Act and hence to assessment of importers, on an equivalent-weight basis, alongside growers to support the research and promotion program. In return for the mandatory assessment of importers, collected at customs, growers agreed to make their own assessment mandatory as well – relinquishing their right to request a refund.

This change was controversial and introduced new tension into the organization. Cotton Incorporated president Nick Hahn was wary of taking on new "owners" with interests that differed from those of the growers, and he fretted about governance problems down the road. (As it turned out, importer representatives would have seats on the Cotton Board but not on the board of Cotton Incorporated.) An influential group of export-oriented growers led by Cotton Incorporated's chairman Fred Starrh argued that the assessment of importers was both fair and essential to the continuation of the research and promotion program. It was also the lever that enabled the grower leadership to deal decisively, once and for all, with the old problem of "free riders" in the ranks. When refunds vanished, everybody paid, which then bestirred another sort of tension in the organization. This involved the uneasy issue of federal oversight, as financing arrangements once construed as voluntary came to resemble a tax, albeit a self-imposed one.

At the time, what mattered most to Cotton Incorporated was the cash. By 1995, the importer assessment was supplying nearly 25 percent of Cotton Incorporated's budget – a much-needed financial infusion. That year, the company established an office of importer relations within its international division in order to develop programs and activities that responded specifically to the needs of the importer community. One of these resulted in a change in the way the Seal of Cotton would be used.

Beginning in 1993, the seal was licensed to importers for use on cotton goods sold in the United States, regardless of country of origin. Domestic mills were far from enthusiastic about this development, though they themselves paid no assessment into the program. Their objection concerned the

[38] Dean Turner, Cotton Incorporated, interview, September 18, 2000.

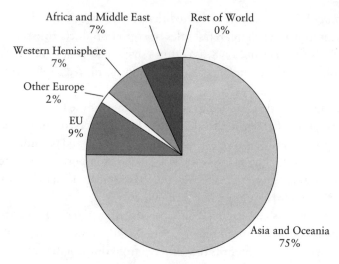

Figure 10. U.S. cotton exports to the world by region, 1991. *Source:* U.S. Department of Agriculture, National Agricultural Statistics Service data.

implicit history of the seal as a denominator of U.S. cotton or cotton products. It had never been policy; Cotton Incorporated never had measured success of the seal by any connection consumers might have made with American-grown cotton – only with cotton content and the qualities associated with it. Yet for years the seal had probably functioned as a kind of "Made in the USA" surrogate. No longer.[39]

Rising import penetration raised serious questions about the long-term viability of the U.S. textile industry, which (through the 1990s) was still the best customer for U.S. upland cotton, typically taking around 60 percent of annual production, 10–11 million bales.[40] To the extent that this home market threatened to decline, the urgency of exports increased. This was especially so for a country like the United States, with its troublesome combination of enormous productive capacity for fiber and relatively low rate of population growth. The tendency for a larger proportion of cotton to be processed within producing countries – even very poor ones like Pakistan[41] – had enormous consequences for the world cotton trade, which

[39] Dean Turner interview, November 1998.
[40] USDA figures. On the prospects for that industry, see Frederick H. Abernathy et al., *A Stitch in Time: Lean Retailing and the Transformation of Manufacturing – Lessons from the Apparel and Textile Industries* (New York: Oxford University Press, 1999).
[41] "Vision of Hope for Pakistan Clothmakers," *Financial Times,* September 19, 2000.

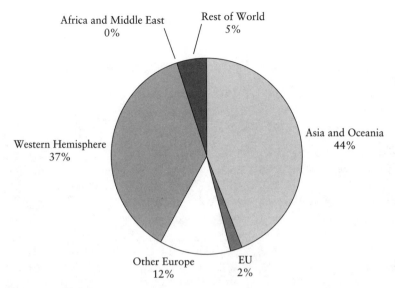

Africa and Middle East
0%

Rest of World
5%

Western Hemisphere
37%

Asia and Oceania
44%

Other Europe
12%

EU
2%

Figure 11. U.S. cotton exports to the world by region, 1999. *Source:* U.S. Department of Agriculture, National Agricultural Statistics Service data.

increased 19 percent between 1960 and 1985. Cotton production over the same period increased much faster, at close to 50 percent. This meant that growers like the Americans, ever looking for expanded exports, found themselves competing for a larger share of a more slowly growing market.[42]

Or *markets,* to be more exact. The vaunted "global" market was really a cluster of regional markets with varying characteristics and potentials. The very location of cotton markets moved around in response to world economic conditions and government policies. China, for instance, which had looked so promising in the early and mid-1990s but then faded as the Communist Party leadership decreed building up domestic cotton growth, appeared by early in the twenty-first century to be readying its return to net importer status.[43] Over the long term, it was reasonable to conjecture that

---

[42] Starbird et al., *U.S. Cotton Industry*; USDA.

[43] Statistics were one thing; actually being there was another. Reported one awed American grower and Cotton Incorporated board member of his visit to the Yellow River Basin:

"I was shocked and stunned at what I saw. Large fields of astounding uniform, weed-free beautiful cotton (except for two or three crabgrass plants and a couple of volunteer sesame plants). Plant spacing was perfect and fertility level high. No growth regulators were used, instead the terminals of the plants were pinched out. Farmers pruned the vegetative branches to allow sunlight penetration into the canopy. In short, incredible cotton!

U.S. cotton has always sought world markets. In the nineteenth century, square-riggers sailing from the cotton-clogged wharves of Galveston, New Orleans, and Savannah carried much of it to the mills of Europe. At the end of the twentieth century, the new pattern of an old trade found containers loaded at West Coast ports bound for the mills of Asia.

China would have to revisit its agricultural priorities, perhaps at the expense of cotton production. With 26 percent of the world's population but just 7 percent of its arable land, China faced a food-versus-fiber (as much as crop-versus-livestock) dilemma. If resolved in favor of more rice and less cotton then this would augur well for U.S. farmers, who had an excess productive capacity in both food and fiber.[44]

"Plus no environmental or labor laws, or any regulatory intervention whatsoever. Talk about limited production costs! And their homes were only 200 square feet or so; thus, living costs quite minimal. We would hope they move to more food production through grains and animal protein." Dale Swinburn (Tulia, Texas) to authors, January 8, 2001.

[44] Nothing was certain, however, and it was possible that the Chinese might have it both ways and frustrate Western exporters yet again. Largely immune, domestically, to safety and environmental constraints, China wholeheartedly embraced genetic engineering and the promise of genetically modified crops, including cotton. With its farmland still typically fragmented into tiny plots where the cost of production was higher than on high-technology Western farms, the Chinese saw genetically modified seed (Monsanto's Bollguard, which produced a plant naturally resistant to bollworm and reduced the need for costly spraying) as a vital competitive weapon. "China Rushes to Adopt Genetically Modified Crops," *New York Times*, October 7, 2000.

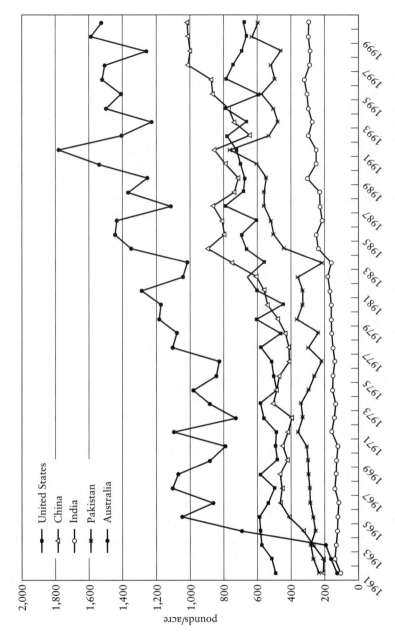

Figure 12. Cotton yields of the world's major producers, 1961–1999. *Source:* U.S. Department of Agriculture, National Agricultural Statistics Service data.

Consider also Turkey, which met 60 percent of the European Union's demand for textiles. Turkey had become the second largest buyer of U.S. cotton at the end of the twentieth century. Economic growth in Russia, meanwhile, promised to rekindle mill consumption there, in all likelihood fed by fiber from the Central Asian republics of the old Soviet Union: Uzbekistan, Azerbaijan, Turkmenistan, and Tajikistan. This in turn promised to lessen the amount of central Asian cotton – which just a few years before had flooded into Europe – and to increase the potential in Europe for substituting fiber exported from the United States. Meanwhile, Australia had a relatively new cotton industry and still a relatively small crop (3 million bales in 1999), but it emerged as a major U.S. competitor in Asia and the Far East, actually displacing the United States as the largest supplier of cotton fiber to Japan by the late 1990s. In addition to a substantial exchange-rate advantage on price, the Australians enjoyed proximity to Asian buyers and competed effectively on quality. As a Southern Hemisphere producer, they were able to make cotton available in the latter half of the crop year, an added advantage when supplies from northern growing regions (including the U.S.) had been spoken for by spring at the latest.[45]

As the world's trading regime moved steadily in the direction of lower barriers to the exchange of goods, services, and capital, the health of U.S. cotton – and of the domestic textile industry that it supplied with fiber – was tied to public policies aimed at making markets freer.[46] The scenarios one could derive from this trend held out hope, if not certainty, for the U.S. textile industry and cotton growers alike.

The World Trade Organization (WTO) mandated elimination of quotas and reduction of tariffs beginning in January 2005, just as NAFTA had done for North America. The movement toward low-cost manufacturing sites in Mexico spurred by NAFTA (much of the U.S. raw cotton exported to Mexico was promptly imported back as textile products) would presumably accelerate under WTO and impose an increasing disadvantage on U.S. mills. The Caribbean Basin Initiative (CBI) created an interim opportunity by establishing, beginning in the fall of 2000, a quota- and tariff-free

---

[45] Cotton Incorporated Strategic Plan, 2001–2005; "Cotton Boom Continues in Australia," *Financial Times,* September 19, 2000.

[46] Imports of raw cotton into the United States were first limited under the Agricultural Adjustment Act of 1933, which employed tariffs and quotas to prevent imports from rendering price support programs ineffective, and such imports remain negligible. In 1999, when U.S. production stood at 17 million bales, imports totaled 100,000.

trading zone among 24 small Western Hemisphere countries and territories that did business with the United States. The hope was that U.S. mills and offshore manufacturers would be able to forge profitable business links between U.S. supply, Caribbean Basin manufacturing centers, and North American consumer markets. If so, the U.S. textile industry would improve its competitive stance against textile imports from Asia and thus remain a steadfast customer for U.S. fiber.[47]

Coupled with the niche opportunities that U.S. mills were prepared to grasp, CBI's approach for sustaining U.S. mill and fiber production looked like sound strategy. The alternative was certainly not attractive. Unless the trend could be arrested that already saw low-cost textile suppliers from Asia dominating U.S. markets for apparel and home fabrics, the prospect for continuing strong domestic mill consumption was not bright. As it faded, demand for the U.S. crop and the price it commanded would fade, too. Such disadvantage for U.S. growers would come in addition to stiffer competition for U.S. fiber exports in Asian markets from Australia, China, Uzbekistan, Turkmenistan, and the hand-picked crops of the African Franc Zone. If, on the other hand, U.S. mills could be sustained as the principal yarn and fabric suppliers to the manufacturing centers of the Caribbean Basin, then U.S. cotton producers could expect to thrive on strong demand from U.S. mills for years to come.[48]

This was a substantial "if." On it depended much, but not quite all, of the future of U.S. growers. The rest depended on continuous strengthening of demand for the large share of U.S. cotton that U.S. mills could not take and that had to go, as it always had, out of the country. Increasing the U.S. amount of world cotton trade upward from its 1999 share of 25 percent would be a function of how well one could provide value-added, after-sale services to key foreign buyers. While U.S. growers faced daunting competitive challenges abroad from both foreign growths and polyester, they remained unique among the world's growers in having their own purpose-built fiber company dedicated to promoting their interests by "selling" the

---

[47] Cotton Incorporated Strategic Plan, 2001–2005. Under CBI rules, in order to obtain preferential quota and tariff treatment, regional trading partners were required to use U.S.-manufactured yarns and fabrics in their garment-making operations. However, the CBI incentive for low-cost regional cut-and-sew operations to continue to "buy American" (U.S. mills were already the principal yarn and fabric suppliers to the region) and thus to consume U.S.-grown cotton would last only until the WTO agreement took effect, which was scheduled for 2005.

[48] Ibid.

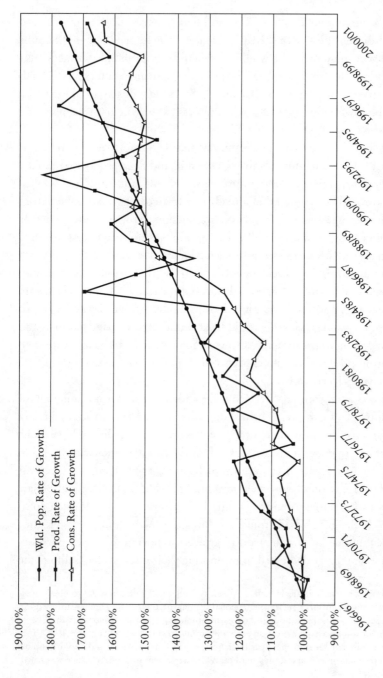

Figure 13. Rate of world population growth versus rates of cotton production and consumption, 1966–2000. *Source:* U.S. Department of Agriculture, Foreign Agricultural Service Division.

Figure 14. U.S. percentage of world cotton consumption, 1961–2000. *Source:* U.S. Department of Agriculture, Foreign Agricultural Service Division.

advantages of high quality, reliable supply, and respect for contracts between buyers and sellers.

Trend lines of cotton use worldwide continued to move downward as the twenty-first century opened. Cotton's share of world fiber use, which stood at 62 percent in 1965, dipped to 45 percent in the late 1970s, stayed below 50 percent through the 1980s, and then remained more or less flat for the dozen years to the end of the century. At the same time, world demand for fiber increased 50 percent.[49] There were at least two ways to interpret such numbers.

As world population rose faster than world cotton production and as cotton lost share in the aggregate, people obviously were being clothed in synthetics or they were going with fewer clothes. There was no denying the appeal of low-cost synthetics in the clothing markets of developing nations. An inexpensive all-synthetic wash-and-wear shirt could have huge appeal to Third World consumers just stepping out of the village economy into the dazzling world of retail. But the bet was that, as developing nations grew richer, consumers there would move up the consumption ladder – just as more affluent Westerners had done before them – to demand style, comfort, and all the rest.

[49] See Starbird et al., *Cotton*; Keith Collins, Chief Economist USDA, speech to Thirteenth Annual EFS Conference, Cotton Incorporated, April 18, 2000.

One thinks again of the push–pull marketing strategy with which Cotton Incorporated had countered the domestic threat from synthetics in the early 1970s; the worldwide challenge today is similar. Then it had proven necessary to push cotton back into the mills (supported with improved breeding programs and fiber research that made cotton once again an attractive raw material for mills to use) and simultaneously pull cotton back into the market by rekindling consumer demand at the retail level, else the mills would pay no attention. Cotton historically had always met and typically exceeded whatever demand the market offered it, and cotton seldom had been caught in short supply. Since the 1950s, however, it had suffered from chronically weak demand. The flatness of cotton's share worldwide, thirty years after Cotton Incorporated first diagnosed the problem at home, suggests that the same push–pull prescription remains a viable strategy for cotton abroad. The marketing opportunity, in such a context, is enormous: to sell the world on the idea of cotton's "natural" superiority. "We have the best fiber," declares Dean Turner, Cotton Incorporated's current head of global marketing. So long as that remains so, American growers will deploy quality as a key competitive weapon.

AFTERWORD

Trends and Cycles

The impact of Cotton Incorporated on the markets for cotton was a remarkable achievement in organizational entrepreneurship. Most basic American agricultural industries – beef, dairy, soybeans, even mushrooms and popcorn – have their "boards," government-sanctioned agencies that promote the uses of commodities, sponsor research on them, and tend to the political interests of farmers who produce them. Cotton has its board, too, but only in cotton is there anything like Cotton Incorporated, which is unique in its organization as an independent, nonpolitical, public–private company wholly dedicated to building markets for its commodity. Though funded by growers of cotton and importers of cotton textiles, it works to stimulate and meet demand along the entire chain of production and distribution, from planting cotton to its final sale in the form of retail consumer goods. In its "total marketing" effort to rebuild cotton's market share, it has fostered substantial scientific, technological, and managerial improvements in the quality and performance of cotton. In doing so, it has enhanced the efficiency not only of the farmers who grow cotton but also of all those who then transform it into thread, then fabrics, and finally consumer goods.

In the three decades since the establishment of Cotton Incorporated, cotton growers have achieved a high measure of sustained impact on consumption in an industry that historically left markets to chance. What is particularly intriguing about this achievement, in formal economic terms, is that the long chain of production and distribution that moves cotton – from the fields and, in the form of value-added products, into the homes of millions of consumers – is substantially lacking in vertical integration. That is, the various stages of production and distribution are generally owned and operated by distinctly independent entities. One exception is the long history in the United States, dating back to Lowell Mills in 1820s

Massachusetts, of combining the spinning and weaving of cotton under common corporate ownership. In that conjunction of producer functions there are genuine scale and operating economies to be realized from managerial coordination, as the conversion of fiber to textiles moves through several closely related stages of production. Most everything else is left to market transactions among independent entities. Some cotton growers may have investments in gins, but this is not necessary to achieve substantial cost reductions or improvements in quality. Mills may invest in warehouses, but it is not crucial that they do so. Clothing and other end-product manufacturers find it best to purchase their textiles on the open market; retail stores, likewise. In other words, cotton growers have come to enjoy considerable vertical influence over their markets without the requirements, or burdens, of vertical control. The evidence is the growth in market share for cotton fibers from 34 percent to 60 percent in a quarter century. As the history described here demonstrates, this was no accident.

Cotton Incorporated has helped growers increase demand and lower their costs in historically demonstrable ways. The one thing that it has not been able to do is influence the price paid for their cotton. Cotton growers live and toil in a fiercely competitive global environment, where prices are pure commodity prices subject only to changes resulting from aggregate cotton production and demand worldwide and from the perceived desirability of alternative fibers. Historical attempts to manage the supply of cotton through the mid-twentieth century, when there was far less worldwide competition than now, never worked very well; today, such attempts would be utterly hopeless. The best that cotton growers can do is to continue what they have been doing: work their costs down and improve fiber quality. The best that Cotton Incorporated can do is to continue persuading final consumers that cotton products are worth buying and to help the mills make it and the farmers grow it more efficiently. Of course, all this is quite a lot to do.

What are the prospects that Cotton Incorporated can do as good a job in the future as it has in the past? Four long-term market and political trends, though hardly inevitable and always reversible, seem to be well underway. First, in the past decade, synthetic fibers have resurfaced in new forms that are more challenging in quality and price. Can cotton defend, let alone increase, its hard-won share of the market in the United States?

Second, more countries are producing cotton and in greater quantity than ever before, so the very landscape on which cotton growers compete

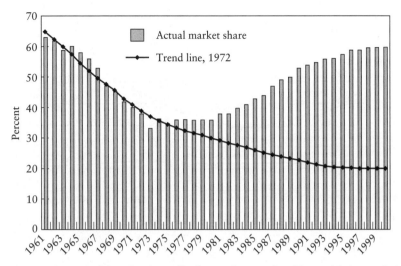

Figure 15. Cotton's share of U.S. market for retail apparel and home fabrics (excluding carpet), 1961–2000. *Source:* Based on data compiled by Cotton Incorporated from industry sources, the NPD Group, and other trade intelligence.

has become increasingly international. Will U.S. cotton growers continue to have an economic interest worth protecting against cotton growers elsewhere? Should production simply be allowed to move to its most efficient locales (low cost balanced by quality) in accordance with the "law" of comparative advantage? Could there be an opportunity to expand U.S. cotton's share around the world, where relatively low per-capita cotton consumption might be expected to rise as people in emerging markets grow more affluent?

Third, the economic deregulation inherent in the 1996 "Freedom to Farm Act" and the progressive globalization of free trade have changed the rules regarding what cotton growers can expect in the form of "protection" in hard times. Will the emergency subsidies, which farmers have come to take for granted in hard times, be allowed to lapse? What the government gives, it can always take away.[1] This applies also to the mandatory assessments or "check-offs" that fund farm promotion and research programs across the

---

[1] A front-page article in the *New York Times* (May 14, 2001) argues that the emergency payments – especially those made to "row-crop" farmers, including cotton growers – have taken on the aspect of a new farm entitlement program. "The phaseouts [of farm subsidies] are a thing of the past." If so, then such payments, which favor large farms, would have to be politically sustainable should crop prices, which have been depressed in recent years, rise substantially in the years to come.

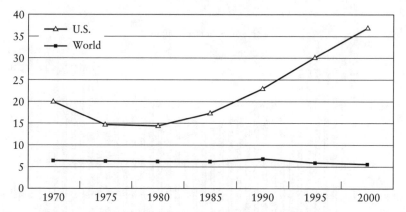

Figure 16. U.S. and world per-capita cotton consumption, 1975–2000. *Source:* Based on data from the U.S. Department of Agriculture, Foreign Agricultural Service Division, and the U.S. Census.

board. Some programs are far more effective than others, and mandatory assessments put into effect for the cotton growing industry in 1991 are subject to renewal via referendum every few years. Should programs lose their observable impact on the marketplace, they will surely lose their investors. In 2000, for example, pork farmers – deciding there was too much "pork" in the Pork Board – voted to pull the plug.

Fourth is the increasing scrutiny to which all government-sanctioned farm programs have become subject. In 1996, the Office of the Inspector General issued a harsh report on the management of expenditures by farm check-off programs – those funded by mandatory assessments. In November 1998, a *Washington Post* article cited some expense-account abuses by cotton officials, repeated some of the complaints of the Inspector General's report, and called into question the effectiveness of programs funded by mandatory assessments. The newspaper asked – with respect to Cotton Incorporated, in particular – why it needed a new $19 million building, why it needed to throw a $400,000 "party" at the Metropolitan Museum of Art, and (even more fundamentally) why the company enjoyed a monopoly on servicing cotton grower and textile importers' marketing needs.[2]

---

[2] The *Washington Post* article, "Cotton Program Soft on Oversight" (November 25, 1998), refers to the Inspector General's report and is written in the tone and style of an exposé. Industry publications were more neutral or even sympathetic in tone. See, for example, "Checkoff Challenge," *California Farmer,* July 1999, and "Checkoffs under Fire," *Progressive Farmer,* April 11, 1999.

The article caused a stir in the USDA, and the Cotton Board along with Cotton Incorporated's board moved quickly to reply. The more than decade-old "Celebration of American Style" in New York helped to move more than $2.2 billion of cotton into the marketplace, as one grower put it.[3] The new research and development facility in Cary, North Carolina, was overwhelmingly supported by the growers' board of directors. The answer to why Cotton Incorporated was the sole recipient of assessments levied by the Cotton Board was implicit in the underlying assumption that such programs are "public goods," even if achieved by private-sector means.[4] (In any case, what other entity has the brand, the franchise, the capability, or the desire to provide the service?) Some of the expense account abuses by Cotton Board officials were real enough, and the salutary effect of their exposure spilled over to Cotton Incorporated. According to Cotton Incorporated's vice-president of administration, Hugh Malone, the result was "better monitoring and more rigorous accounting by our corporate staff. [Secretary of Agriculture Dan] Glickman rode us very hard on this, as he should have."[5] For the vast majority of cotton growers, the issue blew over quickly (there was no move to petition for a renewal of the check-off, as some industry observers had anticipated), though the issue of the check-off continued to fester among many textile importers.

Indeed, such challenges in the market and political system have become increasingly manifest, making Cotton Incorporated's task – if not harder – no less uncertain than it was thirty years ago. The abiding uncertainty might be better understood as a function of two cyclical phenomena that, in a broad sense, characterize the progress of all industries over time.

The first is *the virtuous cycle of competition* – a virtue from society's standpoint but a mixed blessing from the producer's standpoint. As they

---

[3] Ibid. "Robert 'Bob' Coker, Cotton Inc. board member and grower from Yazoo City, Miss., heads the committee that puts on the party [and] he is quick to point out that he paid the $1,500 cost, including airfare to bring his wife along .... Cotton Inc. board Chairman Hugh Summerville, an Aliceville Ala., producer adds that the [guests] 'are invited because they are important to cotton's future.' "

[4] A "public good" is an economic term defined as a good or service that a government deems to be both essential and non-excludable. Non-excludability refers to the condition by which individuals among a class of beneficiaries of a public good cannot decline to receive the benefit, even if they wanted to. National defense, police services, K–12 schooling, and basic postal delivery are traditional examples of public goods as defined by most governments. In this particular case, it may be argued that no cotton grower or cotton textile importer can fail to benefit from the promotional and marketing activities of Cotton Incorporated.

[5] Interview: Hugh Malone, undated.

fought to regain markets they were losing to synthetic fiber producers after World War II, a group of entrepreneurial cotton growers devised an innovative organizational means for increasing demand for their product. To satisfy rising expectations that it created through promotion and advertising, Cotton Incorporated had to foster quality improvements through the entire system of production and distribution. Continuous improvements begat higher expectations in the market for cotton goods, provoked competitive responses from producers of synthetics, and forced marginal land and less efficient producers out of the business.

The second is *the entrepreneurial cycle.* Great innovations often result in great gains to the innovators – but only for a while, because success inevitably breeds competition. At some point (and it is usually hard to tell just when this occurs, except in retrospect), the entrepreneurial cycle that the creators of Cotton Incorporated set in motion more than thirty years ago will have run its course. After thirty years, Cotton Incorporated's total marketing strategy and all its supporting tactics, from the Seal of Cotton to sponsorship of technological improvements, may have begun to reach its growth limits. For several years, market share has remained stable at an impressive but stubborn 60 percent. Has the industry matured? Has the nature of the game shifted from one of expanding markets to one of defending them against erosion? Perhaps so, in the United States at least.

For the foreseeable future, Cotton Incorporated will continue to confront the competition from synthetics producers with persuasive consumer campaigns, deft engineering support, and creative research and development. Its greater apparent opportunity for substantial market growth lies outside the United States. The challenge now for Cotton Incorporated is to cultivate ever more vigorously cotton markets worldwide, since the gap between cotton's international and U.S. market shares suggests a big opportunity for growth. Can the organizational structure that did this so well domestically be adapted to work better globally?

For the most efficient producers of cotton that remain, there are harsh yet salutary lessons to be learned from the history of their industry. There is no time to relax; no time to coast. Entrepreneurs cannot afford to become caretakers of their own achievements. Market victories cannot be taken for granted. In free markets, choices abound and consumers can afford to make them. American cotton, no more a necessity than any of its competitors, is just one of them.

APPENDIX A

Table A. *Cotton Incorporated budget history*
(thousands of dollars)

Year	Total Budget	Marketing	Research	Administration
2000	60,000	40,508	16,688	2,804
1999	60,000	40,920	16,254	2,826
1998	63,000	43,677	16,705	2,618
1997	61,280	41,708	17,097	2,475
1996	61,059	42,033	16,660	2,366
1995	55,096	35,928	16,867	2,301
1994	47,395	30,660	14,525	2,210
1993	45,079	29,381	13,586	2,112
1992	43,107	28,201	12,879	2,027
1991	28,553	18,610	7,901	2,042
1990	26,550	17,890	6,707	1,953
1989	22,407	14,511	5,992	1,904
1988	22,141	14,554	5,732	1,855
1987	18,413	11,569	5,172	1,672
1986	18,545	11,990	4,862	1,693
1985	18,131	10,591	5,016	2,524
1984	18,000	10,772	5,088	2,140
1983	18,000	11,705	5,317	978
1982	22,500	14,208	6,792	1,500
1981	22,884	14,452	7,233	1,199
1980	21,900	15,958	4,847	1,095
1979	17,800	11,467	4,957	1,376
1978	20,500	12,900	6,600	1,000
1977	12,500	8,714	2,904	882
1976/75	28,840	15,730	11,930	1,180
1974	24,000	15,286	8,031	683
1973	20,000	12,161	7,358	481
1972	20,000	8,779	8,561	2,660

Note: 1975 and 1976 are combined because of a changeover
from fiscal-year to calendar-year budgeting.
Source: Cotton Incorporated files.

APPENDIX B

Table B. *Output of top ten cotton-producing countries, 1983–2000*
(thousands of 480-lb. bales)

1983	Bales	Market Share (%)	1984	Bales	Market Share (%)
China	21,300	32.4	China	28,701	32.4
All others	20,214	30.7	All others	25,373	28.6
U.S.	7,771	11.8	U.S.	12,982	14.6
India	6,122	9.3	India	8,360	9.4
Turkey	2,398	3.6	Pakistan	4,630	5.2
Pakistan	2,271	3.5	Turkey	2,664	3.0
Egypt	1,934	2.9	Egypt	1,840	2.1
Sudan	1,020	1.6	Mexico	1,240	1.4
Mexico	1,001	1.5	Australia	1,144	1.3
Syria	888	1.4	Sudan	932	1.1
Argentina	826	1.3	Argentina	786	0.9
Total	65,745	100.0	Total	88,652	100.0

1985	Bales	Market Share (%)	1986	Bales	Market Share (%)
China	19,000	23.7	China	16,300	23.1
All others	16,625	20.7	All others	15,374	21.8
U.S.	13,432	16.7	U.S.	9,731	13.8
India	9,021	11.2	Uzbekistan	7,450	10.6
Uzbekistan	7,936	9.9	India	7,254	10.3
Pakistan	5,587	7.0	Pakistan	6,062	8.6
Turkey	2,379	3.0	Turkey	2,380	3.4
Egypt	1,999	2.5	Egypt	1,850	2.6
Turkmenistan	1,781	2.2	Turkmenistan	1,626	2.3
Tajikistan	1,337	1.7	Tajikistan	1,346	1.9
Australia	1,185	1.5	Azerbaijan	1,203	1.7
Total	80,282	100.0	Total	70,576	100.0

Table B *(cont.)*

1987	Bales	Market Share (%)	1988	Bales	Market Share (%)
China	19,500	24.1	All others	21,762	25.8
All others	17,571	21.7	China	17,400	20.6
U.S.	14,760	18.2	U.S.	12,196	14.5
India	7,140	8.8	India	10,599	12.6
Uzbekistan	6,912	8.5	Uzbekistan	7,605	9.0
Pakistan	6,744	8.3	Pakistan	6,687	7.9
Turkey	2,465	3.0	Turkey	2,835	3.4
Turkmenistan	1,745	2.2	Turkmenistan	1,823	2.2
Egypt	1,614	2.0	Tajikistan	1,332	1.6
Argentina	1,295	1.6	Egypt	1,324	1.6
Australia	1,275	1.6	Mexico	761	0.9
Total	81,021	100.0	Total	84,324	100.0

1989	Bales	Market Share (%)	1990	Bales	Market Share (%)
China	17,400	21.8	China	20,700	23.8
All others	16,473	20.7	U.S.	15,505	17.8
U.S.	12,196	15.3	All others	15,296	17.6
India	10,599	13.3	India	9,135	10.5
Uzbekistan	7,605	9.5	Pakistan	7,522	8.6
Pakistan	6,687	8.4	Uzbekistan	7,317	8.4
Turkey	2,835	3.6	Brazil	3,215	3.7
Turkmenistan	1,823	2.3	Turkey	3,007	3.5
Australia	1,401	1.8	Turkmenistan	2,007	2.3
Tajikistan	1,332	1.7	Australia	1,989	2.3
Egypt	1,324	1.7	Egypt	1,378	1.6
Total	79,675	100.0	Total	87,071	100.0

Table B *(cont.)*

1991	Bales	Market Share (%)	1992	Bales	Market Share (%)
China	26,100	27.3	China	20,700	25.1
U.S.	17,614	18.4	U.S.	16,218	19.7
All others	14,481	15.1	All others	12,016	14.6
Pakistan	10,000	10.4	India	10,775	13.1
India	9,291	9.7	Pakistan	7,073	8.6
Uzbekistan	6,628	6.9	Uzbekistan	5,851	7.1
Brazil	3,445	3.6	Turkey	2,635	3.2
Turkey	2,578	2.7	Brazil	2,113	2.6
Australia	2,306	2.4	Turkmenistan	1,791	2.2
Turkmenistan	1,971	2.1	Australia	1,713	2.1
Egypt	1,338	1.4	Egypt	1,620	2.0
Total	95,752	100.0	Total	82,505	100.0

1993	Bales	Market Share (%)	1994	Bales	Market Share (%)
China	17,200	22.3	China	19,900	23.2
U.S.	16,134	20.9	U.S.	19,662	22.9
All others	11,652	15.1	All others	12,700	14.8
India	9,800	12.7	India	11,148	13.0
Pakistan	6,282	8.2	Pakistan	6,250	7.3
Uzbekistan	6,067	7.9	Uzbekistan	5,778	6.7
Turkey	2,766	3.6	Turkey	2,886	3.4
Egypt	1,909	2.5	Brazil	2,526	2.9
Brazil	1,860	2.4	Greece	1,791	2.1
Turkmenistan	1,850	2.4	Turkmenistan	1,608	1.9
Greece	1,529	2.0	Argentina	1,608	1.9
Total	77,049	100.0	Total	85,857	100.0

Table B *(cont.)*

1995	Bales	Market Share (%)	1996	Bales	Market Share (%)
China	21,900	23.5	China	19,300	21.5
U.S.	17,900	19.2	U.S.	18,942	21.1
All others	14,405	15.5	All others	14,548	16.2
India	13,250	14.2	India	13,918	15.5
Pakistan	8,200	8.8	Pakistan	7,300	8.1
Uzbekistan	5,740	6.2	Uzbekistan	4,750	5.3
Turkey	3,911	4.2	Turkey	3,600	4.0
Greece	2,067	2.2	Australia	2,788	3.1
Australia	1,970	2.1	Egypt	1,568	1.8
Argentina	1,929	2.1	Argentina	1,493	1.7
Brazil	1,791	1.9	Greece	1,382	1.5
Total	93,063	100.0	Total	89,589	100.0

1997	Bales	Market Share (%)	1998	Bales	Market Share (%)
China	21,100	23.0	China	20,700	24.4
U.S.	18,793	20.5	All others	14,073	16.6
All others	15,183	16.6	U.S.	13,918	16.4
India	12,337	13.5	India	12,727	15.0
Pakistan	7,175	7.8	Pakistan	6,300	7.4
Uzbekistan	5,228	5.7	Uzbekistan	4,600	5.4
Turkey	3,650	4.0	Turkey	3,850	4.5
Australia	3,059	3.3	Australia	3,289	3.9
Brazil	1,745	1.9	Brazil	2,100	2.5
Greece	1,650	1.8	Greece	1,783	2.1
Syria	1,650	1.8	Syria	1,539	1.8
Total	91,570	100.0	Total	84,879	100.0

Table B *(cont.)*

1999	Bales	Market Share (%)	2000	Bales	Market Share (%)
China	17,600	20.1	China	20,000	22.6
U.S.	16,968	19.4	U.S.	17,220	19.5
All others	13,038	14.9	All others	12,614	14.3
India	12,337	14.1	India	11,900	13.5
Pakistan	8,600	9.8	Pakistan	8,100	9.2
Uzbekistan	5,180	5.9	Uzbekistan	4,300	4.9
Turkey	3,634	4.2	Turkey	3,700	4.2
Australia	3,400	3.9	Brazil	3,700	4.2
Brazil	3,100	3.5	Australia	3,300	3.7
Greece	2,020	2.3	Greece	1,900	2.1
Syria	1,480	1.7	Syria	1,700	1.9
Total	87,357	100.0	Total	88,434	100.0

Source: U.S. Department of Agriculture, Foreign Agricultural Service Division.

APPENDIX C

The Elastic Cotton Bale

Schoolchildren learn that a bale of cotton is 500 pounds. For official statistical purposes, however, it is 480 pounds, which is the unit used (unless noted otherwise) throughout this study. Why the discrepancy? For much of the twentieth century, the common wrapper for a 500-pound "running bale" was made of jute bound by steel straps, or "ties," which taken all together weighed about 20 pounds. There was nothing precise about the weight of the wrapping, however – nor, for that matter, about the cotton in the package when waste is taken into account. "About 500 pounds" is the best the National Cotton Council could do when it defined a fully wrapped bale of cotton in the year 2001.[1]

Imprecision in measuring a cotton bale has a venerable history. Before 1810 in the United States, "bags" of upland and Sea Island cotton alike were known to vary within a range of 125 to 350 pounds. By 1840, cotton growers had made enough progress toward increasing the size and regularity of the cotton "bale" (generically, the word refers to any compressed and wrapped unit of merchandise) that it reached a rough antebellum norm of 400–450 pounds. In the meantime, as "pressing" cotton into bags shifted from the cotton fields to larger, centralized gin houses, and as the Industrial Revolution made its way to the farm, a rapid series of innovations in hydraulic and steam-powered presses enabled the cotton trade to "standardize" the bale at 500 pounds gross weight by the 1880s.[2] Nonetheless, variations in cotton fiber and press operator idiosyncrasies ensured that perfect standardization would be impossible to achieve.

Even though advances in bagging and strapping material sharply reduced wrapping weight to just 6 pounds by the end of the millennium, the U.S. Commerce Department's lagging standard for the "statistical bale" remained at 480 pounds.

---

[1] See the National Cotton Council's website: ⟨www.cotton.org/ncc/education/cotton⟩.

[2] Two useful histories on ginning technology and its impact on the bale are: Charles A. Bennett, *Cotton Ginning in the United States and Auxiliary Developments* (Dallas: The Cotton Ginner's Journal and The Cotton Gin and Oil Mill Press, 1962), pp. 1–4; Karen Gerhardt Britton, *Bale o' Cotton: The Mechanical Art of Cotton Ginning* (College Station: Texas A&M University Press, 1993), pp. 9ff.

INDEX